THE UNITED NATIONS POLITICAL SYSTEM

THE UNITED NATIONS POLITICAL SYSTEM

Edited by DAVID A. KAY
The University of Wisconsin

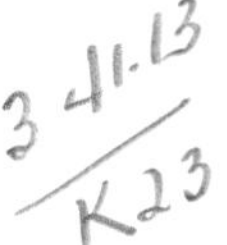

JOHN WILEY & SONS, INC., New York · London · Sydney

Library of Congress Catalog Card Number: 67-29937
GB 471 46110X
Printed in the United States of America

Preface

A distinctive feature of the contemporary international political system is the presence within it of a universal international political organization with aspirations of being an important actor in the system. That this universal international political organization—the United Nations—is an instrument of international politics, susceptible to the same type of political analysis as any other political instrument (whether it be the political party or the diplomatic corps of a state), is the chief motivating factor behind this collection of readings. The United Nations has too often been subjected to blind adulation by its supporters and unthinking abuse by its disparagers, when what it really needs most is a searching analysis of the dynamics of its connections with the international political system and of its own political system.

The United Nations, like the League of Nations before it, emerged as a result of a victorious wartime coalition, which hoped to utilize (to secure the peace) the same great power cooperation that had made the prosecution of the war so devastatingly effective. It was not the shared belief that the great powers would be able to continue their close collaboration, but it was believed that unless they were able to continue it the prospects for peace would indeed be small. When the hopes of great-power cooperation faded soon after the end of World War II, what was left was an arena for interstate cooperation or competition according to agreed guidelines and rules of procedure.

The United Nations, however, does more than engage in world politics in a glass house. Its unique feature (and what makes it of interest to the student of international politics) is the component that is contributed to the overall pattern of action by its own political system. In other words, the United Nations is one instrument of international politics (among many others) by which states choose to carry out their foreign policies; it is also an arena within which the interplay of national power takes place; but both as an instrument and as an arena it contributes something of its own to the action that is taking place.

At least part of the unique contribution made by the United Nations to this process is covered by the felicitous phrase, "parliamentary diplomacy," which

Dean Rusk coined in 1955.[1] This term is used to describe a form of multilateral politics in which four factors are present. First, the international organization must be more than the traditional *ad hoc* conference called to deal with specific items; it must be of a continuing nature with interests and responsibilities broader than the agenda at any given time. The second factor that must be present is regular public debate, open to coverage by the media of mass communications. Thirdly, the process of debate and decision making must be conducted according to agreed rules of procedure "which are themselves subject to tactical manipulation to advance or oppose a point of view."[2] Finally, the organization must, as a matter of regular course, make formal conclusions that can be adopted according to some form of majority voting. The necessity of states advancing or defending their interests in an environment of parliamentary diplomacy is an important part of the international political system. An understanding of the nature of this interconnection between parliamentary diplomacy and international politics is vital to an understanding of the role of the United Nations in the international system.

Another critical relationship that must be comprehended for an adequate understanding of the contribution of the United Nations to world politics is the nature of the linkage between the Members of the United Nations and the Organization itself. If the United Nations is to achieve to any meaningful degree the purposes set out in Article I of the Charter, it must change the environment within which it operates. However, the difficulty of this task is apparent when we realize that the major forces in the environment also happen to be the principal Members of the United Nations. The tension that results from the duality of this relationship accounts for much of the contention over the proper role of the Organization, its employees, and appropriate national strategies in the United Nations.

The multipurpose nature of the Organization itself complicates the student's effort to get an adequate grasp of the nature of the United Nations' political system. The Organization does not deal just with the obvious political questions of disarmament and arms control, the Indian-Pakistan dispute over Kashmir, the incessant conflict of the Arab states and Israel, the problems of decolonization, and problems of East-West conflict, although these questions certainly are enough to compound the difficulties of studying the Organization. The United Nations also deals with a host of other questions that are perhaps less well known but are possibly no less important in terms of the objectives of the Organization or of understanding how it operates. The Organization is involved in the consideration of other diverse topics such as the proper uses of outer space, the problem of

---

[1] Dean Rusk, "Parliamentary Diplomacy–Debate vs. Negotiation," *World Affairs Interpreter,* Vol. XXVI, No. 2 (Summer 1955), 121-122.

[2] *Ibid.*

population control, the problems faced by land-locked territories, and the rights of women. The United Nations also is engaged in operational activities, ranging from malaria control projects in Asia to designing a common set of road symbols that (it is hoped) will be universally adopted.

The objective of this reader, when used in conjunction with one of the several textbooks in the field, is to provide the student with a framework within which to analyze the dynamic processes of the Organization. I chose these readings because, taken together, I believe that they provide this framework; they do not provide (nor was it intended that they should provide) a definitive picture of all of the aspects of the Organization.

This book originated from the stimulus provided by my students at The University of Wisconsin in their own search for an understanding of the political processes of the Organization and where it fits into the fabric of international politics. I greatly value the opportunity that they gave me to try out many of the readings included here and, especially, the manner in which they probed and challenged the conventional wisdom. In an underlying sense, the guidance and friendship of Leland M. Goodrich not only is responsible for this reader but for my larger interest in international organization. Professor Goodrich, both as a teacher and as a model of careful scholarship, provides an important inspiration for his former students.

I express my gratitude to Mrs. Judith Gaudet for long hours of accurate typing of much of this manuscript. I thank Gerald Papke of John Wiley & Sons for his encouragement of this project. Finally, I owe a large debt to my wife Jane not only for the expenditure of so much of her own time in the mundane tasks of preparing a manuscript but, more importantly, for her unfaltering encouragement and good humor during the project.

DAVID A. KAY

Contents

THE UNITED NATIONS POLITICAL SYSTEM

I THE UNITED NATIONS AND THE INTERNATIONAL POLITICAL SYSTEM

In the first selection, Geoffrey Goodwin, provoked by two seminal events in the history of the United Nations (the Middle Eastern and Hungarian crises of 1956), examines the changing role of the United Nations in international politics. He carefully considers the ever-present problem of what the role of the United Nations should be in the security strategy of the great powers in light of the political divisions of the world. Also he examines the vexing problem of the proper relationship between voting and power in a political organization. This article is one of the first to deal with the impact upon the United Nations of the rush to independence of a large number of former colonial territories.

In William Jordan's article, based on his experience in the Secretariat of the United Nations since 1945, we have a subtle analysis of the problems that result from trying to think about an international organization in a world whose principal actors are nation-states. Jordan, after initially examining this problem with reference to the operation of the system of collective security—all for one and one for all—turns to the question of the kind of peace and security system that the United Nations has evolved in this type of world. Very suggestive is his characterization of the United Nations as "an agency for the continuous adjustment of the relations of established and nascent political groupings." The functional manner in which this adjustment takes place and how much of it not only is carried on within the United Nations but is influenced by the process of the United Nations continues to be a matter of vital concern.

The question of what role the United Nations should play in the international political system is reexamined in the final section of this book. However, both of the present selections make out an impressive case for the view that this determination should be made on the basis of the empirical evidence at hand rather than on the basis of an abstract determination of what the Charter intended. It is a role that is strongly influenced by the Cold War and that is essentially political instead of legal.

The Role of the United Nations in World Affairs

Geoffrey Goodwin

Whatever interpretations future historians may place on recent events in the Middle East and Hungary, they can hardly fail to remark that, in addition to bringing the United Nations back into the forefront of world affairs, they sparked off a debate in more than one member country in which, often for the first time since its inception, the organization became an object of bitter political controversy. In Britain, for instance, attitudes which had previously ranged from sympathetic but rather anxious interest at one end to ill-disguised indifference at the other were replaced almost overnight by acrimonious exchanges in which the United Nations frequently seemed to be regarded either as the supreme arbiter of human affairs, defiance of which verged on sacrilege, or as an irresponsible body of humbugs which acted as a positive incitement to lawlessness and injustice. In this emotional upheaval little attention was paid to the real limitations and potentialities of the organization, while even in the more sober atmosphere that now prevails there is still a good deal of ignorance about the major changes it has undergone in recent years in the field of what the Charter calls "peace and security". A brief assessment of the role of the United Nations in world affairs viewed against the background of these changes may not, therefore, be without value even though it must, in the nature of things, be both tentative and provisional.

Three misconceptions about the United Nations that occasionally linger on mainly, but not solely, in the popular mind can be quickly disposed of. The

Geoffrey Goodwin, "The Role of the United Nations in World Affairs," *International Affairs*, Vol. 34, No. 1 (January 1958), pp. 25-37. Reprinted by permission of the author.

first is that the United Nations provides a "halfway house" to world government. The inability of most protagonists of world government to show why a world riven between parliamentary democracies and variegated autocracies should be thought ripe for world government and their reluctance to tackle the equally crucial question of "Who is to do the governing?" does not deter them from adumbrating formulae intended gradually to transform the United Nations into some kind of federal authority–world government by constitutional stealth, as it has been called. Yet, based as it is on the "sovereign equality of all its Members", the United Nations is in almost every respect the very antithesis of world government. Indeed, the deference paid to the principle of national self-determination, the divorce of responsibility from power through the eclipse of the Security Council by the General Assembly, and the incongruities of the principle of "one State, one vote", all suggest that the organization may excite rather than discourage national particularism and individualism.

The second misconception is not unrelated to the first. It is that the United Nations is a world authority endowed with a will of its own and the capacity to enforce that will; that it is, as Professor J. L. Brierly once put it, an "it" rather than a "they".[1] Hence the disposition of some to exclaim "If only the United Nations would do this or that . . .", or to find in the United Nations a convenient scapegoat for the shortcomings of its members. The United Nations is, in fact, a form of multilateral diplomacy, a modernized version of nineteenth-century "conference diplomacy". More particularly it is a diplomatic contrivance to facilitate collective action; and as such it can for the most part do no more than its members collectively are prepared to do. It is true that the Purposes and Principles of the Charter set out the diplomatic rules to which States are expected to conform. But the natural disposition of most States is to harp on those rules which are in line with their own particular national objectives, and to play down the rest. The prospects for collective action usually turn, therefore, far more on the majority's recognition of a coincidence of national interests then on a genuine deference to these rules.

The third misconception is that had it not been for the veto and especially, it is often said, the Soviet Union's abuse of the veto, the collective security system of the Charter could have been made to work, so rendering unnecessary the creation of collective defence arrangements such as N.A.T.O. and its appendages in the S.E.A.T.O. and the Baghdad Pact. Yet it was obvious almost from the start that the organization's contribution to its members' security could be no more than marginal,[2] if only because the Charter's collective security formula was based

[1] J. L. Brierly, "The Covenant and the Charter", in *British Yearbook of International Law*, 1946.

[2] Article 51 of the Charter (recognizing the right of individual and collective self-defence against armed attack), on which the Western defence system is based, was inserted very largely as an insurance against the breakdown of the Charter's security system.

on the assumption of a continuing "Armed Concert" of great Powers. Even at the San Francisco Conference there were signs of disruption in this Concert. The Soviet Union's later frequent resort to the veto merely reflected the speeding-up of this process; it was a symptom, not a source, of great Power antagonisms. In the nuclear world of today which has crystallized into two main power blocs of about equal strength (with the uncommitted Powers nowhere near strong enough to give a clear preponderance to the side on which they might choose to throw their weight), the orthodox collective security picture of an aggressive minority deterred or, if necessary, subdued by a majority coalition of overwhelming might is quite irrelevant. Measures such as the amendment of the veto, the conclusion of military agreements under Article 43, the strengthening of the General Assembly's "Uniting for Peace" machinery, could in no way alter this basic fact.

I

That the United Nations is not of central importance in its members' search for security and that the prospects of world peace turn principally on the effectiveness of global and regional balances of power and on the common fear of thermonuclear warfare has, of course, been accepted doctrine in most of the Western world for some years. This is not to argue, however, that the United Nations contribution to its members' security has been negligible. On the contrary, it has served the Western world well by combatting early American isolationism and by serving as a convenient medium through which American power has been brought to bear on some peripheral danger spots (Iran, Greece, Korea, and perhaps the Middle East today). It has also provided a diplomatic point of contact through which informal and private negotiations have been initiated when normal diplomatic channels have practically broken down (the Berlin blockade and the clearing of the Suez Canal), while it has on several occasions helped to bring fighting to an end (Indonesia and Palestine)—sometimes, as in the case of Korea, by facilitating mediation by an uncommitted Power (India).

Against these achievements must be set, however, the evident incapacity of the Security Council—and *a fortiori* the General Assembly—to secure compliance with its wishes even by those who are neither great Powers nor the latters' "protégés"; the disposition of more than one leading member to behave as if the United Nations were a substitute for a coherent policy or to use it as a convenient depository for insoluble problems (early American and British policies respectively over Palestine); the encouragement given to meddling in private disputes or in "domestic affairs" by far from disinterested third parties; and the interminable wrangling in which delegates have often seemed more intent on scoring points off their opponents than on seeking an accommodation.

It is not surprising, therefore, that even as early as the beginning of 1950 there was a considerable body of opinion in several member countries which suspected that the organization was doing more harm than good. Although United Nations action in Korea temporarily checked this suspicion, the chief lesson of Korea seemed to be the need to strengthen and extend N.A.T.O.'s defences and to ensure that the United Nations would be able to provide the N.A.T.O. Powers with moral support if a similar situation should arise elsewhere.[3]

This was the main purpose of the "Uniting for Peace" Resolution of 3 November 1950. Though ostensibly preserving the primary responsibility of the Security Council in security matters, it was in fact based on the postulate that the Security Council would almost certainly be paralysed by Soviet obstructionism[4] and that, in such an eventuality, the General Assembly could properly act in its place. In the event of a threat to the peace, therefore, the resolution provided, *inter alia,* for the calling of an emergency special session of the General Assembly with a view to the latter "making appropriate recommendations to Members for collective measures, including in the case of a breach of the peace or act of aggression the use of armed force when necessary".[5]

The "Uniting for Peace" resolution registered the final consummation of a trend initiated as far back as September 1947 with General Marshall's proposals for an "Interim Committee" to sit between normal Assembly sessions, the chief result of which has been, of course, that the General Assembly has come to overshadow the Security Council in the field of peace and security as in everything else. The United Nations is now, and has been for several years, an Assembly-centred rather than a Security Council-centred organization, as was the intention of its founders. It is with some of the consequences of this change that the rest of this article will be principally concerned.

II

Unlike the Security Council, the *decisions* of which members have pledged themselves to carry out, the General Assembly can, generally speaking, only make *recommendations,* which members are legally free to ignore. But the

[3]Action could, of course, be taken under Article 51, but the moral backing of the United Nations might help to rally the necessary public support—as the Security Council's endorsement of American action in Korea had done.

[4]The Security Council had only been able to act over Korea because the Soviet delegate was absent and China was represented by a delegate of the rump Nationalist Government.

[5]U.N. General Assembly Official Records, 5th Session, Suppl. No. 20, Resolution 377 (v). Provision was also made for a Peace Observation Commission and for the earmarking of national contingents for service with the United Nations.

significance of this distinction should not be overrated; the sense of legal compulsion behind the Security Council's decisions has not prevented even the less powerful States from ignoring them with impunity.[6] The crucial differences between the two arise from the greater size of the Assembly and from the introduction into it of a system of majority voting, based upon the principle of "one State, one vote", in which no provision is made for the special position of the great Powers. One of the main consequences of this system has been to encourage what might be called "voting power" politics, the aim of which is to muster the number of votes (either a two-thirds or simple majority) required to secure the passage of a resolution. If the prescribed majority can be secured, the minority can then be voted down.

Majority voting owes its introduction chiefly to the conception of the General Assembly as the deliberative assembly–the "town meeting" of the world–the chief function of which would be to crystallize and express "world public opinion". Majority voting–a good democratic device–would enable it to do so unhampered by the veto given to every State, great or small, by the unanimity rule. This analogy between majority rule within a parliamentary democracy and majority rule in an international institution is, however, misleading. Whereas, within certain limits, the dissentient minority within a State is constitutionally compellable, at the international level the majority are neither entitled to impose conformity–a majority vote gives no legal power of coercion–nor do they usually possess either the capacity or the will to do so. Moreover, the degree of agreement as to ends and means on which democratic procedures are predicted rarely, if ever, exists in the international context. More often than not, therefore, the majority's recommendations will carry little or no moral authority in the eyes of the minority. In any case, a minority's conformance with a resolution will in most instances be dictated much more by fear of diplomatic isolation (which may threaten ties of friendship on which a country's security and influence are heavily dependent) or of a threat to a government's position at home (since the resolution may strike responsive chords in domestic opinion or at least serve as useful grist to an Opposition's mill) than by any belief in its intrinsic merits. And it hardly needed the differing responses to the General Assembly's resolution on Suez and Hungary to drive home the point that some States are much more sensitive than others to such considerations.

This is not to dismiss majority voting out of hand. A perpetuation of the unanimity rule of the League would almost certainly have stultified the Assembly as surely as has the veto the Security Council. The present system does at least prevent the Assembly from being hamstrung by the vagaries or calculated

[6]Egypt's defiance of the Council's resolution of 1 September 1951, calling upon her to terminate the embargo on shipping passing through the Suez Canal bound for Israel, is but one example.

obstructionism of a small minority and enable the majority to act with United Nations backing. The real need is for majorities to appreciate the limitations of their arithmetical preponderance and to refrain from passing resolutions which clearly bear little relation to diplomatic realities or which bear invidiously on those States peculiarly sensitive to majority opinion.

III

The chief danger of a divorce between Assembly resolutions and diplomatic realities arises, it is often said, from the excessive egalitarianism of the principle of "one State, one vote" and from the growth of bloc voting. On the face of it it does indeed look quite absurd that the smallest member should have the same voting strength as one of the great Powers. This discrepancy between voting weight and diplomatic weight has led to the advocacy, especially in countries whose responsibilities far outrun their present voting power, of various forms of weighted voting.

The merits of weighted voting can be exaggerated, however. Even were the present status of Assembly recommendations to remain unaltered, weighted voting would almost certainly strengthen the belief, at least in the West, that they have some kind of moral sanction behind them; recent events have shown what an embarrassment such a belief may prove to statesmen of democratic countries who may quite genuinely hold, rightly or wrongly, that their country's interests require them to embark on what they know will prove to be an unpopular course. Thus weighted voting may have an effect quite the reverse of that intended.[7] Moreover, the existing system may in practice be closer to diplomatic realities, since under it the present recommendations evidently represent neither the decisions of a world arbitral tribunal nor the findings of "world public opinion"—even if this can be said to exist. They merely register what might be called a diplomatic consensus, that is, the degree of agreement reached between the diplomatic representatives of the sovereign members of the General Assembly.

Naturally the attention paid by governments to this consensus will turn far more on its composition than on its size; in other words they will look behind the numerical totals to see what the political realities are. Thus the significance of, for instance, the resolution of 2 November 1956 calling for a cease-fire in Egypt and for troop movements to be halted lay not so much in the size of the supporting vote as in the fact that it included the United States and the majority of N.A.T.O., half the Commonwealth, and practically all of Asia, Africa, Latin

---

[7] Especially as its strongest advocates are often those who see in it a step towards giving the General Assembly the power to arrive at decisions binding on its members.

America, and the Middle East.[8] Such an extraordinary consensus of agreement pointed up quite unmistakably the diplomatic isolation of Britain and France as a result of their action. This kind of "mental weighting" is also reflected in the disposition of the small States to look to the great (and to some medium) Powers to take the initiative on major policy questions and in the more frequent representation of these Powers on *ad hoc* committees and sub-committees. For these and other reasons the Assembly's recommendations now usually register the outcome of private negotiation in the lobbies and elsewhere rather than the points scored in the cut and thrust of the public debates; and in these private negotiations it is nearly always the greater Powers that take the lead.

Lastly, whatever the intrinsic merits of weighted voting—and the above arguments do not tell decisively against it—the difficulties of hitting upon an acceptable system of weighting would be formidable indeed. Which criteria should be used in computing voting strength? Population? National or *per capita* income? Territorial area? Contributions to the United Nations budget? If the weighting were based upon a single factor only it would give an entirely false picture of the relative diplomatic weight of States. If, on the other hand, several factors were taken into account, how much weight should be attached to each? And should not the weighting vary according to the particular issue on which the vote is being taken, for most States are bound to be more interested in some issues than others? In face of such uncertainties it might well seem that the present "mental weighting" is not at all a poor substitute for a formalized weighting system.

IV

It is possible, however, that some of the above arguments may be invalidated by the growth of bloc voting in the Assembly and by the disproportionate influence exercised by the Afro-Asian bloc. Bloc voting—and the "horse-trading" between blocs, often irrespective of the merits of a question—has come in for much adverse criticism in Britain. This is not, perhaps, surprising since in this kind of voting game Britain is at a considerable disadvantage (as there is no Commonwealth bloc) compared with the Soviet Union that commands nine votes, the United States that on most issues counts upon the support of sixteen Latin-American republics, and the Afro-Asian group with the largest bloc vote of any.

As is well known, the admission of some twenty new members into the United Nations since December 1955 has radically changed the voting balance within the

[8] U.N.G.A.O.R., 562nd Plenary meeting, p. 34; the resolution was carried by sixty-four votes to five (Australia, France, Israel, New Zealand, United Kingdom) and six abstentions (Belgium, Canada, Laos, Netherlands, Portugal, South Africa). Though abstaining, Canada expressed support for a cease-fire.

Assembly. Previously it was the United States that could usually mobilize the twenty-one votes then necessary to block any resolution on an important issue.[9] Today it is the Afro-Asian group that has a virtual veto since it can muster the twenty-eight votes which can prevent such a resolution from receiving the necessary two-thirds majority (i.e. fifty-five votes if all the eighty-two members are present and voting).[10]

Two caveats should perhaps be entered here. The first is that the manoeuvring for votes which goes on in the Assembly (as it does in most bodies in which majority voting prevails) is on the whole kept within reasonable limits by the growth of these voting blocs. Not only do the latter mark a real if inchoate community of ideas and interests, but their very voting cohesion helps to make the Assembly a less unpredictable and volatile body. And if it be argued that one result of bloc voting is that many members will often put their group loyalties before their own private assessment of the merits of an issue, is this entirely unknown even in the "Mother of Parliaments"? The second is that not only are there a number of countries that do not belong to any bloc but also alignments within the different blocs vary considerably (the Soviet bloc always excepted) according to the issue involved, be it the cold war, colonialism, or economic aid. This is particularly true of the Afro-Asian bloc, in which there are three subgroups. There are the members of S.E.A.T.O. and the Baghdad Pact with eight votes; the "neutralist" countries, led by India and Egypt, also with eight votes; and, lastly, on all issues other than those they would term Western imperialism or colonialism, the "floating" vote of countries like Burma, Cambodia, Ceylon, Ghana, and, perhaps, Malaya. Much of the manoeuvring at the United Nations is designed to secure these "floating votes". Nor is this a peculiarly United Nations exercise. It is part of the normal diplomatic task of trying to find some common denominator between interests which are not, on the face of it, coincidental. And if, in the course of it, Western policies have sometimes to be modified to secure as wide support as possible, this may very well dissuade the United States and its allies from taking too narrow a view of their national interests or from pursuing policies which may alienate the "uncommitted" countries and drive them into the Soviet camp.

However, the main burden of most recent criticism in Britain and elsewhere is not only that the Afro-Asian bloc exercises a voting power quite out of proportion

---

[9] Under Article 18 of the Charter, "Decisions of the General Assembly on important questions shall be made by a two-thirds majority of the members present and voting," while "decisions on other questions, including the determination of additional categories of questions to be decided by a two-thirds majority, shall be made by a majority of the members present and voting."

[10] If the Afro-Asian group, the Latin American group, and the Soviet bloc voted together they could themselves muster a two-thirds majority. This is an unlikely but not an impossible contingency.

to its real power but that some of its members are so animated by anti-Western prejudice as to undermine that respect for "the principles of justice and international law" which the organization is intended to foster. The first part of this criticism is clearly well founded. Yet the exceptional influence that the Afro-Asian countries wield in the Assembly may be both a fairly accurate forecast of the balance of forces which is gradually coming into being in the world and a healthy reminder of the disastrous consequences for the West if the majority of these countries (and especially India) should gravitate towards the Communist camp. The second part of the criticism is more damaging and calls for rather more detailed examination.

V

As has been well described elsewhere,[11] the attempts to adapt the United Nations to the exigencies of the cold war have of recent years been almost overshadowed by a new conflict, in which the whole system of relationships which grew up between Europe and the non-European world over the past three centuries is being called into question. The roots of this conflict are to be found in the growth of national self-consciousness and self-assertiveness among Asian and African peoples at a time when Western Europe's power and influence are on the wane. The colonial Powers would have had to reckon with these new forces irrespective of the United Nations. Nevertheless, it is the case that the organization has tended to provide them with a convenient focus and has consequently tended to function much less as a defence of the *status quo* than as an instrument for speeding up the process by which the destinies of non-European peoples have passed from European hands. And since it is part of the nature of an international organization that its members should tend to identify its aims with their own national objectives, it is to be expected that the Afro-Asian–the "Bandung"–Powers should see in the organization a means of pursuing, not only the general interest in the avoidance of war, but their own particular interest in bringing to an end the last vestiges of European overlordship.

For a country like Britain, which in the last decade has demonstrated in unmistakable fashion her desire to lead her dependent peoples to full nationhood, there need be no fundamental disagreement with the long-term objectives of the anti-colonial group. But there are several ways in which its activities may prove detrimental to British interests. For example, the Anglo-Iranian Oil dispute (1951-1952) and President Nasser's seizure of the Suez Canal pointed up a dilemma with which the Charter confronts States having important property interests abroad. The Charter, in Article 2(4), in effect enjoins members to refrain from the *unilateral* threat or use of force to protect the lives and property of their nationals

[11] Coral Bell, "The United Nations and the West," *International Affairs*, October 1952.

in foreign lands. But what collective means of protection or of redress does the Charter provide as an alternative? Virtually none. Yet both these instances suggest that circumstances may well arise[12] in which a country will feel perfectly justified in using force to safeguard what it regards as a vital overseas interest and yet be disinclined to do so partly from fear of incurring the wrath of the Security Council or, more likely, of the General Assembly. It is arguable that such a deterrent is unlikely to prove very embarrassing if a country's case is obviously a strong one and it plays its diplomatic cards astutely. Also in most instances a deterrent of this kind is all to the good since it can set a check on rash action and serve as an inducement to States to settle their disputes by peaceful means, even under great provacation. The difficulty is that, as United Nations handling of the disputes over Guatemala, Hungary, Kashmir, and Suez has shown, this deterrent is apt to discriminate against the colonial Powers, not only because of their peculiar sensitivity (as parliamentary democracies) to public criticism and their dependence on the goodwill of the United States (where there is both a genuine desire to work through the United Nations and a certain lack of understanding of the colonial Powers' dilemma), but also because of the "double-standard" which appears to be applied by several members of the Afro-Asian group.

The existence of "double-standards" (and of "double-talk") is not surprising in an organization which purports to look after the collective interest but which, in fact, consists of members primarily concerned with looking after their individual national interests. Most delegates will naturally be disposed to apply one standard–given to lofty moral generalities–when their interests are not immediately engaged and another–a thoroughly realistic one–when they are. No doubt partly for this reason, and partly as a result of their own past history, a good many Afro-Asian Powers are very allergic to anything that seems to them to smack of Western imperialism (including so-called dollar imperialism), but are far less sharply critical of the Soviet Union's own brand of imperialism in Eastern Europe and elsewhere. This "double-standard" existed before the United Nations was even thought of and its present incidence should not be exaggerated. The bulk of the Afro-Asian group did in fact support the General Assembly resolution of 14 September 1957 "condemning" Soviet policy in Hungary; and it is reported that several more would have done so if it had been slightly watered down. It should also not be forgotten that both Ceylon and Tunisia were represented on the committee of five which drew up the unanimous Report on the Problem of Hungary,[13] and that it is reported that the honesty of the report was subsequently defended by, amongst others, the Indonesian delegate.[14] Indeed, by providing a medium for disseminating the true facts

[12] It is not the contention here that they existed in either of the two instances mentioned.

[13] G.A.O.R., 11th Session, Supplement No. 18(A/3592). The other countries represented were Denmark, Australia, and Uruguay.

[14] *The Observer,* 15 September 1947.

about the Hungarian tragedy throughout Afro-Asian diplomatic circles, the United Nations has probably done a good deal to dispel some of the illusions still current in these circles about the Soviet Union. It is not too much to hope, therefore, that this particular "double-standard" is on the way out. So long as it persists, however, the Western colonial Powers must be expected to look rather askance at an Assembly in which its practitioners hold the voting balance.

Two related misgivings can only be briefly mentioned. The first arises from the General Assembly's rather cavalier treatment of legal considerations. For this the Afro-Asian group must also accept much of the responsibility; several of them do indeed behave as if international law were a derogation from some higher principle of international justice (for example, national self-determination) or as if legal rights were merely the expression of a vanishing order of international relationships. The existing legal order is not, of course, sacrosanct, and few States will give precedence to legal obligations which run counter to their "vital interests". But it is one thing to decide to evade legal restraints out of sheer political necessity or because they have become manifestly "unjust", and quite another to brush them aside merely because they have become something of an embarrassment. This latter attitude is bound to weaken an important element making for order and stability in international society and is clearly contrary to the prescriptions of the Charter. It is especially disturbing for countries such as Britain, not only because of their ingrained respect for law and their obvious interest in a more orderly world, but also because their legal rights tend to outrun their capacity to defend them.

The second misgiving is best summed up in Sir Winston Churchill's speech of 31 July 1957 on the United Nations[15] in which, with the contrast between the responses to the General Assembly's resolutions on Suez and Hungary in mind, he declared: "Justice cannot be a hit-or-miss system." There will be much sympathy with this thought, especially amongst those who see in the United Nations an instrument not only for avoiding war through the peaceful reconciliation of conflicting interests but also for remedying injustices, particularly those perpetrated by the Soviet Union in Eastern Europe. But would these people have been prepared to spark off a third world war (and to risk defeat in it) by backing the Assembly's exhortations to the Soviet Union with military sanctions?[16] Would they be prepared to go to war with India to enforce a plebiscite in Kashmir which the Security Council has consistently favoured as the first step towards a "just" solution to the problem of Kashmir? Is it their view that a solution could have been found to the Palestine problem in 1948 that would have done justice to both Jews and Arabs, or that solutions can be found today that will do full justice to both Greek and Turkish Cypriots in Cyprus and to both Europeans and Arabs in Algiers? These are very large questions on which there will be many differing opinions. But so, of course,

---

[15] *The Times,* 1 August 1957.

[16] Economic sanctions would clearly have been quite ineffective.

are there many differing conceptions of "justice". This is not to deny that these differing conceptions may sometimes coincide or to argue that justice must invariably give way to the realities of power. Yet it does suggest the need for an awareness both of the subjective element in nearly all conceptions of justice and of the risk that too brash an attempt to remedy an existing injustice may merely lead to conditions in which even greater injustices will flourish.

VI

The United Nations is not today what most people in 1945 expected it to be. The prospects of world peace turn not on the Security Council but on the effectiveness of global and regional balances of power and on the common fear of thermo-nuclear warfare. The primary aim for the West, therefore, must be the more effective unity of Europe within a consolidated N.A.T.O. system, and a sustained effort–for the most part through traditional diplomatic channels–to hammer out a general *modus vivendi* with the Communist world. But there are several ways in which the United Nations can help to counter the inherently unstable and competitive nature of a two-sided balance (as each side seeks to achieve a slight margin of superiority in order to diminish its own sense of insecurity and to strengthen its hand in negotiation).

An obvious instance is disarmament. There is clearly little hope of the institution of a comprehensive disarmament scheme while the problems of a divided Germany or of Formosa's future remain unresolved. But one source of the present tension between the West and the Soviet Union is almost certainly the belief of both that the other may attempt, if an opportune moment should arise, to achieve a quick victory by a surprise "knock-out" blow. A partial disarmament scheme which could provide something of a safeguard against surprise attacks and limit test explosions of nuclear weapons would be of inestimable benefit.[17] The prospects even for such a limited agreement are not particularly encouraging, but the United Nations does, at least, provide a forum where unremitting pressure to this end can be maintained.

There are other more subtle ways in which the organization can exercise a healthy restraining influence. For instance, by encouraging personal diplomacy between Foreign Ministers (and their immediate aides) it may enable them to get to know each other's minds and fears and so act as a brake on mutual suspicion and mistrust; at least it can help to indicate how far a policy can be pursued without precipitating bloodshed. It may make it easier for a State–even for a great Power–to claim that it is modifying its policy in the "general interest" and so to

---

[17] Whether it should include a ban on the production of fissile material for military purposes is more open to question.

climb down from an untenable position without serious loss of face. Nor should its potentialities in moments of crises be underestimated. The creation of the United Nations Emergency Force is an obvious example, for it is difficult to see how such a force could have come into existence had it not been for the United Nations. And although recent experience has shown that the main problems lie not so much in the actual formation of such a force as in obtaining agreement on the political directives for its military commander and in securing the consent of the country in whose territory the force is to be stationed, the present Emergency Force may possibly serve as a model for the future.

However, probably one of the main contributions of the United Nations is to serve as a place where, on the one hand, the statesmen of newly independent countries can learn better to appreciate political realities, and where, on the other hand, the statesmen of the West can gain a closer understanding of the new forces at work in the world. The more moderate tone in recent Assembly debates on Cyprus and Algeria already suggests that many non-European delegates have become much more alive to the complexities of issues to which previously they had thought application of the principle of self-determination provided a certain answer. There are also signs that some at least have grasped the need to strike a balance between their desire for change and the reasonable preservation of established rights and treaty obligations. If these hopes should prove illusory a reassessment of the organization's value would then become necessary. But that is not yet the case.

This is not to deny that the United Nations has many limitations and obvious imperfections. But this is to be expected, given the unruly and turbulent world in which it has to operate; and few of them could be removed merely by formal amendment of the Charter even if that were to prove possible. How its potentialities are used depends first and foremost on the moderation and good sense of its members, not on its precise institutional machinery. The prime need today as perhaps never before, therefore, is for prudent and yet courageous statesmanship. But the United Nations can often serve as a useful navigational aid—a diplomatic lighthouse—warning statesmen of the perils to be avoided, while it still symbolizes, in however dim and inchoate a way, those ideals to which probably the majority of informed opinion in the "free" world feels itself committed. To harp exclusively on the defects and limitations of the United Nations would ill become a country like Britain whose best safeguard for the future is still, as it was in 1907, a national policy that is "so directed as to harmonize with the general desires and ideals common to all mankind, and more particularly that . . . is closely identified with the primary and vital interests of a majority, or as many as possible, of the other nations."[18]

---

[18]Memorandum by Mr. Eyre Crowe, F. O. 371/257, Foreign Office, 1 January 1907, G.P. Gooch and H. Temperley, *British Documents on the Origins of the War,* 1898-1914 (London, H.M.S.O., 1928), Vol. III, pp. 402-3.

Concepts and Realities in International Political Organization

William M. Jordan

The heading under which these observations are brought together may well seem presumptuous. The request made to me was to deal with the subject: "collective security"–a phrase which I am hesitant to use, for it has come to cover the most diverse international political arrangements. The title adopted provides a convenient umbrella under which to bring together a number of general observations on the approach to the problem of maintaining peace.

Just forty years have passed since Leonard Woolf brought together in his two studies, *International Government* in 1916, and *The Framework of a Lasting Peace* in 1917, the proposals which were then being put forward for the maintenance of peace and the body of experience available at that time regarding the working of international institutions. The range of relevant experience was then slender. Thought on the subject had to be based on analogy from the working of national institutions, on the traditions and practices of international law, and on the operation of a few, mainly technical, international agencies. In the past forty years, a vast range of experience has been accumulated, and our problem is now largely one of devising means to view this extensive experience as a whole.

Clarity of thought is made all the more difficult by the great variety of approaches. Numerous case histories of the handling of specific political problems are now available. They have the great merit of facilitating the study of the working of international political organs within the broad framework of conflicting

William M. Jordon, "Concepts and Realities in International Political Organization," *International Organization,* Vol. 11, No. 4 (Autumn 1957), pp. 587-596. Reprinted by permission of *International Organization.*

national policies. But concentration on the detail of an individual case tends to preclude the formulation of generalizations valid for the working of international political organs as a whole. So the endeavor has been made to discern reasonably constant elements in the functioning of international political organs regarding both their internal procedures and their expedients for dealing with problems, and to classify and expound the range of experience under headings indicative of characteristic types of activity. This mode of analysis was commenced in masterful fashion by T. P. Conwell-Evans some thirty years ago,[1] and has been applied in Leland Goodrich and Anne Simons' work, *The United Nations and the Maintenance of International Peace and Security.*[2]

Side by side with these empirical studies are the works concerned with the constitutional instruments under which international political organs operate. But the meticulous study of the texts gives rise only too readily to the defect, so aptly described by M. Geny—that "the idea, completely detached from its object, finds its own release and leads a life of its own, deprived of all contact with the living reality."[3] In works prepared by the Secretariat, such as the *Repertoire of the Practice of the Security Council* and the *Repertory of Practice of United Nations Organs,*[4] the attempt has been made to relate the living reality of the work of the organs to the provisions of the Charter. But the study of the working of essentially political institutions requires a freedom of analysis and exposition which cannot be attained within a framework of constitutional commentary. The utility of such works is limited by reason of the necessary formalism of their approach.

Then there are those whose minds have ranged freely over the realm of experience, either on the basis of actual participation or on the basis of wide study, and who have sought to formulate by intellectual processes which we but dimly understand—we call it reflection, judgment, or intuition—counsels of wisdom which give guidance for the present and future. The diversity of approaches applied to the wide range of experience accentuates the difficulty of any one mind bringing within its focus the extensive knowledge and reflection which has been directed to the subject of international political institutions.

Many new theoretical approaches are being devised for the study of international politics and international political institutions. The advance in modes of

---

[1] T. P. Conwell Evans, *The League Council in Action,* London, Oxford University Press, H. Milford, 1929.

[2] Leland M. Goodrich and Anne P. Simons, *The United Nations and the Maintenance of International Peace and Security,* Washington, Brookings Institution, 1955.

[3] Quoted in Charles de Visscher, *Theory and Reality in Public International Law,* Princeton, New Jersey, Princeton University Press, p. 67.

[4] *Repertoire of the Practice of the Security Council,* 1946-1951, New York, 1954; *Repertoire of the Practice of the Security Council,* Supplement, 1952-57, New York, 1957; *Repertory of Practice of United National Organs,* Vol. I-V, New York, 1955.

political analysis cannot but be of special interest to an international secretariat which increasingly needs to bring to bear a body of corporate thought on the development of the organs which it serves and the political problems which those organs face. Within an international secretariat the great problem is not so much the conflict of national loyalties, but rather the great diversity of mental habits which men and women of different countries bring to their work. We have to strive toward some unity of analytical approach if a corporate body of work is to emerge. Economists have seemingly built up agreed modes of analysis which transcend national boundaries, and the world has come to accept the tradition of current economic analysis by its international servants. In the political field, we are still almost wholly dependent on individual wit and wisdom. I recall that some thirty years ago Graham Wallas, reflecting on the political differences which arose through the devotion of Englishmen to intuitive processes of thought and of Frenchmen to logical reasoning, made a prophecy which might appropriately be quoted:

"...I find myself hoping that some day an art of thought may prevail—perhaps after the horrors of a new Thirty Years' War—in which the psychological truths implied in both types of thinking may be recognized and combined, and the errors of both may in some measure be avoided. If the psychologists ever create such an art, it may be that, a century hence, in gratitude for escape from some world disaster which had seemed to be 'logically' inevitable, a statue will be set up in New York or Paris or Peking, not to the Goddess of Reason, but to 'Psyche', the goddess who presides over the wise direction of the whole thinking organism....

"Sometimes I hope that an art of thought which makes full use of every factor in the human organism may first be developed in America."[5]

In such writing on collective security I find myself puzzled by what appears to me a sometimes bewildering combination of logical and empirical thought. The temptation seems inescapable to define collective security, and thereafter to proceed by an exploration of the logical implications of the definition. But collective security is not a term of law which requires definition. The term is not, I think, to be found in the Charter or in the Covenant of the League of Nations. The process of definition and logical exposition is by no means identical with, and not always reconcilable with, the task of envisaging concretely—almost in physical form—the problem which confronts us and the manner of dealing with it. "De quoi s'agit-il?" was the question which Marshal Foch insistently demanded that his officers pose to themselves when lost in the labyrinths of their own reasoning.

---

[5]Graham Wallas, *The Art of Thought,* London, J. Cape, 1926, p. 185.

The problem is that of ending the institution of war, of establishing arrangements to achieve that goal, and of estimating the prospects of their successful working in practice.

In the inter-war period, the conviction developed that war could most assuredly be brought to an end if a system were established whereby wrongful recourse to war was met by the application of collective counter-measures of overwhelming strength. The essential and indispensable feature of such a system had to be certainty in the operation of sanctions; for without certainty, deterrence could not be assured. The quest for certainty gave rise to long debate concerning the scope of the acts to be included in the definition of wrongful recourse to war and the means whereby the application of the definition to circumstances as they arose could be made automatic. Only in this way could the application of sanctions become an inexorable consequence of the commission of the wrongful act of war.

Such were the arrangements for which the term collective security was coined. That at least is my impression. The Covenant of the League of Nations was not itself a system of collective security in this sense. The Covenant prescribed procedures of pacific settlement which states were required to observe before having recourse to force for the protection of their interests. The sanctions to be applied by Member States were designed to ensure the observance of procedures of settlement.

The conviction that peace might be maintained most surely by establishing machinery for the automatic application of coercive measures against any state which broke the peace arose primarily from the endeavor of France and her allies to convert the League into a system which would provide them with a guarantee of the maintenance of the territorial settlement in Europe. Their thesis was simple. You ask us to disarm. We hold that if we disarm, we shall be unable to defend our frontiers and to maintain the territorial settlements concluded in 1919. In so far as we reduce our national armaments, we must obtain a corresponding degree of protection by the organization of international military assistance. That assistance must be as efficacious for purposes of national defense as national military organization. It must be certain in its application against the disturber of the peace. It must be brought into operation without delay. It must be provided to a degree and in a manner made known in advance, since common plans of defense cannot be devised at a moment's notice. The temper of the time precluded the possibility of discussing the defense of France simply and purely as a problem of checking the resurgence of German power. The immediate preoccupations of France in relation to Germany were translated into general terms such as the defining of aggression and the designation of the aggressor.

The world was left with the conviction that the road to peace lay through the organization of collective security in the sense of automatic application of sanctions against aggression. The success which attended the intellectual effort of

France is indicated by the conviction which arose that the urgent problem was to solve the so-called gap in the Covenant. In fact, there was no gap in the Covenant. The Covenant was simply the Covenant. The gap existed only on the assumption that the Covenant was intended to be a system of collective security complying with the logical French criteria of adequacy. The failure to meet the threat of Hitlerism until it involved the world in a Second World War appeared to confirm the thesis that the road to peace lay in the assured mobilization of collective measures against the aggressor. That failure has led to a state of mind in which the ability of an international organization to take effective measures against aggression tends to be regarded as the primary criterion of its utility and success.

But neither experience nor reflection provides grounds for believing that any system of collective security organized between independent states could provide the certainty which was premised of collective security in the inter-war period. Even the discharge of an obligation is, when the time comes, an act of will. The final decision to apply sanctions must be taken when the occasion arises, in circumstances of discouragement. For the objective of collective security is the maintenance of peace, not ultimate victory. When the moment comes to apply sanctions, the primary purpose of collective security has already been defeated. Participants are in the position of those called upon to pay for the horse after it has left the stable. The legal obligation to apply sanctions is therefore an imperfect measure of the probability of their application. A complete system of sanctions against aggression would indeed seem to require sanctions against those who fail to apply sanctions. When war breaks out, each state is prone to balance the degree of the menace presented to it by the initial outbreak, against the risks involved in joining in collective repression of the wrongdoer. When war breaks out, too, the response of other states is likely to be decisively influenced by the view taken of the soundness of justice of the situation which precipitated it. In the theory of automatic collective security, the obligation arises to engage in coercive action against the state which has placed itself in the position of committing aggression within the definition, without account being taken of the element of provocation, of the surrounding circumstances, or of the natural affinities of feelings between peoples. This is not unjust, it is urged, providing procedures are available for peaceful change. Yet, in fact, in moments of crisis, the course of action followed by a state will be largely swayed by the feelings of sympathy entertained at that moment and by attention to the consequences of immediate action on future relations.

There is then, I think, general agreement that collective security as it was understood would need to be preceded by a conviction on the part of men and women throughout the world that recourse to armed force in any part of the world is a threat to them individually and collectively; and this conviction must be held with sufficient compelling force to enable them to join in common action, whatever the cost to themselves and to their individual countries.

It would be premature to say that these psychological conditions exist. Even if and when these psychological conditions prevail, it would be hazardous to forecast that they will find expression in institutions of collective security automatic in their application. Police action against individuals in communities wedded to the observance of law is no precedent for automatic coercive sanctions against states. This conclusion has been cogently expressed by Oliver Lissitzyn:

"It does not appear that peace has ever been successfully maintained, over appreciably long periods of time, by the application of coercive sanctions to political entities alone. This fact was well known to the framers of the United States Constitution. Federal force has never been used in the United States to enforce a judgment against a state of the Union, and at least one such judgment remained unexecuted. Yet in most federal unions courts have compulsory jurisdiction in disputes between the states and their decisions are usually obeyed. This is attributable to the transfer of the primary allegiance of the individuals from the subordinate entities to the federal Union and to the growth of respect for law."[6]

I should stress that these observations apply only to collective security in the sense of the automatic application of sanctions against aggression. Those who framed the Charter in 1945 wisely avoided any element of automatism. In the Charter the decision to apply enforcement measures was made the prerogative of the Security Council, and was subjected to a voting procedure which would ensure that no such decision would take place against the will of a permanent member. The so-called "veto", at least in relation to Chapter VII, was designed to afford protection as much to lesser states as to the great powers. For it ensured that membership in the UN would not entail for lesser states the burden of a binding obligation to participate in the application of sanctions in circumstances which might involve them in conflict with a great power. Since 1945 the development of nuclear weapons has accentuated the difficulties attending the exercise of coercive power by an international authority.

Should we therefore conclude that the sense of personal identification on the part of men and women with their national communities is so exclusive and unassailable as to render vain the effort to channel the political forces of our time along peaceful lines through the agency of international political institutions? Such would seem to be, if I understood aright, the conclusion of Percy Corbett. He sees a more promising line of advance in the re-orientation of international organization around the focus of human rights. An area of human life should, he proposes, be selected for study, report, and eventually supervision by a supernational agency, and he has pointed to racial discrimination as the most

---

[6]Oliver James Lissitzyn, *The International Court of Justice,* New York, Carnegie Endowment for International Peace, 1951, p. 108.

promising area. "The important thing," he comments, "is the development of effective procedures to which men may increasingly repair in matters which concern them individually and deeply. This is the way to bring international organization out of the high clouds of diplomacy to win for it the common loyalty which is the firm foundation for authority."[7]

"The common loyalty which is the firm foundation for authority" may command our assent as a statement of the goal, without committing us to the road we are invited to travel. I wonder whether Corbett does not underestimate the impact of the principles of the UN Charter. This is not a matter on which we can make confident assertions. Yet we cannot but seek to assess the degree to which the political precepts of the Charter are becoming an element in the structure of thought of men and women throughout the world. The formulation of purposes and principles as obligations to govern the conduct of Member States and to guide the functioning of UN organs was perhaps the outstanding innovation of the Charter as compared with the Covenant of the League. I would feel that there is good reason to hold that within the framework of the UN—granted amidst much contradiction and many conflicts of national interest—the representatives of its Members have in fact striven to translate into practice the general principles of the Organization. The working of the Organization has been shaped not so much by adherence to prescribed procedures as by concern to move, amidst the tense and baffling conflicts of national interest, toward conditions closer to the Charter's standards which command at least verbal homage. These unifying standards are general in scope yet compelling in appeal: the dignity of the human personality, the promotion of economic development, the principle of self-determination, and above all, the renunciation of the use of force.

The maintenance of international peace and security was given priority among the purposes of the Organization. In the service of this objective, two related conceptions were written into the Charter: first, the renunciation of the use or threat of force by Member States, and second, the exercise of force by the Security Council under the provisions of Chapter VII of the Charter.[8] The provisions for placing force at the disposal of the Security Council have not been fulfilled largely because the creation of a powerful international force does not eliminate the problem of the rivalry of great states for predominant influence within it. Yet the very inability of the Organization to develop as an instrument of coercion would seem to have focused attention on Article 2(4) as an anchorage of the Organization's authority. The text of Article 2(4) runs:

"All Members shall refrain in their international relations from the threat or use of force against the territorial integrity or political independence of

[7] P. E. Corbett, *Law and Society in the Relations of States,* Institute of International Studies at Yale University, New York, Harcourt, Brace, 1951, p. 298.

[8] Article 2(4).

and State, or in any other manner inconsistent with the Purposes of the United Nations."

The fear was expressed at San Francisco that this phraseology would leave it open to a Member State to use force in a manner which it claimed to be consistent with the purposes of the UN, but without securing the Organization's assent to such use of force. The Committee of the Conference responsible for the drafting of Chapter I sought to dissipate all doubt by stating in its report: "The unilateral use of force or other coercive measures is not authorized or admitted."[9] Subject to the explicit reservation of the right of self-defense, this interpretation has been ratified in commentaries, notably in the United Kingdom and United States commentaries issued in 1945, and has been markedly fortified by more recent events. Doubt has been expressed whether the renunciation of force can be maintained in practice unless other means are organized for ensuring the protection of the just interests of states. It seems unlikely that this dilemma will receive a solution in general terms; it is a problem likely to demand solution in situations as they arise. Meanwhile, in moments of crisis, Article 2(4) in isolation remains the focal point. For men and women are well aware that national states can now only in limited degree perform their historic function of affording the individual peace and security. These changing political conditions at present express themselves in an undercurrent of anxiety rather than in any modification of traditional social attitudes.

Yet it is significant that, despite the strains and stresses of the post-war years, no nation has yet cared to challenge the existence, nor in a sense the lasting authority, of the UN. We might do well to think of the UN not so much as an institution or organization, but rather as the process of defining the relation of each state to the totality of other states. In recent events do we not discern a deepening conviction that each state is accountable to all for any exercise of force?

A moment ago I referred to the authority of the UN. I did so advisedly, for I feel that the analysis of international relations in terms of power runs into difficult waters in the matter of international institutions. The conception of power politics has played and will continue to play a valuable role in the realistic probing of a wide range of problems in the relations of states, but there is little reason to believe that it can serve to explain the totality of the relations between organized social groups, of which the state is one category. At a further remove, the relations of men and their social groupings are governed by the mental conceptions which command obedience by virtue of the structure of their personalities. The conception of power as the dominating element gives way before the more elusive conception of authority in the general, non-legal sense of that term. It may

---

[9] *United Nations Conference on International Organization,* Vol. VI, p. 459.

well be that our preoccupation with considerations of power constitutes a hindrance to the formulation in general terms of the role which the UN plays in the processes of international relations. Must it not be a main objective of the Organization to give the stamp of approval to social attitudes consonant with the needs of our generation?

From the character of the Charter itself it follows that the Organization is both an instrument for the pursuance of broad social objectives and an agency for the continuous adjustment of the relations of established and nascent political groupings. A variety of descriptive phrases may be employed to depict the net effect of the voluminous debates and formal recommendations through which the Organization expresses itself. They afford an outlet for national tensions and a means whereby assurance may be given by governments to their peoples that steps are being taken for the remedying of national grievances without recourse to force. They furnish a plane on which negotiations may be conducted over and above direct exchanges between states through diplomatic means, and they afford an opportunity to Member States for clarifying the attitudes and intentions of other states on specific problems and their reactions to varying lines of policy. They constitute a forum within which broad considerations of international interest can be formulated and pressed. They are a device whereby vexed problems can be dealt with against the background of a changing concert of powers rather than by a fixed alignment of states. In the process of collective consultation, rigid lines of opposition between defined groups are at least mitigated. Even in circumstances of chronic conflict, they afford the occasion for exchange of views and for negotiations. The scene of these deliberations is now a diplomatic center without parallel. Devices and expedients for the adjustment of the relations of states which defy any standardized approach are formulated according to the exigencies of the moment. The relations of states are by these means rendered more calculable in a world in which these relations are governed by considerations more complex and uncertain than in the past. While it is true that within the arena of the UN efforts are made to win support for national policies and interests, it would be hazardous to contend that national policies remain unmodified by the influence of the generality of states and the precepts of the Organization within whose framework they meet.

The transaction of the multifarious political business which comes before the UN may well be differentiated from its functions on those occasions when the peace of the world as a whole appears to stand in the balance. The courses open to states on the verge of conflict were formulated by Sir Alexander Cadogan when he submitted the so-called Berlin Question to the Security Council in 1948. He recalled briefly the courses of action which appeared to be open to his government: it could passively yield to efforts to deprive it of its authority in Berlin; or it could agree to continue discussions under the conditions of duress established by the Soviet Union. "It is inconceivable," he observed, "that His Majesty's Government, for its part, could consent to either of these courses." "Thirdly," he continued, "His Majesty's Government could themselves resort to force as the only possible way of defending and maintaining their legitimate rights." To do so would be equivalent to adopting the methods of duress of which it complained, and might give rise to unknown consequences. "In all the circumstances," he concluded, "the only step which His Majesty's Government . . . can now take is to bring this matter to the attention of the Security Council as a clear threat to the peace. . . ."[10] In such circumstances the UN is simply the ultimate political council available to the states of the world.

Inquiry as to common elements in the processes whereby the UN has contributed to or was instrumental in maintaining general international peace on the main occasions on which it has been endangered since 1946 seems to yield little harvest. Each occasion has its special history to add to the fund of experience and demands examination in all its particularity. Consider the example of the Uniting for Peace Resolution. It was designed to codify experience in dealing with the attack on the Republic of Korea. Yet the Uniting for Peace Resolution has repeated the experience of the Charter. Its effective contribution has been the provision of an instrumentality through which the purposes of the Charter may be pursued, in this instance, the emergency session of the General Assembly. The detailed provisions of the Uniting for Peace Resolution have remained in large degree inoperative. In October-November 1956, new expedients were devised appropriate to the exigencies of the situation: the establishment of the United Nations Emergency Force (UNEF); the utilization of the services of the Secretary-General for the establishment of the Force, the assignment to him of responsibility for the supervision of its operations, and reliance on him for negotiation with the states concerned regarding the implementation of the Assembly resolutions; and, finally, the institution of an Advisory Committee for consultative purposes. UNEF was a novel conception. The forces of the permanent members were excluded. Its chief responsible officer was appointed by the UN itself and was responsible ultimately to the General Assembly; his authority was so defined as to make him independent of the policies of any one nation. But the creation and operation of the Force was dependent on the attitude and interests of the states directly concerned in the specific circumstances. The applicability of such a device in the future would similarly depend on the special aspects of the crisis which arises.

From the experience on the UN some have concluded that the Organization would be well advised to concentrate exclusively on its function as an arena of international debate and on its role in the peaceful settlement of disputes, and wholly to eschew the application of coercive measures. Doubtless in practice the emphasis has been on stimulating the will of states to settle disputes peacefully and on providing ways and means of settlement not otherwise available. But it is

---

[10] Security Council *Official Records* (3d year), 364th meeting, October 6, 1948, pp. 35-36.

questionable whether the effort to organize force through the agency of an international political organ could be wholly abandoned without the most detrimental repercussions on arrangements for the settlement of disputes. At any time states are open to the temptation to seize possession or to force, their will by recourse to force, and to calculate that a situation once so created will not be reversed. Uncertainty as to the eventual reaction of the Organization constitutes a factor making for restraint, especially in circumstances where the immediate problem is to arrest the outbreak of hostilities or to prevent their spread. The events of the past twelve months leave somewhat incalculable both the degree of political authority exercisable by or through the UN and the manner of its exercise.

It will, I think, be felt that we are experiencing a great modification in the conditions governing the relations of states and the method of conducting those relations. Between the wars it was the common assertion that armaments were the backing of diplomacy, and that war was the conduct of diplomacy by other means. The correlation between the armed power of a state and the feasible objectives of its foreign policy was not difficult to discern. That correlation is now more obscure. Our conception of the state in international politics has been that of a sharply defined entity dealing with other similar defined and enduring entities exclusively through the authorized agency of its foreign minister. This conception by no means corresponds to reality as closely as in the past. It is not only that the concept of self-determination has rudely challenged the integrity of many existing states—a challenge which would have involved the UN in far greater difficulties had the guarantee of territorial integrity been written into the Charter. It is also that issues which arise in international relations tend to transcent national boundaries. The relations of states tend to be defined—for better or for worse—through a process of international public debate of which the UN is a focal point, but which spreads far beyond its walls. It is in the light of such changing circumstances—the incalculability of force in relation to the achievement of political objectives and the attuning of domestic opinion to views entertained in other lands—that the role of international political organization must be estimated.

We are in no position at present to translate the outcome of such changes into precise institutional forms. Instead, the maintenance of peace remains dependent on restraint and wisdom in the formulation of policy both within and without the formal framework of the UN. The situation which confronts us has been aptly summed up by Mr. Menzies in a recent speech in London:

"Every nation, and particularly every great nation, whatever its natural resentment may be at some actions of the United Nations, must face up to the fact of the Assembly and give to the work of that Assembly a very high authority, threshing out its own policy with great care, presenting it with the greatest authority and force, taking the diplomatic opportunities provided by Assembly meetings for securing the widest measure of support for that policy."[11]

May I conclude that an official will necessarily have difficulty in discerning to what extent his appraisal is an objective examination of the institution which he serves and to what extent it is colored by being viewed through official spectacles. That I have wholly escaped the temptation to move from detached analysis to partisan advocacy is more than I would expect. International political organization is the microcosm of the realm of international politics. The detail and the vastness of the canvas may well defeat the effort to see it clearly and to see it whole.

---

[11] *The Times* (London), July 9, 1957.

II THE UNITED NATIONS–ORIGINS AND EVOLUTION

The immediate origin of the United Nations clearly can be traced to the prior experiment in international organization: the League of Nations. Both organizations share a common inception in victorious wartime coalitions that desired to avoid the horrors of another conflict through concerted political action. Gerhart Niemeyer, after noting this historical progression, evaluates the experience of the League not because of any intrinsic interest in it but because of a belief that an accurate understanding of the role of the United Nations cannot be gained without it. In evaluating the experience of the League, Niemeyer rejects as an appropriate criteria of success the aims of the drafters of the League Covenant and the conflicting perceptions of the states that joined the League. The criteria of success that is used in this article is the extent to which the League succeeded in placing "the use of national arms and diplomacy under the control of general principles of law and the common interests of a world order." Using this criteria, the history of the League in dealing with international security crises is subjected to a searching analysis. Led by this analysis, Niemeyer concludes that the League did not measure up very well to the standard of a world community, and calls for further study of the actual impact of international organizations as instruments of international politics.

As Leland M. Goodrich points out, it was quite fashionable at the founding of the United Nations to disparage (or totally overlook) similarities between the League of Nations and the United Nations. The League not only had failed to prevent the Second World War but also had expelled one of the great powers—the Soviet Union—for its attack on Finland. Another of the great powers—the United States—had failed to join the League after a domestic political conflict whose wounds had not yet completely healed. Although this may have been a compelling reason for slighting the League ancestory at San Francisco, students of international organizations should recognize the many similarities of the two organizations. Goodrich, in making this comparison, specifically calls attention to the League in practice rather than the League of the Covenant. For example, the point is often made that in the League the Assembly could make decisions only on the basis of a unanimous vote whereas in the United Nations the General Assembly can make decisions by a two-thirds majority. However, as Goodrich points out, at the first session of the League's Assembly the practice developed of requiring only a simple majority vote on those resolutions expressing a wish. On the basis of a comparison of the two organizations, Goodrich concludes that the United Nations is a "revised League". This conclusion was reached on the basis of comparing the League in practice with the United Nations of the Charter. Students should be attuned to this question: What would be the conclusion of a comparison of the League in practice with the United Nations in practice?

As the United Nations prepared to celebrate its twentieth birthday in 1965, U Thant, from his prespective as the third Secretary-General of the United Nations, compared the development of the League with the development of United Nations. He sees a clear continuation in commitment to the idea that the rush toward interdependence of political communities confers upon every nation the right to discuss the conduct of every other nation and, in certain situations when the resort to violence has taken place, to act in concert to bring the violence to a rapid conclusion. According to Thant, the League failed to put its ideas into consistent practice, but they were reborn in the United Nations. Would Niemeyer conclude that the League failed or the ideas failed? The Secretary-General also observes several significant contrasts in the practices of the two organizations. Because the process of decolonization has resulted in the creation of a number of new nations, the United Nations is more nearly universal in membership than the League. Also Thant detects a more pragmatic and less legalistic response to crises than was the case during the League period. The question remains: To what extent do these changes reflect a real and permanent readjustment of governmental conduct toward the ideals of the Charter?

The Balance-Sheet of the League Experiment

Gerhart Niemeyer

I

International Organization, no longer the exclusive preserve of dreamers and idealists, is now, for better or for worse, one of the palpable realities of world politics. Whether we choose to consider it our best hope or a snare and a delusion or something in between, we are compelled to reckon with its effects, one of which is the foreseeable cost of non-participation in it. Its characteristic features–public debate, parliamentary procedures and resolution, majorities and voting blocs–all have become instruments of undeniable and indeed often painful efficacy in international relations. A review conference for the purpose of evaluating the experience of the first ten years of Charter operations is scheduled for 1955. Meanwhile, institutional developments within the framework of the Charter occur constantly, and call for policy decisions based on a profound understanding of how this or that change is likely to affect the international scene. In this situation, the publication of the first comprehensive history of the League of Nations[1] must be considered a significant event. It invites a fresh look at the record of the entire League experiment and a re-evaluation of the lessons which it presumably has taught us. At the same time, the work as such

Gerhart Niemeyer, "The Balance-Sheet of the League Experiment," *International Organization,* Vol. 6, No. 4 (November 1952), pp. 537-558. Reprinted by permission of *International Organization.*

[1] F. P. Walters, *A History of the League of Nations* (London: Oxford University Press, 1952), 2 vols.

deserves attention as a possible tool for the understanding of the international world in which we live and of our task in shaping instruments for the rational control of that world. The appearance of Mr. Walters' book affords us an opportunity to re-examine our own thinking about the League by means of testing the assumptions and conclusions of his study.

The League of Nations was not in any formal sense the parent organization of the United Nations. At the same time, however, no one familiar with developments in both organizations can deny that the United Nations is essentially a mutation of the League. One need not necessarily agree with those who claim structural similarity between the League and the United Nations[2] in order to recognize a continuity, from one to the other, of institutional purpose. The experience of the League thus has an immediate and direct significance for our understanding of the United Nations and its role in international relations. We may put it as follows: unless we understand how League institutions functioned and evolved, it is hard to acquire a real grasp on what is going on in the United Nations, what forces are at work in it, and what preconceived notions play a role in its day-to-day activities. For example, a considerable number of people who acquired their familiarity with multilateral diplomacy in the League still are active in the United Nations. The lessons that they and others have learned, or believe they learned, in the earlier institution profoundly affect their political decisions in the United Nations, so that a critical evaluation of those lessons is one of the important things a comprehensive history of the League can help us to accomplish.

The deepest meaning of a comprehensive study of the League emerges, however, in the perspective of the future. So long as our attention is focussed on the past, and the present, it is possible to treat the League as a manifestation of certain historical ideas, and to concentrate on those ideas as having shaped its purpose and the structure or as ends which the League sought with greater or lesser success, to realize. In the perspective of the future, this approach will not do. Here the League must be regarded primarily as number one in a series of experiments with instruments of international political control. The United Nations is the number two. After 1955 we may, as a result of the review conference, confront number three and there is no reason to assume that even it would be the last item in the series. With respect to the problems of international organization, this generation finds itself in a situation similar to our 18th and 19th century forebears, as they focussed their attention on legislation as an instrument of rational control of social processes. They needed and undertook, extensive studies not only of the philosophical ideas that ought to shape the laws, but also of the empirical effects that certain laws had upon the social patterns they were intended to control. If such empirical studies, as this writer

[2] See Leland M. Goodrich, "From League of Nations to United Nations", *International Organization,* I, pp. 3-21.

believes, are indispensable means for learning how to use novel instruments of social and political control, then it is imperative that the League, as the first completed experiment in international organization, be subjected to the most painstaking empirical scrutiny.

II

We assume, then, that the League is not of mere historical interest, that it belongs to the category of novel instruments of political control, that its efficacy and even its effects are not yet fully understood, that it was probably the first in a series of similar ventures in which we shall engage, and, because first, merits thoroughgoing appraisal lest the later attempts suffer from ignorance and misunderstanding. We assume, in other words, that the balance of the League experiment must be included as an active item in our present calculations. If this assumption is granted, the lessons to be learned from the League experiment are among the things we should expect to emerge from a history of the institution. For this we should need an appraisal of the League in terms of its functions, an appraisal, i.e., in terms of the expectations, hopes, and purposes under which the organization actually operated.

If what we should need is an evaluation of the performance and results of the League, the first requirement would be a clearly established yardstick of what would constitute success or failure. This yardstick must be determined with elaborate care, for it constitutes the basis of meaningful description and communication about the object of the study. This is the point at which this history of the League first reveals its inherent shortcomings. The underlying philosophy, the concept of the League is never established firmly as a basis of communication. The "purpose" of the League is supposed to emerge from an account of the making of the Covenant, an accumulation of all that was said about and intended for the new institution. Whose purposes, hopes, and expectations are to be considered the true concept of the League? What, after having studied the ideas of the originators and their predecessors, are we to take the League to be, and what would the League take itself to be? The historian mentions Wilson's ideals, British realistic moderation, French acquiescence, American isolationist opposition. He can trace the diverse elements which entered into the Covenant and even assign preponderance to one or the other of them. But after all is said and done, and the League is founded, the historical record leaves us with but a number of differing views as to the hoped-for effects of the League, and without any compelling reason for preferring one to the other as the "true" measure of League performance. Obviously, the function of the League is not a concept that can be derived from any one of these historical and subjective reactions to the Covenant, or, for that matter, from the original intentions of any one of the individuals or groups who had a share in the genesis of the League. Furthermore, the history of the Covenant explicitly mentions only those influences which happened to be vocal at the time and fails to do justice to elements that remained beyond the scope of the Covenant; elements which, however, for this very reason helped to mold the function of the League in actual operations.

Before pursuing our discussion further, we must attempt to do here what Mr. Walters omitted in his study: we must establish a working concept of what the League as an institution was, what "normal expectations" of purposes guided it in day-to-day actions and reactions. This concept can be formulated, on an analytical rather than a historical basis, roughly as follows: the League as an organization of nations, an organization of potentially universal character, centering in a general and representative organ as well as in a small and "executive" organ, based on a Covenant containing elaborate procedures for the peaceful settlement of international disputes, a universal guarantee of territorial integrity, a promise of a grand coalition against any state that illegally resorted to war, and the prospect of eventual universal disarmament–this institution would have to be looked upon as a world community of nations, an entity more than the sum of its parts and something radically different from the traditional pattern of international relations (i.e., a pattern characterized by national power interests, competitive armaments and fluctuating alliances). Irrespective of what Wilson or others chose to say or not to say, the League, so constituted, would necessarily be regarded as intending to place the use of national arms and diplomacy under the control of general principles of law and the common interests of a world order. These features of community so deceptively analogous to the domestic communities in which our daily experiences are cast, would induce a general tendency, among people everywhere, to draw certain possibly subconscious parallels between League and State, to expect from the League results comparable to those of a government, and from its members attitudes similar to those of citizen. This view and its inherent expectations must be regarded as a real commitment. It is reasonable and appropriate to consider this the function or purpose of the League.

It is legitimate to attribute this purpose of "world community" to the League even though there is a perspective in which these expectations appear quixotic, and hence any judgment of the League based on them would be decried as unfair. An international organization making its appearance in a war-weary world and equipping itself with the above-mentioned features makes certain implicit pretensions; and, whether its goals are or are not realizable, it must be judged either a failure or a success in the light of them. The task of the historian may end with this judgment; the task of the political analyst, however, carries beyond the point of a mere verdict. He must proceed with the thesis that even though the League may have failed in terms of its inherent intent, it has been nevertheless a real factor in international relations for a period of time. Its operations therefore must be studied as sources of knowledge not only about international organization, but also about international relations as such. The effects which this organization has had on the attitudes of governments and the policies of nations, as well as the effects which governments and policies have had on the functioning of the organization, are revealing and must be studied with great care, quite apart from the question of the success of League purposes. Unfortunately, this approach to the subject of international organization is not too frequently found in the literature, although it should recommend itself on the ground that it is reasonably free from preconceived notions and ideological fixations. It approaches the subject in somewhat the following mood: "We have here a phenomenon that is new in the history of international relations. It has obviously been established and operated with a specific purpose in mind. We need to know the purpose, but, since this is a new experiment, we also need to know whether an institution of this kind actually furthers and promotes that purpose, and, if it does not, what other effect it has in the real world."

If it is reasonable and desirable that the phenomena of international organization should be analyzed in this manner, it is also meaningful to inquire what a history of the League has to contribute to such a study. The raising of this question does not necessarily impose on the historian of the League a standard or purpose which he would be unwilling to accept and could reject as an unfair basis of judgment, because the question itself is nothing more than a methodological device for finding out what exactly was in the historian's mind when he described the League. Such a device is certainly permissible when the historian does not tell his readers what assumptions and criteria determined his writing. Mr. Walters gives us no direct statement of his philosophic frame of reference. Since he undertakes to describe and explain what went on in the League, one must of necessity ask whether his description looks upon causes and effects beyond the League proper or chooses to ignore what happened outside of the four walls of Geneva. On the whole Mr. Walters appears to have confined his explanation to a narrow Covenant framework. This does not mean that we are never told about decisions in London, Rome, or Washington that affected the League, but that the entire account is cast in the mold of an approval or disapproval that presupposes a picture of reality based on Covenant hopes and expectations. The League plays the hero's role in his story, no less so for its having perished at the end. In the following pages this thesis will be tested by contrasting Mr. Walters' treatment of certain phases of the League with the kind of analysis proposed above. The comparison is meant to raise the fundamental question of the adequacy of Mr. Walters' categories of description and thus, by implication, the question of the accuracy of his account. It also intends to suggest certain other categories which, so this writer believes, would have been better suited to the purpose of grasping what really happened under the League and to the League. To this end we will select events that can be considered "test cases" for the League, always thinking of that institution as an experiment in political control.

One can speak of "test cases" for the League only in the sense that certain events served either to prove or to disapprove the soundness of the basic concept of the League. On the premise that the "world-community" concept, as outlined above, adequately represents the purpose of the League, it is fair and reasonable to select as decisive those moments in League history in which national power interests clashed in violent conflict, rather than to look for evidence of League effectiveness among less political actions (e.g., the financial rescue of Austria, the exchange of certain populations, or the Saar administration). There are those who would invite us to overlook the spectacular dramatic events and to concentrate our attention on the great achievements of the League in economic and social, humanitarian and cultural fields. They would be correct in considering these achievements as the true measure of the League if one were to begin with a different assumption as to what the League purported to be. If, however, one accepts our thesis that the League must be regarded as having been essentially a universal communal organization of nations committed to the maintenance of peace, the assertion of the rule of law over national power interests, and the solidarity of all against any lawbreaking aggressor, it follows that the moments of acute political conflict are the crucial tests and that those other activities, no matter how beneficial, have only marginal significance as regards passing judgment of the League. In this sense, we follow the generally held view that Manchuria and Ethiopia are the two decisive tests of the League. In addition, we should like to include in the discussion a few similar cases: Vilna, the first aggression considered by the Council, a case which the League abandoned in the face of opposition from Russia; Corfu, the first case in which the League bowed to the will of a defiant great power among its members; the Greco-Bulgarian dispute, which was prevented from breaking into open hostility by a simple telegram from the President of the Council; and the Chaco conflict, which the League was unable to stop in spite of complete singleness of mind among its members on the issues of the case.

III

The invasion of Manchuria by Japan came before the League in two phases: the Council dealt with it, under Article 11, from September 1931 to March 1932, and the Assembly handled it, under Article 15, from March 1932 until February 1933. The Council at first passed a resolution calling upon Japan and

China to negotiate directly, meanwhile hoping for the best; later on a Japanese veto prevented it from adopting another resolution pressing for immediate withdrawal of Japanese troops. Finally it appointed the Lytton Commission which had orders to investigate the circumstances of the conflict impartially and with serene detachment from the urgency of the military situation. The Assembly accepted Stimson's proposed nonrecognition doctrine, and, having failed in prolonged attempts at conciliation, adopted a statement based on the Lytton Report condemning Japan for its aggressive action. Neither body at any time contemplated action to stop Japan and protect the territorial integrity of China against the aggressor. Mr. Walters roundly deplores this failure of the League: "The aggression had taken place, vast territories had been torn from the victim, and yet all they (the Members) had done was to refuse to recognize the new state.... In consequence, men's faith in the Covenant as an effective barrier against war had been profoundly shaken. The small powers, in particular, had learned to doubt, not so much the efficacy of the League system, as the will of the great powers to apply it". He leaves little doubt that he identifies himself with this view of the small powers. The great powers failed to lead where they should have led. The United States sinned by remaining aloof from the League, and London, Paris, and Rome by harboring "a certain amount of sympathy for the State which had dared to use its military preponderance to impose its own kind of justice". Mr. Walters does not close his eyes to the difficulty of the situation which the great powers faced in the fall of 1931, paralyzed as they were by economic depression and unsettled conditions in Europe. He can understand why the powers thought they could not risk war with Japan, but in the sense in which he would understand why the man killed his wife, without thereby abandoning the strict demands of the law. What were the policies of the powers, both with respect to the Far East and otherwise? How did they relate to the demands of collective security, and how could they or should they have been changed to fit those demands? Mr. Walters does not instruct us on these matters. The picture he draws is one dominated by the ideal expectations of the Covenant (and in the framework of his study, what other picture could he draw?), and expectations of strong measures justified by "the unanimity of all the disinterested Members". All we learn about the real policies of the powers is that the Members failed to live up to these expectations, the great powers for understandable but nevertheless regrettable reasons of their own, and the small powers because of the "absence of leadership from Britain and France." The implication is that the fulfillment of Covenant expectations by the great powers would have produced generally beneficial results, either in the sense that it would have erected an "effective barrier against war" or that it would have contributed to an evolution toward a generally more desirable state of affairs. Thus the central question about the League as a factor in international affairs is begged rather than raised in a setting of relevant evidence and information.

The other major test case, by contrast, is described as the moment of greatest triumph as well as of tragic downfall. For the application of sanctions against Italy is hailed as the fulfillment of Covenant expectations against a great power. Again Mr. Walters considers the pressure of small powers as the virtuous influence which compelled Britain and France to play their cards according to strict and open League rules rather than according to the poker methods of power politics. Contrary to widely held opinions, he feels that even lacking an oil embargo, perseverance in the already voted sanctions would have sufficed to bring Italy to her knees. It was the sinister influence of the French, and particularly the Hoare-Laval plan, which broke the back of the League action and spelled the ultimate defeat of collective security, a defeat from which the League was never, he alleges, able to recover. Mr. Walters casts his story in terms of a conflict between the forces of good and evil: "To simple minds it seemed evident that a struggle had now begun between the League of Nations and the Fascist regime which could only end by the victory of one and the defeat of the other." He is unable to see any meaning in the policies of countries which "assumed that the policy of sanctions could be carried out in a friendly spirit, without interrupting normal relations with the Italian government in other respects, or destroying the prospects of a settlement by compromise"—a policy which he describes as a "deliberate refusal to face the facts".

Now it is quite possible that there was a deliberate refusal to face the facts, but there are other ways of interpreting the policies in which Switzerland, the United Kingdom, France and other countries agreed. At any rate, a description of facts cast in the mold chosen by Mr. Walters does not yield much information that could enlighten us on the interaction between international organization and national policies. It simply will not do to assume that the defeat of Italy at the hands of the League would have been the preface to a millenium of universal peace, or that the interest of small powers in collective security was (and still is) the touchstone of political wisdom which the great powers ought to have used to guide them in their policy decisions.

The inferences which must be drawn from Mr. Walters' treatment of these (and other) test cases for the League security machinery are fairly obvious. "If the great powers had recognized and done their duty under the Covenant," he seems to be saying, "the confidence of all nations in the League would have been confirmed, and, even if universal peace would not have resulted immediately, definite improvement in international relations would have taken place and the world would have progressed that much further on the road to law and order." If it is not unfair to attribute this thesis to him, one could certainly expect to be shown some evidence for it in the course of League history. A survey of a number of cases involving small powers, in comparison with the major tests of great power conflict, may possibly yield some information in this respect.

IV

In the Vilna case, fighting between Poland and Lithuania occurred first in connection with the Russo-Polish war of 1920 and subsequently as a result of a Polish coup against the former Lithuanian capital of Vilna. The Council proposed an armistice and a plebiscite and began to form an international armed force to supervise them. Faced with a hostile reaction to these measures on the part of Russia and a simultaneous reluctance on the part of Lithuania to submit to a plebiscite at that time, the Council dropped the matter, which remained an open sore in the international situation for many years. In the Greco-Bulgarian conflict of 1925, border incidents between these two countries had led to rising tensions that culminated in the concentration of Greek troops for an impending offensive into Bulgarian territory. Briand, as President of the Council, dispatched a telegram to the parties demanding the immediate cessation of hostilities. The "order" proved effective, the offensive was called off, a commission of observers supervised the cease-fire, and the dispute was eventually settled by peaceful negotiations. The Chaco war between Bolivia and Paraguay (1932-1935) concerned a disputed territory over which there had been sporadic fighting in the past. An effort by a commission dispatched to the scene by the Council to conciliate the dispute was a failure. The League then tried to "starve" both parties of arms and ammunitions by placing an embargo on them. When the war turned in favor of Paraguay, Bolivia brought the matter before the Assembly (under Article 15) and accepted the unanimous report of the League. When Paraguay, trusting more to her arms, rejected the report, the embargo was lifted as far as Bolivia was concerned, whereupon Paraguay left the League, just as Japan had done two years before. The war was finally settled by a group of six American states rather than by League action.

What, if anything, can one infer from these three cases? In the Vilna case the Council was willing to set up procedures of pacific settlement but not to face a case of aggression, or even to insist on the execution of its own decisions when Russia objected. There was loyalty to League principles, but not to the extent of taking steps which would have engaged the great powers in military commitments in a part of the world from which they had just decided to retreat. Not so in the Greco-Bulgarian case, in which the League and the great powers were so much identified that it is difficult to say which influence was decisive in preventing hostilities. However, the Chaco case, which on Mr. Walters' implicit theory should have been settled even more speedily than the Greco-Bulgarian dispute (since the latter constituted such an obvious advance over the Vilna case), was in the end a complete failure as far as the League was concerned, the war continuing until the point of exhaustion was reached. Nevertheless, all were agreed that the Chaco war was undesirable, the report of the Assembly was unanimous, and defiant Paraguay was liable to be treated as an aggressor by the community of nations. In spite of the general condemnation, the force of public opinion was sufficient neither to stop two very small nations from cutting each other to pieces, nor to induce any great power to use its influence as Britain and France had used their influence on Greece in 1925. If the comparison of the three cases does not permit of any other conclusion, it is at least possible to see that the League's success in one (small power conflict) case did not improve its chances of settling the next case on the strength of the precedent.

One is therefore forced to look for other factors which would explain why the League was successful in 1925, but had failed in 1921 and was to fail again in 1932, in dealing with small power conflicts. One cannot help noticing that the Chaco conflict, like the Vilna case, occurred in a region far from the centers of the great League powers, that no vital interests of these powers were endangered in either case, and that active intervention could have been interpreted as an encroachment on the spheres of interest of Russia in the first case, and the United States in the second. By contrast Greece and Bulgaria formed part of a region in which Britain and France were not only interested in maintaining the status quo, but also capable of giving effect to their will. All of which simply emphasizes the fact that even successful collective action under the League did not suspend the laws according to which power conditions the actions of states among each other! This would suffice to place a large question mark beside Mr. Walters' implicit demand that the great powers, instead of carrying in mind the requirements and limitations of their "positions of strength", should follow the example of the small powers, i.e., of nations which in their very nature do not have the same preoccupations and responsibilities.

It would be a further grave mistake, however, to believe that one can conclude, simply, that action under the League was governed by the laws of international power, just as policy was prior to the League, and that therefore the League can be discounted as something which neither added anything to, nor took anything away from international relations as they always have been conducted. A comparison of the three conflicts involving great powers must give rise to doubts about the validity of any such sweeping application of "realistic" dogma. The Corfu incident took place near "home", close to the great power centers and certainly within the sphere of interests vital to both Britain and France. Although the small powers pressed for an assertion of League authority in view of Italy's lawless use of force, and although the Council discussed the case officially, the matter was finally settled not by the League but by the then equivalent of the Conference of Foreign Ministers, and on terms which without regard for law and justice gave Italy most of what she demanded. While this was a clear display of the "solidarity of the big fellows", the Italo-Ethiopian conflict concerned the same set of powers, drawn together by a similar degree of mutually compatible interests (as proved by the tacit Franco-British condonement if not encouragement of Italian preparations for the Ethiopian campaign during the first half of 1935), but this time Britain and France led the collective measures of the League against Italy. Or, if one would analyze the Manchurian situation in power terms, it is clear that Manchuria was far away and there was no prospect of any collective action in the Far East, but nevertheless the League, again with the full endorsement of not only the United Kingdom and France, but also the United States, undertook to condemn and criticize one of the great powers to the point where the power felt compelled to withdraw from the organization. From Corfu to Manchuria to Ethiopia we find a definite increase in the degree of "idealistic" motivation as contrasted with motives based on power considerations. There seems to be no rhyme nor reason in this "evolution", for the first two cases–in which the Covenant was not heeded–occurred during a period when "the political conditions were generally favorable to collective security and confidence in the League was still unbroken, while sanctions against an aggressor were finally attempted when the League was already discredited and world politics (under the impact of the Manchurian debacle, the failure of the Disarmament Conference, the breakdown of Locarno, and the reversion to alliances and "four power pacts") had reverted to a pattern of armaments, pressures, and competitive power maneuvers. Hence it is not possible to explain the "improvement" in the conformity of British and French policies to Covenant expectations from Corfu to Manchuria to Ethiopia as a function of improvements in power relations. Quite obviously, the ideology of the League played a role as an independent factor, inducing these states to actions which would not appear justified from the point of view of relative power.

But can these policies or motives be booked on the side of "improvement"? Is it possible to discern progress in the imposition of sanctions against Italy, despite the fact that the League was unable to prevent the aggressor from destroying his victim? Is there some gain, on the two-steps-forward-one-step-backward theory, which future generations can hope to use as a foundation for a more effective structure of international order? Is there a sense in which the League, in spite of failures and defeats, can be called the "gentle civilizer" of international relations? These are questions which Mr. Walters' book brings to mind and which call for further inquiry into the balance of the League experiment. If, in the following pages, some ideas about these matters are essayed, they ought to be taken as hypotheses and suggestions rather than as contentions, as an invitation to rather than a product of, penetrating research into the problems of international organization.[3]

[3] It would be particularly important to carry on this kind of research with respect to cases under the United Nations, especially the entirely new experience of the Korean action which, of course, lies beyond the scope of this article.

V

1. It does not seem unreasonable to assert that the League, as an international organization dedicated to the "outlawing" of aggression, constituted a commitment of the great powers. The commitment was neither defined nor definable in concrete geographical or military terms. It called for loyalty to a general principle of international order. The outlawry of aggression constituted the very core of the League system, as can be seen from the continuous attempts to define this concept more precisely and to enlist national policies more rigidly in its defense. It has also been seen that the small powers in all cases of League action looked to and depended on the great powers for leadership, even if they themselves sometimes actively demanded to be led with more energy and force than were readily forthcoming. The great powers, on their part, seemed to expect the small powers to refrain from pressing an issue when they (the great powers) were unwilling to incur the responsibilities of action in any given case. Hence to the extent to which the existence of the League established a commitment to resist and repress aggression, this commitment fell specifically on the shoulders of the great powers. It meant that whenever there occurred anything which in general parlance could be classified as aggression, the great powers would find themselves under the assumption that they were pledged to act against the aggressor, regardless of existing limitations of their capacity, other commitments, or specific national interests. Thus the commitment would not in and of itself be based on or confined by, the realities of power. Nevertheless, the commitment was real. And its most peculiar feature was that, though it did not flow from political realities, its fulfillment or non-fulfillment could make and unmake political realities. The great powers thus found themselves committed in a most unreal fashion, but if they failed to honor the responsibility, other nations would immediately draw important inferences about the capacity or determination of the great powers to play their historical role. In other words, the Covenant commitment, like any other commitment, engaged the prestige of the leading League powers, i.e., Britain and France, although, unlike any other commitment, this one had not been conceived in accordance with available resources of power and positions of strength. The League actions in the cases of Manchuria and Ethiopia tested not merely the League, but also the strength and determination of the United Kingdom and France. The latter's "failure of nerve" was taken to be a true measure of their real power which, so Italy, Germany and Japan concluded, was not as great as they claimed it to be. In the sense in which this decrease of British and French prestige caused the revisionist powers to underestimate their opponents and overestimate their own capacities, aggressive tendencies must have been encouraged thereby. Thus Ethiopia can be said to have been set up by Manchuria, and Munich by Ethiopia and Hitler's decision to go into what he

conceived to be an easy war to have been rooted largely in the estimates of French and British strength and determination which the League test cases had yielded.

One might conclude from this that if these highly unrealistic tests had never occurred, and if a show of French and British power for Hitler's benefit had been made within a proper setting of capacities as relating to national interests, Hitler would not have been edged into the two-front war which proved just as disastrous for Europe as it was for Germany. One might, to be sure, argue that had the United Kingdom and France put a full measure of devotion into those two League actions and resisted aggression "as the law commanded," Hitler's fatal misapprehension could also have been avoided. This however, would be to ignore another phase of the League commitment, *viz.* the commitment to maintain "peace," and to support any move, institution, procedure, or tendency enlisted under that fair banner. This means that the commitment to uphold and enforce "the law" in all but minor cases could never assume the form of a deliberate show or threat of force, or even of a hint that the prosecution of League principles might possibly "aggravate the situation". It means, furthermore, that certain measures sentimentally linked to the idea of peace would be taken, again regardless of the realities of the power situation. Thus, e.g., disarmament, perfectly meaningful and sensible in the context of the Pacific Pact of 1922, was pushed with great energy in 1930 and 1932, at a time when the order of Europe was definitely distrubed and Germany was badly straining at the leash. The attempt to attain disarmament without a political settlement was unrealistic, but unilateral disarmament, as practised particularly by the United Kingdom as a gesture of good will, was "worse than a crime, it was a blunder".

2. The double character of the League commitment was reflected in League procedures which envisaged both enforcement and conciliation. The two major test cases for the League are perfect examples of these two purposes defeating each other. Any demand for energetic action could be, and usually was, met with the contention that a peaceful settlement was still possible, and that its prospects must not be endangered by pressure on the part of the League. Both Japan and Italy could always find eager ears for their claims that negotiations were still under way and showed continued promise. Italy was repeatedly assured that there was no intention of pushing sanctions to an extreme and that the hope for a negotiated settlement could always bring about a slowing down or even a suspension of sanctions. At the same time, however, there was an outcry of indignation against the Hoare-Laval plan precisely because it constituted a compromise which, instead of crushing the aggressor, secured for him the fruits of his criminal action. While action was taken in both cases that had a deeply humiliating and antagonizing effect on the two nations in question, great care was taken to pretend that otherwise everything was normal, and that no real hurt to them had been intended. Right in the middle of League action against

Italy, that country was allowed to join with the United Kingdom, France and other League powers in an indignant declaration condemning the kind of step which Germany had taken in re-occupying the Rhineland.

One cannot help concluding from all this that whatever else the League was able to achieve, it was simply incapable of lending itself to a show of force and determination of the kind that would have put Hitler on notice as to the amount of resistance he must reckon with. Successful and consistent enforcement of the League "law" was not within the possibilities of that organization, even if the great powers had acted precisely in line with Covenant expectations. An aggressor, if he only took care to remain in the League and play an active role in its deliberations, could always ward off the worst the League was capable of doing to him simply by dropping a hint that conciliation was still around the corner. The argument that any given League action was likely to endanger world peace was, in general, all that was needed to cause its dilution or postponement. Nor was successful conciliation a realistic possibility in any case of flagrant aggression. While enforcement, as also the condemnation that was its prerequisite, touched the sensitivities of proud nations to the point where nothing but a victory of their arms could satisfy them, conciliatory appeals had little chance of success. On either side, the test cases of the League unavoidably exposed the great powers to the ignominy of failure, to loss of prestige, to contempt for inconsistency, and to charges of immorality. Failure of enforcement could be counted on to result in underestimation of their strength, while failure of conciliation would place them in a humiliating position as suppliants at the feet of aggressors. Failure to attempt enforcement would deprive them of their support among smaller powers and call in doubt their general reputation for loyalty and reliability, while failure of conciliation would draw upon them the charge of a misuse of the League for the promotion of their own power ambitions.

3. If in all these respects it did not immediately remove the conditions and attitudes that usually go under the name of "power politics," the League need not for that reason be called a failure. Nobody could demand or expect more than that the League should set in motion forces and developments that in due course would bring into being a new kind of international system, a system free from the "expectation of violence" and the irrational conflicts of power rivalry. Thus it is highly important to formulate with the greatest possible precision the gradual changes in the attitudes of governments that this expected evolution would demand, and to ask to what extent, if any, such changes actually occurred. Again, these demands can be inferred from the inner logic of the League pattern, as set forth above. Progress toward the full realization of the League ideal would become possible only as governments developed the "habit" of settling their disputes peacefully, of conducting their foreign policies with an increasing awareness of a "general interest" (rather than with a view to the "particular interest" of national competitive power), and of using their force, especially the threat of

force, in solidarity with all others for the defense of the system as such (rather than for the defense of their national positions). This is on the whole the yardstick that Mr. Walters applies in his evaluation of national conduct under the League. He, like most observers, is far from demanding perfection at the outset; he even is willing to accept hypocrisy as "a bow to virtue". This implies that progress is considered possible through a series of unsuccessful League actions, provided of course that on these occasions nations give evidence of their loyalty to League principles and of their good will as regards attempting to obey the rules. But what, clearly, is involved here is the hope that international confidence will, as a result of partially successful actions, "accumulate"—much as, according to the Catholic dogma, merit accumulates through the deeds of saints, to be used as a common treasure for future need.

Moreover, if we compare actual historical events with these expectations, we cannot refuse the great powers anything less than a passing grade. If partial compliance with League expectations is partial success, the great powers did not do badly at all. Italy submitted the Wal-Wal dispute to arbitration. The United Kingdom, so averse to the rigidities of collective security, was ready to use the threat of force (and actual force, if enacted economic sanctions can be classified as such) in defense of the League system against Italy. Bolivia was willing to cooperate with the League in the settlement of the Chaco dispute. China, at least during the Manchurian phase of the conflict, rested her case so completely on League principles that she even refrained from resisting Japanese aggression. Italy and Japan recognized the competence of the League as an agent for peaceful settlement by remaining in the League throughout the duration of their aggression; they actually participated in discussion of the respective conflicts. Both the United Kingdom and France acted in deference to the "general interest" when, contrary to their previous alignment on Italy's side, they led a communal enforcement action against that country. In all these actions, there was a considerable measure of respect for the League as a whole; and if, according to the principle in *magnis voluisse sat est,* a general rally to the cause is a halfway-house on the road to success, even when it falls short of its goal, then the collective application of sanctions against Italy in 1935 should have given great encouragement to the hope for a fully working League.

Actually, the opposite took place. The League ideal required that eventually there should be a general relaxation, a universal *détente,* on the basis of confidence in the "hue and cry" of collective security. It also demanded a general "rationalization" of international politics as a result of the use of multilateral discussion and formalized procedures of settlement. At the beginning there was, moreover, widespread expectation that these benefits would be brought about by increasingly frequent actions of governments bearing witness to their faith in the League. The fact nevertheless remains that the period of greatest confidence in the League, a period of considerable relaxation and "rationalization", came before 1931, particularly between 1925 and 1931, and that during the period from 1931 to 1936, for all the frantic activity in accordance with the demands of the Covenant, there was scant evidence of hope or faith in ultimate success. After 1936, indeed, there was outspoken lack of confidence in the League. In short, the period of greatest reliance on Covenant principles did not, as it was expected to do, coincide with that of most frequent resort to the League as an instrument of international politics. Before 1931, all the great issues had been settled without benefit of League diplomacy or procedures. Disarmament, Reparations, the German problem (Locarno), the problem of the United States (Kellogg Pact), the Japanese problem (Pacific Pact), the Chinese problem (Nine Power Treaty), the Turkish problem (Lausanne), etc.—these, together with the peace treaties and the system of French alliances, had been the cornerstones of the post-war political system, and the fact must be faced that they had not been laid with the help of the League. After 1931, by contrast, the League was used extensively, one could almost say exclusively, as the means of achieving settlement of problems that the great powers were either unable or unwilling to face on their own. But the period yields no evidence of the calm confidence in the victory of League principles that had prevailed before 1931. On the contrary, after the greatest and most impressive display of League solidarity in 1936, hopelessness and despair became general. Hence it is obviously not possible to establish a one-to-one relation between the practice of policies and actions in obedience to League principles and the development of ever-increasing confidence in the League system.

If the degree of confidence under the League system cannot be understood as an evolutionary effect on the Covenant-abiding practices of nations, some other explanation must be found. In terms of what developments can we comprehend the meaning of the high degree of sure confidence in the League during the 'twenties, as contrasted with the ever-declining assurance of the 'thirties? The picture begins to make sense if one recalls that before 1931 the pattern of international politics was ordered by two great systems, the one centering in the Washington agreements and covering the Pacific area, and the other based on the Locarno Pact and covering at least the western part of Europe (with Russia tied in loosely through the 1926 Treaty of Berlin). All the great powers were at this period capable of enjoying a considerable measure of reassurance regarding each other's aims and ambitions, which is what we usually mean when we speak of the "balance of power".[4] Both systems, however, were upset during the early 'thirties. The Washington system, somewhat shaken by the London Conference of 1930, was seriously damaged by Japan's move against Manchuria.

[4]The term, in its proper use, is taken to connote not a mere physical equation of forces, but a mutual understanding about, and acceptance of, the relation between national aspirations and the capacity to realize them in view of other nations' capacity and will to resist. Such a condition is not incompatible with inequality of military strength.

The Locarno system, already in need of repair when Germany obtained full freedom from internal controls and subsequently attempted a partial union with Austria, fell asunder when Hitler left the Disarmament Conference and introduced conscription. After this, there was only the Stresa Front which, together with the Franco-Russian treaty, seemed capable of restoring some measure of security to Europe. But it too disappeared in the course of the Ethiopian conflict.

Now this analysis seems to indicate that the confidence-building effects of collective security did not as a matter of course develop as a result of the spread of those practices called for by the Covenant, since they were strong at the time when the League was realtively little used and in decline at the time when nations more generally resorted to League procedures. Rather, the time of high optimism for collective security coincided with the existence of a balance of power system, and the period of waning faith in the League was that in which the balance was undermined but there was still some hope of regaining it. After every vestige of the balance of power was gone, in 1936, no confidence in collective security remained either. These conjunctures suggest that the expectation of evolutionary development toward a new international order as a result of gradually forming "habit patterns" of governments may not be sound. It also suggests that collective security may actually be dependent on an underlying balance of power, in the sense in which certain scholars have already argued that international law is dependent on a previous stabilization of international power relations.[5] In other words, if it is a truism that collective security requires an awareness of common interest, we must conclude that an abstract idea of common interest (e.g. "order under law") is insufficient, and that only a *concrete political interest* common to the key nations (and yet not offensive to others) can render a system of collective security workable. If the latter hypothesis should turn out to be correct, one would probably arrive at the conclusion that collective security was a practical possibility during the late 'twenties, that, moreover, it might have been re-established in the middle 'thirties provided the United Kingdom and France had consolidated their alignment with Italy and Russia and had obtained Germany's acquiescence in this new power structure, but that it became definitely impossible after 1936. At first glance this hypothesis seems so plausible that one feels tempted to raise the same question from the other side. If the balance of power should turn out to be a prerequisite of a functioning system of collective security, one might wonder whether collective security makes any contribution to the balance of power. It would particularly be interesting to find out whether collective security offers new—and, one would add, reliable—methods by which a system of stable and balanced power relations can be satisfactorily maintained, or, if challenged, restored.

---

[5] See Keeton and Schwarzenberger, *Making International Law Work* (1939), Chapter III and Percy Corbett, *Law and Society in the Relations of States* (1951), pp. 86-87.

4. The question can be put in the following terms: Assuming that a full-fledged pattern of collective security can at best evolve only gradually, and that, therefore, policies pertaining to the old (power-motivated) system are bound to co-exist, for a while, with policies pertaining to the new (collective security) order, and assuming further that, in these circumstances of co-existence, a "balance of power" is at least a helpful and possibly an indispensable adjunct to collective security, what effects do policies pertaining to collective security have on the chances of maintaining or restoring a balance-of-power system? The Manchuria conflict does not offer an unequivocal answer to this question. One would have to assume that neither the United Kingdom nor the United States felt that Japan's action would seriously trouble the existing order of things, since neither of them were ready to take any action to redress the balance. If this had been the case, however, it would have been important to maintain relations with Japan of such character that each side would continue to be reassured about the other's aims and ambitions. Neither the Non-Recognition Doctrine nor the Lytton Report was designed to accomplish this goal. If, on the other hand, the two powers felt that the balance of power was seriously threatened, their inaction under the cover of League solidarity could take the place of the previous Pacific system. The lack of initiative of the great powers in League councils and the resulting complete inaction of the League in all phases of Japan's expansion, however, suggests that this hope was either not held or not allowed to motivate policy. However, all this depends too much on speculation to be of any real value. It is quite different with the Italo-Ethiopian conflict, where concrete evidence is available.

It is a matter of the record that after the summer of 1934 the western powers looked upon Italy as their great and good friend in a common opposition to Germany's resurgence. The Four Power Pact, the Italian action preventing Hitler from conquering Austria in 1934, the Stresa Front and the Franco-Italian agreement (which is said to have implied French condonement of Italy's Ethiopian adventure) form a consistent pattern. There can be no question that the United Kingdom and France hoped to re-establish the European balance of power by establishing a close understanding with Italy. When public pressure either at home or abroad forced the British and French governments to lead collective sanctions against Italy, this understanding was naturally severely taxed, as it would have been even had there been no League action. The attempt to sit on two stools at the same time led, in any case, to a fall between them. Not only Italy's friendship was lost, but also the League was henceforth morally discredited and politically unproductive. Policies pertaining to collective security had definitely contributed to the breakdown of a re-emerging balance of power, and without producing or helping to bring into existence any substitute. One might, to be sure, reject this analysis on the ground that it is based on a single case. If this were true, the analysis would indeed be inconclusive. The Ethiopian incident, however, points to a feature that is characteristic of all policies pertaining to collective security, and must be because of the decisive role played in that system by the concept of aggression. The United Kingdom and France, in 1935, faced two potential aggressors. The balance of power depended on their being able at any time to use one of them as an ally against the other. The concept of aggression forced them to oppose both with equal zeal and, indeed, to oppose the chosen ally at a moment before the prospective enemy had given them any opportunity to use the League against him. This situation may not repeat itself in detail, but the compelling influence of the concept of aggression is a permanent feature of any system of collective security. The chief title of a system of collective security to respect and obedience is, indeed, that it is supposed to operate against any nation guilty of aggression. To the extent to which condemnation of an aggressor would compel countries to cut existing or renounce emerging ties with a nation that appears to them a vital factor in a balance of power, policies pertaining to collective security cannot, obviously, be expected either to sustain or to rebuild patterns of stable power relations. Collective security stakes its hopes on a stability of a different kind.

VI

This brief survey of the League's great trials leads to certain conclusions regarding a realistic appraisal of the League experiment:

1. In order to learn lessons of political relevance from the first experiment in collective security, we must consider the full range of motives that can be attributed to governments. Above all we must explain national policies pertaining to the League in terms of the total situation confronting the various governments at any given time.

2. In explaining the performance of the League, we must endeavor to strike out beyond the beaten paths of conventional theories, testing the validity of these theories against the total amount of available evidence. Mr. Walters, for example, following familiar lines of thought, blames the ineffectiveness of the League in the Manchurian case to a large extent on the "aloofness" of the United States from the League, an attitude which he attributes to the fact that the United States was not a League member. This thesis seems dubious, however, when one finds that the desire of the United States in 1931 to avoid any provocation of Japan in order not to aggravate the situation differed very little from the desire of the United Kingdom in 1935 to avoid undue provocation of Italy. One wonders whether membership in the League really would have induced the United States to adopt policies other than those it actually pursued in the Manchurian and the Ethiopian crises.

3. A summary appraisal of the League as an instrument of international relations must take into account the fact that the League was more than a security organization. The League was a multi-faceted organization. It sought to be a vehicle for disarmament, it aimed to function as a regulator of political change, it rendered administrative and coordinating services in economic, social, and humanitarian fields, and it assumed the role of a monitor of sovereign governments supervising their exercise of authority in certain respects. An appraisal of the total accomplishment of the League requires an answer to the question of whether these branches of activities are in effect (and should be institutionally) independent of each other or are parts of an integrated whole.

We conclude that the balance of the League experiment is still an open question, despite Mr. Walters' comprehensive study. It is not difficult to say that the League failed. Many have said so, and bemoaned the tragedy inherent in the failure. But given that we are continuing to use international organization as an instrument of international order, the saying is not very instructive and the bemoaning not very much to the point. The kind of summing up of the League experiment that we need would appraise the League not merely in terms of an ideal goal but above all as an institution situated in the mainstream of world politics, and intended to affect the conditions of war and peace. We cannot, in other words, claim to have learned much about the League experiment until we know how it has affected the problem of harnessing and controlling the factors of force and their role in the relations of power. This calls for hard-headed scrutinizing of policies and events as they took shape under the influence of the Covenant. If and when such inquiries are undertaken we shall do well to remember that the League, like all political innovations, must be judged not only in terms of what is ideally desirable but also in terms of what, in a given setting of institutions, forces, and dispositions, was—and other things being equal remains—possible.

From League of Nations to United Nations

Leland M. Goodrich

I

On April 18, 1946, the League Assembly adjourned after taking the necessary steps to terminate the existence of the League of Nations and transfer its properties and assets to the United Nations. On August 1, this transfer took place at a simple ceremony in Geneva. Thus, an important and, at one time, promising experiment in international cooperation came formally to an end. Outside of Geneva, no important notice was taken of this fact. Within the counsels of the United Nations, there was an apparent readiness to write the old League off as a failure, and to regard the new organization as something unique, representing a fresh approach to the world problems of peace and security. Quite clearly there was a hesitancy in many quarters to call attention to the essential continuity of the old League and the new United Nations for fear of arousing latent hostilities or creating doubts which might seriously jeopardize the birth and early success of the new organization.

This silence regarding the League could well be understood at a time when the establishment of a general world organization to take the place of the discredited League was in doubt, when it was uncertain whether the United States Senate would agree to American participation, and when the future course of the Soviet Union was in the balance. Though careful consideration had been given within the Department of State to League experience in the formulation of American

---

Leland Goodrich, "From League of Nations to United Nations," *International Organization,* Vol. 1, No. 1 (1947), pp. 3-21. Reprinted by permission of *International Organization.*

proposals, it was quite understandable that officers of the Department, in the addresses which they delivered and reports which they made on the Dumbarton Oaks Proposals, should have for the most part omitted all references to the League except where it seemed possible to point to the great improvements that had been incorporated in the new Proposals. Nor was it surprising, in view of the past relation of the United States to the League and the known antipathy of the Soviet Union to that organization, that Secretary of State Stettinius in his address to the United Nations Conference in San Francisco on April 26, 1945, failed once to refer to the League of Nations, or the part of an American President in the establishment of it.[1] In fact, from the addresses and debates at the San Francisco Conference, the personnel assembled for the Conference Secretariat, and the organization and procedure of the Conference, it would have been quite possible for an outside observer to draw the conclusion that this was a pioneer effort in world organization.[2] Since the United Nations came into being as a functioning organization there has been a similar disinclination on the part of those participating in its work to call attention to its true relation to the League of Nations.

While the circumstances which make it necessary for those officially connected with the United Nations to be so circumspect in their references to the League of Nations can be appreciated, the student of international organization is free, in fact is duty bound, to take a more independent and objective view of the relations of the two organizations. If his studies lead him to the conclusion that the United Nations is in large measure the result of a continuous evolutionary development extending well into the past, instead of being the product of new ideas conceived under pressure of the recent war, that should not be the occasion for despair, as we know from the past that those social institutions which have been most successful in achieving their purposes are those which are the product of gradual evolutionary development, those which in general conform to established habits of thought but which nevertheless have the inner capacity for adaptation to new conditions and new needs.

While progress largely depends upon the discovery and application of new ideas and techniques, it has always been considered the test of practical statesmanship to be able to build on the past, adapting what has been proven to be useful in past experience to the needs and requirements of the changing world. Thus the framers of the American Constitution, while they created much that was new, did not hesitate to draw heavily upon the institutions and principles which were a part of their common background of experience in America and

[1] United Nations Conference on International Organization, Document 15, P/3, April 27, 1945.

[2] For an authoritative description of the Conference, see Grayson Kirk and Lawrence H. Chamberlain, "The Organization of the San Francisco Conference," in *Political Science Quarterly*, LX (1945), p. 321.

in England. At the time of the establishment of the League of Nations, the view was commonly held, certainly with more justification than today in relation to the United Nations, that something really unique was being created. However, we have come to recognize that even the League system was primarily a systematization of pre-war ideas and practices, with some innovations added in the light of war experience. Sir Alfred Zimmern has expressed this fact very well in these words:

"... The League of Nations was never intended to be, nor is it, a revolutionary organization. On the contrary, it accepts the world of states as it finds it and merely seeks to provide a more satisfactory means for carrying on some of the business which these states transact between one another. It is not even revolutionary in the more limited sense of revolutionizing the methods for carrying on interstate business. It does not supersede the older methods. It merely supplements them."[3]

We have come to recognize the various strands of experience—the European Concert of Powers, the practice of arbitration in the settlement of disputes, international administrative cooperation, to mention only a few—which entered into the fabric of the League. Should we be surprised to find that what was true of the League of Nations is even more true of the United Nations?

Those who have thus far attempted a comparison of the United Nations with the League of Nations have, generally speaking, been concerned with pointing out the differences.[4] Furthermore, comparison has been made of the textual provisions of the Covenant and the provisions of the Charter, not taking into account actual practice under the Covenant. Such a basis of comparison naturally leads to an exaggerated idea of the extent of the gap which separates the two systems. If in similar fashion the Constitution of the United States as it existed on paper at the time it became effective in 1789 were compared with the Constitution as it is applied today, the conclusion undoubtedly would be that a revolution had occurred in the intervening period. Obviously, any useful comparison of the League and the United Nations must be based on the League system as it developed under the Covenant. If that is done, it becomes clear that the gap separating the League of Nations and the United Nations is not large, that many provisions of the United Nations system have been taken directly from the Covenant, though usually with changes of names and rearrangements of words, that other provisions are little more than codifications, so to speak, of League practice as it developed under the Covenant, and that still other provisions represent the logical development of ideas which were in process of

[3] Alfred Zimmern, *The League of Nations and the Rule of Law,* London, 1936, p. 4.

[4] See, for example, Clyde Eagleton, "Covenant of the League of Nations and Charter of the United Nations: Points of Difference," in Department of State, *Bulletin,* XIII, p. 263.

evolution when the League was actively functioning. Of course there are many exceptions, some of them important. But the point upon which attention needs to be focused for the serious student of international affairs is that the United Nations does not represent a break with the past, but rather the continued application of old ideas and methods with some changes deemed necessary in the light of past experience. If people would only recognize this simple truth, they might be more intelligent in their evaluation of past efforts and more tolerant in their appraisal of present efforts.

II

Space does not permit a detailed analysis with a view to establishing the exact extent to which the United Nations is a continuation of the League system. All that is attempted here is to consider the more important features of the United Nations system, particularly those with respect to which claims to uniqueness have been made, with a view to determining to what extent in general this continuity can be said to exist.

RELATION TO THE PEACE SETTLEMENT

One point that has been made in favor of the United Nations as a special claim to uniqueness is that its Charter is an independent instrument, unconnected with the treaties which are in process of being made for settling the political and economic issues of World War II.[5] In contrast, it is argued that the League, by virtue of the fact that its Covenant was made at the Paris Peace Conference, and incorporated in each of the peace treaties, was from the beginning so involved in the issues of the peace settlement that it was never able to overcome the initial handicap of being a League to enforce the peace treaties. It is true, of course, that under the Covenant and under other provisions of the peace treaties, the League had placed upon it certain responsibilities in connection with the carrying out of the peace settlement.[6] This connection was not, in the early years of the League, regarded as an unmixed evil. One distinguished observer, while

[5] See, for example, Clyde Eagleton, "Covenant of the League of Nations and Charter of the United Nations: Points of Difference," in Department of State, *Bulletin,* XIII, p. 264.

[6] See, for example, the provision of the Treaty of Versailles relating to the administration of the Saar Basin and the protection of Danzig, *Treaty of Peace with Germany,* Part III, section IV, Annex, chapter II, and section XI.

recognizing that a principal function of the League was "to execute the peace treaties," concluded on the basis of the first years of experience that this connection on balance served a useful world purpose.[7] It might be suggested that the criticism that later came to be made of the League on the ground of its relation to the peace treaties was primarily an attack upon the treaties themselves and would have been directed against any international organization which proved incapable of revising them. Without further arguing this point, however, the question can be raised as to how different will be the relation of the United Nations to the peace settlement following World War II?

While the Charter is a separate instrument and was made at a conference called specially for the purpose, the United Nations will inevitably become intimately and directly associated with the peace treaties once they are made. For one thing the original Members of the United Nations were those states that were at war with one or more of the Axis powers at the time of the San Francisco Conference. Furthermore, the interpretation to date of the provisions of Article 4 of the Charter makes it clear that the conduct of a nonmember state during the war is an important factor in determining whether that state shall be admitted to membership. While Article 107 dissociates the United Nations as a peace organization from action taken in relation to enemy states, once the peace treaties have been made they will become part of the existing economic and political order on the basis of which the United Nations will seek to maintain peace and security. It is difficult to see how an international organization for maintaining peace and security, such as the United Nations is, can do so on any other basis. Furthermore, in connection with the making of the peace treaties, we already see the United Nations being called upon to exercise important functions of administration or guarantee similar to those which the League was asked to perform. Thus the United Nations guarantee of the special regime for Trieste parallels very closely the League guarantee of Danzig in its basic conception, and the proposed role of the United Nations in connection with "territories detached from enemy states in connection with the Second World War"[8] is almost identical to that of the League in relation to "colonies and territories which as a consequence of the late war [World War I] have ceased to be under the sovereignty of the States which formerly governed them."[9]

In this same connection we should consider the respective powers and responsibilities of the two organizations in regard to the revision of the two peace settlements. One serious criticism made of the League of Nations was its ineffectiveness as an instrumentality for the revision of those provisions of the peace treaties which had come to be recognized as unfair and unjust. Under the

[7] W. E. Rappard, *International Relations Viewed from Geneva,* New Haven, 1925, pp. 14-16.

[8] *Charter of the United Nations,* Article 77.

[9] *Covenant of the League of Nations,* Article 12, paragraph 1.

Covenant of the League the Assembly was empowered to advise the revision of treaties which had become "inapplicable" and the consideration of international conditions whose continuation might affect the peace of the world.[10] This provision remained a dead letter from the beginning, due to the Assembly's lack of power of decision and means of enforcement.[11] How much more effective is the United Nations likely to be in this respect? According to Article 14 of the Charter the General Assembly may recommend measures for the peaceful adjustment of any situation, regardless of origin, which is likely to impair friendly relations among nations. While there is no specific mention made of the revision of treaties, the General Assembly is clearly authorized under this Article to discuss any situation having its origin in unsatisfactory treaty provisions and to make recommendations thereon.[12] There is, however, no obligation on the part of Members to accept any recommendation that may be made. Thus the power conferred under this Article does not go substantially beyond that of the Assembly under Article 19 of the Covenant and there is the same chance, if not likelihood, that the United Nations will be ineffective as an instrument for treaty revision. Furthermore, while the Security Council is given broad powers to take necessary action to maintain peace and security, the powers which the Council has to bind Members are limited to those falling within the general category of enforcement action and do not extend to the power to impose upon parties to a dispute or states interested in a particular situation any particular terms of settlement or adjustment. That was made clear in the discussions at San Francisco.[13]

BASIC CHARACTER OF TWO ORGANIZATIONS

The statement has been made that the United Nations is "potentially and actually much stronger" than the League of Nations.[14] That statement might lend itself to some misunderstanding, particularly in view of the fact that it is only one of many statements that have been made suggesting that the United Nations inherently is a more powerful organization and therefore more likely to achieve its purpose by virtue of the specific provisions of its Charter than was the League of Nations.

[10] *Ibid.,* Article 19.

[11] Frederick S. Dunn, *Peaceful Change,* New York, 1937, pp. 106-11.

[12] See discussion in Leland M. Goodrich and Edvard Hambro, *Charter of the United Nations: Commentary and Documents,* Boston, 1946, pp. 104-06.

[13] See Goodrich and Hambro, *op. cit.,* pp. 152-53, 155-59.

[14] Louis Dolivet, *The United Nations: A Handbook on the New World Organization,* New York, 1946, p. 16.

We can start, I think, with the fundamental proposition that the United Nations, as was the League of Nations, is primarily a cooperative enterprise and falls generally within the category of leagues and confederations instead of within that of federal unions. Except in one situation, neither the United Nations nor its principal political organs have the authority to make decisions binding on Members without their express consent. Without this power, it is impossible to regard the organs of the United Nations as constituting a government in the sense of the federal government of the United States. The essential character of the United Nations is specifically affirmed in the first of the principles laid down in Article 2 of the Charter where it is stated that "the organization is based on the principle of the sovereign equality of all its members." This principle was not expressly stated in the Covenant of the League of Nations, but was, nevertheless, implicit in its provisions.

Since both the United Nations and the League of Nations are based primarily upon the principle of voluntary cooperation, the point that needs special consideration is whether, more or less as an exception to the general principle, the the Charter contains provisions which give to the organs of the United Nations greater authority than was vested in the corresponding organs of the League. In this connection a great deal of emphasis has been placed upon the provisions of the Charter regulating voting in the General Assembly and the Security Council. It is, of course, true that under Article 18 of the Charter decisions of the General Assembly can be taken by a two-thirds majority of the members present and voting, instead of by unanimous vote of those present, as was the requirement for the League Assembly. It must be borne in mind, however, that on questions of policy the General Assembly can only recommend, and that consequently any decision taken is a decision to make a recommendation. Also, it is quite unfair to compare these provisions without taking into account the practice of the League Assembly under the Covenant. In several important respects the rule of the Covenant was interpreted so as to bring actual League practice fairly close to the provisions of the Charter.[15] For one thing, it was provided in the rules of the Assembly that a state which abstained from voting was not to be counted as present, with the result that abstention was a means by which certain of the consequences of the unanimity rule could be avoided. More important, however, was the rule which was established in the first session of the League Assembly, that a resolution expressing a wish, technically known as a "voeu," might be adopted by a majority vote. This had the effect of making possible a whole range of Assembly decisions by majority vote which did not differ in any important respect from decisions which may be taken by the General Assembly by majority or two-thirds votes.[16] Furthermore, if should be noted that the

[15]See Margaret E. Burton, *The Assembly of the League of Nations,* Chicago, 1941, pp. 175-205.

[16]See C. A. Riches, *Majority Rule in International Organization,* Baltimore, 1940, p. 24.

League Assembly early came to the conclusion that the decision to recommend an amendment to the Covenant under Article 26 might be taken by a majority vote,[17] with the result that the power of the Assembly to initiate amendments actually could be exercised more easily than under the Charter of the United Nations. Thus it would seem erroneous to view the provisions of the Charter with respect to the power of the General Assembly to make decisions as representing any fundamentally different approach from or any great advance over the comparable provisions of the Covenant of the League of Nations as interpreted in practice.

When we turn our attention to the Security Council we find admittedly that an important change has been made. Under the League Covenant the Council was governed by the unanimity rule except in procedural matters, and this proved a serious handicap, particularly when the Council was acting under Article 11 of the Covenant. It was possible for a member of the Council, accused of threatening or disturbing the peace, to prevent any effective action under this Article by the interposition of its veto, as happened in the case of Japanese aggression in Manchuria in 1931 and the threat of Italian aggression in Ethiopia in 1935. Under the Charter it is possible for a decision to be taken binding Members of the United Nations without their express consent. Furthermore, this decision may require specific acts upon the part of the Members of the United Nations and is not to be regarded as a simple recommendation as was the case with decisions taken by the League Council under Articles 10 and 16.

Nevertheless, there are important points to be kept in mind before we conclude that a revolutionary step has been taken. In the first place, a decision by the Security Council can only have the effect of a recommendation when the Security Council is engaged in the performance of its functions under Chapter VI, i.e., when it is seeking to achieve the pacific settlement or adjustment of a dispute or situation. Furthermore, while the decision of the Security Council with respect to enforcement action under Chapter VII is binding upon Members of the United Nations, including those not represented on the Security Council, such decisions cannot be taken without the concurrence of all the permanent members of the Security Council. Consequently, in a situation comparable to that of Japanese aggression against China in Manchuria in 1931 and the threat of Italian aggression against Ethiopia in 1935, where the League Council admittedly failed on account of the unanimity principle, the Security Council would be prevented from taking any decision. Under the Charter the Security Council has power, which the League Council did not have, to take action against the small powers, but the experience of the past would seem to show that it is not the smaller powers, acting alone, who are most likely to disturb the peace. When dealing with threats by smaller powers acting alone the League Council was

[17] League of Nations, *Records of the Second Assembly,* Plenary Meetings, pp. 733-35. See also, Burton, *op. cit.,* p. 187.

reasonably effective; it failed only when small powers had the backing of great powers. In spite of important changes in the technical provisions of the Charter, one is forced to the conclusion that so far as the actual possession of power is concerned, the United Nations has not advanced much beyond the League of Nations and that in comparable situations much the same result is to be anticipated. In the last analysis under either system success or failure is dependent upon the ability of the more powerful members to cooperate effectively for common ends.

Finally, the provisions of the Charter with regard to amendments and withdrawal follow in all essential respects the provisions of the Covenant and the practices developed thereunder. Under both Charter and Covenant no amendment recommended by the Assembly can become effective until ratified by the great powers. The Covenant was a little more restrictive than the Charter in one respect, requiring ratification by all members of the League whose representatives composed the Council, plus a majority of all other members, thereby giving any Council member a "veto." On the other hand, the Charter, while limiting the "veto" to permanent members, requires approval by two-thirds of the Members of the United Nations. In practice, the charter provisions are not likely to have substantially different results.

Likewise, with respect to withdrawal, the League and the United Nations systems do not differ in any important respect. The Covenant of the League expressly permitted withdrawal under certain conditions which were not, however, enforced in practice.[18] The Charter says nothing about withdrawal but it is understood on the basis of a declaration adopted at San Francisco that the right of withdrawal can be exercised.[19] No doubt influenced by the League practice and conforming to it, it was decided that no legal conditions should be attached to the exercise of this right and that no attempt should be made to force a state to remain a Member, although it was made clear that a moral obligation to continue as a Member exists and that the right of withdrawal should only be exercised for very good reasons.

BASIC OBLIGATIONS OF MEMBERS

Enumerated in Article 2 of the Charter are certain basic obligations of Members of the United Nations. These include the obligation to settle disputes by peaceful means in such a manner that international peace and security are not

---

[18] Article 1, paragraph 2.

[19] For text, see UNCIO, *Verbatim Minutes of the Ninth Plenary Session,* June 25, 1945, Document 1210, P/20, pp. 5-6; for text and comment, see Goodrich and Hambro, *op. cit.*, pp. 86-89.

endangered, the obligation to refrain from the threat or the use of force against the territorial integrity or political independence of any state, and the obligation to give assistance to the United Nations in any action taken under the terms of the Charter. Similar commitments phrased in somewhat different language and with somewhat different meanings were to be found in various Articles of the Covenant.[20] From the point of view of form the Charter does represent a somewhat different approach in that these basic commitments are grouped together as Principles binding upon all Members. The phraseology of the Charter in certain respects undoubtedly represents improvement. For instance, the provision of Article 2, paragraph 4, by which Members are to refrain "from the threat or use of force against the territorial integrity or political independence of any state" represents an advance over the corresponding provisions of the Covenant which made it possible for members to take refuge in the technicality that an undeclared war in the material sense was no war and that therefore such use of armed force did not constitute a "resort to war." On the other hand, in one important respect, the basic obligations of the Members of the United Nations may prove to be less satisfactory since, in the matter of enforcement action, the obligation of the Members of the United Nations is to accept and carry out decisions of the Security Council and to give assistance to the United Nations in any action taken under the Charter, while under Article 16 of the Covenant, the obligation of members extended to the taking of specific measures against any state resorting to war in violation of its obligations under the Covenant. While this obligation was weakened by resolutions adopted by the Assembly in 1921, it nevertheless proved capable of providing the legal basis for important action against Italy in 1935.

III

The element of continuity in the progression from League of Nations to United Nations is perhaps most obvious when we examine the structure of the two organizations. The General Assembly is the League Assembly, from the point of view of the basic principles of its composition, powers and procedures. We have already seen from an examination of voting procedures that the practical difference between the League provisions and their actual application and the Charter provisions has been greatly exaggerated. The powers of the General Assembly, as compared with those of the League Assembly, have been somewhat restricted, it is true. The General Assembly's powers of discussion under Article

---

[20] Articles 10; 12, paragraph 1; 13, paragraphs 1 and 4; 15, paragraphs 1 and 6; 16, paragraphs 1 and 3; and 17.

10 of the Charter and succeeding articles are fully as broad and comprehensive as the League Assembly's powers under Article 3, paragraph 3 of the Covenant. Only in respect to the making of recommendations has the power of the General Assembly been limited, and this, it can be argued, is in line with the practice which developed under the Covenant according to which the Council, and not the Assembly, ordinarily dealt with disputes and situations which endangered peace and good understanding.[21] The significant difference is that under the Charter a party to a dispute cannot by its act alone transfer the dispute from the Council to the Assembly, as was possible under Article 15, paragraph 9, of the Covenant.

The Security Council, from the point of view of composition, is the old League Council. One important change, however, has been introduced into the Charter. The League Council had general responsibilities and functions, whereas the Security Council is a highly specialized organ. Instead of having one council with broad powers as did the League, the United Nations has three, among which the various functions and powers of the League Council are divided. To a certain extent this new set-up was anticipated in League practice. At the time when the League's prestige as a peace and security organization was low, the Assembly created a special committee known as the Bruce Committee to inquire and report on the possibilities of giving the economic and social work of the League greater autonomy. This Committee recommended the establishment of a new organ to be known as the Central Committee for Economic and Social Questions to which would be entrusted the direction and supervision of the work of the League committees in this field.[22] This proposed Committee, while it never was set up, was in effect the forerunner of the present Economic and Social Council.

So far as the Trusteeship Council is concerned, there is a somewhat similar background of development. While the Council was responsible under the Covenant for the supervision of the administration of mandates, in actual practice the Council came to rely very heavily on the Mandates Commission which, under the Charter, has come to be elevated to the rank of a principal organ, responsible not to the Council but to the General Assembly. This very responsibility of the Trusteeship Council to the General Assembly was to some extent anticipated in the practice of the League. Over the protest of some members, the League Assembly early asserted and exercised the right to discuss and express its opinion on mandates questions. While the Council was technically responsible for the enforcement of the provisions of the Covenant, there can be little doubt but what the Assembly exercised a real influence both on Council action and upon the mandatory powers.[23]

[21]See Burton, *op. cit.*, pp. 284-374.

[22]*League of Nations, Monthly Summary,* August 1939, Special Supplement.

[23]See Quincy Wright, *Mandates under the League of Nations,* Chicago, 1930, pp. 133-35.

The Secretariat of the United Nations is clearly a continuation of the League Secretariat, not only in name, but also largely in substance. While the Charter provisions would permit its organization on somewhat different lines, with separate staffs for the principal organs of the United Nations, it seems clear that the conception of a unified Secretariat has prevailed.[24] "The role of the Secretary-General as the administrator of the United Nations derives from that of his counterpart in the League of Nations,"[25] but has clearly assumed greater importance and scope under the provisions of the Charter. Due to political circumstances and the personality of the first holder of the office, the Secretary-General of the League never came to exercise a strong guiding hand in the direction of the League's work. The Charter of the United Nations, however, both expressly and by implication, gives the Secretary-General greater power and seems to expect more constructive leadership from him. More particularly, the role which the Secretary-General will be called upon to play in connection with the coordination of the work of the specialized agencies will require the exercise of initiative and strong leadership.[26]

With respect to the Court, it is clearly recognized that, while it was decided to set up a new Court under a new name, it will be essentially the same as the Permanent Court of International Justice.[27] The fact that this Court is regarded as one of the principal organs of the United Nations does not in substance distinguish it from the Permanent Court. For purposes of expediency it seemed advisable to maintain the fiction that the Permanent Court of International Justice was independent of the League system, but a careful examination of the actual organization and work of the Court will leave no doubt that the Court functioned as fully within the framework of the League as will the International Court of Justice within the framework of the United Nations.

IV

Like the League of Nations, the United Nations is a "general international organization" in the sense that its functions and actions cover the whole range of matters of international concern. Both the Preamble and the statement of

[24] See Report of the Preparatory Commission of the United Nations, PC/20, 23 December 1945, pp. 84-94; Walter H. C. Laves and Donald Stone, "The United Nations Secretariat," *Foreign Policy Reports,* October 15, 1946.

[25] Laves and Stone, *op. cit.,* p. 183.

[26] *Ibid.,* pp. 186 et seq.

[27] UNCIO, Report of the Rapporteur of Committee IV/1, Document 913, IV/1/74 (1). See also Manley O. Hudson, "The Twenty-Fourth Year of the World Court," in *American Journal of International Law,* LX (1946), pp. 1-52.

Purposes contained in Article I of the Charter make this clear. In fact this generality of purpose and function is more explicitly stated in the Charter than it was in the Covenant, though in the practice of the League it came to be fully recognized. The Charter of the United Nations, in its general arrangement and substantive provisions, divides the major activities of the Organization into three categories: (1) the maintenance of international peace and security, by the pacific settlement of disputes and the taking of enforcement measures; (2) the promotion of international economic and social cooperation; and (3) the protection of the interests of the peoples of non-self-governing territories.

THE PACIFIC SETTLEMENT OF DISPUTES

The Charter system for the pacific settlement of disputes,[28] while differing from that of the League in many details of substance and phraseology, follows it in accepting two basic principles: (1) that parties to a dispute are in the first instance to seek a peaceful settlement by means of their own choice; and (2) that the political organs of the international organization are to intervene only when the dispute has become a threat to the peace, and then only in a mediatory or conciliatory capacity.

The obligation which Members of the United Nations accept under Article 2, paragraph 3, is to "settle their international disputes by peaceful means in such a manner that international peace and security, and justice, are not endangered." Under Article 34, paragraph 1, the parties to any dispute "the continuance of which is likely to endanger the maintenance of international peace and security, shall, first of all seek a solution" by peaceful means of their own choice. Furthermore, by the terms of Article 36 of the Statute of the Court, Members may by declaration accept under certain conditions the compulsory jurisdiction of the Court. Declarations made by Members of the United Nations accepting the compulsory jurisdiction of the Permanent Court of International Justice and still in force are declared to be acceptances under this Article.

The legal obligations which Members of the United Nations have thus assumed are substantially the same as the obligations of League members under the Covenant and supplementary agreements. The Covenant itself did not place upon members of the League the obligation to settle all their disputes by peaceful means. However, forty-six states accepted the compulsory jurisdiction of the Permanent Court by making declarations under Article 36 of the Statute.[29] By

[28]For detailed analysis, see Leland M. Goodrich, "Pacific Settlement of Disputes," in *American Political Science Review,* XXXIX (1945), pp. 956-970.

[29]See Manley O. Hudson, "The Twenty-Fourth Year of the World Court," *op. cit.,* p. 33.

Article 2 of the General Pact for the Renunciation of War of 1928 (Kellogg-Briand Pact), the signatories agreed that "settlement or solution of all disputes or conflicts of whatever nature or of whatever origin they may be . . . shall never be sought except by pacific means."

The powers of the United Nations organs for the pacific settlement of disputes are substantially the same as those of the principal organs of the League. Under the Charter, as under the Covenant, the functions of political organs in this connection are limited to discussion, inquiry, mediation and conciliation. It is clear from the words of the Charter and from the discussions at San Francisco, that the Security Council has no power of final decision in connection with its functions of pacific settlement.[30] The Charter does, however, seek to differentiate between the functions and powers of the General Assembly and the Security Council in a way that the Covenant did not do. More specifically it makes the Security Council primarily responsible for the maintenance of peace and security, does not permit a party to a dispute to have the matter transferred at its request to the General Assembly, and limits the power of the General Assembly in principle to that of discussion. This constitutes an important departure from the textual provisions of the League Covenant which gave the Council and Assembly the same general competence and expressly allowed a party, acting under Article 15, paragraph 9, to have a dispute transferred at its request to the Assembly. It is significant, however, that out of some 66 disputes that came before the League, only three were actually brought before the Assembly under this provision. It would thus appear, and this is the conclusion of a careful student of the Assembly,[31] that actual practice under the Covenant resulted in a differentiation of function. This the Charter seeks to make obligatory.

In certain other respects the Charter system departs from the League pattern, but the importance of these differences can be greatly exaggerated. The elimination of the requirement of unanimity in voting theoretically increases the power of the Security Council, as compared with the League Council, in dealing with disputes and situations, but considering that the Security Council can only recommend, and that in League practice, agreement of the great powers was likely to result in the necessary agreement among all members of the Council, the practical importance of this difference is not likely to be great. Furthermore, under the Charter provision is made for the consideration by the Security Council and General Assembly of situations as well as disputes, but this does not mean any increase in the powers of the United Nations organs, particularly the Security Council, as compared with those of the corresponding organs of the League. In fact, it can be argued that the provisions of the Charter suffer somewhat in

---

[30] See UNCIO, Report of the Rapporteur of Committee III/2, Document 1027, III/2/31 (1), p. 4.

[31] See Margaret E. Burton, *The Assembly of the League of Nations,* pp. 284 et seq.

flexibility and capacity for growth, as compared with the corresponding provisions of the Covenant, because of the greater detail and consequent rigidity of certain of its terms. A comparison of experience under the Charter to date in the peaceful settlement or adjustment of disputes and situations with that of the League gives little basis for a confident conclusion that the Charter system is inherently better than, or for that matter, significantly different from that which operated under the terms of the Covenant.[32]

ENFORCEMENT ACTION

It is in respect of enforcement action that the provisions of the Charter seem to offer the most marked contrast to the provisions of the Covenant,[33] but here again when we compare the Charter provisions with the way in which the Covenant provisions were actually applied the differences do not appear so great. The League system, as originally conceived, was based on the principle that once a member had resorted to war in violation of its obligations under the Covenant, other members were immediately obligated to apply economic and financial sanctions of wide scope against the offending state. The Council was empowered to recommend military measures which members of the League were technically not required to carry out. As a matter of fact, in the one case where the provisions of Article 16 were given anything like a real test, the application of sanctions against Italy in 1936, acting under the influence of the resolutions adopted by the Assembly in 1921,[34] the members of the League established a mechanism for the coordination of their individual acts, and proceeded to apply selected economic and financial measures. No recommendation was made by the Council for the application of military measures.[35]

The Charter makes the Security Council responsible for deciding what enforcement measures are to be used to maintain the peace. Obligations arise for

[32]On the operation of the League system, see William E. Rappard, *The Quest for Peace,* Cambridge, 1940, pp. 134-207; Burton, *op. cit.,* pp. 284-374; and T. P. Conwell-Evans, *The League Council in Action,* London, 1929. On the work of the Security Council to date, see Clyde Eagleton, "The Jurisdiction of the Security Council over Disputes," in *American Journal of International Law,* XI (July 1946), pp. 513-33; and United Nations, *Report of the Security Council to the General Assembly* A/93, October 3, 1946.

[33]For analysis of the United Nations system for the enforcement of peace and security, see Grayson Kirk, "The Enforcement of Security," in *Yale Law Journal,* LV (August 1946), pp. 1081-1196.

[34]League of Nations, *Records of the Second Assembly,* Plenary Meetings, p. 803.

[35]For summary of this experience, see *International Sanctions* (A Report by a Group of Members of the Royal Institute of International Affairs), London, 1938, pp. 204-213.

Members of the United Nations only when such decisions have been taken. This is a further development of the principle recognized in the 1921 Assembly resolutions and in the application of sanctions against Italy, that a central co-ordinating agency is needed to insure the taking of necessary measures with the maximum of effectiveness and the minimum of inconvenience and danger to the participating members. However, the provisions of the Charter go much further than did the Covenant in providing for obligatory military measures and advance commitments to place specific forces at the disposal of the Security Council. Even though certain members of the League, notably France, were insistent upon the need of specific military commitments, little was done in League practice to meet this need. The Geneva Protocol of 1924 was one notable attempt to meet this demand, by methods which in certain respects anticipated the Charter, but it never came into force. The framers of the Charter, no doubt recognizing this as a defect in the League system, sought to remedy the deficiency by providing in some detail for military agreements between members of the United Nations and the Security Council, and for a military staff committee to assist the Security Council in drawing up advanced plans and in applying military measures.

It can, however, be queried whether the Charter system will be more effective than the League system, in view of the requirement of unanimity of the permanent members of the Security Council. If we imagine its application in situations such as the Italian-Ethiopian and Sino-Japanese affairs, it is difficult to see how the United Nations would achieve any better results than did the League. Like the League, but for somewhat different technical reasons, the United Nations, in so far as its enforcement activities are concerned, is an organization for the enforcement of peace among the smaller states. If the permanent members of the Security Council are in agreement, it will be possible to take effective action under the Charter. It is not likely that such agreement will be reached to take measures against one of these great powers or against a protégé of such a great power. Consequently the sphere of effective enforcement action by the United Nations is restricted in advance, even more perhaps than was that of the League. Within the area of possible operation, the actual effectiveness of the United Nations system will depend upon political conditions which, if they had existed, would have also assured the success of the League of Nations.[36]

ADMINISTRATION OF NON-SELF-GOVERNING TERRITORIES

Here we encounter new names and phraseology in the United Nations Charter, but the substance is very much the substance of the League mandates system.

[36]See Kirk, *op. cit.,* p. 1082.

There are, of course, important differences. For one thing, Chapter XI, "Declaration Regarding Non-Self-Governing Territories," is definitely an addition. The idea, however, is not new, as it has been accepted by various colonial administrations in recent years, and has found expression both in official statements and in authoritative writings on the subject.[37] However, it is new to have embodied in an international instrument a definite statement of principles binding upon all states engaged in the administration of non-self-governing territories and to place upon such states the additional obligation to make reports to an international authority.

So far as the trusteeship system, strictly speaking, is concerned, it follows in general the lines of the mandates system.[38] The three categories of A. B. and C mandates do not appear, but due to the freedom allowed in the drafting of trusteeship agreements, there can be the same, if not greater, variety of provisions. Like the League mandates system, the institution of the trusteeship system is not made obligatory for any particular territories; it is simply declared applicable to certain territories to the extent that they are placed under it by agreement. Following the practice under the mandates system, the trusteeship agreements, according to the Charter, are to be made by the states "directly concerned." They must in addition have the approval of the General Assembly or the Security Council, depending upon whether or not they apply to strategic areas, but neither organ has any authority to draft and put into effect a trusteeship agreement for any territory without the specific approval at least of the state in actual possession of it.

The machinery for supervision and the lines of responsibility have been changed in that for trusteeship areas other than strategic areas the administrative authorities are responsible to the General Assembly and its agent, the Trusteeship Council. As has been pointed out above, however, this change as compared with the League mandates system, was to some extent anticipated in League practice by the right which the Assembly asserted and exercised to discuss and make recommendations with respect to the administration of mandated territories. There is, however, in the Charter one important power vested in the United Nations organs, though in somewhat qualified form, which the Council and Mandates Commission of the League did not have and the lack of which was regarded as a serious weakness of the League system. I refer to the provision for periodical visits to the trusteeship territories which should make it possible for the Organization to get information on the spot and thereby check upon and supplement the reports of the administrative authorities.

---

[37]Baron Lugard, *The Dual Mandate in British Tropical Africa,* 2nd ed., (London: W. Blackward & Sons, 1923).

[38]For detailed analysis of the United Nations trusteeship system, see Ralph J. Bunche, "Trusteeship and Non-Self-Government Territories in the Charter of the United Nations," in *Organizing the United Nations,* Department of State Publication 2573.

INTERNATIONAL ECONOMIC AND SOCIAL COOPERATION

Perhaps the most important advance of the Charter over the Covenant of the League is to be found in its provisions defining the objectives, policies, machinery and procedure of international economic and social cooperation. In this respect, the Charter offers a wide contrast to the Covenant, which had only three articles dealing specifically with the subject. In fact, the Preamble of the Covenant, containing the statement of purposes of the League, made no specific mention of cooperation in economic and social matters, though the very general phrase "in order to promote international order and cooperation" was relied upon to justify numerous activities for which no express authority was to be found.

It is, nevertheless, true that the League in practice was a quite different matter.[39] It has been generally observed that the most permanently worthwhile activities of the League of Nations were in the field of international economic and social cooperation. There was in the course of the League's existence a tremendous proliferation of organization and an impressive record of substantial achievement in making available necessary information, in promoting administrative and legislative action by member states, and in dealing directly with international economic and social evils by administrative action. We have seen how in 1939 the recognition of the scope and importance of this work led to the proposal that a Central Committee for Economic and Social Questions should be set up to coordinate League activities in this field.

Apart from the provision for a separate economic and social council there is one important organizational difference between the League and United Nations systems, a difference which may prove to be of great importance, depending upon how the provisions of the Charter are applied in practice. Whereas the League technical organizations dealing with health, economic and financial cooperation were developed within the framework of the League and operated under the general direction and control of the principal League organs, the approach of the United Nations has been a different one. This time we have proceeded on the assumption that special needs as they arise should be met by the creation of appropriate autonomous organizations and that subsequently, these organizations should be brought into relationship with each other and with the United Nations by agreements negotiated by the organs empowered to act in such matters. The result is that instead of having a number of technical organizations functioning within the general international organization and subject to the general direction and supervision of its principal organs, as under the League

---

[39] See, for example, Denys P. Myers, *Handbook of the League of Nations* (Boston, World Peace Foundation, 1935) for evidence of the relative importance on a quantitative basis, at least, of the League's economic and social activities during the first fifteen years of the League's existence.

system, we now have a number of specialized inter-governmental agencies, each operating within a defined area and more or less independently of the others.

Such a system clearly has possibilities as to the range and type of action that may be taken which were denied to the League system operating more completely under the influence of political considerations. On the other hand, there are obviously certain advantages in having some effective coordination of the operation of these various agencies as there will be many points at which their interests and activities will overlap.[40] Under the Charter the proposal is to take care of these common concerns by the special agreements referred to above. It is too early to be certain as to what the practical consequences of this approach will prove to be.

V

To the student of international organization, it should be a cause neither of surprise nor of concern to find that the United Nations is for all practical purposes a continuation of the League of Nations. Rather it would be disturbing if the architects of world organization had completely or largely thrown aside the designs and materials of the past. One cannot build soundly on the basis of pure theory. Man being what he is, and the dominant forces and attitudes of international relations being what they are, it is idle to expect, and foolhardy to construct the perfect system of world government in our day. Profiting from the lessons of past experience, we can at most hope to make some progress toward the attainment of a goal which may for a long time remain beyond our reach. The United Nations is not world government and it was not intended to be such. Rather it represents a much more conservative and cautious approach to the problem of world order. As such, it inevitably falls into the stream of institutional development represented by the League of Nations and its predecessors. Different names may be used for similar things, and different combinations of words may be devised to express similar ideas. There may be changes of emphasis, and in fact important substantive changes, deemed desirable in the light of past experience or thought necessary in order to meet changed conditions. But there is no real break in the stream of organizational development.

The student of international organization must recognize the United Nations for what it quite properly is, a revised League, no doubt improved in some respects, possibly weaker in others, but nonetheless a League, a voluntary association of nations, carrying on largely in the League tradition and by the League methods. Important changes have occurred in the world distribution of power,

[40]See Herman Finer, *The United Nations Economic and Social Council,* Boston, 1945, 121 pp.; also Report of the *Preparatory Commission of the United Nations,* PC/20, December 23, 1945, pp. 40-48.

in the world's economic and political structure, in the world's ideological atmosphere. These changes create new problems and modify the chances of success or failure in meeting them, but the mechanics remain much the same. Anyone desiring to understand the machinery, how it operates, the conditions of its success, must look to the experience of the past, and particulary to the rich and varied experience of that first attempt at a general international organization, the League of Nations.

The League of Nations and the United Nations

U Thant

Next year the United Nations will celebrate the twentieth anniversary of its birth in San Francisco. It will have then been in existence for almost exactly the same number of years as the effective life of the League of Nations, its forerunner. Some comparison of the experience and development of the two organizations is therefore timely.

The word "failure" is often applied to the League of Nations, and the history, especially of its early and successful years, is not much studied now, or even mentioned. And yet in the closing years of World War II the victorious allies hastened to organize and build a new international organization which was, in fact, an improved and strengthened version of the old League. It was not the League, or the ideas behind it, that failed. Rather its members, in the critical years of the 1930's, failed to use and support it, and to rally under its banner against aggression and other dangers. It was thus that they finally had to face these dangers separately and in disarray in the terrible first years of the Second World War.

President Woodrow Wilson laid the first draft of the Covenant of the League before the Paris Conference in 1919 with the words "A living thing is born". Despite disaster and unfulfilled promise, these words have proved to be prophetic, as we can see when we look at the world today as represented in the United Nations. For this first great attempt to move toward a "worldwide political and social order in which the common interests of humanity could be seen and served across the barriers of national tradition, racial differences and geographical separation" (as the League's historian, Mr. Frank Walters, has

"The League of Nations and the United Nations" by U Thant, Secretary-General of the United Nations, is reproduced from the *UN Monthly Chronicle,* Vol. I, No. 1 (May 1964).

described it) was a historical event of the very highest importance. The League embodied a concept which has fundamentally altered, in our own century, the entire conduct of international relations and even the general convictions which form the basis of public opinion.

Let us look for a moment at the meaning of this change. Before the League of Nations came into being, it was almost universally held that every state was the sole and sovereign judge of its own acts and was immune from criticism or even questioning by other states. The idea—now generally accepted—that the community of nations had a moral or legal right to discuss and judge the international conduct of its members was not embodied in any treaty or institution until the Covenant. From that time also dates the idea, now almost universally accepted, that aggressive war is a crime against humanity and that it is the interest, the duty and the right of every state to join in preventing it. That these ideas now seem commonplace is a measure of the vision of the authors of the Covenant of the League.

The Covenant was based on other ideas no less important or fundamental—a new respect for the rights of small nations, the recognition of the need for cooperation in social and economic affairs, the habit of public debate on even the gravest diplomatic issues, the formation of an international civil service. It is the lasting achievement of the League that such ideas are an essential part of the political thinking of our world. Thus the League, as the embodiment of certain ideals and ideas, is very much alive and with us today.

In its time the Covenant of the League was a tremendous step forward, a radical change in the concept of international order. It was a response to the bitter, futile and appalling experience of the First World War, and in retrospect it may be thought the step was too far-reaching to provide a firm foothold when new and terrible dangers threatened. When its basic ideas were reborn in the closing years of the Second World War, however, they were supported by a far greater public understanding and by an even more compelling necessity for success.

The world has changed so rapidly in the last 20 years that it is hard to remember what it was like in the 1920's and 1930's. Thus we tend to forget how much, in the context of the inter-war world, the League actually did or attempted, or how important were the new models of international organization and action which it devised and developed. Despite its fluctuating fortunes, the central purpose of the League remained constant—to be the constitutional embodiment of man's aspirations for peace and a rationally organized world. We, in our time, owe an immense debt to those who, in far harder times, kept this idea alive and did as much as they could to build upon it.

I have already mentioned their achievement in the realm of political ideas. In the practical sphere also their efforts made it possible for the United Nations, when it came into being in 1945, to build on firm and already existing foundations. Quite apart from the central political structure, many of the new organizations continued and developed from the old with unbroken continuity. The International Labour Organisation was maintained and the Permanent Court at The Hague re-established as the International Court of Justice. The Economic and Social Council was modelled on plans made by the Bruce Committee in the last days of peace in 1939. The WHO and FAO and UNESCO grew out of the corresponding parts of the League Secretariat, while the Mandates System of the League was taken over by the United Nations Trusteeship System. The League Treaty Series was maintained without interruption by the United Nations, and many other activities such as the control of narcotic drugs and work for refugees passed from the old organization to the new one.

The basis of both the League of Nations and the United Nations is the pledge by sovereign states to cooperate, a pledge which involves some measure of sacrifice of sovereignty in the common interest. Both organizations were designed as an intermediate base between the international relations of traditional diplomacy, which had become obsolescent with the disasters of the First World War, and were proved inadequate, and even dangerous, with the Second World War, and the theoretical, ultimate aim of a world legislature, if not a world government. Both organizations therefore show the weaknesses of a transitional state—great aims with small means, great responsibilities with little authority, great expectations clouded by deep suspicions, and hopes for the future constantly blurred by fears and prejudices from the past.

National sovereignty is, understandably, a jealously guarded possession. The harmonizing of national sovereignty with the wider interest, in a way that is acceptable to the governments and peoples concerned, is the main task, and necessity, of international organization. The League's experience made this necessity clear, and we can already see a considerable advance since 1919. Certain European organizations in particular, such as the Coal and Steel Community and the Common Market, have gone far in the direction of pooling resources, coordinating policy and limiting national sovereignty in certain economic fields.

The Charter shows some formal advances over the Covenant in the matter of sovereignty. For example, it forbids the use of force by a state in a manner inconsistent with the purposes of the Organization and obligates the members to supply armed forces and other assistance to the Security Council and to apply measures called for by the Council.

In the United Nations there have also been practical indications of a changing attitude towards the sanctity of national sovereignty. The acceptance of a United Nations peace-keeping force on the territory of a sovereign state is one such instance, and the provision of contingents of national armies to serve under United Nations command is another. These are small beginnings, but important ones. There is also, I hope, an increasing recognition of the impartiality and objectivity of the United Nations Secretariat. Despite these changes, the United Nations still has only to a very limited extent a separate existence, and possibilities of action, independent of the will of member governments and the policies of member states. In a given situation it can advance no further than the parties concerned permit. As my distinguished predecessor pointed out, its capacity to act is, in fact, still to a large extent restricted by fundamental national reactions.

There were major differences in the origins and environment of the League and the United Nations. The League was directly linked with the outcome of the First World War and was thus, from the first, dominated by the European situation. The Covenant of the League was an integral part of the Treaty of Versailles. The League was therefore an aspect of the postwar settlement, with all the advantages and disadvantages of such a position. The United Nations Charter on the other hand was drafted before the end of the Second World War and expressly *not* a part of the postwar settlement. In a sense the League was thus tied from the first to the *status quo* with strong overtones from the past. The United Nations Charter, on the other hand, starting with a statement of purposes and principles for the guidance of the Organization and its members, looks firmly to the future. It is this difference perhaps more than any other that has given the United Nations its vitality.

The Covenant was a remarkable document for its time. Its articles on the reduction in armaments, on aggression, on the judicial settlement of disputes and resort to the Permanent Court of International Justice, on sanctions and on the use of armed force to protect the covenants of the League, were great political innovations in the world of 1919 and have been taken up and developed in the corresponding articles of the United Nations Charter. Unfortunately, in the critical 1930's the leadership, the confidence and the courage to apply them effectively were lacking, and with disastrous results. The soundness of the principles underlying them was reinforced rather than invalidated by this failure.

In other respects the League's Covenant lacked the dynamism of the Charter. Thus the Covenant lacked a clear statement of such an important objective as development towards self-government or independence, and emphasis on the necessity of economic and social development and human rights as an essential complement to political and juridical, and even military, arrangements to establish a firm basis for peace. The United Nations Charter has provided, in practice, a more flexible instrument than the League Covenant, over a wider field. The abandonment of the over-all rule of unanimity which prevailed in the League Council and Assembly is one symptom of this flexibility. The Security Council has a far wider discretion than the League Council had in determining what constitutes an act of aggression; while the system of specialized agencies makes possible much wider and more functional operation in the economic and social field.

The world of the League was in some ways a far less articulate world than we have today. A large proportion of the world's population was then still in colonial status and played little or no part in the world's affairs. This fact gave a basic lack of representative balance to the League's position as a world organization, which was aggravated by other factors relating to membership. Despite the primary role of President Wilson in its creation, the United States, by one of history's major ironies, was never a member of the League. The USSR only became a member in 1934, at which time both Germany and Japan had given notice of their withdrawal, to be followed two years later by Italy. Thus the major effort to maintain peace and security in a critical time through the League devolved upon France and Great Britain and had an essentially European basis, which deprived it of much of the moral authority of a truly global organization.

In this regard, the history of the United Nations presents a striking contrast in its steady progress toward universality. Existing in a time of rapid historic change, its membership has more than doubled since its inception, and the majority of its 113 members now come from Africa and Asia. It is thus more broadly based and less dominated by the greater powers, although the great powers, of course, play an immensely important role in its activities.

It derives added strength and balance from the activities and efforts of the smaller nations, which protect it to some extent from the buffetings of great power rivalries. Unlike the League, from which 14 countries withdrew during its active history, leaving it with a membership of 53 in 1939, no country has ever withdrawn from the United Nations, however adverse its position in the United Nations might appear to be at any given time.

In its predominantly European setting the successive breaches of the Covenant in the 1930's by Mussolini's Italy, and later, Hitler's Germany, paralyzed the League and rendered it ineffective, while the rise of economic nationalism after the depression of 1929 overwhelmed the promise of its earlier efforts in the economic field. Undoubtedly the mood of the 1930's turned against the system of the League Covenant. It was a bewildering mood, and they were confused and dismal times, when it seemed as if mankind had obsessively condemned itself to learn all over again the clear lessons of the First World War. The League Covenant became the victim of ultra-nationalist propaganda from all sides. This propaganda, actively pursued by many people in positions of power and responsibility, frustrated the League's efforts, grudged its successes and rejoiced in its failures. Confidence in its promise was undermined, and the system went down to a tragic and inglorious defeat. Only after five years of world war did the victorious nations rally themselves to repeat, with a conviction born of horror, the noble experiment.

In practice it could be said that the League tended to be legalistic in the face of crisis, while the United Nations has been pragmatic. Since the Covenant condemned "resort to war", the Japanese action in Manchuria in the early 1930's was justified as a "police action". The world has learned, in the cruelest way, the danger of such euphemisms. The Charter, of course, expressly forbids the threat as well as the use of force. The successful peace-keeping operations of the United Nations have been essentially improvised responses to particularly urgent problems. None of these operations was clearly foreshadowed in the Charter. The world has become a much smaller and more closely interrelated place in the last 30 years, and trouble can now spread and escalate much faster and with infinitely greater devastation. The relatively greater speed and informality in action of the United Nations in meeting danger, as compared to the League, reflects this fact as much as it does the heightened determination of nations to avoid a third and even more terrible war.

There were also inherent reasons for this change of attitude and pace in the changing environment in which the United Nations has worked for its first 19 years. Due partly to the lack of unanimity among the great powers and partly to the radical change in the nature of war resulting from the development of nuclear and thermonuclear weapons, there has been a gradual change in general attitudes on questions of international security in the United Nations.

There has tended to be a tacit transition from the concept of collective security, as set out in Chapter VII of the United Nations Charter, to a more realistic idea of peace-keeping in a changing world. There has also been a change in emphasis, for the time being at least, from the use of the military forces of the great powers, as contemplated in the Charter, to the use in practice of the military resources of the smaller powers, which has the advantage of not entangling United Nations action in the conflicts of the Cold War.

Already the concept of absolute sovereignty of a state is unreal, for no country can now exist in isolation. The Charter of the United Nations has taken away the sovereign right to go to war, or even to threaten the use of force in any international dispute. The International Court provides a tribunal for the judicial settlement of legal questions between nations. Many states have given the International Court a wide compulsory jurisdiction.

In the political field, even when there has been open conflict between states, and armed force has been used or threatened, there has been an increasing tendency for the principles of the Charter of the United Nations, rather than military power, to prevail, and on a number of occasions since 1945, the Charter has been a factor in actually preventing or in halting war. The principles of the Charter are clearly acceptable to most of mankind. The acceptance of their practical application, however, involving as it does concepts of national sovereignty long held sacred, is a longer and more difficult task–a task in which the League of Nations failed. If the United Nations has, so far, had more success and has made practical progress in applying the principles of the Charter, it is largely because public thinking on international issues has made great advances and because the dangers to be avoided are greater than ever.

We are now moving away quickly from the world of compartmentalized self-sufficiency into a world where human solidarity daily becomes more essential. Already in humanitarian questions this solidarity is real, as we can see from international responses to natural and other disasters. It is becoming more real in the economic field, and it is clearly a necessity, though not yet a practical reality, in the political field. Here the governments of the world, associated in the United Nations, must realize the ideals which were already accepted in 1919 in the Covenant of the League and were reaffirmed in 1945 in the Charter of the United Nations.

We can thus see how far the world has actually come since 1919 in making the ideas and ideals of the Covenant of the League of Nations into acceptable reality. If we are to make the next step toward world authority and then onward to a world government, it will be by the growth in authority and prestige of the institutions and agencies of the United Nations, and by the development of the provisions of the Charter and the Statute of the International Court. If we can make those documents accepted as binding law, as every government in the United Nations is pledged to accept, then we are on the right path to world authority.

III THE UNITED NATIONS POLITICAL PROCESS

Students of the United Nations have devoted more attention to examining the outputs of the Organization than to examining the process by which these effects were achieved. This is unfortunate because, as the selections in this part demonstrate, the political process of the United Nations cannot be understood solely in terms of a legislative body or in terms of the normal diplomatic interaction that takes place in the capitol of a major power.

Sir Pierson Dixon, who for several years represented the United Kingdom at the United Nations, examines in his article the diplomatic vector of the process. In quite frank terms he discusses the problems, posed by Soviet tactics, of conducting diplomatic negotiations in the United Nations. He also deals with the problems of determining the proper mixture of private and public negotiations in a forum that by 1958 had grown to 81 members. This has become an even more serious situation since, in 1967, the membership has mushroomed to 122.

The actual instruments by which nations attempt to gain influence in the political process of the United Nations are discussed in David Kay's selection. United Nations diplomacy is distinguished by its heavy emphasis on the drafting of resolutions, amendments, and reports to be voted on by one or the other of its many organs. This emphasis ensures that parliamentary diplomacy plays an important role in the political process of the United Nations. The functions of the missions, caucusing groups, limited-membership organs, negotiations, resolutions, and voting in this process are examined as instruments of influence.

Dag Hammarskjöld, the second Secretary-General, reflecting particularly on his experience during the Congo crisis, recorded shortly before his death his perceptions of how members viewed the political process of the United Nations and its role in world politics. One group of states conceives of the United Nations as being a static conference machinery for discussing the topics that its members feel can benefit from discussion at the international level. The other view, perceived by Hammarskjöld, is that the United Nations is an organization that is a dynamic instrument entrusted by its members with operational tasks in order to prevent or halt outbreaks of violence "in a spirit of objectivity and in implementation of the principles and purposes of the Charter." Hammarskjöld clearly finds that the second conception is more in keeping with the Charter. By means of a perceptive analysis of the principles of the United Nations, an analysis of the nature of its decisions, and an analysis of the character of its structure, he endeavors to explain why this conception is crucial in a divided political world.

Leland Goodrich's article and Hammarskjöld's Oxford address deal with the nature of the role of the Secretariat in the political process of the United Nations. Goodrich, specifically, is concerned with the role of the Secretary-General as it pertains to the United Nations' function of maintaining international peace and security. He traces the changing aspects of the role of the Secretary-General from the time of Sir Eric Drummond in the League through Hammarskjöld in the United Nations. The impact of the Charter's provisions, their interpretation by the various occupants of the office, the changing role of the Organization itself in international politics, the political environment in which the United Nations has functioned, and finally the personality of the various Secretary-Generals are all examined to determine their contribution to the political role of the Secretary-General.

Goodrich questions whether an increased political role for the Secretary-General is compatible with the conception of the Secretary-General as an independent international civil servant. This is precisely the point that Hammarskjöld focused on in his Oxford lecture. Hammarskjöld maintained that the two roles are compatible. He viewed the purposes and principles of the Charter, the previous United Nations decisions, and consultations with the members as providing an agreed basis of action. We can question with Goodrich whether, in a highly divided world, the vague purposes and principles of the Charter (and also precedent) allow a Secretary-General to take action that will be recognized by all states as having been taken in accordance with international impartiality. Certainly the lessons of the Congo lead us to suspect that the price of involvement may be the questioning of the political neutrality of the Secretary-General.

In the final article of this section, Hayward R. Alker, Jr., examines the political process of the General Assembly by means of voting analysis. This article, which uses the techniques of factor analysis, attempts to uncover the principal dimensions of conflict behind the votes at the Sixteenth General Assembly. Then, using correlation and regression techniques, an assessment is made of the relative importance of these dimensions in determining the voting. Factor analysis reveals that four different substantive issues explain 85 per cent of the Assembly votes. The factors that form the basis of most Assembly voting are: self-determination, the Cold War and related membership questions, UN supernationalism, and Moslem questions. This type of analysis is a highly suggestive way for looking at the political process of the Organization and goes considerably beyond the traditional two-dimensional East-West distinction that is so often used.

Diplomacy at the United Nations

Sir Pierson Dixon, K.C.M.G., C.B.

MEANING OF DIPLOMACY

The United Nations being an association of sovereign countries in which the members are pledged under a Charter to work for certain common ends, there can, or should be, no place for the exercise of diplomacy in the classical sense—the conduct of business between states on a basis of national interest. The conception at the root of this world organisation is that the members, far from using it as a place to further their national interests, should subordinate those interests to the attainment of certain ends assumed to be in the common interests of all—peace with justice, development of friendly relations among peoples, and the promotion of the social and economic advancement of peoples. In theory the members should all be out-bidding each other for these ends, but the practice has fallen short of the theory and it is in fact true to say that, at present, diplomacy in the classical sense is commonly practised at the United Nations.

In another sense diplomacy can be defined as the practice of solving international disputes by peaceful rather than warlike means, that is by the methods of negotiation and conciliation. Diplomacy in this sense is a proper international activity at the United Nations and indeed an activity basic to the purposes laid down in the Charter. Although much genuine effort is devoted to utilising the great potential of the United Nations for negotiation and conciliation, and the

---

Sir Pierson Dixon, Permanent Representative of the United Kingdom at the United Nations, "Diplomacy at the United Nations," *International Relations,* Vol. 1, No. 10 (October 1958), pp. 457-466. Reprinted by permission of *International Relations.* This article was originally presented in a lecture series "Diplomacy in a Changing World" sponsored by the Committee on International Relations at the University of Notre Dame, Indiana.

results have been encouraging, the other practice–utilisation of the United Nations for national interests–has been followed by many member states, to the detriment of the practice of negotiation and conciliation and of the operation of the Organisation as a whole.

NATURE OF THE ORGANISATION

The complexities of the international activity pursued at the United Nations derive from the nature of the Organisation itself. The United Nations is a free association of sovereign countries. Containing as it does 81 members it now comes near to representing the totality of the countries of the world, with their many diverse traditions, institutions and interests. It is not a coalition or an alliance with specific and binding conditions. This of course is how it differs fundamentally from an international organisation such as the North Atlantic Alliance where certain nations have joined together for well-defined common objectives and where decisions can be made and are taken in the common interest. If the United Nations functioned with theoretical perfection and all its members conducted their international affairs through the United Nations and subordinated their national interests to the requirements of the U.N. Charter, there would be no need for such regional organisations. But this postulates an ideal, friction-free world, and the framers of the Charter themselves recognised, in Articles 51 and 52, the justification of such collective security arrangements in present conditions.

In practice the United Nations has not developed as we and the United States, who conceived the project, planned and hoped. The plan and hope was that it would provide an international forum in which all members would co-operate for the common ends which I have already mentioned. Difficulties have arisen from a number of factors, in the forefront of which must be placed the way the Soviet Union has treated the United Nations as a place for the promotion of its purely national interests. Then there has been the distortion of the aims of the Charter in favour of anticolonialism and ultranationalism, which has complicated the task of the so-called colonial powers in making the contribution which they wish to make to the purposes of the Charter. And finally, there was developed a double-standard of behaviour as applied to different parts of the world.

For all these complications the United Nations has made and is making an essential contribution to international peace and stability; but in order to understand how it really works and how diplomatic activity is conducted at the United Nations, it is essential to realise how much the task of international diplomacy is complicated by the factors I have listed, which I will now examine in greater detail.

MISUSE OF THE UNITED NATIONS

It is not my purpose to over-stress the past and present difficulties which divide the Communist and the free worlds. On the contrary, we must be forward-looking and seek to clear away the road-blocks of the past. But we must look forward with our eyes open. Our difficulties with the Soviet Union as reflected at the United Nations, have arisen from the fact that a major member has blocked so many serious efforts to deal with world problems and latterly has gone further and exploited the Organisation as a vehicle for its own national ambitions. This has caused the democratic world to consume much time and effort in circumventing and countering these tactics. This has been a major task for our diplomacy and has complicated our efforts to move towards the objectives which the founders of the United Nations had in mind.

Perhaps the greatest damage to the effectiveness of the Organisation has resulted from the behaviour of the Soviet Union in the Security Council, where it has the veto. The Security Council was intended to be an executive arm with major responsibility for peace and security. It has been gravely handicapped in this role by the way the Soviet Union has misused its veto power in order to frustrate some move genuinely designed to preserve peace and security, or to promote some particular national aim of its own.

In the wider forum provided by meetings of the General Assembly during its annual three months session much time has been wasted and useful initiatives have come to nothing owing to the propagandist use to which these meetings have been turned. The Soviet line is to play on the fear of war, using the slogan of peaceful co-existence, and representing the Soviet Union as the true apostle of peace and progress and the Western Powers as aggressive trouble-makers and imperialists. Recently the Russians have intensified this propaganda effort by capitalising their remarkable advances in science and by alternating peace propaganda with intimidation.

In the United Nations our task is not only to counter this kind of propaganda but, in spite of it, to create and maintain conditions favourable to conciliation and agreement. This requires considerable effort and unremitting patience.

One of the principal targets of Soviet diplomacy are the so-called uncommitted countries, and, however, superficial, the Soviet propaganda line about peaceful co-existence may appear, it must be admitted that it has some appeal and wins some support among these countries. The desire of such countries for peace is understandable, but experience teaches that peace is something that has to be striven for; it is not something that can be bought by a paper agreement or by a slogan. Yet it is slogans that are often offered from the platforms of the United Nations.

COLONIALISM

Besides posing as the apostles of peace, the Soviet propagandists also represent themselves as the great anticolonialists and supporters of nationalistic movements. The object is to play on the emotions of the emergent countries of Asia and Africa and to fan prejudices which do not in fact correspond to the realities of the modern world. It is perhaps understandable that some nationalistically-minded colonial territories should be prejudiced against their former overlords in favour of the Soviet Union whose domination they have never experienced. In fact, of course, the countries of America and Europe are profoundly sympathetic to the historical movements in Asia and Africa which have resulted in independence for so many peoples. The Soviet propaganda seeks to represent Great Britain as a would-be colonising Power and the United States as the prime imperialists of to-day. The facts are that the United States is contributing to the progress of under-developed countries in a significant and disinterested way, and Britain for the past century and more has been leading the dependent parts of her Empire to independence. The Soviet Union on the other hand has acquired and consolidated an imperial hold over people of non-Russian race, both in Central Asia and in Eastern Europe.

When the Russians make propaganda on these lines it is of course necessary to answer them in the United Nations. The resulting clash of views clearly does not help to ease world tensions but has the opposite effect. It would be a good thing if there could be an end to name-calling in the United Nations—an appeal which we have more than once made in the past but unfortunately without durable effect. As things are, diplomatic activity at the United Nations has to proceed against the unproductive background of the cold war.

THE DOUBLE STANDARD

I must now mention the controversy which came up on both sides of the Atlantic as a result of the steps which the General Assembly took to deal with the crises in Suez and Hungary in the autumn of 1956.

The General Assembly at that time passed a series of resolutions calling upon British and French forces to withdraw from Egypt and Soviet forces to withdraw from Hungary. The British and French Governments, whose action followed the Israeli attack on Egypt, felt able to comply with the Assembly's resolutions in view of the formation of the United Nations Emergency Force to preserve peace in the area. In the case of Hungary, the Assembly did not judge it worthwhile even to propose such an international force in view of the uncompromising attitude of the Soviet Union. The assembly called on the Soviet Union to withdraw its forces from Hungary and the Soviet Union rested on defiance of the Assembly's request. Attempts to secure compliance have been unavailing. A number of people both in the United Kingdom and other countries considered that the United Nations was applying a double standard in the two cases and that this represented a grave weakening of its moral strength. This view was held by people who supported the Anglo-French intervention in Egypt and by some who opposed it.

The answer which was made was that the General Assembly had in fact acted just as promptly and decisively in the case of Hungary as in the case of Egypt. Indeed, the tone of the Assembly's resolutions on Hungary, including as they did a specific condemnation of the Soviet action as a violation of the Charter, showed clearly that the Assembly recognised a vast difference between the two interventions. The General Assembly, so runs the argument, cannot be blamed if one member State defied its wishes while two others complied, since it possesses no means of enforcing those wishes. This argument is, of course, valid so far as it goes. It amounts to admitting that a double standard was in fact applied, while claiming that this was not because the Assembly had a double standard of truth, but because it was powerless to bring about a different result. The result is to weaken the reputation for even-handed justice which a world organisation evidently should enjoy.

It is sometimes contended that it is illogical that the smallest member States should have the same vote as the greatest and that this imbalance should be corrected by the introduction into the United Nations of a system of weighted votes. I am inclined to think that it would be impracticable to introduce such an innovation. The real remedy lies in the development of a greater sense of responsibility in the United Nations as it is at present constituted. That sense of responsibility, so far as the more powerful nations of the West are concerned, certainly comprises a great respect for the sovereign voice of each independent nation and a recognition of the fine contribution which many of the smaller and less experienced countries of the world are making. In many cases this contribution is out of all proportion to their size or power. It is, in my view, salutary for world peace and international harmony that the voices of the smaller nations should be heard with effect as they can be in a world organisation where the smallest nation has the same vote as the greatest. In return it is desirable that there should be full recognition of the great contribution which the more advanced and more powerful countries can make towards keeping the peace and promoting the economic advancement of peoples.

The tradition of private diplomacy between individual states was a tradition of mutual respect. This was not merely because its practitioners believed in mutual respect as a virtue in itself; they also found that it helped them to bring their business to a successful result. When diplomacy becomes public, this respect is harder to achieve. If every time a diplomat shakes hands with his rival or opponent a photograph of the event appears in the next day's paper with a political implication, then he may decide that it is safer not to shake hands. If an offensive speech wins bigger headlines than a polite speech, there is obviously a temptation to make it. But it is still true that mutual respect is a valuable adjunct to diplomacy. It is indeed essential in the give and take of multilateral diplomacy in a universal organisation, which by its very nature is designed to further, not the interests of individual countries, but the common interests of all.

HOW THE UNITED NATIONS CAN HELP

I thought it necessary to paint in this realistic background in order to help indicate how international relations are conducted in the United Nations as it actually operates at present. Enough has been said to show that widely conflicting interests, as in international relations generally, are active in the United Nations, and that diplomacy is therefore hard put to it to develop the United Nations as a working centre for harmonising the actions of nations and a place where we can make a contribution to peace with justice and the development of friendly relations among peoples.

Within its existing limitations the United Nations is, however, a most valuable institution. It would, I think, be generally admitted that, if it had not been in existence during the past twelve years, the international situation would be graver to-day. Equally there is, I believe, a general and strongly-held conviction—certainly in my country—that the modern world needs an international organisation of this universal character for the purposes of preserving peace and resolving differences between nations.

I will now briefly examine the ways in which in my view the United Nations can contribute in a practical way.

I should perhaps make it clear in parenthesis that I am not in the present context dealing with the important and successful work which the United Nations does in the economic, social and legal fields.

Within the political field it has three main functions:

Threats to the Peace

1. Dealing with threats to the peace and breaches of the peace, that is preventing war breaking out and dealing with it if it does.

As I have shown, the United Nations at present is gravely handicapped in this, its most important function. It is true that it was able to halt aggression in

Korea; but this was only because by a tactical miscalculation the Soviet Delegation was absent from the Security Council and therefore not able to impose its veto when the important decision was taken. Still, much can be done by bringing the force of public opinion to bear. The United Nations failed to keep the peace between Israel and Egypt, or to stop the Soviet invasion and suppression of liberty in Hungary. But the alarm and distress caused by both these events was widespread and widely voiced in the United Nations. The advertisement of world opinion in this way may be a valuable deterrent for the future. The establishment of the United Nations Emergency Force in the Gaza Strip between Egypt and Israel has proved a valuable and practical contribution to the reduction of the tensions surrounding the Palestine question.

Conciliation

2. The United Nations' second main function is to act as a centre of conciliation.

This of course overlaps with the first function: the surest way to prevent a breach of peace is to deal with and resolve the cause of the dispute. The Security Council has been able to make its contribution, particularly in regard to Palestine problems; though it has not, of course, been able, despite strenuous efforts, to make advance towards turning the armistice into a peace. Our diplomacy here consists in patient work, often behind the scenes and not in open Council, in ironing out those differences and dealing with those incidents between Israel and her Arab neighbours which can so easily flare up into war. In this and other cases there has been a genuine common effort by Western and non-Communist powers as a whole, with the invaluable help of the Secretary-General of the United Nations.

The United Nations is also of course potentially a centre of conciliation between the Communist and non-Communist worlds.

It is indeed the obvious centre for such conciliation simply because Communist and non-Communist representatives sit side by side in the various United Nations bodies and are in constant contact in the halls of the United Nations building. There are thus regular means of contact and discussion. In the past the Soviet diplomatic offensive has not been conducive to fruitful discussion, but, on the contrary, has forced the non-Communist countries to defend themselves and struggle for the initiative in this propaganda battle not of their choosing. Nonetheless, the possible openings arising from the mere fact that the Soviet bloc is represented at the United Nations provide possibilities which our diplomacy should constantly bear in mind.

The United Nations can be very helpful in providing a suitable forum, particularly for progress on disarmament. On the other hand it is a mistaken idea that the United Nations is being "bypassed" if some important international problem is dealt with in some other way. All channels for resolving international difficulties should be considered open, and sometimes one medium is more appropriate in the circumstances than another; sometimes a combination of United Nations action with direct inter-state diplomacy is the method most likely to lead to agreement.

Open Debate and Private Diplomacy

I now turn to less clear-cut issues where strains are liable to arise for friendships within the free world when a matter is raised in the United Nations.

I have here particularly in mind so-called colonial questions which arouse a lot of feeling and where even our closest friends appear sometimes to overlook the great changes that are taking place in what used to be the Colonial Empires. This complicates the task of the so-called Colonial Powers in continuing the process of leading dependent peoples to independence.

The difficulties arise largely from the simple fact that they are raised in the United Nations. In the United Nations the proceedings are public and its decisions are taken by voting. This has value when some broad issue of international concern is being debated. But when it is a specific issue affecting the vital interests of a major power, this open procedure can prove awkward. A problem which might be solved by the old-fashioned methods of private, non-publicised diplomacy, often becomes intractable when debated in the United Nations. A relatively minor problem becomes magnified out of proportion of its true importance, owing to the clash of differing views in debate at the United Nations. But private diplomacy is not only unfashionable: it has come to be regarded as positively immoral. This is perhaps because private diplomacy smells of secret diplomacy, and secret diplomacy in the popular mind is plotting behind people's backs. Yet "open covenants *privately* arrived at" is often the best method of agreement. Covenants are often not arrived at at all if they have to be reached through the medium of public debate. The moral for diplomacy at the United Nations is more restraint in advocating the treatment of thorny questions in public debate and greater use of the many alternative media available in the flexible organisation of the United Nations.

Nonetheless private diplomacy is quietly and regularly pursued at the United Nations as well as diplomacy by public debate. My experience is that a preliminary phase of such behind-the-scenes preparation for the public debate in Council, Committee or Plenary is normally the best way of reaching a good result. The helpful role of the Secretary-General in this kind of activity is of very great value. But the view of the majority of the United Nations seems to be that freedom of public discussion must be untrammelled and that every matter is debatable at the United Nations if a member government wishes to bring it up.

My own view is that the United Nations should be rather more selective in its choice of matters to discuss. It should in my opinion consider carefully whether discussion of a particular problem brought before it by a member nation is going to be helpful to the finding of a peaceful solution or whether discussion is against the terms of the Charter itself and is just going to give one group of member nations a chance to make propaganda against another group. It would be foolish not to recognise that discussion of some problems at the United Nations may actually hinder the interests of peace and stability in the area concerned.

An incidental result of indiscriminate discussion at the United Nations is that a strain is placed on relationships between friends, since differing positions have to be advertised publicly on questions which would otherwise never have been raised in public at all.

These differences are accentuated by the procedure in the United Nations—unavoidable in public debate—of expressing an opinion by a vote. A vote can be for, or against, or an abstention. If, for example, the United Kingdom votes for and the United States against, this advertises a serious difference. If one votes for or against and the other abstains, it is clear to the world that some difference exists.

I do not, however, take a negative line about public discussion at the United Nations. Quite the contrary. In a world in which public opinion strongly influences the shaping of policy by governments, discussion at the United Nations can be an immensely influential force even if it produces no immediately definite decisions. If this force of public opinion is used selectively as I have suggested it can be extremely valuable in bringing the pressure of world public opinion to bear when it is needed.

This is indeed the third main function of the United Nations.

Until the international situation improves to the extent of the major countries working together and the United Nations being given executive powers for collective security, I believe that more emphasis should be laid than at present on this third function of the United Nations as a world forum and clearing house for ideas, a place where countries are influenced by the opinions of other countries and by world opinion, a centre where foreign representatives can meet, talk quietly and get to know each other. The General Assembly was conceived by the founders as having that function, while the Security Council was to be primarily the organ concerning itself with matters of peace and security. There is a real danger in attributing to the General Assembly executive attributes which properly belong to the Security Council. The world, with its hundred separate nations, is not a unity, but a diversity. It is diverse by race, creed and national interest. The United Nations, being an association of sovereign nations, cannot do more than reflect the sum total of international relations as they actually exist. At present there are cleavages of varying depths between the nations, and these cleavages inevitably are reflected in the United Nations. It would be a self-delusion to postulate a unity that does not exist and to entrust to the United Nations as it stands the powers of a world executive. Our goal is that degree of world unity which will ensure co-operation instead of rivalry. We shall further it by recognizing the United Nations as it is, with its present limitations. By understanding its immense potentialities we shall reduce the differences that divide the nations of the world to-day.

HOW TO MAKE THE UNITED NATIONS MORE EFFECTIVE

How then can we make the United Nations more effective? Not, I believe, by trying to turn it into a world executive, or by trying to ascribe to the General Assembly the powers of decision and execution which belong to the Security Council. The real remedy lies in the hands of member states, particularly the more powerful ones. But, in the absence of an improvement in international relations, the United Nations will, I think, make its best contribution by running its affairs in accordance with the structure laid down at San Francisco twelve years ago, which provides for a flexible balance between the major organs of the United Nations.

Above all I believe that we need to develop certain techniques to respond to the unsettled state of international relationships and the peculiar conditions of an 81 nation open forum; and I offer in conclusion some reflections on the methods of diplomacy most likely to be successful for the purposes of the United Nations.

In any worthwhile diplomatic activity there are three stages:

1. Appraisal of the facts of the case.
2. Determination of the best course to pursue.
3. A conclusion which is as widely acceptable as possible not only to governments but also to world opinion.

Stage 1 requires a good hard look, a cold appraisal divorced from cant or emotion.

Stage 2 requires cool and skilful judgment taking a long view and often involving the steering of a difficult course between various conflicting interests.

Stage 3 requires thorough consultation with other countries, ranging from the closest friends and allies, through the range of neutrally-minded countries, and extending to those actively opposed. It is also necessary to sound and prepare opinion through the media of public discussion, and to frame the case with due recognition of the fact that it will come under the searchlight of world public opinion at the United Nations.

It often occurs at the United Nations that these processes, essential for a good result, are either ignored or become bedevilled by emotion or propaganda. The would-be cure is then worse than the disease. I have already spoken of the way in which Soviet diplomacy plays on emotions like the fear of war and ultra-nationalism. When the emotions rule, the true purposes of the United Nations are liable to be lost sight of, and international diplomacy becomes diplomacy by slogan. The actions of nations cannot be harmonised by pleas for peace at any price or denunciations of "Imperialism." The result is rather to increase international tension and embitter, not improve, relations between peoples.

As I see it, the basic function of the rather special kind of diplomacy which operates in a universal organisation whose proceedings take place in public, is to arrange that the problems which come within its purview are dealt with by the methods most likely to conciliate the diverse interests involved and most conducive to agreement; diplomacy by patience and planning and not diplomacy by slogan, diplomacy based on a genuine regard for the Charter as a whole and not diplomacy that picks and chooses according to the tactical advantage of the moment.

If we can work out a generally accepted diplomatic approach on these lines at the United Nations we may hope to develop peaceful methods of resolving disputes and promote understanding between peoples at a moment in world history when it has never been so important to find an alternative to agitation and strife.

Instruments of Influence in the United Nations Political Process

David Kay

The political process of the United Nations is a curious blend of parliamentary nomenclature and procedure with great power politics. One of the more interesting and understudied areas of this quasi-parliamentary process is the instrumentation through which a nation makes demands and exercises influence within the United Nations.

MISSIONS AND DELEGATIONS

It is with the permanent missions of the Member States that the immediate responsibility for the advancement of national policy in the United Nations rests.[1] The establishment by members of permanent representation at the headquarters

David A. Kay, Assistant Professor of Political Science, The University of Wisconsin.

[1] During the plenary sessions of the General Assembly and the Economic and Social Council, states are represented by delegations specially accredited to the particular session of the body. The composition of these special delegations varies from country to country. Many states choose to compose them of prominent members of the government while others tend to draw heavily upon their permanent mission when making such appointments. As a general rule the new nations tend to follow the latter practice. Regardless of the composition of the special delegations, they are dependent upon the permanent missions for staff work and expertise in the politics of the Organization. Unless otherwise noted, the author has followed the practice in this section of using the term "missions" to cover the activity of the specially accredited delegations as well as the permanent missions.

of an international organization is a relatively recent innovation in diplomatic practice. In spite of the initial negative reaction of the League Secretariat, permanent delegations–League terminology for what is now called a permanent mission–first put in a large-scale appearance at Geneva. Although as many as forty permanent delegations were accredited to the League of Nations at the height of its activity, their impact appears to have been slight. The leading historian of the League, F. P. Walters, asserts flatly that "the system of Permanent Delegations was of no serious significance in League history."[2]

While the Charter of the United Nations made no mention of a system of permanent missions accredited to the Organization by the Member States, the tempo of post-war diplomacy as well as the fact that the Organization was not located in the capital of one of the Members soon dictated the establishment of such a system.[3] By 1948 forty-one of the then fifty-eight Members had established permanent missions in New York and by October 1966 this figure had risen to 120 of the 121 Members.[4] Walters' assessment of permanent missions during the League period would be repeated by few, if any, observers of the role played by such missions in the United Nations.

Within the United Nations political system at least four distinct functions as instruments of political influence are performed by all of the permanent missions. The feverish activity which constantly surrounds each mission can be functionally separated according to its contribution to (1) national policy formation, (2) the design and execution of the tactics of parliamentary diplomacy, (3) the collection and reporting of information, and (4) the dissemination of propaganda.

Although each permanent mission serves as its government's advisor on United Nations affairs, this does not automatically assure that the mission's views will be given decisive weight in the determination of national policy. The foreign policy process today has become such a complicated and interrelated web that what seems decisive in New York may not seem so in London or Cairo. An additional handicap which all the missions struggle under in influencing the course of national policy is that their geographical isolation from the national capitals where the broad policy is determined severely limits their personal intervention in the policy-making process where personal influence often counts for much. Even as articulate a mission head as Adlai Stevenson found that the two hundred miles

---

[2]F. P. Walters, *A History of the League of Nations* (London: Oxford University Press, 1952), p. 199.

[3]The only hint of such a system is in Article 28(1), which states: "The Security Council shall be so organized as to be able to function continuously. Each member of the Security Council shall for this purpose be represented at all times at the seat of the Organization."

[4]Sydney D. Bailey, *The General Assembly of the United Nations. A Study of Procedure and Practice* (ed. rev.; New York: Frederick A. Praeger, 1964), p. 13. United Nations Document ST/SG/SER.A/195, October 1966.

separating New York and Washington was sufficient to keep him out of touch with decision-making in Washington.[5]

The very nature of United Nations diplomacy with its heavy emphasis on the drafting of resolutions, amendments and reports to be voted on by one or the other of the numerous organs of the United Nations ensures that the execution of the tactics of parliamentary diplomacy will be a principal focus of the activity of the permanent missions. An unceasing round of private negotiations is the most pervasive form of this activity. It is in the design and execution of the tactics of parliamentary diplomacy that the permanent missions excel. As a member of the United States mission has noted,

". . . a delegation's role in the formulation of tactics and in the precise manner of implementing policy is usually decisive. The tactical situation varies so rapidly from day to day, and the calculation of probable voting and of the attitudes of other countries is so crucial in achieving a successful result, that tactics must be left reasonably flexible. Even such a question as when to inform other delegations of a country's policy can be a critical decision. Such factors as the order in which various people are approached, the concessions which a delegation can make within the limits of its authorization, and the level and timing of moves are best judged as closely to the necessary action as possible, both in time and distance."[6]

Of course, when dealing with a system in which new issues are constantly arising and the terms of old ones are constantly shifting, the mission's acknowledged control over the tactics to be followed often results in its having *de facto* control of policy as well. Few missions operate under detailed instructions as to tactics, and even in regard to policy the guide lines are usually broad enough to allow the mission a certain amount of discretion. As one might imagine, this inability to exercise detailed control is often the despair of home governments. The sentiments once echoed by Prime Minister Macmillan are probably generally shared in many capitals:

". . . the [resolutions] come flooding in, they are very long and complicated and, with the best will in the world, they really do present quite a difficulty to the delegations in New York and to Governments overseas.

"This is, of course, not made easier by the time factor, and the curious rules of procedure which are not, like ours, worked out after many generations. Amendments are moved in New York of which we in the capital cities have hardly seen the text—perhaps we get it on the telephone—and in situations in

---

[5] Theodore C. Sorensen, *Kennedy* (New York: Harper & Row), 1965, pp. 287-288.

[6] Richard F. Pedersen, "National Representation in the United Nations," *International Organization*, Vol. 15, No. 2 (Spring 1961), p. 260. For a similar assessment, see John G. Hadwen and Johan Kaufman, *How United Nations Decisions Are Made* (2d ed. rev.; New York: Oceana Publications, 1962), p. 34.

which we are unable to appreciate the full implications. Many of the member Governments, I can assure the House, have given up the task in despair and give no instructions to their representatives. Some have given permanent instructions to their representatives to abstain."[7]

A third function of the permanent mission is the constant collection and reporting of information on the wide range of questions that face the Organization. Every mission desires to know the probable line of conduct of the over one hundred other Members and all of them would like to stay at least one step ahead of any likely crisis issue. The exchange of information on issues and policies with other missions and the reporting of this information takes a considerable proportion of the time of each mission. In addition to collecting and exchanging information with other missions, contacts must be maintained with the Secretariat for the same purposes.

Finally, every mission is engaged in public relations campaigns directed to the other missions, the Secretariat, foreign governments and foreign and domestic public opinion. One major difficulty is that these various campaigns directed at different audiences must be waged simultaneously, and what may be suitable for one audience may not be for another. Indicative of the extent of this public relations effort is the fact that the verbatim records of the General Assembly and its subsidiary organs now exceed 40,000 pages a year.[8] In addition to speeches, most missions consider it necessary to hold periodic press conferences and to issue a stream of press releases on the views of their governments on the questions before the United Nations.

Starting in 1955 and reaching a peak in 1960, the rush to independence in Africa and Asia began to be reflected in the membership statistics of the United Nations. In 1954 only 60 states were members of the Organization whereas by the end of 1961 this figure stood at 104. By the early 1960's when the majority of these new states entered the Organization, the permanent mission system was already well established, and it was assumed that as a matter of course they would also establish missions in New York. In general, this expectation was followed, and through the end of 1966 no new nation remained without a permanent mission for more than one year. However, these missions tended to be quite small. For example, the average number of diplomatic personnel in all the missions of the new nations in 1960 was only 3.6, and by 1966 this figure had risen to only 5.5. By comparison, during the period 1964-1966 the average size of the permanent missions of Argentina, Brazil, Guatemala, Mexico, and Uruguay taken as a group was 9.0. The Soviet Union leads all states with a permanent mission that

[7] Great Britain, *5 Hansard's Parliamentary Debates* (Commons), vol 653, February 5, 1962, pp. 53-54.

[8] Richard P. Hunt, "At the U.N.–13,000,000 Words a Year," *New York Times Magazine*, December 9, 1962, p. 33.

during the period 1964-1966 averaged 53.66 people. During this same period the average for the United States was 44.66, for the United Kingdom it was 22.33, and for France 15.33.

This figure for the new nations is somewhat overstated since it was a common practice for the new nations to appoint their Ambassadors to the United States as heads of their permanent missions. In 1961 seventeen of the thirty-seven new nations listed their Ambassadors to the United States as heads of their permanent missions, and as late as 1964 thirteen of the forty-eight new states still followed this practice. In spite of great exertion on their part, most such heads of delegations forced to fill two key posts are only able to maintain close contact with United Nations affairs during the annual sessions of the General Assembly and in some cases not even then.

There are several reasons for the small size of the permanent missions of the new nations. One manifestation of economic underdevelopment and social backwardness is a shortage of trained personnel. This shortage has meant that the new nations have in general tried to keep most of their talented personnel at home to staff key ministries and departments and to ration the remainder out among various international commitments. Important limits have been placed upon the size of missions by the shallowness of the pool of available talent.

Another limiting factor on the size of these missions has been their financial cost. Stoessinger in his study of United Nations financing calculated the average cost of maintaining a mission in New York at $100,000.[9] That this figure is probably much closer to a minimum rather than an average is indicated by Stoessinger's own use of Indonesia's and Mexico's annual expenditures of $270,000 each to illustrate the cost of a small mission.[10] Whatever the true minimum cost of a mission, many new nations have believed the cost of a large establishment in New York to be greater than any potential benefits and have kept the size of their missions very small.

The more interesting questions relate not strictly to the size of the missions of the new nations but to how they have functioned in the political system of the United Nations. One would expect that to the extent that the permanent mission system represents a functional response to requirements of the United Nations political system the tasks performed by the new nations' missions would duplicate those performed by the missions of other states. With certain important variations, this has been the case. As was noted earlier, each mission in its capacity as its government's advisor on United Nations affairs plays an important role in shaping the foreign policy of its government. While this is as true for the new nations as for the other Members of the United Nations, there are certain

[9] John G. Stoessinger *et al., Financing the United Nations System* (Washington; Brookings Institute, 1964), p. 71.

[10] *Ibid.;* The average size of the Mexican and Indonesian missions during Stoessinger's study was eleven.

significant distinctions. For the older and generally larger nations with a longer history of diplomatic involvement and consequently more international commitments, the United Nations is seldom the dominant concern of their foreign policy. Recommendations from the missions of these older nations must contend with the recommendations from other elements of their national foreign policy-making system. Most of the new nations, however, face a significantly different situation. Having been independent for a shorter period, they generally have fewer international commitments. More importantly, for the vast majority of the new nations the United Nations forms both the chief arena and the major instrument of their foreign policy; it is only within the United Nations confines that they can speak and vote on a basis of equality with the world's larger powers. This tends to give a much greater weight in the determination of policy to the advice emanating from the missions of the new nations. This tendency is greatly reenforced by the limited size of the foreign offices of these new states which, when combined with their geographic separation from New York, effectively limits the scope of their supervision of the missions. In general, the missions of the new nations have significantly fewer instructions as to policy and tactics and consequently have greater latitude of action than the other missions.[11] This degree of discretion does vary, however, according to the nature of the issue under consideration. On colonial issues and questions of economic aid and development only the vaguest of instructions are issued to these missions. On the other hand, when the issue involved is one with significant East-West overtones, the missions of most new nations seek to obtain instructions from their governments, or if this is impossible, they abstain. Thus, the missions of the new nations play a much larger role than the missions of other states in determining the shape of their national policy as expressed in the United Nations.

Faced with only limited diplomatic representation abroad, many of the new nations have broadened the traditional function of the permanent mission in collecting and reporting information into a distinctly new function. Unable to afford the costs in money and trained manpower needed to maintain diplomatic representation in over a hundred capitals, these new nations have used the opportunity provided by the concentration in New York of diplomatic representatives from most members of the international community to complete their diplomatic network. The head of a typical mission from a new state may find himself also serving as his country's Ambassador to the United States and *de facto* representative to eighty or more other states.

The strain placed on the small missions of the new nations is obvious. With,

---

[11]Robert E. Riggs, *Politics in the United Nations, A Study of United States Influence in the General Assembly* (Urbana, Ill.: The University of Illinois Press, 1958), p. 20. Hayward R. Alker, Jr. and Bruce Russett, *World Politics in the General Assembly* (New Haven, Conn.: Yale University Press, 1965), pp. 218-219. Thomas Hovet, Jr., *Africa in the United Nations* (Evanston, Ill.: Northwestern University Press, 1963), pp. 218-222.

on the average, fewer than five diplomatic personnel, these missions must shoulder the burden of representing their nation, in a quite literal sense, before the world. The audience, both governmental and private, available to a permanent mission of a new nation in New York is larger than that in any of the world's capitals. In addition to this heavy representational burden, the mission of a typical new nation bears the responsibility for the successful advancement of its nation's foreign policy in the United Nations as well as advising the government on future policy. The heavy and time-consuming schedule of plenary and committee meetings during Assembly session is followed by an almost equally heavy load of *ad hoc* committees when the Assembly is not in session. In all of these tasks the mission is not only grossly understaffed in New York but is inadequately backstopped at home with research and other assistance.

The growth of the permanent mission system has both reflected and assisted the evolution of the United Nations into a continuous diplomatic conference. As the organization has acquired more operational tasks permanent missions have become essential instruments for constantly monitoring and influencing these activities. Permanent missions also serve a psychological function as a token of a Member's concern and interest in the Organization. However, the principal function of the missions remains at the present time the advancement of national policy aims through the United Nations.

CAUCUSING GROUPS

As early as the San Francisco Conference the pressures of having to decide which states were to serve on the limited-membership organs of the United Nations had resulted in an inchoate system of geographical groupings.[12] By the 1950's under the impetus of an expansion in the concerns of the Organization and the pressures inherent in parliamentary diplomacy toward frequent voting, these informal groupings of Member States were caucusing for periodic discussions of issues before the United Nations.[13] It is these caucusing groups which possess varying degrees of organization but meet with some degree of regularity for the

[12] Writing in 1951, M. Margaret Ball noted: "The spectre of bloc voting has haunted the United Nations since the Charter was first debated at San Francisco. Since then, the influence of certain groups of states in affecting the outcome of elections has occasioned considerable comment, and it has been suggested that the same groups have been inordinately powerful in deciding substantive issues." M. Margaret Ball, "Bloc Voting in the General Assembly," *International Organization*, Vol. 5, No. 1 (February 1951), p. 3.

[13] Thomas Hovet, Jr., who has done much of the pioneering work in this area, draws a distinction between blocs and caucusing groups. He applies the term bloc only to "a group

purpose of discussing United Nations issues that form the principal element of the group system in the United Nations political process.[14]

At least four functions of the caucusing groups in the political process of the United Nations can be discerned. A principal function of these groups remains the selection of candidates for election to the limited-membership organs of the United Nations. In an examination of twelve years of the General Assembly's electoral practice, Norman J. Padelford found that group association and the concerted political action associated with it played a decisive role in the process.[15] Operating in the context of the "gentlemen's agreements" that have developed for the allocation of the elective posts of the Organization, the caucusing groups in their elective function have fulfilled a quasi-official role in the structure of the Organization. Certainly as the United Nations has grown larger the only thing preventing the *de facto* disenfranchisement of a large number of Members with respect to the limited-membership organs has been the development of indirect representation through the caucusing groups.

Caucusing groups have also functioned in the United Nations as convenient centers for the exchange and, to varying extents, the harmonization of views on issues before the Organization. Particularly as the cultural, economic and ideological diversity of the United Nations increased, these groups began to function as important arenas for the preliminary consideration of issues among states possessing a broadly similar outlook. Of decisive importance in the caucusing groups' development of this function is the pressure, inherent in the majority voting rules of parliamentary diplomacy, to accent the resolution-passing power of the Assembly. As long as resolutions were rare and their passage required unanimity, as in the League, there was little point to engaging in extensive

---

of states which meets regularly in caucus and the members of which are bound in their votes in the General Assembly by the caucus decision." Only the Soviet group meets Hovet's criteria of a bloc. The other groups which meet regularly in caucus but lack bloc discipline are referred to by Hovet as caucusing groups. Thomas Hovet, Jr., *Bloc Politics in the United Nations* (Cambridge: Harvard University Press, 1960), pp. 31-32. However, as both terms refer to states engaged in the same activity, i.e., periodic meeting within some degree of organizational structure, the more inclusive term "caucusing group" is used in this study to cover both the Soviet bloc and the other caucusing groups. For a discussion of the confused terminology in this area, see Arend Lijphart, "The Analysis of Bloc Voting in the General Assembly: A Critique and a Proposal," *The American Political Science Review,* Vol. LVII, No. 4 (December 1963) pp. 902-904.

[14]Various special interest groups, ranging from land-locked states to economically underdeveloped states, may temporarily coalesce for a particular resolution, but as these groupings do not consider the broad range of issues before the United Nations, it seems more appropriate to consider these special interest groups as a normal product of the negotiations process.

[15]Norman J. Padelford, *Elections in the United Nations General Assembly, A Study in Political Behavior* (Cambridge: Center for International Studies, Massachusetts Institute of Technology, 1959), p. 67.

preliminary consideration of issues among one's friends.[16] But when these conditions changed such consideration became incumbent for the effective exercise of political influence.

As greater emphasis was placed on passing General Assembly resolutions the caucusing groups began to assume responsibilities for the initiation and coordination of efforts to obtain action on issues of special interest to their group. Thus, the move at the seventh session to add for the first time to the General Assembly's agenda the question of race relations in South Africa was initially made in the Afro-Asian caucus, and the accompanying draft resolution was a product of the caucus.[17] To a limited extent this emerging function of the caucusing groups compensates for the lack of clearly defined leadership centers within the General Assembly.

Starting with the large membership increases of 1955, the caucusing groups began to play an important tutorial function in the political process of the United Nations. Upon their admission to the Organization, the new Members found themselves immediately welcomed into an ongoing group of similar states which seemed far less imposing than the Organization as a whole. In exercising this function the caucusing groups contributed significantly to the inculcation of the new Members with the mores and procedures of United Nations diplomacy. More importantly in terms of the exercise of political influence, the caucusing groups helped structure the activity of the new Members. Left to themselves the overworked missions of many of these new Members when faced with the plenitude of issues dealt with each year might have diluted their influence in a flurry of undirected activity. Although in no sense able to prevent all of the confusion that inevitably surrounds first immersion into the diplomacy of the Organization, the caucusing groups have fulfilled an important socialization function in assisting the adjustment of new Members to this political process.

As instruments in the exercise of political influence, the caucusing groups had by 1960 developed important functions in regard to elections to United Nations organs, the preliminary discussion of issues, initiating and coordinating action on issues of special interest and the initiation of new Members into the political mores and folkways of United Nations diplomacy. Although they varied greatly in structure and frequency of meetings, nine caucusing groups could be identified in the United Nations as of 1967. These nine caucusing groups are the: African; Afro-Asian; Arab; Benelux; Commonwealth; Eastern European; Latin American; Scandinavian; and Western European.

Considerable overlapping of membership existed among the caucusing groups with the Arab and African groups being only subgroups of the Asian-African

---

[16] Hovet, *Africa in the United Nations, op. cit.,* p. 13.

[17] United Nations Documents A/2183, 15 September 1952; A/AC.61/L.8/Rev. 2, 19 November 1952.

group. As of 1966 ten states, Austria, China, Finland, Greece, Ireland, Israel, Portugal, Spain, the United States and Yugoslavia, were not represented in any of the caucusing groups.

The most interesting of the caucusing groups is probably the Afro-Asian group, whose origin can be traced back to 1951. The Asian-African group, as it was then called, grew out of the search by these states in early 1951 for a basis of negotiations to end the Korean conflict.[18] After the Bandung Conference of 1955 and the Suez crisis of 1956 the process of caucusing among the Asian, Arab and African members of the Organization had developed sufficiently for these states to be identified as a caucusing group.[19] During Assembly sessions the group normally meets at least once a week with the chairmanship rotating alphabetically among the members.[20] Formal organization from the beginning was kept to a minimum with the emphasis being placed upon informal discussions.

The African group emerged as a result of the Accra Conference of Independent African States held in April 1958. The Conference directed the eight African countries which were then United Nations Members to instruct their permanent missions to consult together on matters of common concern.[21] Great pains were taken to emphasize the fact that the African group was remaining in the Asian-African group and was only constituting a separate group for the purpose of discussing strictly African affairs. Unlike the Asian-African group, the African group chose to establish an elaborate organization bearing the unlikely title of The Informal Permanent Machinery.[22] The Informal Permanent Machinery provided for a Co-ordinating Body, composed of the permanent representatives of all the African states that are United Nations members, and a Secretariat, composed of four of the African states elected for two-year terms. Although the procedures of the African group are in theory more precise and formal than those of the larger group in operation, the practice has been so informal "that some of the newer African Members of the United Nations, especially those with small delegations, may be completely unaware that they are part of the formally organized Informal Permanent Machinery.[23]

[18]Geoffrey Goodwin, "The Expanding United Nations, I.–Voting Patterns," *International Affairs* (London), Vol. 36, April 1960, p. 181.

[19]Israel, China and South Africa were excluded from the beginning.

[20]Hovet, *Block Politics in the United Nations, op. cit.,* pp. 84-85. Samaan Boutros Farajallah, *Le Groupe Afro-Asiatique Dans Le Cadre Des Nations Unies* (Geneve: Libraire Droz, 1963), pp. 13-41.

[21]Hovet, *Africa in the United Nations, op. cit.,* p. 75. Farajallah, *op. cit.,* pp. 41-71. The eight initial members were Ethiopia, Ghana, Liberia, Libya, Morocco, Sudan, Tunisia and the United Arab Republic.

[22]Hovet, *Africa in the United Nations, op. cit.,* pp. 80-82.

[23]*Ibid.,* p. 82. Both Hovet and Farajallah provide in the pages cited excellent discussions of the formal mechanisms and divisions that have developed in these groups.

Whereas in 1959 the Asian-African group had comprised only 34.1 percent of the United Nations membership, by 1964 this figure had risen to 50.4 percent, and in early 1967 it stood at 52.1 percent. Indicative of the increased African influence on the combined caucus is the shift in names after 1960 from the Asian-African group to the Afro-Asian group. This sharp rise in the size of these two caucusing groups resulting from the admission of the new nations has certainly increased the potential of the Afro-Asian and African caucusing groups to serve as effective instruments of political influence.

While the great influx of former colonial states has increased the size of the Afro-Asian caucusing group, it has caused a relative decline in the size of the majority of the other caucusing groups. The Eastern European caucusing group composed 11.8 percent of the membership of the United Nations in 1955 but by 1966 this figure had fallen to 6.61 percent. The Arab group, while increasing in absolute size during the period 1955-1966 from eight to twelve members, fell in relative size from 10.5 percent of the United Nations membership in 1955 to 9.9 percent in 1966. Of all the caucusing groups the Latin American group has experienced the sharpest relative decline in size. In 1955 the Latin American caucusing group represented 26.31 percent of the Organization's membership but by 1966 only 18.1 percent. Only that most amorphous of all caucusing groups, the Commonwealth, has been spared a relative decline in size during this period. Because many of the African states that joined the United Nations after 1955 had been British colonies they became members not only of the African Afro-Asian caucusing groups but also of the Commonwealth group. While the Commonwealth only represented 10.5 percent of the United Nations membership in 1955, it had increased to almost 20 percent in 1966.

LIMITED-MEMBERSHIP ORGANS

While the three councils, Security, Economic and Social, and Trusteeship, played a significant role in the political process of the United Nations from the very beginning, it was only as the Organization undertook an increased number tasks and its membership grew that other limited-membership organs gained a significant role in its political process.[24] For the United Nations, limited-membership organs, whether they be called commissions, committees or subcommittees, provide an effective means of ensuring that certain problems receive continuous attention. It was for this purpose that such bodies as the Committee

[24] Catherine S. Manno, "Problems and Trends in the Composition of Nonplenary UN Organs," *International Organization*, Vol. 19, No. 1 (Winter 1965), pp. 37-55.

on South West Africa and the Eighteen Nation Committee on Disarmament were established by the General Assembly. Limited-membership organs also provide an effective means of securing expert advice on technical subjects for the Assembly. Both the General Assembly and the Economic and Social Council have been responsible for the proliferation of a host of select bodies, such as the International Law Commission, the Population Commission and the Statistical Commission, all designed to gain expert opinion on technical questions. While the practice varies as to whether such experts sit in their individual capacity or as representatives of governments, few would argue that nationality plays a minor role in the selection of such bodies.

The General Assembly, the only United Nations organ in which all Members are represented, has been loath to make use of limited-membership bodies to expedite its work while it is in session. In spite of a doubling in its size in twenty years, the Assembly's main committees still remain committees-of-the-whole.[25] This reluctance to approve a large-scale use of select committees during the Assembly's session stems from the understandable desire of many states to protect their "sovereign equality" in the one body of the United Nations where all states are represented. However, the Assembly's aversion to limited-membership organs is strictly limited to the period in which it is in session. The necessity of providing continuous attention to sensitive subjects and the need for expert advice has forced the Assembly to spawn numerous limited-membership organs.

As instruments of influence within the political process of the Organization, these limited-membership organs play two noteworthy functions. The very fact that such organs are established in order to provide continuous attention to a subject ensures that their members will have a greater opportunity to exercise influence than those states which are not members. For example, when the Committee on South West Africa was established in 1953 to conduct negotiations with the South African Government and to submit annual reports to the Assembly on conditions in South West Africa, it was obvious to all that the members of the Committee would play a central role in the United Nations handling of the question. Certainly as Catherine Manno has noted, the heated arguments in the Assembly over the composition of these limited-membership organs is significant evidence that the Member States believe the bodies wield important influence.[26]

---

[25] The General Assembly has seven main committees, each of which consists of representatives of all Member States. The main committees are as follows: First Committee (Political and Security Questions); Special Political Committee; Second Committee (Economic and Financial Questions); Third Committee (Social, Humanitarian, and Cultural Questions); Fourth Committee (Trusteeship Questions); Fifth Committee (Administrative and Budgetary Questions); Sixth Committee (Legal Questions).

[26] Manno, *op. cit.*, p. 37.

Not only do these limited-membership organs by their continuous attention to a problem provide greater opportunities for influence, but as they have taken upon themselves the preliminary formulation of United Nations programs and policies they have become useful instruments for influencing the course of final United Nations action. The Commission on Human Rights is but one of many available examples of a limited-membership organ constantly called upon to draft preliminary programs for the consideration of its parent body. Since its establishment in 1947 the Commission, composed of only eighteen representatives, has prepared for Assembly consideration the Universal Declaration on Human Rights, draft covenants on civil and political rights and on economic, social and cultural rights and a series of objective and general comments, conclusions and recommendations on the status of human rights in the world. The ability of the parent body to amend or to totally disregard its offspring's recommendations remains unquestioned, but the fact remains that those states represented on such organs have the greatest opportunity to exercise influence during the formative stages of drafting a program or policy.

Because of their continuing concern with selected problems and their role in the preliminary formulation of United Nations programs and policies, the subsidiary organs are important instruments in the exercise of political influence in the United Nations.

NEGOTIATIONS

In the assertion of demands and in exercising influence to obtain them, negotiations play a central role. The very nature of United Nations diplomacy with its heavy emphasis on the drafting of resolutions, amendments and reports to be voted on by one or the other of its organs ensures this key role for negotiations.[27] In spite of the heavy schedule of public meetings associated with United Nations activity, the negotiating process is overwhelmingly private. Hadwen and

[27] "The public debate, and the decisions reached gain added significance when the attitudes presented in public result from practically uninterrupted informal contacts and negotiations. Thus, it does not belittle the importance of the formal proceedings in the General Assembly, the Councils and other United Nations organs if it is understood that, to an increasing extent, their role has come to provide for a public confrontation of views which have developed in negotiations under the forms, and for the registration of a resulting consensus, or, when this has not been achieved of a difference of opinion with the relative support apparent from the votes." Dag Hammarskjöld. United Nations General Assembly *Official Records,* 14th Session, Supplement No. 1A (A/4132/Add.1, August 1959), "Introduction to the Annual Report of the Secretary-General on the Work of the Organization, 16 June 1958–15 June 1959," p. 2.

Kaufman in discussing the role of personal relations in the private meetings in which most negotiations are conducted wrote:

"In such meetings personal relations are paramount. If a delegate is to be effective it is necessary for him to know and approach the right person in the right delegation at the right time. If this approach is made under conditions of pressure and decisions are urgent, close personal understanding between the individuals concerned is of special importance."[28]

The private nature of the negotiation process reflects the desire of the participants to ensure their freedom of maneuver. However, the ability of any of the participants even in private negotiations to force an issue to a public test of strength through the simple device of pushing for a vote on the question gives to United Nations negotiation an element of openness not always found in diplomatic negotiation outside the confines of the Organization. Regardless of a nation's devotion to private negotiation, the possibility of an ultimate public test makes it incumbent upon all states to maintain a rather close correlation between public and private positions for fear of inviting such a public test which would publicize the discrepancy.

Negotiations are strongly influenced by the orientation of most activity towards the ultimate adoption of a resolution. A general tendency towards compromise emanates from the fact that, with the exception of a few matters, the United Nations can only make recommendations. Those who favor a given course of action desire to see it supported by the largest number of states possible in order that the recommendation may have the maximum weight behind it. On the other hand, those opposed to a given course of action would prefer, in most cases, not to be forced to take a public stand against the majority of the United Nations. These two factors combine to produce an inherent bias toward compromise in the negotiation process of the Organization.[29]

In the negotiating process the Afro-Asian states, in common with other small powers, lack the resources to pose creditable threats of direct action vis-á-vis other states as a means of gaining support within the Organization. Also, there is little in the way of tangible benefits outside the Organization that the Afro-Asian states can offer in exchange for support. However, there are two potent bargaining devices that the Afro-Asian states do have in the negotiating process. First, on many issues in the Assembly the new nations have the opportunity to play the great powers off against each other. The reasoning behind this strategy is usually that if the West (East) does not support resolution X and the East

---

[28] Hadwen and Kaufman, *op. cit.*, p. 36. These authors, both of whom served as members of permanent missions, lay heavy emphasis on the private, informal nature of United Nations negotiations. This opinion is shared by all observers of this aspect of United Nations diplomacy. Also see Pederson, *op. cit.*, p. 264.

[29] Hadwen and Kaufman, *op. cit.*, p. 65.

(West) does, then the West (East) will suffer a permanent loss of influence with the Afro-Asian states. Secondly, the large number of votes commanded by the Afro-Asian states on those issues on which they are relatively united provides them with a strong bargaining device. It has become very much a quixotic effort to flatly oppose the Afro-Asian states on questions such as decolonization and economic development where they already have sufficient votes to secure the adoption of their proposals. The wiser negotiating strategy for the other Members has been to support these initiatives while bargaining on the details of the proposal. The ultimate appeal to numbers in the parliamentary process of the Organization provides the Afro-Asian states with a strong negotiating position on those issues on which they are united.

With the rapid expansion of United Nations membership produced by the sudden emergence of the new nations, negotiations become more important and at the same time more difficult. With larger membership the public bodies of the Organization became submerged in their own debate and concerted action could only be arranged through private negotiations. Effective use of private negotiations as an instrument of political influence requires, however, an intimate knowledge of the personnel and positions of the other missions. This knowledge can only be gained through prolonged contact. Many of the new missions operating with fewer than five people simply have lacked the personnel to acquire this experience. On the other hand, even the large missions of the older states have found this sudden inflow of so many new states difficult to cope with in terms of developing the personal contacts necessary for private negotiations.

RESOLUTIONS AND VOTING

The remaining two instruments of influence to be surveyed exist in tandem in the United Nations political system. In the final analysis it is the procedure of adopting formal conclusions embodied in a resolution through some form of majority voting that distinguishes United Nations diplomacy from the diplomacy practiced in the various capitals of the world.

A draft resolution submitted either by a single state or a group of states represents in its clearest form the policy preferences of its sponsors. In the United Nations political system resolutions are the necessary instruments for translating policy preferences into United Nations decisions and are viewed as the logical end toward which much of the activity of the Member States is directed. The activities of the permanent missions, the caucusing groups and the various organs of the United Nations all bear the imprint of this ultimate "parliamentary test."

Most resolutions are drafted in New York on the basis of guide lines approved by the national governments with the right of final approval being held by the home government.[30] While individual sponsorship allows a state to put forward a draft resolution without the necessity of accepting compromise in the drafting stage, the political impact gained from a long list of co-sponsors is such that few delegations, other than the major powers, are willing to submit a draft without at least a few co-sponsors.[31]

As an instrument of political influence a draft resolution has the advantage of shifting the terms of debate and negotiations towards the positions of the draft's sponsors and providing a bargainable commodity. Whereas United Nations discussions and negotiations tend to have an amorphous quality before the introduction of draft resolutions, they tend to take on something of the crass air of the market place after their introduction. Both qualities are to a large extent the products of parliamentary diplomacy. In the period before a draft is introduced no state is willing to fully reveal its position for fear of robbing itself of potential bargaining power in the drafting process. On the other hand, once a draft or drafts are introduced the eventual necessity of obtaining a two-thirds majority on "important questions" for the adoption of a resolution exerts a strong force towards compromise. It is this drive to compromise in an atmosphere where "*the why* and *the how* is often much more important than *the what*" that gives a nit-picking air to much United Nations activity.[32]

Permeating all of this activity is the prospect of the ultimate "parliamentary test" in which all members of the General Assembly have but one vote. When United Nations activity in the form of resolutions is viewed as the logical product of the Organization's political system, then each state's vote is its final instrument of influence within the system.

---

[30] *Ibid.*, p. 37.

[31] For an interesting study of the strategy of sponsorship of General Assembly resolutions, see A. Glenn Mower, Jr., "The Sponsorship of Proposals in the United Nations General Assembly," *Western Political Quarterly,* Vol. 15 (December 1962), pp. 661-666.

[32] Hadwen and Kaufman, *op. cit.*, p. 49. Emphasis is in the original.

Two Differing Concepts of United Nations Assayed

Dag Hammarskjöld

I

Debates and events during the year since the publication of the last report to the General Assembly have brought to the fore different concepts of the United Nations, the character of the Organization, its authority and its structure.

On the one side, it has in various ways become clear that certain members conceive of the Organization as a static conference machinery for resolving conflicts of interest and ideologies with a view to peaceful coexistence, within the Charter, to be served by a Secretariat which is to be regarded not as fully internationalized but as representing within its ranks those very interests and ideologies.

Other members have made it clear that they conceive of the Organization primarily as a dynamic instrument of governments through which they, jointly and for the same purpose, should seek such reconciliation but through which they should also try to develop forms of executive action, undertaken on behalf of all members, and aiming at forestalling conflicts and resolving them, once they have arisen, by appropriate diplomatic or political means, in a spirit of objectivity and in implementation of the principles and purposes of the Charter.

Naturally, the latter concept takes as its starting point the conference concept, but it regards it only as a starting point, envisaging the possibility of

Dag Hammarskjöld, "Two Differing Concepts of United Nations Assayed," *United Nations Review,* Vol. 8, No. 9 (September 1961), pp. 12-17. Reprinted by permission of *United Nations Review.*

continued growth to increasingly effective forms of active international cooperation, adapted to experience, and served by a Secretariat of which it is required that, whatever the background and the views of its individual members, their actions be guided solely by the principles of the Charter, the decisions of the main organs and the interests of the Organization itself.

The first concept can refer to history and to the traditions of national policies of the past. The second can point to the needs of the present and of the future in a world of ever-closer international interdependence where nations have at their disposal armaments of hitherto unknown destructive strength. The first one is firmly anchored in the time-honored philosophy of sovereign national states in armed competition of which the most that may be expected in the international field is that they achieve a peaceful coexistence. The second one envisages possibilities of intergovernmental action overriding such a philosophy, and opens the road toward more developed and increasingly effective forms of constructive international cooperation.

It is clearly for the governments, members of the Organization, and for these governments only, to make their choice and decide on the direction in which they wish the Organization to develop. However, it may be appropriate to study these two concepts in terms of the purposes of the Organization as laid down in the Charter and, in this context, also to consider the character and significance of the decisions of the Organization as well as its structure.

II

The purposes and principles of the Charter are set out in its preamble and further developed in a series of articles, including some which may seem to be primarily of a procedural or administrative nature. Together, these parts of the Charter lay down some basic rules of international ethics by which all member states have committed themselves to be guided. To a large extent, the rules reflect standards accepted as binding for life within states. Thus, they appear, in the main, as a projection into the international arena and the international community of purposes and principles already accepted as being of national validity. In this sense, the Charter takes a first step in the direction of an organized international community, and this independently of the organs set up for international cooperation. Due to different traditions, the state of social development and the character of national institutions, wide variations naturally exist as to the application in national life of the principles reflected in the Charter, but it is not too difficult to recognize the common elements behind those differences. It is therefore not surprising that such principles of national application could be transposed into an agreed basis also for international behavior and cooperation.

In the preamble to the Charter, member nations have reaffirmed their faith "in the equal rights of men and women and of nations large and small," a principle which also has found many other expressions in the Charter.

Thus, it restates the basic democratic principle of equal political rights, independently of the position of the individual or of the member country in respect to its strength, as determined by territory, population or wealth. The words just quoted must, however, be considered as going further and imply an endorsement as well of a right to equal economic opportunities.

It is in the light of the first principle that the Charter has established a system of equal votes, expressing "the sovereign equality of all its members," and has committed the Organization to the furtherance of self-determination, self-government and independence. On the same basis, the Charter requires universal respect for and observance of human rights and fundamental freedoms for all "without distinction as to race, sex, language or religion."

It is in the light of the latter principle—or, perhaps, the latter aspect of the same basic principle—that the Charter, in Article 55, has committed the members to the promotion of higher standards of living, full employment and conditions of economic and social progress and development as well as to solutions of international economic and related problems. The pledge of all members to take joint and separate action, in cooperation with the Organization, for the achievement of these purposes has been the basis for the far-reaching economic and technical assistance channeled through or administered by the Organization, and may rightly be considered as the basic obligation reflected also in such economic and technical assistance as member governments have been giving, on a bilateral basis, outside the framework of the Organization.

It would seem that those who regard the Organization as a conference machinery, "neutral" in relation to the direction of policies on a national or international basis and serving solely as an instrument for the solution of conflicts by reconciliation, do not pay adequate attention to those essential principles of the Charter to which reference has just been made. The terms of the Charter are explicit as regards the equal political rights of nations as well as of individuals and, although this second principle may be considered only as implicit in the terms of the Charter, they are clear also as regards the demand for equal economic opportunities for all individuals and nations. So as to avoid any misunderstanding, the Charter directly states that the basic democratic principles are applicable to nations "large and small" and to individuals without distinction "as to race, sex, language and religion," qualifications that obviously could be extended to cover also other criteria such as, for example, those of an ideological character which have been used or may be used as a basis for political or economic discrimination.

In the practical work of the Organization these basic principles have been of special significance in relation to countries under colonial rule or in other ways under foreign domination. The General Assembly has translated the principles into action intended to establish through self-determination a free and independent life as sovereign states for peoples who have expressed in democratic forms their wish for such a status. Decisive action has in many cases been taken by member governments, and then the United Nations has had only to lend its support to their efforts. In other cases, the main responsibility has fallen on the Organization itself. The resolution on colonialism, adopted by the General Assembly at its fifteenth session, may be regarded as a comprehensive restatement in elaborated form of the principle laid down in the Charter. Results of developments so far have been reflected in the birth of a great number of new national states and a revolutionary widening of the membership of the Organization.

The demand for equal economic opportunities has, likewise, been—and remains—of special significance in relation to those very countries which have more recently entered the international arena as new states. This is natural in view of the fact that, mostly, they have been in an unfavorable economic position, which is reflected in a much lower per capita income, rate of capital supply and degree of technical development, while their political independence and sovereignty require a fair measure of economic stability and economic possibilities in order to gain substance and full viability.

In working for the translation into practical realities in international life of the democratic principles which are basic to the Charter, the Organization has thus assumed a most active role and it has done so with success, demonstrating both the need and the possibilities for such action.

Further, in the preamble to the Charter it is stated to be a principle and purpose of the Organization "to establish conditions under which justice and respect for the obligations arising from treaties and other sources of international law can be maintained." In these words—to which, naturally, counterparts may be found in other parts of the Charter—it gives expression to another basic democratic principle, that of the rule of law. In order to promote this principle, the Charter established the International Court of Justice, but the principle permeates the approach of the Charter to international problems far beyond the sphere of competence of the Court. As in national life, the principle of justice—which obviously implies also the principle of objectivity and equity in the consideration of all matters before the General Assembly or the Security Council—must be considered as applicable without distinction or discrimination, with one measure and one standard valid for the strong as well as for the weak. Thus, the demand of the Charter for a rule of law aims at the substitution of right for might and makes of the Organization the natural protector of rights which countries, without it, might find it more difficult to assert and to get respected.

The principle of justice can be regarded as flowing naturally from the principles of equal political rights and equal economic opportunities, but it has an independent life and carries, of itself, the world community as far in the direction of an organized international system as the two first-mentioned principles. It has deep roots in the history of the efforts of man to eliminate from international life the anarchy which he had already much earlier overcome on the national level, deeper indeed than the political and economic principles which, as is well known, were much later to get full acceptance also in national life. Long before the United Nations and long before even the League of Nations, governments were working toward a rule of justice in international life through which they hoped to establish an international community based on law, without parliamentary or executive organs, but with a judicial procedure through which law and justice could be made to apply.

The Charter states and develops the three principles mentioned here as a means to an end: "to save succeeding generations from the scourge of war." This adds emphasis to the concept, clearly implied in the Charter, of an international community for which the Organization is an instrument and an expression and in which anarchic tendencies in international life are to be curbed by the introduction of a system of equal political rights, equal economic opportunities and the rule of law. However, the Charter goes one step further, drawing a logical conclusion both from the ultimate aim of the Organization and from the three principles. Thus, it outlaws the use of armed force "save in the common interest." Obviously, the Charter cannot, on the one side, establish a rule of law and the principle of equal rights for "nations large and small" and, on the other hand, permit the use of armed force for national ends, contrary to those principles and, therefore, not "in the common interest." Were nations, under the Charter, to be allowed, by the use of their military strength, to achieve ends contrary to the principle of the equality of members and the principle of justice, it would obviously deprive those very principles of all substance and significance. One practical expression of this approach, which may be mentioned here, is that the organs of the United Nations have consistently maintained that the use of force, contrary to the Charter as interpreted by those organs, cannot be permitted to yield results which can be accepted as valid by the Organization and as establishing new rights.

In the Charter, the right to the use of force is somewhat more extensive than may seem to be the case from a superficial reading of the phrase "save in the common interest." Thus, apart from military action undertaken pursuant to a decision of the Security Council for repression of aggression—that is, for upholding the basic Charter principles—the Charter opens the door to the use of armed force by a nation in exercise of its inherent right to resist armed attack. This is a point on which, both in theory and in practice, the development of international law is still at a very early stage. As is well known, no agreement has been reached on a definition of aggression, beyond that found in Article 2, paragraph 4, of the Charter, and the Organization has several times had to face situations in which, therefore, the rights and wrongs in a specific case of conflict have not been clarified. It would be a vitally important step forward if wider agreement could be reached regarding the criteria to be applied in order to distinguish between legitimate and illegitimate use of force. History is only too rich in examples of armed aggression claimed as action in self-defence. How could it be otherwise, when most cases of armed conflict are so deeply rooted in a history of clashes of interests and rights, even if, up to the fatal moment of the first shot, those clashes have not involved recourse to the use of armed force?

In recognition of this situation and in the light of historical experience, the Charter makes yet another projection into international life of solutions to conflicts tested in national life, and establishes the final principle that the Organization shall "bring about by peaceful means and in conformity with the principles of justice and international law, adjustment or settlement of international disputes or situations which might lead to a breach of the peace." This principle, as quoted here from Article 1 of the Charter, is further developed specifically in Article 33, which requires parties to any dispute, the consequence of which is likely to endanger the maintenance of international peace and security, to "seek a solution by negotiation, inquiry, meditation, conciliation, arbitration, judicial settlement, resort to regional agencies or arrangements, or other peaceful means of their own choice." It is in this sphere that the Security Council has had, and is likely to continue to have, its main significance, both directly as a forum before which any dispute threatening peace and security can be brought up for debate and as an organ which directly, or through appropriate agents, may assist the parties in finding a way out and, by preventive diplomacy, may forestall the outbreak of an armed conflict. It seems appropriate here to draw attention especially to the right of the Security Council under Article 40 to "call upon the parties concerned to comply with such provisional measures as it deems necessary or desirable" for the prevention of any aggravation of a situation threatening peace and security, and to the obligation of members to comply with a decision on such measures.

It is in the light of the approach to international coexistence in our world today, which is thus to be found in the Charter, that judgment has to be passed on the validity of the different conceptions of the Organization which in recent times have become increasingly apparent. As already pointed out, the basic principles regarding the political equality of nations and their right to equal economic opportunities are difficult to reconcile with the view that the Organization is to be regarded only as a conference machinery for the solution, by debate and joint decisions, of conflicts of interest or ideology. It seems even more difficult to reconcile these principles with a view according to which equality among members should be reflected in the establishment of a balance between power blocs or other groupings of nations. The same difficulty is apparent as regards the principle of justice and the principle of prohibiting the use of armed force.

It is easier to apply the conference concept to the principle of prevention of conflict through negotiation, but also on this point the difficulties become considerable if it is recognized that such solutions as may be sought by the Organization should be solutions based on the rules of equality and justice.

III

The General Assembly, the Security Council and other collective organs of the United Nations have features in common with a standing international diplomatic conference, but their procedures go beyond the forms of such a conference and show aspects of a parliamentary or quasi-parliamentary character.

While decisions of a conference, in order to commit its participants, must be based on their subsequent acceptance of the decisions, the organs of the United Nations act on the basis of voting, with the decisions being adopted if supported by a majority. However, the decisions of the Assembly have, as regards member states, only the character of recommendations (except for financial assessments and certain other types of organizational action) so that obligations like those arising out of an agreement, coming into force after a conference, do not normally flow from them. But although the decisions, legally, are only recommendations, they introduce an important element by expressing a majority consensus on the issue under consideration.

Naturally, such a formula leaves scope for a gradual development in practice of the weight of the decisions. To the extent that more respect, in fact, is shown to General Assembly recommendations by the member states, they may come more and more close to being recognized as decisions having a binding effect on those concerned, particularly when they involve the application of the binding principles of the Charter and of international law.

Both those who regard a gradual increase in the weight of decisions of the General Assembly as necessary, if progress is to be registered in the direction of organized peaceful coexistence within the Charter, and those who oppose such a development, have to recognize that, with certain variations in individual cases, the practice still is very close to the restrictive Charter formula. Experience shows that even countries which have voted for a certain decision may, later on, basing themselves on its character of merely being a recommendation, refuse to follow it or fail to support its implementation, financially or in other respects.

What has been said applies generally to the collective organs of the Organization, but, as is well known, the Charter has gone one step further beyond the conference concept, in the direction of parliamentary concept, in the case of the Security Council. In Article 25 member states of the United Nations have agreed to "accept and carry out the decisions of the Security Council in accordance with the present Charter," thus, by agreement, making the decisions of the Council mandatory, except, of course, when such decisions take the form of "recommendations" within the terms of Chapter VI or certain other Articles of the Charter. They have further, in Article 49, undertaken to "join in affording mutual assistance in carrying out the measures decided upon by the Security Council."

This agreed mandatory nature of certain Security Council decisions might have led to a demand for unanimity in the Council, a unanimity which was the rule for the Council of the League of Nations. Even so, however, the arrangement would have gone beyond the conference principle with its requirements that no decision reached in an international organ should be binding on an individual member short of his agreement. With the present arrangements, requiring a majority of seven and the concurring votes of the permanent members, a bridge between the traditional conference approach and a parliamentary approach is provided by the commitment in Article 25 to agree to the carrying out of the decisions in the Council which should be considered as giving the Council its authority by general delegation as indeed stated in Article 24, paragraph 1.

What clearly remains within the Council of the traditional conference and agreement pattern is the condition that its decisions of a nonprocedural character must be supported by the unanimous vote of the five permanent members, thus avoiding for those members the risk of being bound by a decision of the Council which has not met with their agreement. It may be observed that this special position for the permanent members, apart from other reasons, has the justification that, without such a rule, the other members of the organization, in complying with a Security Council decision, might find themselves unwillingly drawn into a big power conflict.

In spite of the delegated authority which the Council may be considered as exercising, and the condition that decisions must be agreed to by the permanent members, the experience of the Organization, as regards the implementation of Council decisions, is uneven and does not indicate full acceptance in practice of Article 25. In this case also, examples can be given of a tendency to regard decisions, even when taken under Chapter VII, as recommendations binding only to the extent that the party concerned has freely committed itself to carry them out; there is here a clear dichotomy between the aims of the Charter and the general political practice at its present stage of development. Such cases refer not only to members outside the Council, or, perhaps, members inside the Council, who have not supported a specific decision, but also to members within the Council who have cast their votes in favor of a decision but who later on are found to reserve for themselves at least a right to interpret the decision in ways which seem to be at variance with the intentions of the Council. The ambiguity of this situation emerges with special force in cases where such attitudes have been taken by permanent members of the Council, who are considered to shoulder the responsibility for the maintenance of peace and security which is reflected in the special position they hold within the Council. Obviously, the problem whether the intended legal weight is given to decisions of the Security Council arises in practice not only in cases of noncompliance but also in cases of a refusal to shoulder the financial consequences of a decision of the Council.

These observations—which have been limited to a reminder of the Charter rules and a factual reminder also of the experiences in practice—point to a situation which in any evaluation of the United Nations must be given the most serious consideration by members. For the judgment on the various concepts of the United Nations which are put forward, it is one thing to note what the Charter stipulates; it is an entirely different but ultimately more important question as to what the situation is in practice and what, in fact, is the weight given to decisions of the Organization when they go beyond the conference pattern of agreement.

For those who maintain the conference concept of the Organization, it is natural to side-step the mandatory nature of decisions by the Security Council. For those who take a different view, it is equally natural and essential to work for a full and general acceptance of the Charter rules. Were those to be right who hold that the Charter, on the points discussed here and, maybe, also as regards the five basic principles discussed in the first part of this introduction, is ahead of our time and the political possibilities which it offers, such a view still would not seem to justify the conclusion that the clear approach of the Charter should be abandoned. Rather, it would indicate that member nations jointly should increase their efforts to make political realities gradually come closer to the pattern established by the Charter.

In the light of such considerations, the significance of the outcome of every single conflict on which Organization has to take a stand and the weight given to its decisions in such a conflict stand out very clearly. A failure to gain respect for decisions or actions of the Organization within the terms of the Charter is often called a failure for the Organization. It would seem more correct to regard it as a failure of the world community, through its member nations and in particular those most directly concerned, to cooperate in order, step by step, to make the Charter a living reality in practical political action as it is already in law.

Were such cooperation, for which the responsibility naturally rests with each single member as well as with all members collectively, not to come about, and were the respect for the obligations flowing from Article 25 of the Charter to be allowed to diminish, this would spell the end of the possibilities of the Organization to grow into what the Charter indicates as the clear intention of the founders, as also of all hopes to see the Organization grow into an increasingly effective instrument, with increasing respect for recommendations of the General Assembly as well.

What this would mean for the value of the Organization as protector of the aims, principles and rights it was set up to further and safeguard is obvious. The effort through the Organization to find a way by which the world community might, step by step, grow into organized international cooperation within the Charter must either progress or recede. Those whose reactions to the work of the Organization hamper its development or reduce its possibilities of effective action may have to shoulder the responsibility for a return to a state of affairs which governments had already found too dangerous after the First World War.

IV

The growth of the United Nations out of the historic conference pattern—which, as observed earlier in this introduction, at all events naturally remains the starting point in all efforts of the Organization—is clearly reflected in what, in the light of experience, may seem to be a lack of balance in the Charter. While great attention is given to the principles and purposes, and considerable space is devoted to an elaboration of what may be called the parliamentary aspects of the Organization, little is said about executive arrangements. This does not mean that the Charter in any way closes the door to such arrangements or to executive action, but only that, at the stage of international thinking crystallized in the Charter, the conference approach still was predominant, and that the needs for executive action, if the new Organization was to live up to expectations and to its obligations under the Charter, had not yet attracted the attention they were to receive in response to later developments.

The key clause on the executive side may be considered to be Article 24, in which it is said that "in order to assure prompt and effective action by the United Nations, its members confer on the Security Council primary responsibility for the maintenance of international peace and security."

On that basis the Security Council is given the right, under Article 29, to establish such subsidiary organs as it deems necessary for the performance of its functions, the right under Article 40 to decide on so-called provisional measures, the right to use, for the purposes of the Charter, under certain conditions, armed forces made available to the Council, the right under Article 48 to request from governments action on the Council's behalf, as well as the right to request of the Secretary-General to "perform . . . such functions as are entrusted to him" by the Council.

The various clauses here briefly enumerated open a wide range of possibilities for executive action undertaken by, and under the aegis of, the Security Council. However, no specific machinery is set up for such action by the Council, apart from the Military Staff Committee, with planning responsibilities in the field of the possible use of armed force by the Security Council under Chapter VII of the Charter. In fact, therefore, the executive functions and their form have been left largely to practice, and it is in the field of the practices of the Organization that cases may be found in the light of which it is now possible to evaluate the ways in which the Organization may develop its possibilities for diplomatic, political or military intervention of an executive nature in the field.

The forms used for executive action by the Security Council—or when the Council has not been able to reach decisions, in some cases, by the General Assembly—are varied and are to be explained by an effort to adjust the measures to the needs of each single situation. However, some main types are recurrent. Subcommittees have been set up for fact-finding or negotiation on the spot. Missions have been placed in areas of conflict for the purpose of observation and local negotiation. Observer groups of a temporary nature have been sent out. And, finally, police forces under the aegis of the United Nations have been organized for the assistance of the governments concerned with a view to upholding the principles of the Charter. As these, or many of these, arrangements require centralized administrative measures, which cannot be performed by the Council or the General Assembly, members have to a large extent used the possibility to request the Secretary-General to perform special functions by instructing him to take the necessary executive steps for implementation of the action decided upon. This has been done under Article 98, as quoted above, and has represented a development in practice of the duties of the Secretary-General under Article 97.

The character of the mandates has, in many cases, been such that in carrying out his functions the Secretary-General has found himself forced also to interpret the decisions in the light of the Charter, United Nations precedents and the aims and intentions expressed by the members. When that has been the case, the Secretary-General has been under the obligation to seek guidance, to all possible extent, from the main organs; but when such guidance has not been forthcoming, developments have sometimes led to situations in which he has had to shoulder responsibility for certain limited political functions, which may be considered to be in line with the spirit of Article 99 but which legally have been based on decisions of the main organs themselves, under Article 98, and thus the exclusive responsibility of member states acting through these organs. Naturally, in carrying out such functions the Secretariat has remained fully subject to the decisions of the political bodies.

This whole development has lately become a matter of controversy, natural and, indeed, unavoidable in the light of differences of approach to the role of the Organization to which attention has been drawn earlier in this introduction. While the development is welcomed by member nations which feel a need of growth as regards the possibilities of the Organization to engage in executive action in protection of the Charter principles, it is rejected by those who maintain the conference concept of the Organization. The different opinions expressed on the development are only superficially related to this or that specific action and the way in which it is considered to have been carried through. They are also only superficially related to the choice of means used for translating decisions into action. The discussion regarding the development of executive functions is basically one confronting the same fundamentally difficult concepts of the Organization and its place in international politics, which could be seen also in the different attitudes toward the legal weight of decisions of the Organization.

It is in this context that the principle embodied in Article 100 of the Charter is of decisive significance. This principle, which has a long history, establishes the international and independent character of the Secretariat. Thus, it is said that the Secretary-General and the staff of the Secretariat "shall not seek or receive instructions from any Government or from any other authority external to the Organization," and that they "shall refrain from any action which might reflect on their position as international officials responsible only to the Organization." In the same Article, the members of the United Nations undertake to respect "the exclusively international character of the responsibilities of the Secretary-General and the staff and not to seek to influence them in the discharge of their responsibilities."

The significance of the principle stated in Article 100 is a dual one. It envisages a Secretariat so organized and developed as to be able to serve as a neutral instrument for the Organization, were its main organs to wish to use the Secretariat in the way which has been mentioned above and for which Article 98 has opened possibilities. But in doing so, the principle also indicates an intention to use the Secretariat for such functions as would require that it have an exclusively international character.

In the traditional conference pattern, participants in a meeting are mostly serviced by a secretariat drawn from the same countries as the participants themselves, and constituting a mixed group regarding which there is no need to demand or maintain an exclusively international character. It is therefore natural that those who favor the conference approach to the United Nations tend to give to Article 100 another interpretation than the one which the text calls for, especially in the light of its historical background and its background also in other clauses of the Charter.

There is no reason to go more deeply into this special problem here. Suffice it to say that, while the Organization, if regarded as a standing diplomatic conference, might well be serviced by a fully international Secretariat but does not need it, the other approach to the Organization and its role cannot be satisfied with anything less than a secretariat of an exclusively international character, and thus cannot be reconciled with a secretariat composed on party lines and on the assumption that the interests represented in the main organs in this manner should be represented and advocated also within the Secretariat. Thus, again, the choice between conflicting views on the United Nations Secretariat is basically a choice between conflicting views on the Organization, its functions and its future.

In order to avoid possible misunderstandings, it should be pointed out here that there is no contradiction at all between a demand for a truly international Secretariat and a demand, found in the Charter itself, for as wide a "geographical" distribution of posts within the Secretariat as possible. It is, indeed, necessary precisely in order to maintain the exclusively international character of the Secretariat that it be so composed as to achieve a balanced distribution of posts on all levels among all regions. This, however, is clearly something entirely different from a balanced representation of trends or ideologies. In fact, if a realistic representation of such trends is considered desirable, it can and should be achieved without any assumption of political representation within the ranks of the Secretariat, by a satisfactory distribution of posts based on geographical criteria.

The exclusively international character of the Secretariat is not tied to its composition but to the spirit in which it works and to its insulation from outside influences, as stated in Article 100. While it may be said that no man is neutral in the sense that he is without opinions or ideals, it is just as true that, in spite of this, a neutral Secretariat is possible. Anyone of integrity, not subjected to undue pressures, can, regardless of his own views, readily act in an "exclusively international" spirit and can be guided in his actions on behalf of the Organizations solely by its interests and principles and by the instructions of its organs.

V

After this brief review of the principles of the Organization, of the character of its decisions and of its structure, especially as regards arrangements for executive action, presented only as a background for the consideration of what basic concepts and approaches should guide the development of the Organization, it may be appropriate, in conclusion, to give attention to the activities of the Organization and their relevance to the current international situation.

For years the Organization has been a focal point for efforts to achieve disarmament. This may still be considered as the main standing item on the agenda of the General Assembly. However, in recent years these efforts of the Organization have been running parallel to other efforts which are either outside of it or only loosely tied to the work of the United Nations. This may be justified on the basis that a very limited number of countries hold key positions in the field of armaments, so that any effort on a universal basis and by voting, to reach a decision having practical force, would be ineffective, unless founded on a basic agreement between those few parties mostly concerned. Therefore, direct negotiations between these countries are an essential first step to the solution, through the United Nations, of the disarmament problem, and do not in any way derogate from the responsibilities or rights of the Organization.

The situation may serve as an example of a problem which has become increasingly important in the life of the Organization: the right way in which to balance the weight of the big powers and their security interests against the rights of the majority of member nations. Such a majority naturally cannot expect the big powers, in questions of vital concern to them, with their superior military and economic strength, automatically to accept a majority verdict. On the other hand, the big powers cannot, as members of the world community, and with their dependence on all other nations, set themselves above, or disregard the views of, the majority of nations. An effort to balance the big power element and the majority element is found in the Charter rules regarding the respective competence of the General Assembly and the Security Council and regarding the special position of the big powers within the Council. Other efforts to solve the same problem are reflected in the way in which the disarmament problem has been attacked in recent years. No fully satisfactory or definitive formula has been found, but it must be sought, and it is to be hoped that when the time comes for a Charter revision, agreement may be reached on a satisfactory solution.

What is true of the disarmament problem is, of course, true also of those more specific questions in which security interests of big powers are or may be directly involved, as for example the Berlin problem. The community of nations, represented in the United Nations, has a vital interest in a peaceful solution, based on justice, of any question which—like this one—unless brought to a satisfactory solution, might come to represent a threat to peace and security. However, the problem of the balance to be struck between the rights and obligations of the big powers and the rights and obligations of all other nations applies, in a very direct way, also to this problem which is now so seriously preoccupying the minds of all peoples and their leaders. The United Nations with its wide membership is not, and can, perhaps, not aspire to be, a focal point in the debate on an issue such as the Berlin question, or in the efforts to solve it, but the Organization cannot, for that reason, be considered as an outside party which has no right to make its voice heard should a situation develop which would threaten those very interests which the United Nations is to safeguard and for the defence of which it was intended to provide all member nations with an instrument and a forum.

Reference has already been made in this introduction to the work of the Organization devoted to furthering self-determination, self-government and independence for all peoples. In that context it was recalled that the General Assembly, at its last session, adopted a resolution regarding the colonial problem which elaborates the basic principles of the Charter to their application to this problem.

This is, likewise, a question which for years has been before the General Assembly and it is likely to remain a major item until a final result is achieved which reflects full implementation of the basic principles in the direction indicated by last year's resolution. Experience has shown that peaceful progress in that direction cannot be guaranteed solely by decisions of the General Assembly or the Security Council, within the framework of a conference pattern. Executive action is necessary, and neither the General Assembly nor the Security Council—which has had to deal with situations in which the liquidation of the colonial system has led to acute conflict—has abstained from such action in support of the lines upheld. As in the past, executive action by the Organization in the future will undoubtedly also be found necessary if it is to render the service expected from it under the terms of the Charter.

It is in conflicts relating to the development toward full self-government and independence that the Organization has faced its most complicated tasks in the executive field. It is also in the case of executive action in this context that different concepts of the Organization and of its decisions and structure have their most pointed expressions. As regards this specific aspect of the work of the United Nations, the front line has not been the usual one between different bloc interests, but more one between a great number of nations with aims natural especially for those which recently have been under colonial rule or under other forms of foreign domination, and a limited number of powers with other aims and predominant interests. This seems understandable if one takes into account that a majority of nations wishes to stand aside from the big power conflicts, while power blocs or big powers tend to safeguard their positions and security by efforts to maintain or extend an influence over newly emerging areas. The United Nations easily becomes a focal point for such conflicting interests as the majority looks to the Organization for support in their policy of independence also in relation to such efforts, while power blocs or countries with other aims may see in the United Nations an obstacle in the way of their policies to the extent that the Organization provides the desired support. How this is reflected in the attitude toward the development of the executive functions of the United Nations can be illustrated by numerous examples. It may be appropriate in this context to say in passing a word about the problem of the Congo and the activities of the United Nations in that country.

Different interests and powers outside Africa have seen in the Congo situation a possibility of developments with strong impact on their international position. They have therefore, naturally, held strong views on the direction in which they would like to see developments in the Congo turn and—with the lack of political traditions in the country and without the stability which political institutions can get only by being tested through experience—the doors have been opened for efforts to influence developments by supporting this or that faction or this or that personality.

True to its principles, the United Nations has had to be guided in its operation solely by the interest of the Congolese people and by their right to decide freely for themselves, without any outside influences and with full knowledge of facts.

Therefore, the Organization, throughout the first year of its work in the Congo, up to the point when Parliament reassembled and invested a new national Government, has refused—what many may have wished—to permit the weight of its resources to be used in support of any faction so as thereby to prejudge in any way the outcome of a choice which belonged solely to the Congolese people. It had also had to pursue a line which, by safeguarding the free choice of the people, implied resistance against all efforts from outside to influence the outcome. In doing so, the Organization has been put in a position in which those within the country who felt disappointed in not getting the support of the Organization were led to suspect that others were in a more favored position and, therefore, accused the Organization of partiality, and in which, further, such outside elements as tried to get or protect a foothold within the country, when meeting an obstacle in the United Nations, made similar accusations.

If, as it is sincerely to be hoped, the recent national reconciliation, achieved by Parliament and its elected representatives of the people, provides a stable basis for a peaceful future in a fully independent and unified Congo, this would definitely confirm the correctness of the line pursued by the United Nations in the Congo. In fact, what was achieved by Parliament early in August may be said to have been done with sufficient clarity. It is a thankless and easily misunderstood role for the Organization to remain neutral in relation to a situation of domestic conflict and to provide active assistance only by protecting the rights and possibilities of the people to find their own way, but it remains the only manner in which the Organization can serve its proclaimed purpose of furthering the full independence of the people in the true and unqualified sense of the word.

The United Nations may be called upon again to assist in similar ways. Whatever mistakes in detail and on specific points critics may ascribe to the Organization in the highly complicated situation in the Congo, it is to be hoped that they do not lead members to revise the basic rules which guide the United Nations activities in such situations, as laid down in the first report of the Secretary-General to the Security Council on the Congo question, which the Council, a year ago, found reason unanimously to commend.

Closely related to a policy aiming at self-government and independence for all is the question of economic and technical assistance, especially during the first years of independence of a new member state. The United Nations and its agencies and affiliated organs have at their disposal only very modest means for the purpose, but a rich experience has been gathered and the personnel resources are not inconsiderable.

Last year the Economic and Social Council and the General Assembly had to consider proposals designed to open up new possibilities for the Organization to respond to the demands of member governments facing all the problems of newly achieved independence. Naturally, the problems which are of special importance for such countries are basically the same as those which face all countries which have been left behind in economic development. Therefore, the urgent attention required by newly independent countries in this respect can in no way justify a discrimination in their favor against other countries with similar difficulties.

This year the General Assembly will have before it proposals initiated by the Scientific Advisory Committee and endorsed by the Economic and Social Council for a conference, under United Nations aegis, intended to provide possibilities for a break-through in the application of the technical achievements of present times to the problems of the economically less developed countries. It is sincerely to be hoped that, in the interest of international cooperation and the acceleration of the economic progress of those countries, this proposal will meet with approval of the General Assembly.

So far, the economic and technical activities of the United Nations have been less influenced by the conflict between different concepts of the role of the Organization than its activities in other fields. However, it is impossible to isolate the economic and technical problems from the general question discussed in this introduction. While receiving countries should have full freedom to take assistance from whatever source they find appropriate, they should not be barred, if they so wish, from getting all the assistance they need through United Nations channels or under United Nations aegis. The Organization is far from being able to meet all such demands, as donor nations continue to show a strong preference for bilateral approaches on a national or a group basis. Again, the problem arises of the basic concept of the United Nations. With the conference approach to the work of the Organization a choice is made also in favor of bilateral assistance, while the alternative approach opens the door to a development under which international assistance, in implementation of the principle of equal economic opportunities for all, would be channelled through the Organization or its related agencies to all the extent that this is desired by the recipient countries and is within the capacity of the Organization.

Basic to the United Nations approach to economic and technical assistance is the principle, under all circumstances, that, although the Organization has to follow its own rules and maintain its own independence, its services are exclusively designed to meet the wishes of the recipient government, without the possibility of any ulterior motives and free from the risk of any possible influence on the national and international policies of that government. Whatever development the executive activities of the Organization may show in the field, there should never be any suspicion that the world community would wish or, indeed, could ever wish to maintain for itself, through the United Nations, a position of power or control in a member country. Were political groups in a country really to believe in such a risk, the explanation would seem to be that, as has indeed happened in the case of governments of member countries with long-established independence, they may find it difficult to accept the judgment of the majority of the nations of the world as to what in a specific situation is necessary in order to safeguard international peace and security, when such a judgment appears to be in conflict with the immediate aims of the group. With growing respect for the decisions of the Organization and growing understanding of its principles, the risks for such misinterpretations should be eliminated.

The Political Role of the Secretary-General

Leland M. Goodrich

For the purposes of this discussion, the political role of the Secretary-General is defined in somewhat narrow terms. It is not intended to discuss his role in the development of policy generally, which would be a possible way of viewing the subject. Rather, attention will be given to the role of the Secretary-General in the discharge of one of the major responsibilities of the United Nations–the maintenance of international peace and security. Consequently, the role of the Secretary-General in developing and executing policies and programs of economic and social development, which has come to be one of the major fields of activity of the Organization, will not be touched upon, except incidentally.

I

The League Covenant gave the Secretary-General a very limited role in the maintenance of international peace. Apart from performing secretarial functions at meetings of the Council and Assembly, his powers were limited to summoning meetings of the Council, under Article 11, upon request of any member of the League, and to making arrangements for a full investigation and consideration of any dispute submitted under Article 15. While a liberal interpretation of Covenant provisions might have justified a larger role for the Secretary-General,

---

Leland M. Goodrich, "The Political Role of the Secretary-General," *International Organization,* Vol. 16, No. 4 (Autumn 1962), pp. 720-735. Reprinted by permission of *International Organization.*

particularly more active participation in the deliberations of the Assembly, both the first Secretary-General, Sir Eric Drummond, and his successor, Joseph Avenol, chose to take a conservative view of the Secretary-General's responsibilities. In doing this, they undoubtedly met the wishes of most governments.

Nevertheless, one should not underestimate the influence which the Secretary-General, and in particular, Sir Eric Drummond, did exercise through private and confidential contacts with representatives of Member governments at Geneva. As the Organization's highest ranking official who was continuously on the job, thoroughly familiar with League procedures and practice, and the trusted confidant of governments, Sir Eric Drummond was in the position to exercise substantial influence on the course of League activity in keeping the peace.

In the drafting of the Charter of the United Nations, there appears to have been general agreement among participating governments that the chief administrative officer of the Organization—whatever his title might be—should be given a more important political role than his League predecessor.[1] It was agreed at Dumbarton Oaks that the Secretary-General, in addition to being the chief administrative officer of the Organization and performing secretarial functions at all meetings of the General Assembly and the Councils, should report annually on the work of the Organization and be empowered to bring before the Security Council on his own initiative any matter which in his judgment threatened international peace and security. This last provision was apparently adopted as a result of dissatisfaction with the operation of the League Covenant provision which permitted only Member States to bring matters to the attention of the Council. The Dumbarton Oaks proposals regarding the powers of the Secretary-General were approved at San Francisco with the added provision (Article 98 of the Charter) that the Secretary-General "shall perform such other functions as are entrusted to him" by the General Assembly and the Councils. In addition, more detailed guarantees of the independence and international character of the Secretary-General and his staff were adopted than were embodied in the Dumbarton Oaks proposals.

By the choice of Trygve Lie, Members of the Organization made it quite clear that they expected the Secretary-General to have an important political role, as Mr. Lie's past experience and personal qualities—well known to Member governments—gave assurance that he would not be content with the anonymous and predominantly passive role that Sir Eric Drummond had accepted. Mr. Lie, in his subsequent account of his stewardship, tells us that on taking office he "had no calculated plans for developing the political powers of the office of Secretary-General," but that he "was determined that the Secretary-General should be a

[1] See Ruth Russell and J. E. Mather, *A History of the United Nations Charter* (Washington: Brookings Institution, 1958).

force for peace."[2] He professes to have been fully aware of the limits imposed upon him—"limits of the Charter's text and, even more, the limits imposed by the realities of national and international life." He chose to proceed pragmatically, "in the light of developments."

It is not necessary here to review in detail the various political initiatives which Mr. Lie took with a view to making the United Nations more effective as an instrument of peace and creating conditions which in his judgment would improve the prospects of peace. It is clear that his efforts did not meet with a high degree of success. Nevertheless, there was no inclination on the part of Member governments to challenge his right under the Charter to take these initiatives. Some governments disagreed with the substance of his proposals and views, and faced with this kind of opposition, Mr. Lie did not have the resources of power and influence at his disposal that would have enabled him to give effect to his initiatives. His "was a moral power, not a physical one, and moral power in this world is not conclusive."[3] The Soviet boycott of Lie, which was a decisive factor in forcing his resignation in 1952, reflected, of course, disapproval of the posture Lie had taken in the Korean affair, and consequent unwillingness to agree to his reappointment, but not a denial of his right as Secretary-General under the Charter to take important political initiatives.

During the early years of his tenure, Mr. Hammarskjöld[4] was more cautious and circumspect than Mr. Lie had been in his public utterances and actions in the cause of peace. He evidenced a fuller recognition in practice of the limits enforced upon him by the need of a substantial measure of agreement among interested Member governments and of the dangers to which he exposed himself and the influence of his office by taking bold initiatives which ended in failure. The emphasis during this early period was on "quiet diplomacy" and "a diplomacy of reconciliation," with full recognition, however, that the Organization was more than an instrument of "conference diplomacy," and that the Secretary-General had a positive duty to seek the implementation of the purposes and principles set forth in the Charter.

While Hammarskjöld played an important positive political role, even though a relatively unpublicized one, during these early years, his emergence as an independent political force, serving not only as the agent of Member governments, but also as the faithful exponent of United Nations purposes and principles, became clearly established with the middle east crisis of 1956. First of all, it is to be noted that the Secretary-General, by his statement before the Security Council

---

[2] Trygve Lie, *In the Cause of Peace* (New York: Macmillan, 1954), p. 42.

[3] *Ibid.*

[4] On Mr. Hammarskjöld's conception of the office, see Joseph P. Lash, "Dag Hammarskjöld's Conception of His Office," *International Organization*, Summer 1962 (Vol. 16, No. 3), pp. 542-566.

on October 31, 1956,[5] made it clear that he would only serve on the basis of full acceptance and respect for the purposes and principles of the Charter, and that if the Member governments, more particularly the permanent members of the Security Council, were not prepared to act on the same assumption, they could draw the necessary consequences. Secondly, the resolutions, adopted by the General Assembly after the question of Israeli, British, and French military action had been submitted to that organ in accordance with the "Uniting for Peace" resolution, placed important responsibilities on the Secretary-General to secure the implementation of the Assembly's request for a cease-fire and the withdrawal of British, French, and Israeli forces, and to undertake the organization and direction of a United Nations force to facilitate that withdrawal and assist in creating conditions favorable to peace. Finally, in the discharge of these responsibilities, the Secretary-General acted in strict accordance with the resolutions of the General Assembly and the purposes and principles of the Charter as he interpreted them. It is particularly to be noted that he resolutely opposed any attempt to make the withdrawal of forces conditional in any sense, firmly maintaining that the United Nations could not condone a change in the *status juris* if that change resulted from military action contrary to the Charter, and that the UN Emergency Force (UNEF) could not be used as a means of forcing a settlement of controversial political matters in the interest of one or more parties.

Hammarskjöld's success in the middle east in 1956 and 1957 undoubtedly encouraged him to develop further his peace-keeping role when trouble broke out in Lebanon in 1958. This time the Soviet Union and the United States were on opposite sides, with United States intervention in Lebanon being attacked by Moscow as a violation of the Charter. After the Soviet representative on the Security Council had vetoed the Japanese draft resolution proposing an increase in the United Nations Observer Group in Lebanon (UNOGIL) to facilitate American withdrawal, on the grounds that it did not go far enough in requiring immediate American withdrawal, Hammarskjöld proceeded on the basis of his own liberal interpretation of the relevant Charter provisions and of the views expressed by the representatives of governments to do on his own responsibility what the draft resolution would have authorized him to do if it had been adopted. Furthermore, he made it clear that the purpose of the Observer Group was to protect Lebanese independence as well as to prevent infiltrations from outside. The latter had been the declared purpose of the Security Council in initially establishing UNOGIL.

In the *Introduction* to his report for 1958-1959, Mr. Hammarskjöld undertook to expound his views regarding the changing political role of the United Nations, and more particularly that of the Secretary-General. He noted that:

[5] Security Council *Official Records* (11th year), 751st meeting, October 31, 1956, pp. 1-2.

"while the statement of objectives in the Charter is binding and so are the rules concerning the various organs and their competence . . . it is not necessary to regard the working methods indicated in the Charter as limitative in purpose. . . . The United Nations, as a living organism, has the necessary scope for a continuous adaptation of its constitutional life to the needs [of the Organization]".[6]

In this connection, he called attention to the "special diplomatic and operational functions" with which the Secretary-General had been entrusted by various decisions of the General Assembly and Security Council, and to recent instances where the Secretary-General had dispatched personal representatives at the request of governments without authorization by the Assembly or Council. He concluded:

"Thus, the wider functions, which in specific cases have been exercised by the Secretary-General, fully maintain the character of the United Nations as an Organization whose activities are wholly dependent on decisions of Governments. On the other hand, the development reflects an incipient growth of possibilities for the organization to operate in specific cases within a latitude of independence in practice given to it by its Member Governments for such cases".[7]

Hammarskjöld's visit to Laos in late 1959 and his establishment of a personal representative there on his own authority and independently of Council action were in line with the above interpretation of his role.

It was, of course, in July 1960 and the months following that the Secretary-General's political role assumed its most advanced and, at the same time, controversial form. While this marked the first formal use of the Secretary-General's power under Article 99 of the Charter, the special significance of the Congo experience did not lie in this fact. Rather, it lay in the wide discretionary powers which were vested in the Secretary-General by the resolutions of the Security Council and the General Assembly, the failure of these organs to give the Secretary-General specific directives for dealing with rapidly changing and unanticipated circumstances, and, in the absence of these directives, the willingness of the Secretary-General to look in other directions for guidance and in effect to make himself an independent interpreter and executor of the will of the Organization. As Hammarskjöld explained in his address at Oxford University on May 30, 1961, "unforeseen and unforeseeable problems . . . made it necessary for [him] repeatedly to invite the Council to express themselves on the interpretation given by the Secretary-General to the mandate" contained in the Security Council's resolution of July 13, 1960. This need for interpretation resulted especially from the politically charged situation which arose because of the

---

[6]General Assembly *Official Records* (14th session), Supplement No. 1A, p. 2.

[7]*Ibid.*, p. 3.

secession of Katanga and the disintegration of the central government of the Republic of the Congo. Failure of the Security Council to give him more specific instructions placed upon him the necessity of choosing between two unpleasant alternatives: refusing to proceed further unless specific instructions were forthcoming, which required a harmonization of Member government views impossible to achieve; or proceeding on the basis of his best judgment, reached after appropriate consultations, as to the course of action most consistent with the declared policies of the Organization, the purposes and principles of the Charter, and the body of legal doctrine and precepts that had been generally accepted by states.

Clearly the assumption of this kind of responsibility in situations where the important interests of major powers are involved carries a considerable degree of risk for the Secretary-General. As Trygve Lie was forced to recognize, the limits of the political role of the Secretary-General are defined not only by the provisions of the Charter but also by the facts of international life. The turn which events in the Congo took in late August and early September 1960, was bound to make more unhappiness in Moscow, and the Secretary-General, as the result of the responsibilities he had chosen or been forced to assume, offered a convenient scapegoat. Hammarskjöld's tragic death had probably at least one fortunate consequence in that it permitted the question of the future role of the Secretary-General to be considered in relation to a new personality who was not himself a subject of bitter controversy. The appointment of U Thant as Acting Secretary-General did not mean, however, that all basic issues had been resolved.

II

To understand and explain the evolution of the political role of the Secretary-General in the work of the United Nations, it is necessary to consider a variety of factors, the relative importance of which can only be a matter of subjective judgment. These factors include the provisions of the United Nations Charter, the way these provisions have been interpreted and applied in reference to varying needs and circumstances, the nature of the Organization itself, the political environment in which the Organization has functioned, and not of least importance certainly, the personality of the Secretary-General himself and the extent to which he is able to gain the confidence of Member governments.

The Charter of the United Nations provides a much more favorable legal basis for the development of an important political role for the Secretary-General than did the League Covenant. In the first place, the Secretariat is declared to be one of the principal organs of the Organization, thus placing it in this respect in a position of equality with the General Assembly and the Councils instead of in a position of dependence or subservience. The Secretary-General is declared to be the chief administrative officer of the Organization; this and other Charter provisions guarantee him an independent status and protect him and his staff against improper influence by Member governments. His powers are defined in considerable detail by the Charter itself. Thus, in addition to being the chief administrative officer, he performs secretarial functions for the General Assembly and the Council; he is required to make an annual report to the General Assembly on the work of the Organization; he appoints his staff; he may bring to the attention of the Security Council any matter which "in his opinion" may threaten international peace and security, and he "shall perform such other functions as are entrusted to him" by the General Assembly and Councils.

Of equal importance to the actual provisions of the Charter in explaining the evolution of the Secretary-General's role is the manner in which these provisions have been interpreted. While Sir Eric Drummond took a narrow view of his powers under the Covenant according to accepted principles of treaty interpretation, successive Secretaries-General of the United Nations have interpreted their powers liberally. In doing so they have followed the practice of other organs. In fact one of the notable features of United Nations development has been the practice not too commonly or widely challenged of interpreting the Charter of the United Nations as a constitution and not simply as a treaty. Chief Justice Marshall's rule of interpretation according to which a wide choice of means is permitted to achieve a legitimate purpose has been widely utilized. The justification which Hammarskjöld offered of his trip to Laos and the establishment of a United Nations presence in that country was a case in point. Hammarskjöld's view was that in order to discharge his responsibility under Article 99, he must be allowed to carry out appropriate investigations and make arrangements for being constantly informed regarding developments in critical areas. Another example was Hammarskjöld's reliance on his general Charter powers and not on his authority under the General Assembly resolution in negotiating with the Peking Government in 1954 over the release of American prisoners.[8]

Closely related to the legal bases of the Secretary-General's Charter powers and helping to explain the liberal way in which they have been interpreted is the conception of the nature of the Organization which has gained wide acceptance. As Hammarskjöld pointed out in the *Introduction* to his 1961 report, which in a sense may be regarded as his final testament, there have been two competing views regarding the nature of the United Nations. On the one hand, it has been regarded as "static conference machinery" for resolving conflicts, while on the other hand it has been viewed as:

"a dynamic instrument of governments through which they, jointly and for the same purpose, should seek such reconciliation but through which they should

---

[8] Lash, *op. cit.*, p. 548.

also try to develop powers of executive action, undertaken on behalf of all members, and aiming at forestalling conflicts and resolving them, once they have arisen, by appropriate diplomatic means, in a spirit of objectivity and in implementation of the principles and purposes of the Charter."[9]

This view has had wide acceptance, particularly among the newer nations. Its acceptance carries with it recognition of the General Assembly and the Councils as more than diplomatic conferences, as possessing some of the characteristics of parliamentary organs, and also encourages, if it does not necessitate, expanding the political role of the Secretary-General, both in respect to his own independent initiatives and more particularly in respect to his executive role in carrying out tasks assigned to him.

Without question, a most important factor in explaining the development of the political role of the Secretary-General has been the political environment in which the United Nations has functioned. In the maintenance of international peace and security there is little doubt that the original intent of the framers of the Charter, translated into the clear terms of that document, was to make the Security Council the executive organ. It was to perform this role not only in the sense that it could take initial decisions regarding measures to be adopted, but also in that it could carry out, with the assistance of the Military Staff Committee in military measures, the detailed execution of these decisions. From the beginning, however, the Council was unable to discharge its responsibilities as initially intended due to the deepening divisions between the Soviet Union and the major non-Communist powers, as evidenced by the mounting number of Soviet vetoes. As a result, responsibility came to be increasingly assumed by the General Assembly. The "Uniting for Peace" resolution represented a forthright assumption by the General Assembly of responsibility in this area.

The General Assembly, however, lacked the powers of the Security Council, more particularly the power to take decisions binding on Member States. Furthermore, the Assembly by its very nature—its size, the variety of interests represented, and its operating procedures—was incapable of exercising its powers directly and continuously. Thus, in dealing with the Greek, Palestine, and Korean questions, it established subsidiary organs to perform certain duties continuously and, to the extent necessary, on the spot. In 1956, however, when called upon to deal with the outbreak of hostilities in the Middle East, it requested the Secretary-General to act on its behalf in performing functions which it could not carry out itself. This was not the only course open to it—it might have followed its earlier practice of appointing a person outside the Secretariat or setting up a committee or commission to do the work. No doubt the confidence which Mr. Hammarskjöld had inspired in discharging earlier responsibilities was an important, if not the decisive factor, in explaining this decision.

---

[9] General Assembly *Official Records* (16th session), Supplement No. 1A, p. 1.

In the *Introduction* to his 1959 report, Mr. Hammarskjöld, in commenting on the developing functions of the Secretariat, and the decisions of the General Assembly and the Security Council delegating various tasks to the Secretary-General, sought to reassure those who might be somewhat disturbed by this trend by asserting that "these decisions should not, of course, be considered as setting precedents changing the constitutional balance among the various organs of the United Nations."[10] However, it would seem quite clear that the constitutional balance initially envisaged by the authors of the Charter was in process of change from the very beginning as the result of the impotence of the Security Council resulting from the Cold War and from the assumption of growing responsibilities in the peace and security field by the General Assembly. And certainly during Mr. Hammarskjöld's tenure of office, the Secretary-General on his own initiative, as well as at the request of the other organs, took on responsibilities which substantially alerted the practical relationship of the Secretariat to the Security Council and the General Assembly. Mr. Hammarskjöld, on numerous occasions, made it clear that the powers he was exercising flowed from his interpretations of his responsibilities as Secretary-General under the Charter and did not have their necessary basis in decisions of the Security Council or the General Assembly.

In the light of this development, which was facilitated, if not made necessary, by the Cold War, it is not surprising that the Soviet Union, realizing that the interpretation and application of the purposes and principles of the Charter in sensitive areas involving the conflicting interests of major powers could have serious political consequences, concluded that its right of veto in the Security Council was in fact being circumvented and that under the new constitutional practice some means had to be found to control the new center of power and influence—the office of the Secretary-General.

Another aspect of the postwar political environment influencing the development of the Secretary-General's political role has been the political awakening of Asia and Africa, the liquidation of colonial rule, and the emergence of new independent states, all desirous of becoming, and quickly accepted as, Members of the United Nations. This has resulted in a changed balance of influence in the Organization, and in a great increase in the relative influence of Members with an interest in using the Organization for protection against the revival of imperialism, and for constructive development purposes. Furthermore, these new states generally seek to avoid involvement in the Cold War, while at the same time the major parties to the ideological conflict are desirous of having their good will and support. The result has been an emphasis on United Nations projects and programs that require the development and utilization of the executive capacity of the Organization. This naturally suggests an enlarged role for

---

[10]General Assembly *Official Records* (14th session), Supplement No. 1A, p. 5.

the Secretary-General and his staff, not only in the carrying out of economic and social programs, but also in laying the basis for political viability, as in the Congo.

These new states, having only recently succeeded in achieving independence from colonial rule, are anxious that outside assistance should not lead to the reinstatement of that control. Whether it is for assistance in economic and social development or for aid in establishing the conditions of internal security and order and providing protection against outside intervention, for the most part they prefer United Nations assistance and look to the Secretary-General as the one who can most safely be trusted with the organization and direction of that assistance. This attitude not only encourages initiatives by the Secretary-General and the use of his office to carry out programs approved by the Assembly and the Councils, but it also provides the Secretary-General himself with an important political support that he can use in defending himself against criticism by major Member governments, especially those seeking some selfish advantage for themselves. It is highly significant that Mr. Hammarskjöld in defending himself against Soviet attacks over his conduct on the Congo operation, chose to appear as the defender of the small states and to make his offer of resignation to them, and did not, as in 1956, place his future in the hands of the major powers.

Finally, mention should be made of the personality factor as contributing to the development of the political role of the Secretary-General. During the League period, even though the role of the Secretary-General was narrowly defined both in theory and practice, the first occupant of the office, Sir Eric Drummond, exercised a very considerable influence by the sheer force of the confidence that he inspired. He became the trusted confidant of states even though he insisted on maintaining a formal relationship of subordination and anonymity. Trygve Lie, during his period of service, acted on the assumption that the Secretary-General had a more positive role to play and did not hesitate to express his views on controversial matters and to take initiatives on his own responsibility. Nevertheless, his actual influence on the other organs and on the decisions and conduct of Member governments was not large. Mr. Hammarskjöld, on the other hand, was able, through a combination of skillful diplomacy and the full exploitation of the powers vested in him, to make the office of Secretary-General a major influence in the discharge of the Organization's responsibility for keeping the peace. His high intelligence, proved diplomatic skill, and moral integrity inspired confidence and encouraged governments to trust him with the performance of delicate diplomatic and executive tasks that hitherto had been performed by subsidiary organs of the General Assembly or the Security Council. Not until he was placed in a position, in handling the Congo affair, where he had to take decisions that should have been taken by the Security Council itself, or the General Assembly, was he subjected to attacks and accusations by a major power which he was able to withstand temporarily, but which, had it not been for his untimely death, might have led to the same consequences as in the case of his predecessor.

It is too early to evaluate with any confidence the relative importance of the personality factor in the development of the political role of the Secretary-General. While Hammarskjöld's personality was undoubtedly an important factor in explaining the growth of the Secretary-General's influence and importance during his tenure, other factors, as we have seen, were at work. His successor, U Thant, is obviously in a less strong position than was Hammarskjöld in his first term, since he has been designated Acting Secretary General to serve only for the remainder of Hammarskjöld's second term. Nevertheless, his record to date in the choice of advisers and the definition of their relations to him, in views that he has expressed in controversial matters and proposals that he has made, and in the appreciation of the possibilities and limitations of his office, is reassuring to those who believe that the Secretary-General has an important independent role in the maintenance of international peace and security.

III

The development of the political role of the Secretary-General in recent years raises questions, affecting not only the future of the Secretariat but also of the Organization itself, that need serious consideration. The first of these is whether this enlargement of the Secretary-General's personal responsibilities to the point where, as in certain stages of the Congo operation, he is giving practically all his time to handling one particular matter and is called upon to take decisions affecting the important interests of Member governments, is wholly to be welcomed. While the liberal interpretation of the Charter allows this, it does not require it. Had it not been for the great prestige of Mr. Hammarskjöld and his readiness to take on great responsibilities in the Congo, other methods would in all likelihood have been used. In earlier situations where the General Assembly or the Security Council was called upon to deal with critical situations, subsidiary organs were set up and utilized to perform various peace-keeping functions on behalf of the parent organ. Calling upon the Secretary-General to undertake these tasks may expose him to the risk of antagonizing influential governments. It makes too easy the evasion of responsibility by the political organs (the Security Council and the General Assembly). It places such a heavy demand on the Secretary-General's time and energy that he may be forced to neglect other important responsibilities resting upon him. Furthermore, as the political power and influence of the Secretary-General grows, the difficulty of finding a person to fill the job who is equally acceptable to the major governments in a politically and ideologically divided world is bound to increase. Even if the unity of the office is maintained, and the destructive results of a "troika" arrangement are avoided, there still remains the possibility of either prolonged deadlock in the choice of a person or the selection, as a last act of desperation, of a weak person.

However, there are definite advantages in having the Secretary-General perform major political functions in the peace and security field. He is an official continuously on the job, presumably possessing qualifications of a political and personal nature which equip him for difficult diplomatic and administrative tasks. He has in the Charter a legal basis for taking initiatives and assuming responsibilities. He has at his disposal a large and well qualified staff, representing a variety of experiences and national points of view. He is, therefore, in the position, acting directly or through his chosen representatives, to mobilize a variety of skills and experiences, and with the traditions of an impartial and highly qualified international service to support him, to command the confidence and trust of governments.

Although the Secretary-General is dependent on governments for support, his position is not one of complete impotence. National governments may stand between him and the people they represent, but the same governments in their relations with each other do not always have common views nor speak with one voice. It is therefore possible for the Secretary-General to play one group against the other and, by skillful diplomacy, achieve an effective support. In 1956 in the Suez affair, Hammarskjöld, acting for the General Assembly, had the support of the United States and the Soviet Union, though perhaps for different reasons, as well as that of other Members. Thus, the British and French governments had no real alternative to yielding before this array of power and influence. In 1960 the Soviet Union reluctantly gave its support initially to the Congo operation, even though it may have had some doubts as to whether the United Nations would vigorously pursue the line it advocated of ousting the agents of "Western imperialism." Later, it probably did not carry its opposition to Hammarskjöld to the full limit for fear of antagonizing the Asian and African states that were supporting him.

It must, however, be recognized that there are limits to the responsibilities that the Secretary-General can be expected to assume. His political position is not sufficiently strong to permit him to oppose a major power, except under circumstances which permit him to exercise effective counter-influence. Like the Pope, he has no fighting battalions at his command and is restricted largely to the use of skillful diplomacy. The Secretary-General is not in the position of a popularly elected head of state who has a large constituency to which he can appeal in case of conflict with rival authorities. Yet, although governments may treat him as expendable, such treatment damages the whole organization which he represents. It is therefore desirable that governments, through their actions in the General Assembly and the Security Council, do not place upon him the responsibility for taking decisions on questions of vital importance to them on which they are unable to agree and are unwilling in fact to accept his decision. The reverse is also true—the Secretary-General should not willingly assume responsibilities that are beyond his effective power and influence.

If the Secretary-General is to assume large responsibilities in conducting negotiations and in supervising and directing peace-keeping operations such as UNEF and the UN operation in the Congo (ONUC), it is essential that he have adequate political guidance. This guidance initially should be found in the resolutions of the Security Council and the General Assembly. However, the directions contained in such resolutions may not prove adequate for dealing with rapidly changing and unforeseen situations. It is inevitable that the Secretary-General should exercise a certain amount of discretion in discharging his responsibilities. Consultation with his top advisers in the Secretariat should help inform him of national views and other considerations to be taken into account. The maintenance at the Headquarters of the United Nations of permanent missions by Member governments provides the Secretary-General with means of direct contact with, and of informing himself regarding, the views of Member governments. The use of an advisory committee, composed of representatives of governments most directly concerned, as was established by the General Assembly in the Middle East crisis and by the Secretary-General in 1960 during the Congo crisis, is another possible means of keeping the Secretary-General continuously informed regarding the views of governments. While the Secretary-General cannot escape the necessity of a personal decision if important responsibilities of a diplomatic and executive nature are placed upon him, he must realize that his position is not comparable to that of head of state, above all, to that of the President of the United States. His actual influence on a given situation is bound to be determined largely by his intelligent and skillful use of methods that are essentially diplomatic in nature, and a major concern of his must always be to act on the basis of an adequate consensus among interested governments, a consensus which he himself may well have had a major share in forming.

The increased political role of the Secretary-General raises basic issues regarding the compatibility of such a role with the conception of an independent international civil servant. In the British tradition, the civil servant is protected against criticism by the assumption of responsibility by his political superior. This protection is afforded the Secretary-General only to the extent that he has back of him the agreement of governments.

Mr. Hammarskjöld appears to have taken the position that the purposes and principles of the Charter and United Nations precedents constituted a body of agreement upon which he could base decisions on matters not adequately covered by the resolutions of the political organs. This view, however, is open to the possible criticism that the purposes and principles of the Charter, and even the precedents of the United Nations, are so general in form, or so controversial in content, and consequently open to such a variety of interpretations, that any application of them to a factual situation in a highly charged political atmosphere constitutes a political act of a kind that a civil servant should not or at least cannot safely perform. To liken the decision taken in such a situation to that of a judge, as Hammarskjöld did in his Oxford University address, is somewhat misleading, as, first of all, the judge customarily has clearer guidance from written law and precedents; and secondly, when he ventures into the realm of policy, he does so on the basis of being part of a government with effective power, which is not the position of the Secretary-General.

Premier Khrushchev, in his appearance before the fifteenth session of the General Assembly, drew the conclusion that, since the Secretary-General had followed a course of which the Soviet Union disapproved and which amounted to a circumvention of the veto—the Security Council not having authorized him to proceed as he had—the appropriate remedy was to politicize the Office of Secretary-General by introducing the same safeguards against actions displeasing to the Soviet Union that existed in the case of the Security Council. His "troika" proposal would have accomplished this result. Fortunately, the proposal received little support outside of the Communist bloc. The circumstances surrounding the appointment of U Thant as Acting Secretary-General and his statements and conduct since suggest that the independence and integrity of the Office have been preserved. Such concessions as were made to give assurance that the Acting Secretary-General would have broadly representative advisers did not seriously weaken the independent responsibilities of the Secretary-General himself in discharging the duties of his Office.

It is, however, quite clear that the political responsibilities of the Secretary-General and his staff cannot be enlarged without at the same time raising doubts in some quarters at least as to whether a Secretariat with such important political responsibilities can be treated in the same way as a British civil service, protected against the political consequences of its acts by the principle of ministerial responsibility. This doubt arises more particularly with respect to the Secretary-General himself, and his top advisers and assistants in peace and security matters. Hammarskjöld recognized that the assumption by the Secretary-General of responsibilities of decision in controversial political matters was likely to expose him and his staff to criticism and attack. His position was that the Secretary-General could not be accused of a lack of neutrality because he found it necessary to take such decisions in the absence of adequate guidance from the Security Council or the General Assembly. As stated in his Oxford University address, his contention was that if the Secretary-General kept his feelings and emotions under the strictest observation, was careful not to allow his sympathies and antipathies to influence his judgment, and was guided solely "by the common aims and rules laid down for, and by, the Organization he serves and by recognized legal principles, then he has done his duty, and then he can face the criticism which, even so, will be unavoidable." He likened the role of the Secretary-General to that of a judge in this respect, a comparison which as we have seen is not altogether valid.

It is surely not just coincidental that the increase in the political role of the Secretary-General and his staff should be paralleled, not only by attacks upon Hammarskjöld and a near crisis in the choice of his successor, but also by increasingly urgent demands on the part of Members' "underrepresented" in the Secretariat that their nationals be appointed to Secretariat posts in larger numbers and particularly to the more important political positions. The arguments for balanced geographical distribution within the Secretariat are bound to carry greater weight and be more difficult to resist as the political role of the Secretary-General and his staff increases. Even in the League period, when the Secretary-General and his staff behaved very much in the tradition of British civil servants, demands for wide geographical distribution, especially in the higher echelons, were repeatedly made and generally respected. There should be no surprise that the demand is now much more insistent with the development that has taken place in the Secretary-General's role.

Notwithstanding the attacks to which it has been subjected, the ideal of an independent international civil service headed by a Secretary-General committee to furthering the purposes, principles, and interests of the Organization is in conception a valid one and capable of a large measure of practical achievement as events have demonstrated. It would be a retrogression to allow the Secretariat to degenerate into an inter-governmental service under the impact of government criticism and pressure. There is no present likelihood that this will happen, as too many governments are committed to the idea of an international civil service as expressed in the Charter. Nevertheless, there are serious dangers ahead—possible deadlock over the appointment of a successor to U Thant, a Soviet boycott if his term should be extended by General Assembly action alone or deterioration of Secretariat morale and efficiency as the result of too rapid introduction of new personnel to achieve wider and more balanced geographical distribution and use of fixed term appointments to the extent that promotions are seriously blocked and the career service weakened. The likelihood of such misfortunes will certainly be greatly reduced if governments assume their responsibilities in the General Assembly and Security Council and do not place upon the Secretary-General or make it necessary for him to assume responsibilities beyond his powers and of such a nature as to expose him to serious political attack. Furthermore, the Secretary-General himself must recognize that his executive powers are not comparable to those of the American President, that he has no organized constituency or direct means of support, that to play the game of bloc politics in addition to requiring great skill can be exceedingly dangerous, and that his real power and influence must be based largely on his ability to convince governments that their best interests are served by working together through the United Nations' instrumentalities in furtherance of the common purposes and principles set forth in the Charter.

The International Civil Servant in Law and in Fact

Dag Hammarskjöld

I

In a recent article Mr. Walter Lippmann tells about an interview in Moscow with Mr. Khrushchev. According to the article, Chairman Khrushchev stated that "while there are neutral countries, there are no neutral men", and the author draws the conclusion that it is now the view of the Soviet Government "that there can be no such thing as an impartial civil servant in this deeply divided world, and that the kind of political celibacy which the British theory of the civil servant calls for, is in international affairs a fiction".[1]

Whether this accurately sums up the views held by the Soviet Government, as reflected in the interview, or not, one thing is certain: the attitude which the article reflects is one which we find nowadays in many political quarters, communist and noncommunist alike, and it raises a problem which cannot be treated lightly. In fact, it challenges basic tenets in the philosophy of both the League of Nations and the United Nations, as one of the essential points on which these experiments in international co-operation represent an advance beyond traditional "conference diplomacy" is the introduction on the international arena of joint permanent organs, employing a neutral civil service, and the use of such organs for executive purposes on behalf of all the members of the organizations. Were it to be

---

Dag Hammarskjöld, "The International Civil Servant in Law and Fact," Lecture delivered at Oxford on 30 May 1961. Reprinted by permission of Clarendon Press, Oxford, England.

[1] *New York Herald Tribune,* 17 April 1961, pp. 1-2.

considered that the experience shows that this radical innovation in international life rests on a false assumption, because "no man can be neutral", then we would be thrown back to 1919, and a searching reappraisal would become necessary.

II

The international civil service had its genesis in the League of Nations but it did not spring full-blown in the Treaty of Versailles and the Covenant. The Covenant was in fact silent on the international character of the Secretariat. It contained no provisions comparable to those of Article 100 of the Charter, and simply stated:

"The permanent Secretariat shall be established at the Seat of the League. The Secretariat shall comprise a Secretary-General and such secretaries and staff as may be required."[2]

In the earliest proposals for the Secretariat of the League, it was apparently taken for granted that there could not be a truly international secretariat but that there would have to be nine national Secretaries, each assisted by a national staff and performing, in turn, the duties of Secretary of the Council, under the supervision of the Secretary-General. This plan, which had been drawn up by Sir Maurice Hankey, who had been offered the post of Secretary-General of the League by the Allied Powers, was in keeping with the precedents set by the various international Bureaus established before the war which were staffed by officials seconded by Member countries on a temporary basis.

It was Sir Eric Drummond, first Secretary-General of the League, who is generally regarded as mainly responsible for building upon the vague language of the Covenant a truly international secretariat. The classic statement of the principles he first espoused is found in the report submitted to the Council of the League by its British member, Arthur Balfour:

"By the terms of the Treaty, the duty of selecting the staff falls upon the Secretary-General, just as the duty of approving it falls upon the Council. In making his appointments, he had primarily to secure the best available men and women for the particular duties which had to be performed; but in doing so, it was necessary to have regard to the great importance of selecting the officials from various nations. Evidently, no one nation or group of nations ought to have a monopoly in providing the material for this international institution. I emphasize the word 'international', because the members of the Secretariat once appointed are no longer the servants of the country of which they are citizens, but

[2] Article 6 of the Covenant of the League of Nations.

become for the time being the servants only of the League of Nations. Their duties are not national but international."[3]

Thus, in this statement, we have two of the essential principles of an international civil service: (1) its international composition, and (2) its international responsibilities. The latter principle found its legal expression in the Regulations subsequently adopted which enjoined all officials "to discharge their functions and to regulate their conduct with the interests of the League alone in view" and prohibited them from seeking or receiving "instructions from any Government or other authority external to the Secretariat of the League of Nations".[4]

Along with the conception of an independent, internationally responsible staff, another major idea was to be found: the international Secretariat was to be solely an administrative organ, eschewing political judgements and actions. It is not at all surprising that this third principle should have originated with a British Secretary-General. In the United Kingdom, as in certain other European countries, a system of patronage, political or personal, had been gradually replaced in the course of the nineteenth century by the principle of a permanent civil service based on efficiency and competence and owing allegiance only to the State which it served. It followed that a civil service so organized and dedicated would be non-political. The civil servant could not be expected to serve two masters and consequently he could not, in his official duties, display any political allegiance to a political party or ideology. Those decisions which involved a political choice were left to the Government and to Parliament; the civil servant was the non-partisan administrator of those decisions. His discretion was a limited one, bound by the framework of national law and authority and by rules and instructions issued by his political superiors. True, there were choices for him, since neither legal rules nor policy decisions can wholly eliminate the discretion of the administrative official, but the choices to be made were confined to relatively narrow limits by legislative enactment, Government decisions and the great body of precedent and tradition. The necessary condition was that there should exist at all times a higher political authority with the capacity to take the political decisions. With that condition it seemed almost axiomatic that the civil service had to be "politically celibate" (though not perhaps politically virgin). It could not take sides in any political controversy and, accordingly, it could not be given tasks which required it to do so. This was reflected in the basic statements laying down the policy to govern the international Secretariat. I may quote two of them:

"We recommend with special urgency that, in the interests of the League, as well as in its own interests, the Secretariat should not extend the sphere of its

---

[3]*League of Nations Official Journal,* vol. i, June 1920, p. 137.

[4]Article I of the Staff Regulations of the Secretariate of the League of Nations, 1945 edition.

activities, that in the preparation of the work and the decisions of the various organisations of the League, it should regard it as its first duty to collate the relevant documents, and to prepare the ground for these decisions without suggesting what these decisions should be; finally, that once these decisions had been taken by the bodies solely responsible for them, it should confine itself to executing them in the letter and in the spirit."[5]

"Une fois les décisions prises, le rôle du Secrétariat est de les appliquer. Ici encore, il y a lieu de faire une distinction entre application et interprétation, non pas, à coup sûr, que je demande au Secrétariat de ne jamais interpréter; c'est son métier! Mais je lui demande, et vous lui demanderez certainement tous, d'interpréter le moins loin possible, le plus fidèlement possible, et surtout de ne jamais substituer son interprétation à la vôtre."[6]

Historians of the League have noted the self-restraining role played by the Secretary-General.[7] He never addressed the Assembly of the League and in the Council "he intended to speak . . . as a Secretary of a committee and not more than that".[8] For him to have entered into political tasks which involved in any substantial degree the taking of a position was regarded as compromising the very basis of the impartiality essential for the Secretariat.

True, this does not mean that political matters as such were entirely excluded from the area of the Secretariat's interests. It had been reported by Sir Eric Drummond and others that he played a role behind the scenes, acting as a confidential channel of communication to Governments engaged in controversy or dispute, but this behind-the-scenes role was never extended to taking action in a politically controversial case that was deemed objectionable by one of the sides concerned.

III

The legacy of the international secretariat of the League is marked in the Charter of the United Nations. Article 100 follows almost verbatim the League regulations on independence and international responsibility barring the seeking or

---

[5] Report of Committee No. 4 ("Noblemaire Report"), League of Nations, Records of the Second Assembly Plenary Meetings, p. 596.

[6] Statement by M. Noblemaire at the 26th plenary meeting of the League Assembly, 1 Oct. 1921, League of Nations, Records of the Second Assembly, Plenary Meetings, p. 577.

[7] F. P. Walters, *A History of the League of Nations,* pp. 559 ff.; Egon F. Ranshofen-Wertheimer, *The International Secretariat,* pp. 48-49; Stephen M. Schwebel, *The Secretary-General of the United Nations,* pp. 6 ff.

[8] Proceedings of the Conference on Experience in International Administration, Washington, Carnegie Endowment, 1943, p. 11.

receiving of instructions from States or other external authority. This was originally proposed at San Francisco by the four sponsoring powers–China, the USSR, the United Kingdom, and the United States–and unanimously accepted.[9] The League experience had shown that an international civil service, responsible only to the Organization, was workable and efficient. It had also revealed, as manifested in the behaviour of German and Italian Fascists, that there was a danger of national pressures corroding the concept of international loyalty. That experience underlined the desirability of including in the Charter itself an explicit obligation on officials and Governments alike to respect fully the independence and the exclusively international character of the responsibilities of the Secretariat.

It was also recognized that an international civil service of this kind could not be made up of persons indirectly responsible to their national governments. The weight attached to this by the majority of members was demonstrated in the Preparatory Commission London, when it was proposed that appointments of officials should be subject to the consent of the government of the Member State of which the candidate was a national.[10] Even in making this proposal, its sponsor explained that it was only intended to build up a staff adequately representative of the governments and acceptable to them. He maintained that prior approval of officials was necessary, in order to obtain the confidence of their governments which was essential to the Secretariat, but once the officials were appointed, the exclusively international character of their responsibilities would be respected. However, the great majority of Member States rejected this proposal, for they believed that it would be extremely undesirable to write into the regulations anything that would give national governments particular rights in respect of appointments and thus indirectly permit political pressures on the Secretary-General.[11]

Similarly, in line with Article 100, the Preparatory Commission laid emphasis on the fact that the Secretary-General "alone is responsible to the other principal organs for the Secretariat's work", and that all officials in the Organization must recognize the exclusive authority of the Secretary-General and submit themselves to rules of discipline laid down by him.[12]

The principle of the independence of the Secretariat from national pressures was also reinforced in the Charter by Article 105, which provides for granting officials of the Organization "such privileges and immunities as are necessary for

---

[9] Documents of the U.N. Conference on International Organization (hereinafter referred to as UNCIO), vol. 7, p. 394. See also summary record of 18th meeting, Committee I/2 (2 June 1945) in UNCIO, vol. 7, pp. 169-70.

[10] U.N. Preparatory Commission (1946), doc. PC/AD.54.

[11] U.N. Preparatory Commission, Committee 6, 22nd and 23rd meetings, Assembly records, pp. 50-51.

[12] Report of the Preparatory Commission (1946), p. 85, para. 5, and p. 86, para. 9.

the independent exercise of their functions in connexion with the Organization". It was in fact foreseen at San Francisco that in exceptional circumstances there might be a clash between the independent position of a member of the Secretariat and the position of his country, and consequently that an immunity in respect of official acts would be necessary for the protection of the officials from pressure by individual governments and to permit them to carry out their international responsibilities without interference.[13]

In all of these legal provisions, the Charter built essentially on the experience of the League and affirmed the principles already accepted there. However, when it came to the functions and authority of the Secretary-General, the Charter broke new ground.

In Article 97 the Secretary-General is described as the "chief administrative officer of the Organization", a phrase not found in the Covenant, though probably implicit in the position of the Secretary-General of the League. Its explicit inclusion in the Charter made it a constitutional requirement—not simply a matter left to the discretion of the organs—that the administration of the Organization shall be left to the Secretary-General. The Preparatory Commission observed that the administrative responsibility under Article 97 involves the essential tasks of preparing the ground for the decisions of the organs and of "executing" them in co-operation with the Members.[14]

Article 97 is of fundamental importance for the status of the international Secretariat of the United Nations, and thus for the international civil servant employed by the Organization, as, together with Articles 100 and 101, it creates for the Secretariat a position, administratively, of full political independence. However, it does not, or at least it need not, represent an element in the picture which raises the question of the "neutrality" of the international civil servant. This is so because the decisions and actions of the Secretary-General as chief administrative officer naturally can be envisaged as limited to administrative problems outside the sphere of political conflicts of interest or ideology, and thus as maintaining the concept of the international civil servant as first developed in the League of Nations.

However, Article 97 is followed by Article 98, and Article 98 is followed by Article 99. And these two Articles together open the door to the problem of neutrality in a sense unknown in the history of the League of Nations.

In Article 98 it is, thus, provided not only that the Secretary-General "shall act in that capacity" in meetings of the organs, but that he "shall perform such other functions as are entrusted to him by these organs". This latter provision was not in the Covenant of the League. It has substantial significance in the Charter, for it entitles the General Assembly and the Security Council to entrust

---

[13]UNCIO, vol. 7, p. 394, Report of Rapporteur of Committee I/2.

[14]Report of U.N. Preparatory Commission, p. 86, para. 12.

the Secretary-General with tasks involving the execution of political decisions, even when this would bring him—and with him the Secretariat and its members—into the arena of possible political conflict. The organs are, of course, not required to delegate such tasks to the Secretary-General but it is clear that they *may* do so. Moreover, it may be said that in doing so the General Assembly and the Security Council are in no way in conflict with the spirit of the Charter—even if some might like to give the word "chief administrative officer" in Article 97 a normative and limitative significance—since the Charter itself gives to the Secretary-General an explicit political role.

It is Article 99 more than any other which was considered by the drafters of the Charter to have transformed the Secretary-General of the United Nations from a purely administrative official to one with an explicit political responsibility. Considering its importance, it is perhaps surprising that Article 99 was hardly debated; most delegates appeared to share Smut's opinion that the position of the Secretary-General "should be of the highest importance and for this reason a large measure of initiative was expressly conferred".[15] Legal scholars have observed that Article 99 not only confers upon the Secretary-General a right to bring matters to the attention of the Security Council but that this right carries with it, by necessary implication, a broad discretion to conduct inquiries and to engage in informal diplomatic activity in regard to matters which "may threaten the maintenance of international peace and security".[16]

It is not without some significance that this new conception of a Secretary-General originated principally with the United States rather than the United Kingdom. It has been reported that at an early stage in the preparation of the papers that later become the Dumbarton Oaks proposals, the United States gave serious consideration to the idea that the Organization should have a President as well as a Secretary-General.[17] Subsequently, it was decided to propose only a single officer, but one in whom there would be combined both the political and executive functions of a President with the internal administrative functions that were previously accorded to a Secretary-General. Obviously, this is a reflection, in some measure, of the American political system, which places authority in a chief executive officer who is not simply subordinated to the legislative organs but who is constitutionally responsible alone for the execution of legislation and

[15] Letter from Field-Marshal Jan Christian Smuts to Mr. H.W.A. Cooper, 15 Dec. 1949, quoted in Schwebel, *The Secretary-General of the United Nations* (1952), p. 18.

[16] *Ibid.* at p. 25. See summary record of 48th meeting of Committee of Experts of the Security Council, UN doc. S/Procedure/103, particularly statement of the representative of Poland. Also Virally, 'Le Rôle politique du Secrétaire général des Nations Unies', *Annuaire Francais de Droit International,* vol. iv (1958), p. 363 and footnote 2; Simmonds, 'Good Offices and the Secretary-General', *Nordisk Tidsskrift for International Ret* (1959), vol. xxix, fasc. 4, pp. 332, 340, and 341.

[17] Schwebel, *op. cit.* at p. 17.

in some respects for carrying out the authority derived from the constitutional instrument directly.

The fact that the Secretary-General is an official with political power as well as administrative functions had direct implications for the method of his selection. Proposals at San Francisco to eliminate the participation of the Security Council in the election process were rejected precisely because it was recognized that the role of the Secretary-General in the field of political and security matters properly involved the Security Council and made it logical that the unanimity rule of the permanent Members should apply.[18] At the same time, it was recognized that the necessity of such unanimous agreement would have to be limited only to the selection of the Secretary-General and that it was equally essential that he be protected against the pressure of a Member during his term in office.[19] Thus a proposal for a three-year term was rejected on the ground that so short a term might impair his independent role.

The concern with the independence of the Secretary-General from national pressures was also reflected at San Francisco in the decision of the Conference to reject proposals for Deputies to the Secretary-General appointed in the same manner as the Secretary-General. The opponents of this provision maintained that a proposal of this kind would result in a group of high officials who would not be responsible to the Secretary-General but to the bodies which elected them.[20] This would inevitably mean a dilution of the responsibility of the Secretary-General for the conduct of the Organization and would be conducive neither to the efficient functioning of the Secretariat nor to its independent position.[21] In this action and other related decisions, the drafters of the Charter laid emphasis on the personal responsibility of the Secretary-General; it is he who is solely responsible for performing the functions entrusted to him for the appointment of all Members of the Secretariat and for assuring the organ that the Secretariat will carry out their tasks under his exclusive authority. The idea of a "Cabinet system" in which responsibility for administration and political functions would be distributed among several individuals was squarely rejected.

It is also relevant in this connexion that the provision for "due regard to geographical representation" in the recruitment of the Secretariat was never treated as calling for political or ideological representation. It was rather an affirmation of the idea accepted since the beginning of the League Secretariat that the staff of the Organization was to have an international composition and that its basis would be as "geographically" broad as possible.[22] Moreover, as clearly indicated

[18]UNCIO vol. 2, pp. 691-3.

[19]*Ibid.*, vol. 7, pp. 343-7, 387-9. Report of the Rapporteur of Committee I/2.

[20]*Ibid.*, p. 386.

[21]*Ibid.* See also summary record of 12th meeting of Committee I/2, *ibid.*, p. 106.

[22]*Ibid.*, pp. 505, 510-11.

in the language of Article 101, the "paramount consideration in the employment of the staff" should be the necessity of securing the highest standards of efficiency, competence, and integrity. This terminology is evidence of the intention of the drafters to accord priority to considerations of efficiency and competence over those of geographical representation, important though the latter be.

To sum up, the Charter laid down these essential legal principles for an international civil service:

It was to be an international body, recruited primarily for efficiency, competence, and integrity, but on as wide a geographical basis as possible;

It was to be headed by a Secretary-General who carried constitutionally the responsibility to the other principal organs for the Secretariat's work;

And finally, Article 98 entitled the General Assembly and the Security Council to entrust the Secretary-General with tasks going beyond the *verba formalia* of Article 97—with its emphasis on the administrative function—thus opening the door to a measure of political responsibility which is distinct from the authority explicitly accorded to the Secretary-General under Article 99 but in keeping with the spirit of that Article.

This last-mentioned development concerning the Secretary-General, with its obvious consequences for the Secretariat as such, takes us beyond the concept of a non-political civil service into an area where the official, in the exercise of his functions, may be forced to take stands of a politically controversial nature. It does this, however, on an international basis and, thus, without departing from the basic concept of "neutrality"; in fact, Article 98, as well as Article 99, would be unthinkable without the complement of Article 100 strictly observed both in letter and spirit.

Reverting for a moment to our initial question, I have to emphasize the distinction just made. If a demand for neutrality is made, by present critics of the international civil service, with the intent that the international civil servant should not be permitted to take a stand on political issues, in response to requests of the General Assembly or the Security Council, then the demand is in conflict with the Charter itself. If, however, "neutrality" means that the international civil servant, also in executive tasks with political implications, must remain wholly uninfluenced by national or group interests or ideologies, then the obligation to observe such neutrality is just as basic to the Charter concept of the international civil service as it was to the concept once found in the Covenant of the League. Due to the circumstances then prevailing the distinction to which I have just drawn attention probably never was clearly made in the League, but it has become fundamental for the interpretation of the actions of the Secretariat as established by the Charter.

The criticism to which I referred at the beginning of this lecture can be directed against the very Charter concept of the Secretariat and imply a demand for a reduction of the functions of the Secretariat to the role assigned to it in the League and explicitly mentioned in Article 97 of the Charter; this would be a retrograde development in sharp conflict with the way in which the functions of the international Secretariat over the years have been extended by the main organs of the United Nations, in response to arising needs. Another possibility would be that the actual developments under Articles 98 and 99 are accepted but that a lack of confidence in the possibility of personal "neutrality" is considered to render necessary administrative arrangements putting the persons in question under special constitutional controls, either built into the structure of the Secretariat or established through organs outside the Secretariat.

IV

The conception of an independent international civil service, although reasonably clear in the Charter provisions, was almost continuously subjected to stress in the history of the Organization. International tensions, changes in governments, concern with national security, all had their inevitable repercussions on the still fragile institution dedicated to the international community. Governments not only strove for the acceptance of their views in the organs of the Organization, but they concerned themselves in varying degrees with the attitude of their nationals in the Secretariat. Some governments sought in one way or another to revive the substance of the proposal defeated at London for the clearance of their nationals prior to employment in the Secretariat; other governments on occasion demanded the dismissal of staff members who were said to be inappropriately representative of the country of their nationality for political, racial, or even cultural reasons.

In consequence, the Charter Articles underwent a continual process of interpretation and clarification in the face of pressures brought to bear on the Secretary-General. On the whole the results tended to affirm and strengthen the independence of the international civil service. These developments involved two complementary aspects: first, the relation between the Organization and the Member States in regard to the selection and employment of nationals of those States, and second, the relation between the international official, his own State, and the international responsibilities of the Organization. It is apparent that these relationships involved a complex set of obligations and rights applying to the several interested parties.

One of the most difficult of the problems was presented as a result of the interest of several national governments in passing upon the recruitment of their nationals by the Secretariat. It was of course a matter of fundamental principle that the selection of staff should be made by the Secretary-General on his own responsibility and not on the responsibility of the national governments.[23] The interest of the governments in placing certain nationals and in barring the employment of others had to be subordinated, as a matter of principle and law, to the independent determination of the Organization. Otherwise there would have been an abandonment of the position adopted at San Francisco and affirmed by the Preparatory Commission in London.

On the other hand, there were practical considerations which required the Organization to utilize the services of governments for the purpose of obtaining applicants for positions and, as a corollary of this, for information as to the competence, integrity, and general suitability of such nationals for employment. The United Nations could not have an investigating agency comparable to those available to national governments, and the Organization had therefore to accept assistance from governments in obtaining information and records concerning possible applicants. However, the Secretary-General consistently reserved the right to make the final determination on the basis of all the facts and his own independent appreciation of these facts.[24]

It may be recalled that this problem assumed critical proportions in 1952 and 1953 when various authorities of the United States Government, host to the United Nations Headquarters, conducted a series of highly publicized investigations of the loyalty of its nationals in the Secretariat.[25] Charges were made which, although relating to a small number of individuals and largely founded upon inference rather than on direct evidence or admissions, led to proposals which implicitly challenged the international character of the responsibilities of the Secretary-General and his staff.[26] In certain other countries similar proposals were made and in some cases adopted in legislation or by administrative action.

In response, the Secretary-General and the Organization as a whole affirmed the necessity of independent action by the United Nations in regard to selection and recruitment of staff. The Organization was only prepared to accept information from governments concerning suitability for employment, including information that might be relevant to political considerations such as activity which would be regarded as inconsistent with the obligation of international civil servants.[27] It was recognized that there should be a relationship of mutual confidence and trust between international officials and the governments of Member States.

---

[23] Report of the Preparatory Commission, p. 86, para. 15; GA resolution 13 (I), 13 Feb. 1946.

[24] Report of the Secretary-General on Personnel Policy (30 January 1953), UN doc. A/2364, para. 7 and Annex I.

[25] See Hearings of the Sub-committee of the Committee on the Judiciary of the U.S. Senate on "Activities of U.S. Citizens employed by the United Nations" (1952).

[26] *Ibid.* at pp. 407-11. See also Bill S. 3, 83rd Congress, First Session.

[27] Report of the Secretary-General on Personnel Policy, UN doc. A/2533, paras. 69-70.

At the same time, the Secretary-General took a strong position that the dismissal of a staff member on the basis of the mere suspicion of a Government of a Member State or a bare conclusion arrived at by that Government on evidence which is denied the Secretary-General would amount to receiving instructions in violation of his obligation under Article 100, paragraph I of the Charter "not to receive in the performance of his duties instructions from any Government".[28] It should be said that, as a result of the stand taken by the Organization, this principle was recognized by the United States Government in the procedures it established for hearings and submission of information to the Secretary-General regarding U.S. citizens.[29]

A risk of national pressure on the international official may also be introduced, in a somewhat more subtle way, by the terms and duration of his appointment. A national official, seconded by his government for a year or two with an international organization, is evidently in a different position psychologically—and one might say, politically—from the permanent international civil servant who does not contemplate a subsequent career with his national government. This was recognized by the Preparatory Commission in London in 1945 when it concluded that members of the Secretariat staff could not be expected "fully to subordinate the special interests of their countries to the international interest if they are merely detached temporarily from national administrations and dependent upon them for their future".[30] Recently, however, assertions have been made that it is necessary to switch from the present system, which makes permanent appointments and career service the rule, to a predominant system of fixed-term appointments to be granted mainly to officials seconded by their governments. This line is prompted by governments which show little enthusiasm for making officials available on a long-term basis, and, moreover, seem to regard—as a matter of principle or, at least, of "realistic" psychology—the international civil servant primarily as a national official representing his country and its ideology. On this view, the international civil service should be recognized and developed as being an "intergovernmental" secretariat composed principally of national officials assigned by their governments, rather than as an "international" secretariat as conceived from the days of the League of Nations and until now. In the light of what I have already said regarding the provisions of the Charter, I need not demonstrate that this conception runs squarely against the principles of Articles 100 and 101.

This is not to say that there is not room for a reasonable number of "seconded" officials in the Secretariat. It has in fact been accepted that it is highly desirable to have a number of officials available from governments for short periods,

---

[28] UN doc. A/2364, para. 94.

[29] UN doc. A/2364, pp. 35-36, containing Executive Order No. 10422; as amended by Executive Order No. 10459, UN doc. A/2533, appendix to Annex I.

[30] Report of the Preparatory Commission, p. 92, para. 59.

especially to perform particular tasks calling for diplomatic or technical backgrounds. Experience has shown that such seconded officials, true to their obligations under the Charter, perform valuable service but as a matter of good policy it should, of course, be avoided as much as possible to put them on assignments in which their status and nationality might be embarrassing to themselves or the parties concerned. However, this is quite different from having a large portion of the Secretariat—say, in excess of one-third—composed of short-term officials. To have so large a proportion of the Secretariat staff in the seconded category would be likely to impose serious strains on its ability to function as a body dedicated exclusively to international responsibilities. Especially if there were any doubts to the principles ruling their work in the minds of the governments on which their future might depend, this might result in a radical departure from the basic concepts of the Charter and the destruction of the international civil service as it has been developed in the League and up to now in the United Nations.

It can fairly be said that the United Nations has increasingly succeeded in affirming the original idea of a dedicated professional service responsible only to the Organization in the performance of its duties and protected so far as possible from the inevitable pressures of national governments. And this has been done in spite of strong pressures which are easily explained in terms of historic tradition and national interests. Obviously, however, the problem is ultimately one of the spirit of service shown by the international civil servant and respected by Member Governments. The International Secretariat is not what it is meant to be until the day when it can be recruited on a wide geographical basis without the risk that then some will be under—or consider themselves to be under—two masters in respect of their official functions.

V

The independence and international character of the Secretariat required not only resistance to national pressures in matters of personnel, but also—and this was more complex—the independent implementation of controversial political decisions in a manner fully consistent with the exclusively international responsibility of the Secretary-General. True, in some cases implementation was largely administrative; the political organs stated their objectives and the measures to be taken in reasonably specific terms, leaving only a narrow area for executive discretion. But in other cases—and these generally involved the most controversial situations—the Secretary-General was confronted with mandates of a highly general character, expressing the bare minimum of agreement attainable in the organs. That the execution of these tasks involved the exercise of political judgement by the Secretary-General was, of course, evident to the Member States themselves.

It could perhaps be surmised that virtually no one at San Francisco envisaged the extent to which the Members of the Organization would assign to the Secretary-General functions which necessarily required him to take positions in highly controversial political matters. A few examples of these mandates in recent years will demonstrate how wide has been the scope of authority delegated to the Secretary-General by the Security Council and the General Assembly in matters of peace and security.

One might begin in 1956 with the Palestine armistice problem, when the Security Council instructed the Secretary-General "to arrange with the parties for adoption of any measures" which he should consider "would reduce existing tensions along the armistice demarcation lines".[31]

A few months later, after the outbreak of hostilities in Egypt, the General Assembly authorized the Secretary-General immediately to "obtain compliance of the withdrawal of foreign forces".[32] At the same session he was requested to submit a plan for a United Nations Force to "secure and supervise the cessation of hostilities", and subsequently he was instructed "to take all . . . necessary administrative and executive action to organise this Force and dispatch it to Egypt".[33]

In 1958 the Secretary-General was requested "to despatch urgently an Observation Group . . . to Lebanon so as to ensure that there is no illegal infiltration of personnel or supply of arms or other matériel across the Lebanese borders".[34] Two months later he was asked to make forthwith "such practical arrangements as would adequately help in upholding the purposes and principles of the Charter in relation to Lebanon and Jordan".[35]

Most recently, in July 1960, the Secretary-General was requested to provide military assistance to the Central Government of the Republic of the Congo. The basic mandate is contained in a single paragraph of a resolution adopted by the Security Council on 13 July 1960 which reads as follows:[36]

"The Security Council

. . . .

2. *Decides* to authorize the Secretary-General to take the necessary steps, in consultation with the Government of the Republic of the Congo, to provide the Government with such military assistance, as may be necessary, until, through

---

[31]Security Council resolution S/3575 of 4 April 1956.

[32]General Assembly resolution 999 (ES-I) of 4 November 1956.

[33]General Assembly resolutions 998 (ES-I) of 4 November 1956 and 1001 (ES-I) of 7 November 1956.

[34]Security Council resolution S/4023 of 11 June 1958.

[35]General Assembly resolution 1237 (ES-III) of 21 August 1958.

[36]Security Council resolution S/4387 of 13 July 1961.

the efforts of the Congolese Government with the technical assistance of the United Nations, the national security forces may be able, in the opinion of the Government, to meet fully their tasks."

The only additional guidance was provided by a set of principles concerning the use of United Nations Forces which had been evolved during the experience of the United Nations Emergency Force.[37] I had informed the Security Council[38] before the adoption of the resolution that I would base any action that I might be required to take on these principles, drawing attention specifically to some of the most significant of the rules applied in the UNEF operation. At the request of the Security Council I later submitted an elaboration of the same principles to the extent they appeared to me to be applicable to the Congo operation.[39] A report on the matter was explicitly approved by the Council,[40] but naturally it proved to leave wide gaps; unforeseen and unforeseeable problems, which we quickly came to face, made it necessary for me repeatedly to invite the Council to express themselves on the interpretation given by the Secretary-General to the mandate. The needs for added interpretation referred especially to the politically extremely charged situation which arose because of the secession of Katanga and because of the disintegration of the central government which, according to the basic resolution of the Security Council, were to be the party in consultation with which the United Nations activities had to be developed.[41]

These recent examples demonstrate the extent to which the Member States have entrusted the Secretary-General with tasks that have required him to take action which unavoidably may have to run counter to the views of at least some of these Member States. The agreement reached in the general terms of a resolution, as we have seen, no longer need to obtain when more specific issues are presented. Even when the original resolution is fairly precise, subsequent developments, previously unforeseen, may render highly controversial the action called for under the resolution. Thus, for example, the unanimous resolution authorizing assistance to the Central Government of the Congo offered little guidance to the Secretary-General when that Government split into competing centres of

[37] See "Summary Study of the experience derived from the establishment and operation of the Force: report of the Secretary-General", U.N. doc. A/3943, General Assembly, Official Records, 13th session, annexes, agenda item 65.

[38] See Security Council, Official Records, 15th year, 873rd meeting, para. 28.

[39] First report by the Secretary-General dated 18 July 1960 on the implementation of the Security Council resolution of 13 July 1960, U.N. doc. S/4389, p. 4.

[40] See para. 3 of Security Council resolution S/4405 of 22 July 1960.

[41] See Memorandum on implementation of Security Council resolution of 9 Aug. 1960, U.N. doc. S/4417 and addenda; Security Council, Official Records, 15th year, 884th and following meetings.

authority, each claiming to be the Central Government and each supported by different groups of Member States within and outside the Security Council.

A simple solution for the dilemmas thus posed for the Secretary-General might seem to be for him to refer the problem to the political organ for it to resolve the question. Under a national parliamentary régime, this would often be the obvious course of action for the executive to take. Indeed, this is what the Secretary-General must also do whenever it is feasible. But the serious problems arise precisely because it is so often not possible for the organs themselves to resolve the controversial issue faced by the Secretary-General. When brought down to specific cases involving a clash of interests and positions, the requited majority in the Security Council or General Assembly may not be available for any particular solution. This will frequently be evident in advance of a meeting and the Member States will conclude that it would be futile for the organs to attempt to reach a decision and consequently that the problem has to be left to the Secretary-General to solve on one basis or another, at his own risk but with as faithful an interpretation of the instructions, rights, and obligations of the Organization as possible in view of international law and the decisions already taken.

It might be said that in this situation the Secretary-General should refuse to implement the resolution, since implementation would offend one or another group of Member States and open him to the charge that he has abandoned the political neutrality and impartiality essential to his office. The only way to avoid such criticism, it is said, is for the Secretary-General to refrain from execution of the original resolution until the organs have decided the issue by the required majority (and, in the case of the Security Council, with the unanimous concurrence of the permanent members) or he, maybe, has found another way to pass responsibility over on to Governments.

For the Secretary-General this course of action—or more precisely, non-action—may be tempting; it enables him to avoid criticism by refusing to act until other political organs resolve the dilemma. An easy refuge may thus appear to be available. But would such refuge be compatible with the responsibility placed upon the Secretary-General by the Charter? Is he entitled to refuse to carry out the decision properly reached by the organs, on the ground that the specific implementation would be opposed to positions some Member States might wish to take, as indicated, perhaps, by an earlier minority vote? Of course the political organs may always instruct him to discontinue the implementation of a resolution, but when they do not so instruct him and the resolution remains in effect, is the Secretary-General legally and morally free to take no action, particularly in a matter considered to affect international peace and security? Should he, for example, have abandoned the operation in the Congo because almost any decision he made as to the composition of the Force or its role would have been contrary to the attitudes of some Members as reflected in debates, and maybe even in votes, although not in decisions?

The answers seem clear enough in law; the responsibilities of the Secretary-General under the Charter cannot be laid aside merely because the execution of decisions by him is likely to be politically controversial. The Secretary-General remains under the obligation to carry out the policies as adopted by the organs; the essential requirement is that he does this on the basis of his exclusively international responsibility and not in the interest of any particular State or groups of States.

This presents us with the crucial issue: is it possible for the Secretary-General to resolve controversial questions on a truly international basis without obtaining the formal decision of the organs? In my opinion and on the basis of my experience, the answer is in the affirmative; it is possible for the Secretary-General to carry out his tasks in controversial political situations with full regard to his exclusively international obligation under the Charter and without subservience to a particular national or ideological attitude. This is not to say that the Secretary-General is a kind of delphic oracle who alone speaks for the international community. He has available for his task varied means and resources.

Of primary importance in this respect are the principles and purposes of the Charter which are the fundamental law accepted by and binding on all States. Necessarily general and comprehensive, these principles and purposes still are specific enough to have practical significance in concrete cases.[42]

The principles of the Charter are, moreover, supplemented by the body of legal doctrine and precepts that have been accepted by States generally, and particularly as manifested in the resolutions of UN organs. In this body of law there are rules and precedents that appropriately furnish guidance to the Secretary-General when he is faced with the duty of applying a general mandate in circumstances that had not been envisaged by the resolution.

Considerations of principle and law, important as they are, do not of course suffice to settle all the questions posed by the political tasks entrusted to the Secretary-General. Problems of political judgement still remain. In regard to these problems, the Secretary-General must find constitutional means and techniques to assist him, so far as possible, in reducing the element of purely personal judgement. In my experience I have found several arrangements of value to enable the Secretary-General to obtain what might be regarded as the representative opinion of the Organization in respect of the political issues faced by him.

One such arrangement might be described as the institution of the permanent missions to the United Nations, through which the Member States have enabled

[42] See, for example, references to the Charter in relation to the establishment and operation of UNEF: U.N. doc. A/3302, General Assembly, Official Records, first emergency special session, annexes, agenda item 5, pp. 19-23; U.N. doc. A/3512, General Assembly, Official Records, eleventh session, annexes, agenda item 66, pp. 47-50. See also references to the Charter in relation to the question of the Congo: U.N. doc. S/PV. 887, p. 17; U.N. doc. S/PV. 920, p. 47; U.N. doc. S/PV. 942, pp. 137-40; U.N. doc. S/4637 A.

the Secretary-General to carry on frequent consultations safeguarded by diplomatic privacy.[43]

Another arrangement, which represents a further development of the first, has been the advisory committee of the Secretary-General, such as those on UNEF and the Congo, composed of representatives of Governments most directly concerned with the activity involved, and also representing diverse political positions and interests.[44] These advisory committees have furnished a large measure of the guidance required by the Secretary-General in carrying out his mandates relating to UNEF and the Congo operations. They have provided an essential link between the judgement of the executive and the consensus of the political bodies.

VI

Experience has thus indicated that the international civil servant may take steps to reduce the sphere within which he has to take stands on politically controversial issues. In summary, it may be said that he will carefully seek guidance in the decisions of the main organs, in statements relevant for the interpretation of those decisions, in the Charter and in generally recognized principles of law, remembering that by his actions he may set important precedents. Further, he will submit as complete reporting to the main organs as circumstances permit, seeking their guidance whenever such guidance seems to be possible to obtain. Even if all of these steps are taken, it will still remain, as has been amply demonstrated in practice, that the reduced area of discretion will be large enough to expose the international Secretariat to heated political controversy and to accusations of a lack of neutrality.

I have already drawn attention to the ambiguity of the word "neutrality" in such a context. It is obvious from what I have said that the international civil servant cannot be accused of lack of neutrality simply for taking a stand on a controversial issue when this is his duty and cannot be avoided. But there remains a serious intelluctual and moral problem as we move within an area inside which personal judgement must come into play. Finally, we have to deal here with a question of integrity or with, if you please, a question of conscience.

The international civil servant must keep himself under the strictest observation. He is not requested to be a neuter in the sense that he has to have no

[43]See Introduction to the Annual Report of the Secretary-General on the Work of the Organization, 16 June 1958–15 June 1959, p. 2, U.N. doc. A/4132 add. I, General Assembly, Official Records, fourteenth session, Supplement No. IA.

[44]UNEF Advisory Committee, established by General Assembly resolution 1001 (ES-I). The Advisory Committee on the Congo was established by the Secretary-General and recognized by the General Assembly and in the Security Council's various resolutions.

sympathies or antipathies, that there are to be no interests which are close to him in his personal capacity, or that he is to have no ideas or ideals that matter for him. However, he is requested to be fully aware of those human reactions and meticulously check himself so that they are not permitted to influence his actions. This is nothing unique. Is not every judge professionally under the same obligation?

If the international civil servant knows himself to be free from such personal influences in his actions and guided solely by the common aims and rules laid down for, and by the Organization he serves and by recognized legal principles, then he has done his duty, and then he can face the criticism which, even so, will be unavoidable. As I said, in the final test, this is a question of integrity, and if integrity in the sense of respect for law and respect for truth were to drive him into positions of conflict with this or that interest, then that conflict is a sign of his neutrality—and not of his failure to observe neutrality—then it is in line, not in conflict with his duties as an international civil servant.

Recently it has been said, this time in Western circles, that as the International Secretariat goes forward on the road of international thought and action, while Member States depart from it, a gap develops between them and they grow into mutually hostile elements; and this is said to increase the tension in the world which it was the purpose of the United Nations to diminish. From this view the conclusion has been drawn that we may have to switch from an international Secretariat, ruled by the principles described in this lecture, to an intergovernmental Secretariat, the members of which obviously would not be supposed to work in the direction of an internationalism considered unpalatable to their governments. Such a passive acceptance of a nationalism rendering it necessary to abandon present efforts in the direction of internationalism symbolized by the international civil service—somewhat surprisingly regarded as a cause of tension—might, if accepted by the Member Nations, well prove to be the Munich of international co-operation as conceived after the First World War and further developed under the impression of the tragedy of the Second World War. To abandon or to compromise with principles on which such co-operation is built may be no less dangerous than to compromise with principles regarding the rights of a nation. In both cases the price to be paid may be peace.

Dimensions of Conflict in the General Assembly

Hayward R. Alker, Jr.

Although there has been considerable work on voting patterns in the United Nations,[1] almost none of it has contributed cumulatively to existing theories of international relations. Methodological problems or a descriptive intent have often stood in the way of such advancement. For example, the main findings of

---

Hayward R. Alker, Jr., Yale Univeristy, "Dimensions of Conflict in the General Assembly," *The American Political Science Review,* Vol. LVIII, No. 3 (September 1964), pp. 642-657. Reprinted by permission of the author and *The American Political Science Review.* An earlier version of this paper was delivered at the Annual Meeting of the American Political Science Association, New York City, September 1963. In addition to the Computation Center, M.I.T., and the Yale Computer Center, where the calculations presented here were performed, the author is indebted to Karl W. Deutsch, Ernst B. Haas and Bruce M. Russett for helpful comments, and to Bruce Russett and the Yale Political Data Program for collecting most of the variables in Table IV. The Data Program's work is supported by the National Science Foundation.

[1] For example, M. Margaret Ball, "Bloc Voting in the General Assembly," *International Organization,* Vol. 5, No. 1 (February, 1951), pp. 3-31; Jan F. Triska and Howard E. Koch, Jr., "Asian-African Coalition and International Organization: Third Force or Collective Impotence?" *Review of Politics,* Vol. 21, No. 2 (April, 1959), pp. 417-55; Geoffrey Goodwin, "The Expanding UN; I-Voting Patterns," *International Affairs,* Vol. 36, No. 2 (April, 1960), pp. 174-87; Leroy N. Rieselbach, "Quantitative Techniques for Studying Voting Behavior in the UN General Assembly," *International Organization,* Vol. 14, No. 2 (Spring 1960), pp. 297-304; Arend Lijphart, "The Analysis of Bloc Voting in the General Assembly: A Critique and a Proposal," this REVIEW, Vol. 57, No. 4 (December, 1963), pp. 902-17; Robert E. Riggs, *Politics in the United Nations* (Urbana, University of Illinois Press, 1958); Thomas Hovet, Jr., *Bloc Politics in the United Nations,* (Cambridge, Harvard University Press, 1960), and *Africa in the United Nations* (Evanston, Northwestern University Press, 1963).

Thomas Hovet, Jr.'s *Bloc Politics in the United Nations,* the most comprehensive work to date, are based on trends in the voting cohesion of regional and caucusing groups in the Assembly and time-series data on how often these groups vote with the majority.

Voting with the majority, as used by Hovet—and Riggs before him—is a poor measure of national power in the General Assembly because of the problems associated with discovering the extent to which nations are "satellites" or "chameleons."[2] Hovet himself has recognized the chameleon-like nature of the Soviet Union:

"It would be a serious misjudgment . . . to conclude that the high degree of cohesion of these African groups and factions with the Soviet Union means that the Soviet Union dominates their voting behavior. . . . The policy of the Soviet Union is to associate itself with the proposals and statements of the African states, especially when these issues are of vital interest to Africa, and at the same time to stress the fact that the United States is not a friend of Africa."[3]

If this is true, voting with the majority cannot be used as a measure of Soviet power. The trouble with an alternative inference, that the Africans have influenced the Russians, is that the Russians *want* to be persuaded. If exercising power means getting someone else to do something he otherwise would not do, neither the Soviets nor the Africans have appreciably influenced each other. Within the majority, then, it is not clear who is more powerful; nor do voting percentages indicate very clearly the deprivations suffered by the minority.

This problem aside, Hovet and Riggs have made a significant contribution to the study of power and of group cohesion in distinguishing among the various kinds of issues before the Assembly. As Dahl has clearly shown,[4] groups have more power on some kinds of issues than on others. In terms of such Charter-based issue-categories as "collective measures, including regulations of armaments, etc.," "peaceful settlement," "economic questions," "human rights," "self-determination" or "administrative, procedural or structural" questions, comparative and trend studies of the functional areas of group cohesion and influence are possible.[5]

Conclusions from such analyses, however, are often controversial. One problem is that of making reproducible and widely acceptable assignments of roll calls

---

[2] These distinctions are made by Robert Dahl, "The Concept of Power," *Behavorial Science,* Vol. 2, No. 3 (July, 1957), pp. 201-15.

[3] *Africa in the United Nations,* pp. 181-85.

[4] Robert Dahl, *Who Governs?* (New Haven, Yale University Press, 1963).

[5] See Hovet, *Bloc Politics in the United Nations, op. cit.,* pp. 130-88. Ernest B. Haas has used to advantage a somewhat more specific set of issue-groupings in an analysis of the "coverage" of different conventions ratified by members of the International Labor Organization. See his "System and Process in the International Labor Organization, A Statistical Afterthought," *World Politics,* Vol. 14, No. 2 (January, 1962), pp. 339-52.

to the "correct" issue category. Some observers, for instance, would like to consider Tibet a question involving self-determination and human rights.[6] Others might refer to it as a basically political controversy, related to the cold war. To take another example, is a resolution recommending negotiations on West Irian primarily one about "peaceful settlement," "self-determination" or a structural attempt to establish a certain kind of negotiating committee? Perhaps it is all of these. But *multiple* assignments on the basis of the language of the resolution raises another problem: the relative "importance" of the various parts and implications of a particular roll call. In fact most of the disagreement expressed in the General Assembly is about just this question: which Charter norms should be applied in what manner in a particular situation? "What kind of self-determination and for whom?" has been a basic controversy in both the Tibetan and the West Irian questions. Whether or not "self-determination" or "domestic jurisdiction" or the need for "peaceful settlement" is most appropriate to an African conflict situation is always a matter of debate.

If agreement on the relevant Charter *norms* is often difficult, perhaps one can be more objective in describing the political *conflicts* which a voting alignment contains. These conflict categories can be used in combination with objective verbal, structural or functional classifications to test various theories about the substance and causes of international conflict.

Thinking in terms of international conflicts brings up another question which is unanswered in most studies of group cohesion: in what voting context did these positions occur? Telling us that Latin Americans were divided on "self-determination" questions like West Irian or South Africa does not tell us about the positions of the other main participants such as the United States, Russia, Indonesia, the Netherlands or South Africa. We would need to know how these and other states voted before we can say that Cold War or anticolonial perceptions dominated the voting. Simply measuring group cohesion on heterogeneous issue-categories, we cannot be very sure who disagreed with whom, to what extent, and about what kinds of issues.[7]

---

[6] Sydney Bailey has presented an interesting discussion of the different tactical approaches to this issue in "The Question of Tibet," *The General Assembly of the United Nations* (New York, 1961), ch. 10.

[7] Hovet, *Bloc. Politics, op. cit.*, p. 112, feels it "premature" to attempt any formal conclusions about the implications of the total phenomenon. He does suggest, however, that with its mixed blessings the "bloc" phenomenon is likely to increase and should be better understood. Fortunately in *Africa in the United Nations* considerably more attention is given to the specific issues on which group members disagree and how their votes are related to the American and Soviet positions. This methodology is much more useful than the *ad hoc* verbal descriptions of group differences that supplemented the bar graphs in *Bloc Politics.* Arend Lijphart, *op. cit.*, pp. 913-17, has also studied voting cohesion with the positions of other states in mind. His Figure 2 seems quite clearly two-dimensional. The proper dimensionality of UN voting patterns is discussed in detail below.

Another major omission in previous analyses of voting patterns in the General Assembly has been a comparative analysis of the various proposed influences on Assembly voting. One can argue with Hovet that group loyalties and pressures are important determinants of voting behavior, but unless one has a measure of the actual voting *positions* of different states on such major conflicts as the Cold War in the UN, the relative impact of caucusing-group influences and domestic social, economic and political considerations cannot be compared. Many current theories of international politics suggest that racial, economic, geographic and military variables are also at work in influencing voting positions. Ernst Haas, for example, has characterized the UN as a multi-phase system "whose characteristics and evolutionary potential must be specified in terms of the changing environment in which it operates."[8]

This paper will concentrate on two aspects of contemporary politics in the General Assembly. Factor analysis will be used in an attempt to uncover the principal dimensions of conflict underlying votes at the Sixteenth General Assembly and the location of states on these main issues. The relative importance of the various determinants of voting behavior suggested above will then be assessed, using correlation and regression techniques.[9] Findings from these analyses will serve both as a test of several hypotheses in international relations theory and as a basis for further studies of conflict and consensus, cohesion and power in the General Assembly.[10]

---

[8]Ernst B. Haas, "Dynamic Environment and Static System: Revolutionary Regimes in the United Nations," in Morton Kaplan (ed.), *The Revolution in World Politics* (New York, 1962), p. 178. Italics omitted.

[9]Neither of these techniques is new to political science. Glendon Schubert has factor-analyzed judicial votes in "The 1960 Term of the Supreme Court: A Psychological Analysis," this REVIEW, Vol. 56, No. 1 (March, 1962), pp. 90-107; see also Duncan MacRae, Jr., and James A. Meldrum, "Critical Elections in Illinois: 1888-1958," this REVIEW, Vol. 54, No. 3 (September, 1960), pp. 669-83. Regression is a basic deductive technique in *The American Voter.* See Stokes, Campbell and Miller, "Components of Electoral Decision," this REVIEW, Vol. 52, No. 2 (June, 1958), pp. 367-87. A readable summary of both techniques may be found in Hubert Blalock, Jr., *Social Statistics* (New York, 1960), chs. 17-19 and 21. What is new about these techniques is the ease with which they may be applied. The seventy roll call factor analyses reported here took eleven minutes on the IBM 7090. The regressions took less than a minute each on the IBM 709.

[10]Hayward R. Alker, Jr. and Bruce M. Russett, *World Politics in the General Assembly* (New Haven: Yale University Press, 1965). Power measurements are facilitated by the use of both the conflict dimensions presented below and additional information on the sponsorship of resolutions and the intensity of involvement of different groups on these conflicts. Voting cohesion may satisfactorily be measured in terms of mean deviations on the factor scores presented below.

I CONFLICTS IN THE GENERAL ASSEMBLY

The Sixteenth General Assembly met intermittently, from September 1961 through June 1962. Seventy important votes from this session were chosen for intensive analysis. They include all distinct, non-unanimous, non-procedural, plenary roll calls, as well as 26 of the most important committee votes. Grouped according to the main committee of the Assembly in which they were originally discussed, these votes are briefly described on the left-hand sides of Tables 1 and 2.[11]

Each conflict underlying more than one of these votes could be described by a *set of correlations* between the conflict and each of the 70 selected roll calls (r_{jk} for roll call j and voting component k). If two such sets of correlations were themselves uncorrelated, we could say these conflicts were distinct. Each roll call could then be analyzed in terms of a set of its own correlations with separate voting components. Tables 1 and 2 contain these kinds of correlations: the *vertical* sets of correlations describe distinct conflicts in the General Assembly; the *horizontal* rows give each roll call's correlations with the conflict alignments.

Table entries were calculated in the following manner. Voting positions on each roll call ("Yeses," "Abstains" and "Nos") were quantified as ranks with zero means and unit standard deviations. These positions (V_{ji} for roll call j and country i) were assumed to result from a summation of underlying conflict positions (C_{ik} for conflict k) after multiplication by a *set of coefficients* (a_{jk}) indicating the relevance of each conflict to each roll call. These coefficients, called "conflict loadings" or "factor loadings" can be presented in as many rows as there are roll calls and in as many columns as there are general conflicts in Assembly voting.[12]

---

[11]Designating plenary meetings as the "Eighth Committee" and the Special Political Committee as the "0th Committee," the first digit of the identification numbers for each roll call in the Tables corresponds to the Committee in which the vote occurred; the numbers after this digit refer to the order of occurrence of the roll call within the Committee. "S.C.E.A.R." stands for the Scientific Committee on the Effects of Atomic Radiation; "P.D.R." symbolizes the People's Democratic Republic of Korea; and "S.C.17" refers to the Special Committee of 17 set up at the Fifteenth Session to implement the Declaration on the Granting of Independence to Colonial Countries and Peoples. "UNCURK" is the United Nations Commission for the Unification and Rehabilitation of Korea, while "CINSGT" is the author's label for the Committee on Information from Non-Self-Governing Territories.

[12]Symbolically the model of voting positions used in factor analysis is

$$V_{ji} = \sum_k a_{jk} C_{ik} + u_{ji},$$

where u_{ji} is the unexplained voting position of country i on roll call j. For more details on the roll calls and methods described above, see Hayward R. Alker, Jr., *Dimensions of Voting in the General Assembly* (Ph. D. Dissertation, Department of Political Science, Yale University, 1963). Harry H. Harmon, *Modern Factor Analysis* (Chicago, University of Chicago Press, 1960), ch. 9, derives the "principal component" method of factor analysis used in this article.

Table 1 Dimensions of Conflict at the 16th General Assembly: Unrotated Factor Matrix

Roll Calls		Factor								
		I	II	III	IV	V	VI	VII	VIII	IX
8004.	Censure South Africa	.63	.33	−.36	.02	.09	−.03	−.11	−.11	−.00
8022.	Sanction South Africa	.84	.25	−.28	−.13	.01	−.01	.05	.06	−.03
8023.	Security Council & S. Africa	.88	.28	−.22	−.13	−.04	−.03	.00	.01	.07
8024.	No arms to South Africa	.83	.22	−.15	−.21	−.05	.04	.18	.07	−.02
8025.	No petroleum to S. Africa	.85	.21	−.20	−.16	−.03	.00	.20	.11	−.05
8027.	Oman self-determination	.84	.06	−.16	.26	−.11	−.05	−.02	−.01	.10
0018.	Reconstitute Pal. Con. Com.	.38	−.03	−.00	.04	−.11	−.57	.32	.49	−.14
8045.	Reconstitute Pal. Con. Com.	.72	−.01	.01	.39	−.07	−.24	.01	.14	−.20
8046.	Protect Arab refugees	.77	−.02	.07	.38	−.13	−.18	−.00	.03	−.17
8047.	U.N.R.W.A.	−.64	.20	−.03	−.32	.33	−.22	.11	.16	.17
8048.	U. S. Palestine Resolution	−.70	.22	−.02	−.28	.26	−.17	.11	.22	.08
0003.	Czech Res. on S.C.E.A.R.	.81	−.09	.01	−.12	−.12	−.02	−.07	−.04	−.06
8006.	Czech Res. important?	−.87	.05	.02	.03	−.03	−.02	.16	.00	.00
8007.	Admit Mauritania	−.77	.17	−.14	−.28	.16	−.04	.05	−.16	−.00
8029.	China question important?	−.74	.19	−.49	.04	−.21	−.10	.09	−.16	.00
8030.	China Declaration	.67	.15	.54	−.25	.05	.17	−.17	.16	.07
8031.	Seat People's Rep. of China	.63	.16	.55	−.32	.02	.11	−.15	.14	−.00
8032.	Representation of China	.74	−.13	.45	−.27	.15	.12	−.12	.15	.02
8008.	Stop 50 megaton bomb	−.55	.64	.17	−.03	−.34	.04	−.14	.09	−.02
1010.	General & complete Disarm.	.88	.04	.03	−.11	−.08	.05	−.03	−.09	−.16
8009.	Regrets tests; need treaty	−.01	.86	.12	.15	.10	.18	−.04	−.06	.07
8010.	Regrets rejection of US-UK	−.70	.50	−.07	−.04	−.17	−.08	.11	−.07	.02
8012.	De-nuclearize Africa	.70	.06	.43	.17	.06	.10	.24	−.14	.07
8016.	Nuclear vs. Humanity	.87	.31	−.11	−.11	.04	.05	.06	−.07	.04
1023.	Non-nuclear club	.67	.10	.41	.17	.19	.12	.22	−.19	.01
8044.	Question of Algeria	.68	.16	.43	.12	.14	.03	.27	−.20	.04
1026.	P.D.R. & UNCURK	−.75	.32	−.25	.02	−.22	−.05	.11	−.11	.13
8054.	Report of UNCURK	−.88	.25	−.18	−.01	−.08	−.00	.14	.08	−.01
8055.	Deplores Hungary	−.92	.07	.04	.20	−.04	−.04	.05	.04	.05
8064.	Non interference (Cuba)	.86	−.08	.23	.09	−.01	−.06	−.10	.09	−.06
8065.	Friendly relations with Cuba	.92	.05	.10	−.11	−.00	−.02	.00	.12	−.09
2002.	Trade Conference	.88	.23	−.06	−.17	−.09	−.03	.15	−.06	−.03

2005.	Primary commodities	.44	.41	–.10	.25	.41	.08	.14	.16	.37
8038.	Study trade conference	–.74	.37	–.03	–.17	–.14	.00	.07	–.06	.11
2010.	Special int. devel. agency	.57	.38	–.42	.34	.21	–.02	–.12	.12	–.04
2015.	Conference on patents	–.58	–.21	.36	–.37	–.16	.05	.28	.00	–.21
8039.	Capital & technical assist.	–.25	.74	.09	.01	–.14	–.03	–.28	.16	.05
8041.	Population & econ. devel.	.53	–.13	.38	–.23	.00	–.17	.27	.04	.25
8001.	Tibet on agenda	–.83	.31	–.03	.04	.10	.02	.15	–.04	–.01
8043.	Resolution on Tibet	–.79	.44	–.17	–.06	.06	–.03	.19	–.02	.00
3001.	Absentee marriage	–.02	–.38	–.33	–.17	.50	–.28	–.11	–.16	–.33
3007.	"Hatred and hostility"	.78	.17	–.31	–.15	.03	–.05	–.16	.04	–.02
3013.	Safeguard right of reply	.68	–.17	.10	–.07	–.29	–.07	.17	–.26	–.16
8011.	Algerian prisoners	.78	.30	.10	–.15	.04	.08	.34	–.04	.06
8017.	1962 end of colonialism	.91	–.05	–.05	–.19	.07	–.01	.03	–.01	–.04
8019.	W. Irian self-determination	–.74	.11	–.25	–.34	.13	.17	–.04	–.03	–.08
8020.	Commission on W. Irian	–.78	.09	–.26	–.31	.09	.14	–.10	.01	–.07
8021.	Indian res. on W. Irian	.76	.01	.24	.40	.08	–.08	.05	–.10	.09
8035.	Regrets Port. non-compliance	–.83	–.29	.20	.09	.04	.02	–.07	.00	–.15
8037.	Renew CINSGT	–.26	.84	.15	.08	–.04	.14	–.03	.07	–.07
4009.	Swedish res. on South Africa	–.80	–.12	.34	.18	–.05	.01	.17	.03	–.07
8066.	Ask SC 17: S. Rhodesia SGTP	.87	.32	–.27	–.05	–.03	–.00	.03	–.01	.04
8068.	S. Rhodesia on agenda	.84	.34	–.25	–.04	–.04	–.06	.05	–.07	.03
8073.	"1 man 1 vote" S. Rhodesia	.86	.24	–.16	–.14	–.10	.02	.09	–.07	–.01
8075.	Regret UK on S. Rhodesia	.73	.40	–.30	.10	.06	.03	.04	–.10	.02
8056.	Condemn Portugal	.92	.04	–.05	–.13	.02	–.07	.03	–.01	–.07
8058.	Report on Angola	.80	.03	–.03	–.08	.04	–.10	–.07	–.02	.11
8059.	Angola & SC 17	.89	.16	–.08	–.00	–.00	–.10	–.05	–.06	.02
4001.	Burundi Prime Minister	–.88	–.24	.18	.01	.04	.02	.06	.11	–.05
4021.	Rwanda & Burundi sovereign	–.82	.01	–.12	.09	–.05	.11	.12	.09	–.09
8069.	Evacuate R. & B. by 1 Jul. 62	.95	.02	–.01	–.11	.00	–.10	.00	–.04	–.03
8070.	Rwanda & Burundi Evacuation	.30	.40	–.05	.21	.46	.29	.16	.03	–.49
4023.	Rwanda & Burundi Evacuation	–.30	.73	.06	.20	.04	.19	.01	.31	–.18
8071.	$2 million to S.G. for R. & B.	–.24	.66	.26	–.16	–.22	–.00	.03	–.08	–.30
5004.	5 Secretariat members/country	.57	.56	.07	–.02	–.33	.01	–.13	.02	–.03
8049.	Congo expenses and I.C.J.	–.74	.39	.20	.14	.14	–.19	.05	–.08	.00
8051.	Congo cost	–.42	.55	.43	.07	.12	–.37	–.22	–.20	–.01
8052.	U.N.E.F. expenses	–.50	.45	.43	–.02	.13	–.33	–.24	–.19	.06
8053.	Budget for year 1962	–.39	.60	.29	–.21	.16	–.28	–.02	–.15	–.14
8033.	Conf. on consular relations	.91	–.06	.06	–.15	.01	–.04	–.18	.03	–.02

Table 2 Dimensions of Conflict at the 16th General Assembly: Rotated Factor Matrix

Roll Calls		Factor								
		I	II	III	IV	V	VI	VII	VIII	IX
8004.	Censure South Africa	.77	.02	.00	.17	.16	.08	−.11	.03	−.09
8022.	Sanction South Africa	.88	−.10	.19	.13	.05	−.11	.03	−.03	−.11
8023.	Security Council & S. Africa	.91	−.06	.25	.16	.06	−.07	.06	−.06	−.00
8024.	No arms to South Africa	.82	−.12	.28	.08	−.05	−.15	.14	−.15	−.11
8025.	No petroleum to S. Africa	.84	−.14	.24	.11	−.02	−.20	.11	−.13	−.14
8027.	Oman self-determination	.67	−.19	.15	.51	.17	−.06	.09	−.07	.02
0018.	Reconstitute Pal. Con. Com.	.24	−.08	.09	.19	−.01	−.85	−.02	−.03	.03
8045.	Reconstitute Pal. Con. Com.	.43	−.12	.19	.65	.08	−.33	−.06	−.02	−.13
8046.	Protect Arab refugees	.45	−.12	.23	.71	.03	−.22	−.03	−.07	−.08
8047.	U.N.R.W.A.	−.33	.28	−.18	−.67	.18	−.18	−.18	−.01	.09
8048.	U.S. Palestine Resolution	−.38	.32	−.21	−.65	.13	−.21	−.10	.06	.01
0003.	Czech Res. on S.C.E.A.R.	.60	−.25	.40	.30	−.14	−.03	−.01	−.04	.06
8006.	Czech Res. important	−.64	.25	−.44	−.33	−.05	−.02	.05	−.01	.00
8007.	Admit Mauritania	−.37	.28	−.40	−.59	−.08	.13	−.18	.02	.03
8029.	China question important?	−.22	.20	−.83	−.30	−.10	.05	.01	.15	.09
8030.	China Declaration	.34	.13	.86	.12	.00	.03	.15	−.09	.00
8031.	Seat People's Rep. of China	.33	.16	.84	.08	−.09	−.01	.11	−.09	.01
8032.	Representation of China	.33	−.17	.87	.12	−.01	−.03	.01	−.11	−.01
8008.	Stop 50 megaton bomb	−.22	.79	−.21	−.16	−.12	.04	.30	.20	.06
1010.	General & Complete Disarm.	.69	−.16	.42	.33	−.18	.01	−.01	−.10	−.08
8009.	Regrets tests; need treaty	.24	.76	−.04	−.02	.25	.20	.17	−.13	−.23
8010.	Regrets rejection of US-UK	−.26	.59	−.51	−.32	−.09	.00	.12	.01	.05
8012.	De-nuclearize Africa	.31	−.03	.48	.42	.05	.01	.11	−.52	−.10
8016.	Nuclear vs. humanity	.85	−.02	.29	.17	.07	.01	.04	−.19	−.09
1023.	Non-nuclear club	.31	.00	.47	.38	.09	.06	.01	−.53	−.19
8044.	Question of Algeria	.35	.07	.46	.30	.05	−.00	.02	−.58	−.12
1026.	P.D.R. & UNCURK	−.29	.37	−.67	−.32	−.04	.07	.15	.05	.14
8054.	Report of UNCURK	−.47	.35	−.58	−.43	−.03	−.04	.11	.12	−.05
8055.	Deplores Hungary	−.72	.31	−.47	−.22	.07	−.00	.07	.08	.03
8064.	Non-interference (Cuba)	.48	−.17	.57	.49	.03	−.13	−.01	−.07	−.02
8065.	Friendly relations with Cuba	.67	−.15	.54	.29	−.04	−.17	.02	−.09	−.08
2002.	Trade conference	.83	−.06	.31	.19	−.11	−.11	.07	−.23	−.04

2005.	Primary commodities	.44	.11	.11	.03	.67	−.04	.11	−.25	−.19
8038.	Study trade conference	−.34	.48	−.41	−.45	−.09	.07	.14	.03	.12
2010.	Special int. devel. agency	.67	.06	−.09	.30	.43	−.05	−.08	.13	−.29
2015.	Conference on patents	−.60	.05	.03	−.38	−.51	−.10	.09	−.14	.01
8039.	Capital & technical assist.	.06	.78	−.07	−.10	.12	.02	.18	.26	.03
8041.	Population & econ. devel.	.23	−.16	.51	.05	−.02	−.26	.07	−.43	.25
8001.	Tibet on agenda	−.49	.43	−.47	−.39	.05	.05	.01	−.04	−.12
8043.	Resolution on Tibet	−.32	.48	−.56	−.49	.03	−.01	.03	−.02	−.10
3001.	Absentee marriage	.01	−.38	−.08	−.18	−.03	−.03	−.74	.12	−.14
3007.	"Hatred and hostility"	.82	−.13	.22	.13	.06	−.03	−.08	.13	−.02
3013.	Safeguard right of reply	.45	−.26	.23	.40	−.39	−.05	.01	−.27	.09
8011.	Algerian prisoners	.69	.01	.35	.09	−.01	−.11	.17	−.44	−.13
8017.	1962 end of colonialism	.72	−.30	.45	.19	−.04	−.08	−.07	−.13	−.05
8019.	W. Irian self-determination	−.32	.16	−.35	−.65	−.12	.20	−.07	.22	−.10
8020.	Commission on W. Irian	−.36	.16	−.38	−.63	−.10	.18	−.06	.29	−.06
8021.	Indian res. on W. Irian	.37	−.09	.35	.63	.23	−.05	−.02	−.33	−.03
8035.	Regrets Port non-compliance	−.85	.05	−.20	−.15	−.12	.06	−.11	.14	−.02
8037.	Renew CINSGT	.04	.84	−.11	−.11	.08	.07	.23	.02	−.24
4009.	Swedish res on S. Africa	−.84	.19	−.21	−.10	−.10	−.05	.08	−.09	−.04
8066.	Ask SC 17:S. Rhodesia SGT?	.91	−.04	.16	.21	.09	−.05	.06	−.07	−.06
8068.	S. Rhodesia on agenda	.90	−.00	.13	.22	.06	−.06	.02	−.12	−.04
8073.	"1 man 1 vote" S. Rhodesia	.86	−.07	.23	.20	−.07	−.04	.09	−.15	−.05
8075.	Regret UK on S. Rhodesia	.82	.05	.02	.23	.18	.04	.01	−.12	−.16
8056.	Condemn Portugal	.76	−.21	.40	.25	−.05	−.12	−.07	−.12	−.04
8058.	Report on Angola	.65	−.17	.37	.24	.10	−.05	−.07	−.10	.10
8059.	Angola & SC 17	.77	−.09	.31	.34	.06	−.05	−.06	−.11	.02
4001.	Burundi Prime Minister	−.85	.06	−.22	−.30	−.07	−.04	.00	.09	−.01
4021.	Rwanda & Burundi sovereign	−.58	.14	−.49	−.30	−.05	.00	.11	.14	−.14
8069.	Evacuate R. & B. by 1 Jul. 62	.75	−.20	.42	.31	−.03	−.11	−.08	−.15	.02
8070.	Rwanda & Burundi Evacuation	.30	.19	.09	.10	.12	.04	−.15	−.13	−.81
4023.	Rwanda & Burundi Evacuation	−.05	.70	−.14	−.09	.16	−.08	.26	.15	−.44
8071.	$2 million to S.G. for R.& B.	.01	.75	−.04	−.11	−.35	−.01	.10	−.03	−.14
5004.	5 Secretariat members/country	.64	.41	.21	.28	−.10	−.02	.24	.04	.03
8049.	Congo expenses and I.C.J.	−.51	.61	−.32	−.20	.11	−.02	−.13	−.10	−.01
8051.	Congo cost	−.28	.83	−.01	−.00	.07	.01	−.30	−.08	.17
8052.	U.N.E.F. expenses	−.36	.76	.02	−.11	.07	.06	−.29	−.06	.23
8053.	Budget for year 1962	−.12	.76	−.03	−.29	−.10	−.06	−.27	−.13	.01
8033.	Conf. on consular relations	.65	−.23	.56	.29	−.02	−.04	−.08	.01	.06

For the case of standardized voting scores and uncorrelated voting components, $r_{jk} = a_{jk}$; *thus Tables 1 and 2 can be interpreted both as correlations between roll calls and voting components, and as factor loadings.*

Factor analysts have traditionally sought to extract distinct sets of factor loadings, each explaining a maximum proportion of the correlations among variables (in our case, roll calls). A sequential procedure for determining uncorrelated columns of as many high factor loadings as possible can be derived using the calculus. In Table 1 the resulting columns of *a*'s are presented in the same order as the amount of voting variance they explain. For any particular column, factor loadings will have the same signs when "Yeses" represent the same point of view.

In this kind of analysis some analysts who believe that a Cold War alignment is paramount in all voting at the United Nations would expect correlations between all Assembly roll calls and this factor to be nearly unity. More sophisticated students of UN affairs suggest that at least two distinct voting conflicts underlie particular roll calls in differing degrees. Ernst Haas has interpreted Assembly politics in terms of a "balancing" process between Cold War demands and the political economic and anti-colonial demands of the under-developed countires.[13] John Stoessinger considers the two principal conflicts of our time to be the struggle between the Communist and the non-Communist worlds, and between the "new nationalism" of Asia, Africa and the Middle East and the waning empires of Europe.[14] In a similar way, Lincoln Bloomfield has described the General Assembly as:

"... a prime political forum for the nations which remain outside the East-West camps and pursue their own goals of political independence, economic improvement and racial dignity. In this situation what might be called the North-South conflict cuts across the East-West issues and makes its own powerful demands on American diplomacy at the same time offering frequent opportunities for the Soviets to seize the political initiative."[15]

The Most Frequent Conflicts in Assembly Voting Behavior. Looking at what is called the unrotated factor matrix in Table 1, we see that a single conflict, which we shall call "East vs. West," did in fact dominate most issues before the United Nations, with the exception of budgetary concerns. By adding up squared correlations in the first column of Table 1, we can say that this one factor accounts for the equivalent of 37 entire roll calls. This represents about 53 per cent of all votes cast on the seventy roll calls being analyzed or about 64 per cent of

---

[13]Ernst Haas, "Regionalism, Functionalism, and Universal International Organization," *World Politics*, Vol. 8, No. 2 (January, 1956), pp. 238-63.

[14]John G. Stoessinger, *The Might of Nations* (New York, 1961).

[15]Lincoln Bloomfield, *The United Nations and United States Foreign Policy* (Boston, 1960), p. 10.

"explainable" voting alignments.[16] Prominent among the variety of issues loading above 0.60 on this "East-West" factor are South Africa, Palestine, Chinese membership, disarmament, Hungary, Korea, West Irian, Southern Rhodesia, Angola, and Rwanda and Burundi.

A second conflict, "explaining" about 13 per cent of the "interpretable" voting variation, was paramount on several resolutions dealing with nuclear testing, economic aid, the renewal of the Committee on Information from Non-Self-Governing Territories, other votes on Rwanda and Burundi, and most of the questions regarding the financing of the Congo Operation.

The inferred alignments of the main states and regional groupings in the Assembly on these two factors are plotted in Figure 1.[17] Looking at Figure 1 helps to suggest why Bloomfield's "North-South" and "East-West" labels have been chosen from among various possibilities to identify the two most frequent conflicts in the Assembly. With only a few obvious exceptions, the similarity between inferred voting positions of states and regional groupings and their geographical locations in a two-dimensional map of the world are rather striking. West Europeans, Latin Americans, Afro-Asians and the Soviet Bloc are almost entirely in their correct quadrants. The most notable exceptions are that South Africa and France are farther "North" than the other "colonial" countries; non-colonial Scandinavians are farther "South"; and pro-West Asians are farther "West" because of their ties with the United States. Note how the Soviet Union was very "Northern" on the 50-megaton bomb issue; she joined a few extreme colonial powers on the renewal of the Committee on Information from Non-Self-Governing Territories, and agreed further with these states on economic aid, and financing UN operations in the Congo and Rwanda and Burundi.

Another significant finding, however, is that besides these two major voting alignments, the matrix in Table 1 suggests that other conflicts and disagreements underlay voting positions at the Sixteenth Assembly. In fact, seven other alignments were found in the factor analysis, accounting for about 23 per cent of the "interpretable" voting variation. Like those noticed above, they can perhaps be interpreted by looking at the votes loading heavily on them in the factor matrix and by looking at the inferred policy positions (factor scores) of states on them.

---

[16] All uncorrelated factors underlying or "explaining" more than the variance of a single roll call were extracted and are presented in Table I. For the rationale for stopping factoring at this point, see Harry H. Harmon, *op. cit.*, ch. 14. The variances "explained" by these nine dimensions of conflict are 37.0, 7.8, 4.2, 1.8, 1.4, 1.4, 1.1, 1.0, leaving only 17% of all voting "unexplained."

[17] In matrix notation the equation(s) in footnote 12 can be written as $\hat{V} = AC$. When A is not a square matrix, component scores are given by the equation $C = (A'A)^{-1} A'V$. See Henry Kaiser, "Formulas for Component Scores," *Psychometrika*, Vol. 27 (March, 1962), pp. 83-8. As calculated here, these sets of factor scores are very nearly uncorrelated with each other.

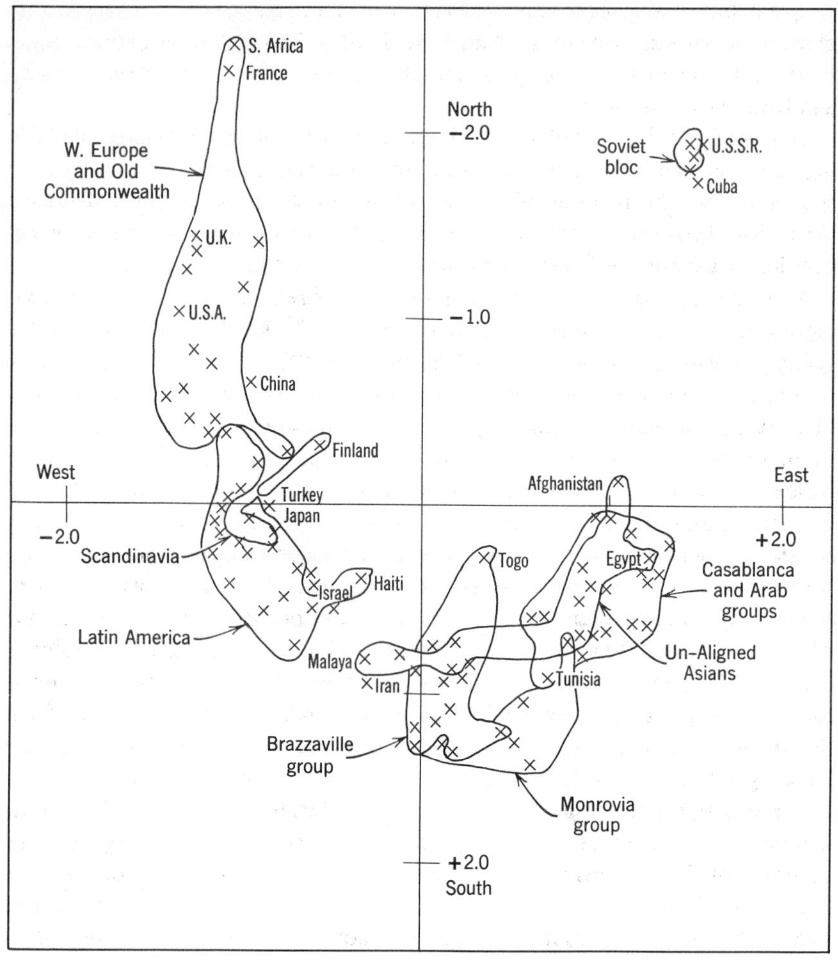

Figure 1. Unrotated factor scores on the East-West and North-South conflicts at the Sixteenth General Assembly.

The third principal conflict, for instance, contains aspects of the Cold War, including Chinese membership in the United Nations, uncaptured by the first two factors.

A Substantive Interpretation of Assembly Conflicts. One way to get a "better look" at the specific content of the first two as well as the remaining factors would be somehow to adjust the factor matrix, keeping the factors uncorrelated, so that each roll call would load very highly on *just one* factor. Such a new factor would be purely and simply interpretable in terms of the common content of, and voting positions on, the roll calls correlating heavily with it. Keeping the same number of voting dimensions, it is possible to find new sets of factor loadings approximating such an ideal factor matrix containing only zeros or ones. This can be done objectively by the use of Kaiser's "normal varimax" rotation technique for obtaining a factor matrix with a "simple structure."[18]

Geometrically, this technique can be visualized in terms of a space of dimensionality sufficient to explain all the main components of Assembly voting. Keeping the same configuration of roll calls in this space, its perpendicular axes can be rotated until the roll calls have the desired loadings (coordinates) on the factor axes. Although the rotated sets of coordinates would still be uncorrelated, they would no longer come in the order of maximum additional voting behavior "explained." Rather, the axes are rotated to a position where their substantive, as opposed to their behavioral, meaning should be most clear. Whether or not these newly perceived conflicts will have any relation to the functional committees where they occurred should also be more clearly discernible than was possible in the unrotated factor matrix.

Before turning to the rotated factor matrix, it may be helpful to recall several existing theoretical conceptions of the multi-dimensional conflict process in the General Assembly. George Liska has suggested that international organization may be treated as part of a "dynamic interplay of institutional military-political, and socio-economic factors and pressures," constituting to a greater or lesser degree, a "multiple equilibrium."[19] Writing in 1956, Ernst Haas suggested that the functional and security claims of the different regional systems have emerged as "the source of the actual functioning of universal international organizations" and that a "balancing" or equilibrium process in both regional groups and the international system connect the two together.[20] Something of the specifics of how a variety of controversies interact in UN votes is suggested by the following prescription of an experienced diplomat for predicting voting behavior:

"Apart from genuine satellites . . . there are other cases where reasonably safe predictions may be made, but on the basis of a more complex calculus. Thus Pakistan . . . as a member of CENTO [likes] to vote with the West, but is also sensitive to Afro-Asian opinion, particularly sensitive to opinion in Moslem countries and strong on self-determination (Kashmir). A Western canvasser can therefore safely count on Pakistan's vote in a direct East-West controversy (Cuba, Hungary) but must make separate calculations if relevant racial, religious or colonial

[18] See Harmon, *loc. cit.* A further step, not taken in this article, would be to find the simplest factor structure using correlated (oblique) factors.

[19] George Liska, *International Equilibrium* (Cambridge, Harvard University Press, 1957).

[20] Ernst B. Haas, "Regionalism," *op. cit.*, esp. pp. 238-41, 160-63.

factors are involved. For example, in a 'colonialist' issue where the 'Moslem' factor tells on the 'colonialist' side (Cyprus), or where the Kashmir issue comes into play (Goa), the West may reasonably expect Pakistan's support. On the other hand, on a straight racial issue (apartheid), or an issue where a Western power is, or has been, in conflict with Moslem populations (Suez, Algeria, Tunisia, Israel) Pakistan will be . . . the most anti-colonialist Afro-Asian. On such issues where both anti-colonialism and the Cold War are involved–for example the Soviet moves on the liquidation of colonialism–accurate prediction of a Pakistan vote becomes impossible."[21]

While not dealing explicitly with the different functional nature of these conflicts, this quotation, as we shall see, is very suggestive of a set of adequate political categories for describing substantive conflicts in the General Assembly.

Turning to the rotated factor matrix in Table 2, we see that most factors are quite simply structured and also remarkably clear in their substantive content. The first four of them, all relatively frequent conflicts in the General Assembly, will receive more detailed consideration.[22] It should be made clear that these interpretations are based on the author's judgment, with which others may disagree; under the assumptions of the model being used, however, the factors themselves are objectively derived from actual voting behavior.

New factors need new names; we shall call the first *"self-determination"* because it consists of most of the anti-colonial demands of the Afro-Asian states regarding South Africa, Angola, Southern Rhodesia and Rwanda-Burundi. Boxing the factor loadings greater than 0.60 in magnitude helps substantiate this description. The economic component of Afro-Asian "self-determination" demands is also brought our clearly by the high loadings of votes 2002, 2010 and 2015 on trade, aid and patent inquiries. Their desire for more jobs and a greater voice in the Secretariat explains why vote 5004 also loads on this factor. Vote 3007 found a similar group of states opposing the advocacy of racial hatred, as an incitement to discrimination and hostility.

Although it is important to distinguish "self-determination" questions from "East-West" alignments, it is clear from comparing the first columns of Table 1 and Table 2 that our new perspective is not yet very different from the earlier one. Almost all of the votes loading highly on the "self-determination" conflict also were closely correlated with characteristic "East-West" voting positions as summarized in Figure 1. The main difference is that quite a few Cold War

---

[21] Conor Cruise O'Brien, *To Katanga and Back* (London, Hutchinson, 1962), p. 18.

[22] These rotated factors "explain" the equivalent of 22.7, 8.7, 10.2, 7.6, 1.8, 1.4, 1.6, 2.4, and 1.6 roll calls respectively.

controversies—Tibet, Cuba, Korea and especially Chinese membership—load more heavily on the new third rotated factor which we shall now examine.

It is quite clear from the boxed entries in the third column of the rotated factor matrix that the proper representation of China forms the largest part of a second distinct conflict in the General Assembly. We shall therefore identify the third factor as *Cold War membership* controversies. The usual alignment on this question at the Sixteenth Assembly pitted the United States, Latin America (except Cuba), most of the Brazzaville group, pro-Western Asians and most Western Europeans against India, Scandinavians, the Soviet bloc and most other Afro-Asians. A slightly confounding feature of the voting was that it was not clear on votes 8030 and 8031 that a declaration to remove Nationalist China was also binding. On these two votes the Soviet bloc, Cuba and several other states in favor of admission abstained; on vote 8032, however, they took their customary positions.

One of the most interesting results of this analysis is the degree to which such *bona fide* Cold War issues as Hungary, Cuba, disarmament and Korea overlapped the self-determination and Cold War membership conflicts. Granting "recognition" to the People's Democratic Republic of Korea at UNCURK meeting (vote 1026) was mostly a Cold War membership question; inviting everyone to a conference on consular relations (vote 8033), however, looks slightly more like a self-determination issue. As we have already noted, one reason for this phenomenon has to do with the similarity between East-West and self-determination controversies. Their relations to the Cold War membership controversy may be brought out more clearly by examining more closely the behavior of the Soviet Bloc, of the Latin Americans and of the Brazzaville group of Africans. It is clear that Soviet disarmament moves were designed to invoke an increasingly East-West or anti-European response: votes 8006 and 1010 called for a modest approval of the work of the UN Scientific Committee on the Effects of Atomic Radiation and for "general and complete disarmament;" vote 8016 summarizes the plenary voting on several paragraphs to the effect that the use of thermonuclear weapons is contrary to the laws of humanity and the Charter. Russia joined an almost solid Afro-Asian caucus in supporting the resolution. Most Afro-Asians also supported a preambular paragraph invoking the principles of non-intervention and self-determination regarding Cuba (vote 8064). On the other hand, almost solid Arab-African abstentions greeted a Western resolution (8055) deploring the disregard of Assembly resolutions regarding Hungary. The distinctive feature of the Chinese membership votes was that the Brazzaville group of states either abstained or backed the American position, while Scandinavians, the Casablanca group and non-aligned Asians did not.

Another reason why "self-determination" and some Cold War alignments have become similar is that Latin Americans, who in previous years have often voted in favor of "self-determination," were much less inclined to do so at the Sixteenth

Assembly. They were probably reacting both to increased Soviet initiatives on "self-determination" questions and to the new, powerful and more radical African members of the Assembly. Thus they abstained on vote 8066 requesting the Committee of 17 to consider Southern Rhodesia and opposed a Soviet initiative (8069) on troop evacuations from Rwanda-Burundi.

Mongi Slim, the President of the Sixteenth General Assembly, has called the United Nations a "supranational framework within which conflicts of interest between nations could be at least attenuated, if not solved."[23] The main reasons for identifying the second rotated factor as *"UN supranationalism"* are the heavy loadings of crucial UNEF and Congo budgetary questions on it. The increasingly supranational role the United Nations has played in the Suez situation and the Congo crisis has been a major subject of controversy in the General Assembly, related to self-determination and the Cold War, but also distinct from them. Along with the enhancement of United Nations authority in these and related areas as a result of her activities there, some colonial states, such as France, Portugal, Belgium and South Africa have joined with the Soviet Bloc in obstructing the supranationalist strivings of the smaller UN members. Alone among the Great Powers, the United States has usually backed such initiatives. As such, these conflicts cut squarely across the East-West struggle. States normally close to the Soviet Union, such as Yugoslavia, Ghana, Guinea, India and Indonesia, voted against her on the apportionment of UNEF costs (vote 8052), the Congo authorization for 1962 (8051), a request for the Soviet Union to refrain from exploding her fifty megaton bomb (8008) and an expression of regret at the resumption of nuclear tests (8009). Belgium, France, South Africa, Portugal, and even the United States (on nuclear testing) opposed at least some of these resolutions. Votes 4023, 8071 and 8072 discussed above, also represent a successful "supranational" effort by the majority of UN members, despite Soviet objections and certain colonial hesitations, to ease the birth pains of Rwanda and Burundi in what might have become another Congo situation. Finally, votes 8039, requesting one percent of National Products in "capital" and technical assistance, and 8037, renewing the Committee of Information on Non-Self-Governing Territories, represent similar small-power aspirations and Great Power objections.

The fourth major component of UN voting, which we might call the *"Moslem factor"* after Conor Cruise O'Brien, is composed of Palestine and West Irian mediation attempts.[24] On these questions the Soviet Bloc supported Arab demands, Old Europeans and Latin Americans were somewhat divided, and most

---

[23] Cited in N. J. Padelford and R. Emerson, *Africa and World Order* (New York, 1963), p. 45.

[24] The West Irian roll calls were all in plenary meetings but are listed in Tables 1 and 2 with other colonial questions because they were discussed in terms of the Declaration on the Granting of Independence to Colonial Countries and Peoples.

importantly, the Brazzaville states, objecting to Arab and Indonesian notions of "self-determination," refused to support the majority of Afro-Asians.[25]

We may describe the remaining five voting components in lesser detail. Factor VI reflects certain Latin, Benelux and Scandinavian misgivings about the composition of the Conciliation Commission (vote 0018, discussed above). The ninth rotated factor is limited to residual colonial misgivings about intervention in Rwanda and Burundi (vote 8070). These same European colonial states have usually been the ones refusing to support anti-colonial domestic intervention by the United Nations in condemning *apartheid* (perhaps what O'Brien would call a "race factor"). About half of the West European and Old Commonwealth states were isolated on vote 2005 concerning commodity regulations, probably because of the definite anti-Common Market flavor of Second Committee discussions (Factor V). A more peculiar coalition of the Soviet Bloc and several Latin Americans appeared in voting on marriage rules in the Third Committee (vote 3001, Factor VII). Finally, the coalition of conservative Westerners with conservative Afro-Asians (the Brazzaville group) on votes 8012, 1023 and 8044 is probably due to special "French concerns" on nuclear testing and Algerian problems (Factor VIII).

Some Comparisons. This paper has empirically characterized the principal conflicts in the General Assembly. The results of the unrotated and the rotated factor analyses shed some light on current interpretations of international politics. Looking at frequent voting alignments, one-factor theories were found at best to describe 64 per cent of explainable Assembly voting. Again focusing on voting behavior more than substantive interpretations, a two-dimensional geopolitical picture was offered that corresponded quite closely to several previous descriptions of current international politics. East-West and North-South alignments (as shown in Figure 1) together underlie about 77 per cent of interpretable Assembly voting behavior. Because the unrotated factors were more easily identified by looking at voting alignments, the geopolitical interpretation was given a behavioral label.

In looking at the same spatial configuration of roll calls from a different perspective (the simply structured factor matrix in Table 2), *four* different substantive issues were found: self-determination, Cold War and related membership questions, UN supranationalism, and Moslem questions (in the Near and Far East). Going beyond an increasingly popular two-dimensional view of world politics, this four-dimensional perspective helps to explain 85 per cent of generally interpretable Assembly voting. It also has the advantages of clearer substantive

---

[25] An important argument for both this fourfold substantive classification and the two-dimensional geopolitical interpretation offered earlier is that similar analyses seem appropriate for the Second, Seventh and Twelfth General Assemblies. *Cf.* Alker, *op. cit.*, or Alker and Russett, *op. cit.* (forthcoming).

meaning than the unrotated factor matrix[26] and of labels corresponding quite closely to several interpretations of Assembly politics offered by diplomatic participants. O'Brien, for example, missed only supranationalism among these four factors, while he also distinguished one of the most important remaining conflicts.

Several of the rotated factors also turn out to be more functionally specific than the East-West and North-South divisions. From the rotated factor matrix (Table 2) it is clear that self-determination issues pervade the General Assembly. Supranationalist votes are found in disarmament, economic, and especially Trusteeship and Fifth Committee contexts. The Special Political and Fourth Committees were the scene of Moslem demands evoking alignments unlike the usual anti-European or anti-West self-determination response; Cold War issues, including Chinese membership, have been largely "political" questions.

To some extent controversies in the Assembly with particular functional bases have produced "cross-cutting conflicts" as suggested by Chadwick Alger and others.[27] Problems of enlarging the scope of UN activities in these areas have divided both East and West. Negative agreements between colonial powers and the Soviet bloc on North-South or supranationalist issues have temporarily brought opponents in the East-West struggle closer together. But on major political conflicts issues such as ONUC and UNEF, increments to UN authority have come not so much from an indirect functional approach to world peace, as from American policy decisions to cooperate with the developing countries in opposition to other colonial powers and the Soviet bloc. Russian commitment to the symbols of self-determination has to some extent influenced the anti-colonial states; but this commitment has also restricted Soviet movements with supranationalist consequences. With anti-colonial Afro-Asians against Soviet or American intervention in the Congo, the Soviet Union gradually and belatedly had to withdraw from her support of the UN Congo operation.[28] Subsequent Russian financial vetoes have been only partly successful in preventing the UN from performing its peacekeeping role.

---

[26] Analyses of the East-West conflict in simple behavioral terms often run into the same confusion that Hovet notes regarding similar Soviet and Afro-Asian voting behavior: they do not distinguish Cold War from self-determination issues. Empirically, the "substantive" and "behavioral" viewpoints are complementary. Each roll call can be checked as to both its rotated and unrotated components. Correlating factor loadings or factor scores makes this relationship explicit. The East-West and North-South correlations of self-determination factor scores are 0.74 and 0.43. The same numbers for the Cold War alignment are 0.50 and -0.20; for Moslem questions they are 0.39 and -0.12; and for supranationalism factor scores -0.25 and -0.86.

[27] Chadwick Alger, "Non-Resolutional Consequences of the United Nations and Their Effect on International Conflict," *Journal of Conflict Resolution,* Vol. 5, No. 2 (June, 1961, pp. 128-47.

[28] Early Soviet support of Security Council resolutions on the Congo is sometimes overlooked. See Alexander Dallin, *The Soviet Union at the United Nations* (New York, 1962), ch. 10.

II CORRELATES AND CONSEQUENCES OF ASSEMBLY CONFLICTS

The suggestion that *political* conflicts preoccupy members of the United Nations implies that the national interests of UN members, shaped as they are by domestic, regional, political, economic and ethnic considerations, are more causally determinative ot UN policy positions than caucusing-group pressures at the UN. There is, for instance, a considerable degree of overlap between geographic regions and active groups at the United Nations in the case of Africans, Latin Americans, West Europeans and the Soviet Bloc. The Commonwealth and Casablanca groups are those with the least geographical basis. The analysis below is directed toward testing just how well caucusing-group memberships and national political variables, the "environment" of the UN system, correlate with voting positions there. Hovet, for example, in *Bloc Politics in the United Nations,* has suggested that environmentally based "common interest groups" operate in the UN in addition to the more formalized caucuses. Among these groups he includes "underdeveloped countries," "colonial powers," "anti-colonial states" and Moslem states."[29] In another context, Ernst Haas has suggested that the nature of a state's political system (democracy, oligarchy or totalitarianism), its region, its state of economic development and its Cold War allegiance might be helpful foci for studying international voting and ratification behavior.[30] Bruce Russett has found that military cooperation (alliances and the stationing of troops), economic interdependence (as measured by shares of export and import trade) and foreign aid are partial determinants of conflict policies in international relations.[31]

Turning to Table 3, we see that group memberships do correlate quite highly with factor scores on all but the Cold War membership controversy in the General Assembly. The table brings out quite clearly the regional identification of the protagonists in all conflicts but that one. We can thus confirm, from the higher entries in the table, our earlier interpretations that the East-West controversy is most clearly a contest between Old Europeans and the Soviet bloc; that the North-South conflict pits Africans, Arabs and Asians against the Soviet bloc and, to a lesser extent, against Old Europeans; but these Africans, particularly the Casablanca states, oppose Old Europeans on self-determination issues. Casablanca, Arab and Brazzaville states took very different positions on Moslem questions (Palestine and West Irian); while on the supranationalist alignment

---

[29]The chart on page 126 summarizes membership in both kinds of groupings in 1959.

[30]Ernst Haas, "System and Process in the International Labor Organization: A Statistical Afterthought," *loc. cit.*

[31]Bruce M. Russett, "The Calculus of Deterence," *The Journal of Conflict Resolution,* Vol. 7, No. 2 (June, 1963), pp. 97-109, and *Community and Contention: Britain and America in the Twentieth Century* (Cambridge, 1963), ch. IV.

Table 3 Correlations between Group Memberships and Factor Scores on the Main Conflicts in the 16th General Assembly[a]

Group Memberships	Unrotated Factor Scores		Rotated Factor Scores			
	East vs. West	North vs. South	Self-Determination	Cold War	Moslem Questions	UN Supranationalism
1. Old Europeans	−.58*	−.43	−.74*	.10	−.25	−.08
2. Latin caucus	−.38	.07	−.21	−.36	.00	.06
3. Soviet Bloc	.50*	−.63*	.20	.27	.13	−.79*
4. Arab caucus	.36	.17	.19	.05	.55*	.12
5. Casablanca group . . .	.05	.37	.53*	−.22	−.56*	.09
6. Brazzaville group . . .	.32	.18	.18	.24	.33	.20
7. Africans	.22	.49	.62	−.02	−.45	.26
8. Asians	.10	.23	.03	.01	.20	.27

[a]Point biserial correlations over 0.50 in magnitude have been asterisked for convenience. The rotated factor scores referred to in this table and elsewhere in this paper are slightly intercorrelated (below 0.10) because Russian abstentions on Chinese membership have been considered affirmative votes and because self-determination scores have been revised to take into account the positions of extreme colonial powers on two nearly unanimous roll calls not included in the factor analysis.

the Soviet bloc and to a lesser extent Old Europeans opposed an Afro-Asian majority.[32]

The search for a more adequate explanation of the "reasons for" or the "environmental determinants of" Cold War voting brings us to Table 4. The large number of asterisked entries suggest immediately that, except for Moslem questions, we can explain each of the major conflicts in the United Nations with "environmental variables" at least as accurately and probably more cogently than with caucusing group variables. Thus on East-West voting a military alliance with the United States is an extremely good predictor of voting behavior (the correlation is 0.77). Describing this conflict (but not the Cold War and Chinese membership issue) as "democracies versus totalitarians" also has some truth to it. An excolonial

[32]Arend Lijphart, *op. cit.*, has correctly pointed out the limitations of arbitrarily chosen groups in the study of Assembly politics. The groupings of states used in Table 3 represent combinations of regular and *ad hoc* caucusing units and regional interest groups. They serve as a convenient compromise between inductively found groupings (as in Figure 1) and Hovet's list of regular caucusing groups (*Africa in the United Nations,* p. 74.). Old Europeans are a frequently united group of West Europeans, Old Commonwealth members, the United States and South Africa; Mongolia is considered only a member of the Soviet bloc; Turkey and Cyprus are considered Asian states. Arabs, Africans and Asians have been exclusively defined with respect to each other, Old Europeans and the Soviet bloc. Yugoslavia, Israel and Nationalist China have not been listed with any group.

Table 4 Correlations between Environmental Variables and Voting Positions on the Main Conflicts in the 16th General Assembly[a]

Environmental Variables	Unrotated Factor Scores		Rotated Factor Scores			
	East vs. West	North vs. South	Self-Determination	Cold War	Moslem Questions	UN Supranationalism
Economic Variables						
9. Recent U. S. aid	–.18	.17	–.13	–.26	.16	.19
10. Postwar U. S. aid	–.44	–.13	–.48	.05	–.12	.05
11. Percent trade with U. S.	–.49	.18	–.29	–.45	.00	.20
12. Percent trade with U. S., U. K., France	–.28	.63*	.22	–.39	–.33	.53*
13. Recent Soviet aid	.50*	–.05	.18	.46	.21	–.09
14. Postwar Soviet aid. . . .	.54*	–.03	.19	.47	.28	–.03
15. Percent trade with Soviet Bloc	.57*	–.63*	.19	.38	.20	–.76*
16. Per capita G.N.P. (1955)	–.43	–.46	–.59*	.09	–.19	–.20
17. G.N.P. (1955)	–.01	–.34	–.11	.03	.02	–.25
Political Variables						
18. U. S. military ally	–.77*	.13	–.68*	–.35	–.17	.08
19. Communist state	.59*	–.56*	.24	.38	.20	–.68*
20. Democracy	–.52*	.04	–.47	–.09	–.17	.27
21. Totalitarian regime . . .	.45	–.44	.22	.29	.11	–.53*
22. Colonial Power (since 1917)	–.43	–.46	–.50*	–.11	–.05	–.16
23. Ex-colony (since 1917).	.51*	.58*	.67*	.11	.06	.37
Sociological Variables						
24. Percent European descent	–.28	–.65*	–.57*	.20	–.12	–.42
25. Percent Negro	.15	.41	.52*	–.04	–.45	.19
26. Percent Moslem	.41	.29	.34	.04	.41	.19

[a]Aid figures are in per capita U. S. dollars; recent aid is from 1957 to 1961 or 1962 (in the Soviet case); trade figures are based on 1961 data. The numbering of variables is continued from Table 3. Sources, definitions of variables, data, and estimates of inaccuracies are available from the Yale Political Data Program. N for this table and the previous one is 101, except for correlations with variables 9, 10, 11, 13, 14 where *a priori* missing data reduced it to 100 or 91. Throughout this and previous tables, Honduras, Gabon and Tanganyika have been omitted because of their high voting absenteeism.

past is also relevant, particularly regarding the self-determination aspects of the East-West alignment. Soviet aid and trade and to a lesser extent similar variables for the Western Big Three are also correlated with East-West voting. A significant finding is that in each of the two main geopolitical conflicts, *trade, not aid,* is the better predictor of voting behavior. As we shall see below, the "environmental" approach to UN voting using such key variables in world politics as trade, aid and military alliances will predict East-West voting positions with just as much accuracy as caucusing group memberships more immediate to the actual voting.

Trade, colonial past, per capita Gross National Product (an indicator of economic development) and the percentage of a nation's population that is of European descent, probably with similar sympathies, are suggestive correlates of North-South voting, but they raise the important question of their relative explanatory importance when the remaining variables are controlled for, a question regression analysis can be used to answer.

Turning to the substantive conflicts in the Assembly, racial variables, economic development, colonial history and American military alliances all influence policy positions (factor scores) on self-determination. Trade and aid, as indicators of what might be best described as a two-way process of interdependence rather than just "buying votes," help improve our understanding of the reasons for Cold War membership alignments. Even from the simple correlations in Table 4 it is evident that *Soviet* (not American) aid either in years since 1957 or in the entire post-World War II period is a good predictor of voting for Communist Chinese membership in the United Nations. Whether the Soviets should be regarded as influential in "buying votes" or as only "rewarding" their friends is a more difficult question which will not be discussed here. On Moslem questions, racial and religious variables do seem to underly the voting pattern, but these have also been modified by caucusing group policy decisions, as we saw in Table 3. As an indicator of economic interdependence, trade with the Big Three (but not Western military alliances this time) correlates highly with supranationalism. Even though data for within-Bloc trade seem to underestimate Bloc solidarity, trade with the Soviet Bloc is as high a correlate of the anti-supranationalist position as was Soviet Bloc membership. From Table 4 it also appears that both democracies and ex-colonial states have contributed to the growth of the United Nations in the present era.

Correlations cannot be considered causal explanations until the observer has controlled for the effects of other possibly relevant variables. Multiple regression analysis takes an important step in that direction: it provides a linear model for explaining a "dependent" variable, such as East-West voting positions, as the sum of distinctive contributions from several "independent" variables, such as foreign aid and military alliances. For individual nations, residual differences between actual and predicted values of the dependent variable can be calculated and subjected to further analysis; for the entire UN membership, squared multiple correlation coefficients indicate the percentage of voting variation explained by the model.[33]

In a regression equation each coefficient of an independent variable tells the direction and the amount of the average change in the dependent variable associated with a unit change in only that one independent variable. The units of the independent variables may be either *concrete,* in policy terms such as dollars of aid or membership in the Latin American caucusing group, or *standardized* to reflect what on a worldwide scale appear as equiprobable changes.[34] When several logically prior variables are each distinctively related to Assembly voting positions on a particular conflict, a linear regression equation provides a simple but attractive theoretical statement of a multivariate explanatory relationship.

In regression equations 1 through 4, abbreviated alphabetic labels taken from Table 4 denote both the independent and the dependent variables. The dependent variables, standardized voting ranks, can be interpreted as distances (roughly, inches) along either axis of Figure 1 or of a similar picture for rotated Cold War and supranationalism alignments. Taken from among the most promising explanatory variables in Table 4, the combinations of independent variables are not exhaustive, but only intended to test several explanations of UN voting reviewed earlier in this article.[35]

---

[33]The R^2s for equations 1 to 4 below are exceptionally high ones in social research. The multiple correlation coefficient of the East-West model is 0.88. The equation explains 78% of the major voting alignment in the General Assembly. Similarly, the North-South Model explains 70%, the Cold War and supranationalism models 48% and 44% respectively. Even for factor scores in their present largely uncorrelated form (see note to Table 3), high correlations with the rotated self-determination conflict indicate that influences affecting these policy positions differ from those which determine Cold War membership alignments.

Using regional and caucusing-group variables that are much more immediate to the voting (see Table 3), the corresponding R^2s are roughly similar: 0.79, 0.78, 0.30 and 0.72. Cold War membership alignments can be explained better by more distant environmental variables, like aid and trade, than by caucusing-group memberships. Supranationalism and self-determination (with group membership regressions explaining 72% and 85% respectively) definitely reflect a good deal of group cohesion. Group cohesion by itself, however, is a poor predictor of what a group has agreed on, for which additional explanations, like equations 1 to 4, are required.

[34]In the case of a standardized dependent variable, standardized B-coefficients are obtained by multiplying a concrete b-coefficient times the standard deviation of its independent variable. B-coefficients are comparable; b-weights are not.

[35]In these equations b-coefficients are given with the independent variables, B-weights are given below them in parentheses. The concrete units for dichotomous variables (e.g., alliances) are 1 or 0; for aid figures they are $100 per capita; for per capita G.N.P. $1,000; and for all percentage figures, 100%. It should be noted that the communist "independent" variables are highly intercorrelated, enough so that further analysis using a single index of communist ties might be desirable.

$$\begin{aligned} EW = &- .29PUSA + .74RUSA + .23TWUUF - .96USALY + 2.00PSBA \\ &\quad (-0.31) \quad (0.02) \quad (0.05) \quad (-0.47) \quad (0.24) \\ &- .23RSBA + 1.35TWSB + .58COMM \\ &\quad (-0.02) \quad (0.28) \quad (0.20) \end{aligned} \tag{1}$$

$$\begin{aligned} CWM = &.50PUSA - 1.44RUSA - .15TWUUF - .63USALY + 1.85PSBA \\ &\quad (0.54) \quad (-0.04) \quad (-0.03) \quad (-0.31) \quad (0.22) \\ &+ 1.46RSBA + 1.01TWSB + .20COMM \\ &\quad (0.14) \quad (0.21) \quad (0.07) \end{aligned} \tag{2}$$

$$\begin{aligned} NS = &.71TWUUF + .50EXECY - 1.50TWSB - .38COMM \\ &\quad (0.15) \quad (0.25) \quad (-0.31) \quad (-0.13) \\ &- .40EURDS - .39PCGNP \\ &\quad (-0.18) \quad (-0.16) \end{aligned} \tag{3}$$

$$\begin{aligned} UNSUP = &.57EXECY + .44DEM - .96TOT - .11COLP - .49PCGNP \\ &\quad (0.28) \quad (0.22) \quad (-0.41) \quad (-0.04) \quad (-0.19) \end{aligned} \tag{4}$$

Equation 1 tells us, for instance, that either a Western military alliance or one hundred dollars of postwar Soviet Bloc per capita aid (Syria, Guinea and Ghana have received about half this amount) would polarize UN voting patterns on the East-West controversy. Since 1957, however, both Soviet and American aid have moved toward the uncommited, away from their own camps. The effect of an increase in trade with the Big Three is roughly one-fifth as large as for a similar Soviet-bloc trade increase. Although the standardized coefficients are similar, dollar for dollar, Soviet aid has been much more strongly related to East-West voting alignments in the United Nations. An "alliance" of communist political-economic systems in Cuba, Guinea, Mali and the Soviet Bloc also had a considerable Eastern influence in 1961 and 1962. Looking specifically at the Cold War membership aspects of the East-West alignment, equation 2 states the opposite tendencies of long-term and short-term American aid, the anti-communist pull of an American military alliance, and consistent relationships between long term *and* recent Soviet aid and voting on Chinese representation in the Assembly.

The third equation tells us that being 100 percent of European descent makes for only about a fourth as much Northern voting as would total trade with the Soviet Bloc. Being a communist state creates about as much Northern voting as a per capita G.N.P. of a thousand dollars. Being an ex-European colony and trading about 70 percent of the time with the Western Big Three would together move a state about an "inch" (on Figure 1) in the Southern direction. On the related supranationalism conflict, ex-colonial status and political democracy are both about equally strong "causes" of supranationalist voting, while totalitarian and developed states tend to demur. An analysis of residuals shows that even equation 4 underestimates the supranationalist tendencies of the Casablanca and Brazzaville groups, as well as the anti-supranationalist tendencies of the Soviet bloc.

Deterministic as the coefficients in the factor matrix and the regression equations just given may seem, they represent opportunities for domestic politicians and foreign service diplomats to reshape international politics by changing these relationships. In the last two decades "issues" on the world scene have been perceived differently (loaded on different factors in succeeding years) with dramatically different consequences; and environmental variables (like military alliances) have become increasingly or decreasingly "influential" in determining policy positions. American foreign aid has increased in its relevance to the Cold War struggle in the UN, but still remains fairly uncorrelated on a world-wide basis with this conflict. If it were to become highly correlated in this manner, an effective neutral and supranationalist role for the anti-colonial countries would be increasingly difficult. South African racial policies have become increasingly East-West and self-determination issues with foreboding consequences; West Irian remained distinct enough from these contests for some progress to be made. The Soviet Union failed significantly to make the Congo crisis into an anti-European and anti-American self-determination issue, although she and the Casablanca states tried to do so. Many of the elements of such a conflict were certainly there; but fortunately (for us) Russia misperceived Afro-Asian and American supranationalist predispositions. The danger with Cold War issues like Hungary and Tibet is that they will become increasingly perceived as anti-Western self-determination conflicts; the American opportunity—and challenge for our policymakers—is to persuade others and ourselves of the United Nations' universal supranationalist possibilities.

IV THE UNITED NATIONS AS AN ACTOR IN WORLD POLITICS

A. THE MAINTENANCE OF PEACE AND SECURITY

B. THE DECOLONIZATION STRUGGLE

C. ECONOMIC AID AND DEVELOPMENT

A. The Maintenance of Peace and Security

The United Nations is a multifaceted organization with a complex mix of operational, supervisory, and informational activities under its aegis. But none of its activities have attracted more public attention than the ones directed toward the maintenance of international peace and security and, specifically, the ones that involve the deployment of military contingents under the flag of the United Nations. The readings in this section are oriented toward this specific aspect of the United Nations activities in the peace and security field.

Lester B. Pearson, whose key role in the creation of the United Nations Emergency Force in the Middle East (UNEF) in 1956 earned him a Nobel prize, examines the institutional practice that culminated in the creation of UNEF. The great power conflict between East and West, by 1950, had paralyzed the Charter scheme for the maintenance of international peace and security—at least, as it applied to the great powers or states allied with them. Korea proved to be an exception because of the Soviet boycott of the Security Council, but one so unlikely to be repeated that a search was launched for alternative means of United Nations action in the event that the Security Council found itself deadlocked by a great power veto. The result of this search was the Uniting for Peace Resolution, which allowed the General Assembly to be called into emergency session and to make recommendations for the maintenance of international peace and security in the cases where the Security Council found itself deadlocked by a veto. Finally, reflecting on the experience of the United Nations through 1956, Pearson develops some tentative principles governing the establishment of a United Nations force.

Inis L. Claude, Jr., in a broader perspective, examines the various theories underlying the use of force by the United Nations. Although the Charter speaks of the use of force by the Organization only in those cases where the great powers have concurred in Security Council decisions directed at threats or breaches of the peace, in actual practice states are most ready to have the Organization use force when it serves the states' purposes in the international political system and are most reluctant for the Organization to use force when it would not serve these purposes. The states that do not envision their own interests as being best served by a stable world order based on respect for the territorial integrity and political independence of their neighbors are likely to be less favorably disposed toward United Nations action than the states who do envision a stable world order as serving their own interests. In light of this, Claude examines what we could reasonably expect to be the role of the United Nations in the military-security field. He has little hope for using the United Nations as an instrument against one of the great powers or even in defense of one small state that is being attacked by another. The most likely military role foreseen for the Organization is in operations "designed to assist the great powers in keeping the Cold War cold."

In 1964 John W. Holmes studied the repertory of United Nations peacekeeping experience up to that time and extracted a set of viable generalizations about its operation. Although the Organization's peacekeeping experience is diverse, it bears little resemblance to the commonly circulated idea of an "international police force." Even though the United Nations activities have been remarkably successful in stopping the fighting in a number of instances, it has a less-than-enviable record in obtaining permanent solutions to the various conflicts. These peacekeeping activities have been plagued (as peaceful settlement projects have been, historically) by the dilemma of choosing between peace and justice. Finally, Holmes looks ahead and projects where past trends in United Nations peacekeeping activities are most likely to lead.

In Stanley Hoffmann's article we are given a masterful analysis of the first two years of the United Nations peacekeeping activities in the Congo. By breaking down this most confusing of all peacekeeping operations into five phases, the pattern of the operation is revealed without imparting an excessively artificial order to the flow of events. On the basis of this experience, lessons are drawn concerning the role of the United Nations, the policy of Dag Hammarskjöld, and the behavior of member states. The analysis of Dag Hammarskjöld's handling of the crisis is a particularly fascinating study of the role of the Secretary-General in the vortex of international politics. Hoffmann's thesis was that Hammarskjöld chose a minimal operation in the Congo. He did this in order to maximize the political support from the Members for the operation, but a minimal operation could only maximize turmoil in the field that, in turn, reduced the political support for the operation. The thesis poses a real challenge to the persons who may be charged with organizing future peacekeeping endeavours. Peacekeeping operations, as they have progressed to date, require (at every stage) the consent of the host states, of the great powers, and of the suppliers of troops. The withdrawal of this consent can mean either the termination of the operations or a period of severe turmoil over the purposes of the operations which, at times, may threaten the existence of the very organization that spawned the peacekeeping effort. If it develops that the achievement of this consent conflicts with the measures that are necessary to deal with the problem at hand, then the entire peacekeeping approach may be vitiated.

Herbert Nicholas, in appraising the course of the peacekeeping activities of the United Nations, first asks why Suez and the Congo are the only major crises in which the response has been the creation of a United Nations force. In the cases of Hungary and Goa, no thought was given to the creation of a United Nations force, and in Korea what was created was a United Nations command that was a cover for a United States-led force. Both Korea and Hungary share the distinction of having been within the perceived spheres of vital interests of differing superpowers, and this vitally constrained the extent of the United Nations role. Goa was not fertile ground for a United Nations force because to act in defense of Goa would have meant acting in defense of colonialism–an impossibility, in view of the political balance of the United Nations in the 1960s.

If the United Nations chose not to act in Hungary or Goa, why did it respond to the Suez and Congo crises by establishing a United Nations force? In the case of Suez, Nicholas finds that the motivation to action resides in the traditional concern of the United Nations for the area, in its position outside the zones of direct great-power conflict, and because no interested power could impose a solution alone. Nicholas concludes that most of the trouble experienced by the United Nations in the Congo flowed from an attempt to apply the legacy of UNEF to the Congo. This analysis places us on guard because it is an all-too-easy application of the lessons of one peacekeeping operation to the problems of another operation.

Force for U.N.

Lester B. Pearson

Peace, one might think, is not the sort of human occupation which should normally require supervision. Yet the United Nations, instead of concentrating on more positive and progressive activities, has ever since its inception been engaged in supervising a kind of peace which has not been much more than the absence of fighting–and not always even that. Now policing a peace–or an armistice–can be an essential international function, at times a dramatic one. It cannot be denied that the United Nations has been successful in this function in some important cases. However, action in this field has been largely pragmatic and *ad hoc.* I believe–and recent events have strengthened my belief–that the time has come when we should seek ways to enable the United Nations to pursue this work in a more organized and permanent way.

The world's alarm last November over events in Egypt–intensified, if that were possible, by the frustrating situation in Hungary–galvanized the General Assembly into establishing a United Nations Emergency Force, an action which until then had not been thought practicable or probable. We must now do everything possible to ensure that this action is successful in achieving the desired results. If we fail in this, a damaging blow–perhaps a fatal one–will be dealt to the whole concept of supervising the peace and avoiding hostilities through the United Nations Assembly. If we succeed, then we must build on that success so that when we are faced in the future with similarly complicated and dangerous situations we can avoid the hasty improvisations of the last autumn.

The United Nations was brought into being primarily as a cooperative endeavor on the part of many nations to seek in collective action the security for which

---

Reprinted by special permission from *Foreign Affairs,* Vol. 35, No. 3 (April 1957), pp. 395-404.

mankind hungered and which the facts of life in the modern world denied to each nation individually. To achieve this the founders of the United Nations recognized the necessity of having military forces at its disposal and they wrote into the Charter provisions which they hoped would bring them into being. Over the years, however, these provisions have developed in ways far removed from the intentions of their authors.

Under the Covenant of the old League of Nations, the Assembly and the Council had concurrent jurisdiction over the peaceful settlement of disputes and recommendations of enforcement action. Under the Charter of the United Nations, however, the Security Council has primary responsibility in this field and, within certain well-defined limits, has the power to direct members to take action. The League Covenant made no provision for the compulsory enforcement of its decisions; any decision which might require the use of force could be taken only with the unanimous approval of all members, including the state against which it was to be directed. Every member of the League had the right of veto over collective action. That, of course, was a guarantee of futility.

The Charter of the United Nations, however, took what was hoped would prove to be a great step forward. The concentration in the Security Council of power to make certain decisions and enforce them gave the new organization immense potential for quick and decisive action—at least in theory. Actually, in the conditions of cold war the veto possessed by each permanent member of the Council was almost as effective in preventing action as if all members had had it.

Despite the dangers inherent in the irresponsible use of the veto, there was hope that the Security Council would prove effective. One reason for hope was that its decisions were to have behind them an overwhelming superiority of armed force deriving primarily from the forces of the Great Powers themselves. In addition, other members of the organization undertook to make armed forces available to the Council, on its call and in accordance with special agreements. These forces were to be organized collectively by the Military Staff Committee of the Security Council, composed of the Chiefs of Staff of the permanent members.

As early as 1947, however, the Military Committee became deadlocked over the issue of the contributions to be made by the Great Powers themselves to the collective force of the United Nations. Their disagreement merely reflected the general breakup of their wartime cooperation and its replacement by the fears and dissensions of the cold war. With no Great Power agreement it is not surprising that the Military Staff Committee also failed to draw up the special agreements between the Council and other members envisaged under Article 43 of the Charter, and upon which the whole military structure of the United Nations was originally meant to rest. As a result, the United Nations today entirely lacks that particular type of international force envisaged in the Charter.

In spite of its inability to use force to implement its decisions, the Security Council was nevertheless able to intervene with some success in the dangerous situations in Iran, Greece, Indonesia, Kashmir and Palestine. Then came the outbreak of hostilities in Korea and a temporary but significant change in the pattern of United Nations action to preserve the peace–a change made possible by two accidents of history. First, the U.S.S.R., with its veto, was absent from the Security Council when the decision to intervene was taken. Second, at the moment of the outbreak of hostilities in Korea a United Nations Commission was on the spot, able to report and advise on the facts of the situation. The U.S.S.R., however, is not likely again to vacate its seat in the Council, and there are many dangerous areas in the world where the United Nations maintains no observation agency. The type of Security Council action against aggression in Korea, therefore, is not likely to be repeated. In any event, the United Nations character of that action was as much symbolic as it was real, because the United States supplied most of the forces and exercised most of the control over them. In so far as the possibility of using the United Nations for collective security was concerned, Korea was both an encouragement and a warning.

By the time of the Korean operation, it had become clear that where an important, not to say vital, political interest of a Great Power was at stake, that Power would not readily subordinate its decision to a collective judgment. Because of this, and because of the veto, the earlier idea of collective security through the Security Council became impossible to realize. To escape from the dilemma thus created, many members of the United Nations suggested that questions which the Council was unable to resolve might be referred to the General Assembly; and they advocated that other forms of force than that provided for under Article 43 of the Charter be organized to carry out United Nations decisions.

Even earlier, at the very first session of the General Assembly in October 1946, the Canadian delegation had voiced its concern that the Security Council and the Military Staff Committee had failed to make substantial progress towards a conclusion of the special agreements with individual members required to implement Article 43. It urged that these bodies proceed with all possible speed to equip the Security Council with forces.

In the following Assembly of 1947, Mr. St.-Laurent, then Canadian Secretary of State for External Affairs, said: "Nations in their search for peace. . . will not and cannot accept indefinitely and unaltered a Council which was set up to ensure their security, and which, so many feel, has become frozen in futility and divided by dissension. If forced, they may seek greater safety in an association of democratic and peace-loving states willing to accept more specific international obligations in return for greater national security. Such associations, if consistent with the principles and purposes of the Charter, can be formed within the United Nations." The provisions of the Charter, he added, "provide a floor under, rather than a ceiling over, the responsibilities of Member States. If some prefer to go even below that floor, others need not be prevented from moving upwards."

It was the Canadian hope that such a development would not be necessary. If it were unnecessary it would certainly be undesirable.

As we have seen, however, hopes for ensuring collective security were not fulfilled. The Security Council remained powerless to provide such security and the Assembly was unorganized for this purpose. In view of the undiminished threat from the Soviet Union, which had a preponderance in armed forces and pursued aggressive policies, certain members of the United Nations sought for a regional means of providing for their mutual defense within the framework of the organization. The North Atlantic Treaty, for example, was created and exists only because of the failure to attain a really effective system of collective security on a universal basis.

The search for means to establish a universal system nevertheless continued. Against the sombre background of events in Korea, members of the United Nations reviewed again the collective security machinery available, with the result that in the autumn of 1950 the Assembly adopted a resolution which potentially was of great importance. The Uniting for Peace Resolution, as it came to be called, meant simply that the General Assembly had decided to provide machinery for utilizing certain powers which it already possessed. The resolution did not itself constitute any revolutionary departure in interpreting the Charter; it was conceived simply as a practical measure designed to meet certain situations in which the purposes of the United Nations might be frustrated by the negative attitude of a permanent member of the Security Council. The General Assembly was to be used for security purposes only when the Security Council failed to perform, or was prevented from performing, its primary function. If the Council acted, nothing in the resolution would interfere with its action.

But if the Security Council did not act, what then? Were we to admit frankly the failure of our United Nations peace machinery and fall back entirely upon regional collective security arrangements such as NATO? While filling a gap, these obviously were limited in scope or character. Surely, it was thought, some way could be found for the United Nations to provide a force which would at least halt a drift to war by helping to carry out an Assembly recommendation when the Security Council failed to act. True, according to the Charter the Assembly had no legal power of enforcement and could act only by recommendation. Nevertheless, in terms of persuasiveness and moral force, the Assembly's recommendations, if responsibly conceived and generally accepted (two very weighty provisos), would carry as much weight as those of the Security Council—perhaps more. So why not at least make available some machinery which might carry them out?

Such was the background of the Uniting for Peace Resolution. It provided, among other things, that an emergency session of the Assembly might be called on 24 hours' notice for the purpose of making recommendations if the Security Council had failed to agree on means of resisting a breach of the peace or an act of aggression. It also called for the establishment of a Collective Measures Committee to study methods which might be used to strengthen the collective security machinery. Moreover—and this was a foundation on which we could have built—the resolution recommended that each member state maintain elements within its armed forces for prompt use as United Nations units, and that a panel of military experts be appointed by the Secretary-General for advisory and organization purposes.

The Collective Measures Committee recommended in the resolution was set up and it developed a set of principles designed to help maintain and strengthen the United Nations collective security system through Assembly action. The Secretary-General asked member governments to survey their resources to determine the nature and scope of the assistance they might render and to report on the progress made. The result was discouraging. In all, 37 governments replied to his communication. Simple acknowledgments were received from 15 governments; 8 indicated that they could not participate at all in the projects being studied by the Committee, or gave only limited and conditional acceptance of the measures contemplated; 11 took certain minimum steps (largely in connection with the earmarking of forces for Korea) and gave assurances of active support for the principle of the Uniting for Peace Resolution. The Canadian Government stated that its special force, raised for service in Korea, would be available for whatever action might be necessary anywhere in order to carry out military obligations under the Charter.

By the Uniting for Peace Resolution, the Assembly also provided for a Peace Observation Commission to observe and report on the situation in areas of international tension. So far it has not been used.

As a whole, the efforts of the Collective Measures Committee were sterile. With the General Assembly's adoption of its third report on November 4, 1954, it concluded its work. Another series of studies had been accumulated and now were laid away in files and vaults. The United Nations, nine years after its founding, still had no force at its disposal to implement its decisions—even to "secure and supervise" a cease-fire and armistice.

Nevertheless, the Uniting for Peace Resolution remained on the books; and almost six years later, in November 1956, in circumstances very different from those contemplated by its authors, it enabled the General Assembly to meet and discuss in emergency special session the serious situation in the Middle East. The Assembly still was ill-prepared to take on responsibilities for "peace supervision" through police action. The Uniting for Peace Resolution recommended the earmarking of forces for its use in peace and police action, but nothing had been done. When the need for these forces was upon us we had to embark on an improvised experiment, starting literally from nothing. There was neither precedent nor organization available to the Assembly in carrying out the new responsibility thrust upon it.

In a sense this was due to the unexpected nature of this responsibility. With fighting actually going on and threatening to spread, quick action was required. In the crisis, an Assembly resolution set up a United Nations Emergency Force and authorized the Secretary-General to organize it within 48 hours. Due largely to the devotion, energy and intelligence of the Secretary-General and his assistants, the Force was in fact brought into being at once. This amazing example of international improvisation showed what can be done by the United Nations when the collective will to action is strong and united. Moreover, the Force has so far proved effective for the purpose it was meant to achieve, the securing and supervising of a cease-fire.

Nevertheless, these purposes were very different from those originally contemplated in the Charter. What we faced in the Assembly last November was the necessity of organizing quickly a force, not to fight, but to ensure that fighting would not be resumed. We were trying to implement, if not a new concept of United Nations supervisory action, certainly an enlarged one.

Such a concept has already stirred interest and hope and optimism. Some of this optimism is exaggerated, because it does not take sufficiently into consideration the limitations under which the Assembly must act. There can be no certainty that the U.N.E.F. will complete successfully the tasks that have been or may be given to it. It may fail, either because it does not secure the right kind of collective backing in the Assembly or because it becomes the victim of Middle Eastern politics. If so, the failure will extend far beyond the immediate situation. It will destroy confidence in the effectiveness of the United Nations in the whole field of security. On the other hand, its success might well lead to further steps in developing means to supervise the peace.

Whatever may be the ultimate result, the intervention of the United Nations through an Emergency Force in November 1956 was certainly an indispensable prerequisite to the acceptance of a cease-fire and the subsequent withdrawal of Anglo-French and Israeli forces from Egyptian territory. Its action also emphasized, however, the need to be better prepared to meet future situations of a similar kind. Even if governments are unable to give the United Nations a "fighting" force ready and organized to serve it on the decision of the Security Council, they should be willing to earmark smaller forces for the more limited duty of securing a cease-fire already agreed upon by the belligerents. We might in this way be able to construct a halfway house at the crossroads of war, and utilize an intermediate technique between merely passing resolutions and actually fighting.

The first step would seem to be to create a permanent mechanism by which units of the armed forces of member countries could be endowed with the authority of the United Nations and make available at short notice for supervisory police duties. It is not suggested that the present Emergency Force should become a permanent force or, indeed, that its functions should be extended beyond those laid down in the relevant Assembly resolutions. We should, nevertheless, build upon the experience of this enterprise. Otherwise, I repeat, we shall only go back again to the situation in which we found ourselves last November, when everything had to be improvised, when there was no precedent for making units available, no administrative and financial procedure and no organization to which the Secretary-General could turn in the task given him by the Assembly of putting a United Nations force into a dangerous and delicate situation. We improvised successfully then. We cannot reasonably expect the same degree of success a second time.

We now have at our disposal a body of experience from which can be developed some tentative principles governing the establishment of United Nations machinery and, as required, a Peace Supervision Force. Among these principles—some of which I have already referred to—the following strike me as forming an essential minimum.

Member governments, excluding the permanent members of the Security Council, should be invited to signify a willingness in principle to contribute contingents to the United Nations for purposes that are essentially noncombatant, such as, for example, the supervision of agreed cease-fires and comparable peace supervisory functions.

Since the Security Council is charged with the primary responsibility for the maintenance of peace, members who have sought and secured election to the non-permanent seats on it would normally be expected to be among those signifying a willingness to contribute contingents to such a force.

For effective organization, there would have to be some central United Nations machinery. The Secretary-General should have a permanent Military Adviser who, with a small staff, might assume responsibility for the direction of other truce supervision arrangements which have been or might be agreed on.

If at any time a Peace Supervision Force were constituted, the Secretary-General would require an advisory committee similar to that which now assists him in connection with the U.N.E.F. in Egypt.

While such a force is not primarily a fighting force, it must be capable of defending itself once it is in the field, since the inherent duty of a commander is to preserve the safety of his men. It should also include the necessary administrative and supporting elements to enable it to function effectively as an entity.

A force to deal with a particular situation could be established by a resolution either of the Security Council or of the General Assembly. Presumably it would be associated with efforts made by the United Nations towards assisting in the settlement of the dispute. These efforts in turn could be furthered by a revitalized Peace Observation Commission given real responsibility to investigate disputes. In a sense, a Peace Supervision Force would be an extension in space of the Peace Observation Commission and the subordinate bodies it was expected to produce.

By its very nature such a force would not be expected to fight its way into a country. Indeed, since it would be deployed upon recommendation of the United Nations, it could enter a country only with the consent of the government of that country. This consent would normally take the form of an agreement between the government concerned and the Secretary-General acting on behalf of the United Nations. To facilitate the negotiation of such agreements, and also to expedite the creation of a force when required, the Secretary-General should be requested to draw up model agreements regarding the financial, administrative and legal procedures which would govern the operations of a Peace Supervision Force. The agreement recently negotiated between the United Nations and Egypt on arrangements concerning the status of the U.N.E.F. in that country would provide a very useful example of what can be done in this regard.

It is my firm conviction that the sort of machinery I have outlined, and the kind of United Nations force that would be expected to function through it, are practicable, are within the competence of the General Assembly, and might be of great value in avoiding, ending or limiting hostilities. The early arrival of a United Nations force of this kind at a scene of emergency would give assurance to the fearful and hope to the dispairing. It would act as the United Nations policeman and his watchdog.

How these arrangements would function would, of course, depend on the circumstances of the particular emergency to be met. Actually, there is nothing so very new in all this. The United Nations has on more than one occasion provided teams of truce observers or supervisors and has now set up an emergency force to enlarge that activity where the danger of renewed fighting, pending the working out of a settlement, required it. A synthesis and systematization of these two concepts would provide a base of departure for the future.

As always, in the last resort, individual governments must determine whether the best laid plans of the United Nations are to succeed or fail. If a plan anything like that which I have outlined is to succeed, governments must, both within and outside the United Nations, follow policies consistent with its objectives and its capabilities. The very least each of our governments can now do, it seems to me, is to draft, in accordance with our respective constitutional processes, whatever measures are required to place us in a better position to support agreed decisions of the United Nations in an emergency. Are we to go on from crisis to crisis improvising in haste? Or can we now pool our experience in our resources, so that the next time we, the governments and peoples whom the United Nations represents, will be ready and prepared to act?

United Nations Use of Military Force

Inis L. Claude, Jr.

There are two possible ways of approaching the question of the purposes of the United Nations. One is to concentrate on the Charter—to treat this formal constitutional document as an authoritative and meaningful expression of the goals which the world organization seeks to achieve and toward which it must be presumed to be working. The Charter, of course, was not handed down from on high, but was formulated by states. Thus, this approach appears to suggest that the Charter was, in 1945, a valid statement of a real consensus among the original members as to what the UN should be and do. As for the present, it suggests that the same conception of the UN is held by the expanded membership of the organization—that the consensus has been widened but not substantively altered or, alternatively, that the UN is an entity sufficiently autonomous to function in accordance with the original consensus, whether or not that consensus, or *any* consensus, still prevails among its members.

The second approach is to focus upon the political interests and purposes of the members of the UN—to proceed upon the assumption that the words of the Charter are less determinative than the policies of the states. Following this approach, we may expect to find that the purposes of the organization are not fixed, but are continuously redefined as states develop new agreements among themselves as to what ends they wish or expect the UN to serve. Moreover, we may expect to find that the organization's purposes are as ambiguous as they are mutable, for it is altogether unlikely that the members have ever been, are now, or ever will be in full agreement concerning the uses to which this international

Inis L. Claude, Jr., "United Nations Use of Military Force," *Journal of Conflict Resolution,* Vol. 7, No. 2 (June 1963), pp. 117-129. Reprinted by permission of the author and the *Journal of Conflict Resolution.*

instrument should be put. In these terms, the explorer of the UN's purpose must wrestle with change and conflict, renouncing the expectation of finding the purposes of the organization conveniently spelled out for him.

Adopting the first course, we may ask what the Charter says with respect to the use of military force. What are the purposes to which 51 states ostensibly subscribed in 1945 and which they, along with 59 additional states, now purport to regard as appropriate and acceptable? The UN is intended to discourage the irresponsible, national use of military force—aggression, in short. It recognizes the legitimacy of defensive action by victims of attack and by other states which may wish to join in that reaction to aggression, but it undertakes to make such defense unnecessary by making offensive action unlikely. In a variety of ways, the UN undertakes to prevent aggression. Its purpose is to deprive states of anything to fight *about*—by inhibiting the development of, and promoting the elimination of, conditions that might make for conflict, and by facilitating the settlement of difficulties that have reached the critical "dispute" stage. By promoting disarmament negotiations, the organization expressed the urge to deprive themselves and each other of anything to fight *with.* Thus far, this analysis suggests that the UN is concerned with the use of force by states, acting on their own. The Charter goes on, however, to say something about the use of force by the UN, or, more accurately, by states acting under its auspices. The two subjects are closely interrelated; provisions calling for the use of force by or on behalf of the UN are integral parts of the scheme for inhibiting aggressive national action and thereby reducing the necessity for individual or collective defensive action. The Charter purports to classify the national use of force under three headings: that which is required, that which is prohibited, and that which is permitted. Insofar as it requires members to provide coercive support for the world organization, the Charter adopts the view that the responsible use of force for international purposes is the ultimate antidote for the irresponsible use of force for national purposes.

The Charter does not in fact go very far in this direction. It pays lip service to the ideal of erecting a collective security system, which would promise to cope with any prohibited use of force by invoking the requirement for the actual creation or operation of such a system. At most, it contains a plan for developing a system under which the UN may mobilize collective action against *minor* aggressors in circumstances which find the major powers unanimously disposed to support or at least to tolerate such action. The crucial provisions pertinent to this scheme, Articles 43 and 45, which contemplate agreements on military contingents to be placed at the disposal of the Security Council by states, have become dead letters but have not been formally erased. The Charter does *not*, it should be emphasized, either provide or promise a system for UN action or UN-sponsored action to repress aggression launched or supported by any of the major powers. The famous veto clause of Article 27 expresses the founding fathers' rejection of the attempt to require member states to join forces under the UN banner for resistance to great-power aggression; the "individual or collective self-defense" clause of Article 51, a permissive clause, expresses the judgment of the founding fathers as to what can and must be done under such circumstances. The Charter, in short, prohibits but does not purport to prevent the most dangerous sort of aggression—that undertaken by or under the auspices of a major power.

We might summarize this reading of the Charter by saying that it speaks much more decisively about the use of force by the UN. The purpose of the UN is to discourage the irresponsible, disruptive use of force by states. The organization itself is to use, or to sponsor the use of, force only when—or if—the great powers concur in the implementation of Articles 43 and 45 and subsequently in Security Council decisions regarding particular cases.

Shifting to the second of the approaches to analysis of the purposes of the UN discussed at the beginning, which stresses the policies of states rather than the words of the Charter, one may express doubts as to whether the statesmen who drafted the Charter were as unanimously and unreservedly dedicated to the creation of an effective peace-preserving organization as they said they were. Equally, one may doubt whether the purposes stated in the Charter are in fact the purposes which all or most member states now wish the UN to pursue and hope that it may realize. There is conflict over the purposes for which the organization is to be used—conflict deriving not from differing interpretations of the Charter but from differing national interests, or conceptions of national interests.

There is no difficulty in securing general condemnation of aggression in the abstract, and agreement that the UN should discourage, if not effectively prevent or suppress, aggression. In concrete terms, however, one state's aggression is always another state's "legitimate use of force to defend vital national interests." What states really want is the imposition of effective international restraint upon the military ventures of "others," not of themselves or of states intimately associated with themselves. It can hardly be imagined that the Soviet Union wishes the UN to be capable of inhibiting Communist conquest of Laos. India presumably does not regret that the organization failed to protect Goa against Indian invasion. The United Arab Republic does not aspire to make the UN an effective guarantor of the integrity of Israel. The United States would have limited enthusiasm for the project of making the UN a bulwark against any possible American attack upon Cuba. With respect to its own resorts to force, actual or potential, every state wants to secure at least the tolerance of the UN, even better the blessing of the UN, and at best such substantial support and reinforcement as the organization might provide.

States vary, of course, in their ability and disposition to use force for the promotion or protection of their interests as they see them. They vary also in the degree to which they conceive their interests as compatible with a stable world order in which respect for the territorial integrity and political independence of all states is enshrined and effectuated as a basic principle. I would argue, for instance, that Washington's view of the national interest of the United States is much more compatible with and conducive to that kind of global system than Moscow's view of the interests and purposes which Soviet policy is to serve. I do not suggest that all states are equally bellicose and aggressive. Nevertheless, it seems to me quite clear that every state has to contemplate the possibility that it might, under some circumstances, feel impelled to take military action that would seem to it absolutely necessary for the protection of vital national interests but might not be regarded as legitimate by the political organs of the UN. States *do* contemplate this possibility; consequently, they do not genuinely commit themselves without reservation to the proposition that they will never resort to force in the face of international disapproval expressed through the UN; consequently, they are not ultimately dedicated to the purpose of enabling the UN—that is, its member states—to control the unilateral resort to military action by any and all states, including themselves.

If I am correct in attributing this attitude to states, then it follows that states must have reservations about conferring upon the UN an extensive legal competence and actual capability to exercise a coercive function. One does not fully endorse the principle of the international use of force unless one fully repudiates the policy of the national use of force, for it must be presumed that a militarily effective UN might frustrate one's state in its efforts to safeguard its vital interests—interests which the state may regard as justifying the national use of force but which a sufficient number of the members of a UN political organ might not so regard.

I submit that this is the actual situation today. We must resist the temptation to take too seriously the simple proposition that the world is divided into two groups of states, one of which (including, most prominently, the Soviet Union) opposes the strengthening of the UN, and the other of which (led by the United States) favors the development of that organization as an international repository of coercive authority and power.

It is easy enough to demonstrate that the Soviets oppose that development. It is perhaps less self-evident that the United States does not favor that development. I would argue, however, that the record shows that the United States favors a UN which can give permissive endorsement and lend moral and perhaps more tangible varieties of support to military actions which we regard as necessary and legitimate; I look in vain for evidence that the United States wishes to equip the UN with either the formal competence or the effective capability to prevent this country and its allies from fighting whenever we may feel it necessary to fight, or to require us to fight when we are not disposed to do so. In the case of Korea, the UN gave an international blessing to, and stimulated the mobilization of multilateral support for, a military reaction to Communist aggression which we felt impelled to undertake. We valued this marginal assistance, and attempted, in the Uniting for Peace plan, to maximize the possibility that such international aid might be rendered to upholders of similarly worthy causes in the future. This was, however, a far cry from endorsing the actual creation of, or expressing the willingness to accept the onerous obligations of, a full-fledged collective security system. The United States has subsequently supported the quasi-military interventions of the UN in the Middle East and the Congo, but these can hardly be characterized as manifestations of, or even as preliminary approaches to, the establishment of a UN capacity to use international military force to squelch illicit national resorts to force.

It might be noted that the United States has, since 1960, stated for the public international record that it regards an effective international coercive mechanism as an essential part of a world system characterized by general and complete disarmament. Perhaps I may be forgiven if I choose to treat this more as an exercise in logic than as a statement of policy. It seems to say that the United States advocates the establishment of a world government—but it should be noted that President Kennedy, in his State of the Union address in January, 1962, described our goal for the future as "a peaceful world community of free and independent states" or "a free community of nations, independent but interdependent".[1] Moreover, another spokesman for the Administration declared that: "The ultimate question at issue is whether this small planet is to be organized on the principles of the Communist bloc or on the basis of voluntary cooperation among independent nation-states. . . . We expect this planet to organize itself in time on the principles of voluntary cooperation among independent nation-states . . ."[2] These statements seem to belie the proposition that American policy is dedicated to the creation of a global governmental authority entrusted with supreme coercive power. In any case, the completely disarmed world to which this proposition is linked is not our world. In dealing with the world as it is, and with the UN as it is and seems to be becoming, the United States betrays little enthusiasm for making the use of military force by the UN the central element in plans for the safeguarding of American security and the maintenance of world peace.

The purpose of this paper is not to speculate about what the world would be like if it were utterly different from what it is. Focusing on the existing situation and the existing global institution, let us ask what role can reasonably be assigned to the UN in the military-security field.

First, there is the question of the possible use of the UN as a military instrument for dealing with great-power aggression; in our terms, this refers to the possibility of the organization's serving as a defensive bulwark against aggressive action launched by, or supported by, the Soviet Union or Communist China. My

---

[1] John F. Kennedy, "The State of the Union," *Department of State Bulletin,* Vol. 46, 1962, pp. 159-163.

[2] Walt W. Rostow, "The Domestic Base of Foreign Policy," *ibid.,* pp. 835, 838.

response to this is quite negative. We rely, quite properly in my judgment, upon our national power and our alliances for security against this threat. The UN was not designed to cope with this sort of problem, and I see no point in criticizing the organization for not doing what it was not supposed to do, or in regretting its inability to do what it was, from the start, constitutionally debarred from attempting to do. Nor do I see any point in trying to transform the UN into an organization appropriate for this role. The UN is not a NATO, and if we undertake to make it a kind of super-NATO, we may sacrifice its values as a global institution without in fact succeeding in making it a valuable free-world institution. We need not choose between global and free-world organizations. We have both kinds, and we need both kinds, to perform different types of functions. If NATO is defective, the answer is to improve NATO, not to attempt to convert the UN into a NATO-like institution.

I am arguing, in short, that the task of providing a military deterrent against Communist expansionism is a task for a coalition of allies, not for a general international organization that includes Communist states and uncommitted states among its members. The usefulness, actual and potential, of the UN lies in other realms. Conceivably, of course, the UN may lend helpful support to the Western coalition, as it did in the case of Korea. We cannot count on this, however, given the increasing numerical strength of the uncommitted states in the UN. Moreover, I have serious doubts as to whether it would be, on balance, advantageous to the West to have the UN function as a reliable endorser of our position in contests with the Soviet bloc. Insofar as the UN habitually plays that role, it tends to take on the appearance of a pro-Western institution, thereby endangering its potential usefulness as neutral ground, or an impartial instrument, in the Cold War. I shall return to this point later.

Secondly, we might ask whether the UN has a significant capability for dealing militarily with clashes between states which lie outside the alignments of the Cold War and the spheres of interest of the major Cold War antagonists. This is precisely what the UN was intended to have, as is indicated by the plan for making national units available for use by the Security Council, stated in Article 43 of the Charter. The question, then, is whether this plan can or should be revived, or a different scheme be substituted for it. The outlook is not encouraging. The early negotiations regarding the implementation of Article 43 indicated that neither the Western powers nor the Soviet Union trusted the other to participate loyally, without ulterior motives, in a collective UN force.[3] Since this mutual distrust has become stronger rather than weaker, it seems perfectly evident that any anti-aggression force assembled by the UN would have to exclude units from the major powers and their most intimate allies. This observation suggests a

[3] Inis L. Claude, Jr., *Power and International Relations* (New York: Random House, 1962), pp. 175-190.

major limiting factor–the pervasiveness of the Cold War. It is extremely difficult to conceive of an international conflict in our time which the Western and Soviet blocs would not regard as at least potentially related to their competitive struggle; in virtually any case that can readily be imagined, UN military action against an aggressive state would be likely to evoke conflicting reactions from the Soviet Union and the United States. Even though these powers might be excluded from participation in the action, they might well find themselves at odds concerning the propriety of the action, the identity of aggressor and victim, and the nature of the political result which the UN should endeavor to promote. The world is too small to provide a wide zone of indifference between the major contestants. In short, an attempt by the UN to deal coercively with almost any conflict would probably be assimilated to an attempt to deal coercively with great-power struggles.

Thus, I see little scope for UN military action in defending one small state divorced from Cold War blocs against another one. Moreover, I see little evidence that the neutralist members of the UN are prepared to institute and effectuate a collective security arrangement among themselves, even assuming that the major powers would be willing to stand dispassionately aside. I would not be willing to advise the leader of any state to base his security policy upon the expectation that a UN force might be mobilized to defend his country against aggression.

What if the UN were equipped with a permanent military force of its own, a force designed to defeat aggressors, and thus ceased to be dependent upon the willingness of states to contribute, or to permit others to contribute, military contingents for UN actions? This possibility seems to me to have no relevance to the problem of restraining great powers. Military power must rest upon a base–a territorial, demographic, social, political, economic, industrial, scientific base. The only base capable of producing and sustaining a military establishment able to match that of a great power is another great power. Concretely, only the United States–or, more broadly, the Western coalition–is able to generate the force required to balance that possessed by the Sino-Soviet bloc. The United States, or the Western coalition, might be rechristened the United Nations, but the change would be both literally and figuratively nominal. The UN is not a New World which can be called in to redress the balance of the old.

Might such a UN force be relevant to the problem of restraining minor aggressors? Possibly–but let us note again how little is really changed by the device of switching from national contingents to an international military organization. Assume that enlistments from major powers are forbidden, so that the question of the force's being internally subverted to the service of one or another of the major powers does not arise. Nevertheless, the critical political issues remain: Who will control the force? Against what state will it be used in a given situation? For what purpose will it fight? Toward what political result will it press? Neither great nor small powers will be indifferent to such issues, or be satisfied with the simple-minded answer that the UN will exercise policy direction and will use the force to achieve the purposes stipulated in the Charter. The retort to this answer is, of course, that the UN is owned and operated by states. Which states will control the UN policy organs that direct the force? The documentary purposes of the Charter are less important than the political purposes of the states which dominate the policy process. There is nothing in the nature of an international military force that makes its use a less contentious issue in a world of political conflict than the use of an assemblage of national units.

More generally, I think we must be on guard against the illusion that a UN fighting force would somehow enable us to escape from national states—from their quarrels and conflicting policies and purposes, from their power. As I have suggested, such a force would not be any less an instrument of states for being labeled an instrument of the UN, for states constitute the UN and their rivalries permeate the policy process of the organization. Moreover, a force which is sustained by the UN is in fact dependent upon states for its sustenance. This is true not only in the general sense that financial support of the UN and its various activities is derived predominantly from states, but also in the more specific sense that the supplies and equipment necessary for transforming a group of men into an effective military unit must come from states. We are back again to the problem of the power base. An army without a country generates no more military power than a country without an army. A UN armed force must be based upon thin air unless it is grounded in dependence upon the very states over which it is supposed to exercise independent authority. Whatever power a UN force might wield would be, in effect, borrowed national power. This is to say that the establishment of a UN force for countering aggression would not in any real sense represent the creation of an autonomous central authority, emancipated from dependence upon the support and cooperation of states and able to function coercively without regard to the policies and attitudes of states.

It might be argued that, given the new technology of warfare which enhances the significance of ready striking power, the problem of the power base has lost, or is losing, its importance. Thus, the UN might gain an impressive military status simply by acquiring a stock of missiles and nuclear warheads, without the necessity of developing the supportive foundations traditionally required by a military establishment. Leaving aside the question of the willingness of states to endow the UN with such a striking force, I think it is clear that this suggestion reflects an exaggerated notion as to the military significance of a finished and finite supply of weapons and delivery vehicles, divorced from the resources and facilities implicit in the concept of the power base. It relies upon a static conception of military force, at precisely the moment in history when military technology has become unprecedentedly dynamic, when the rate of obsolescence has been dramatically accelerated. The current arms race is not primarily a competition in quantitative accumulation, but in qualitative development of military means;

national leaders are not intent upon expanding "over-kill" capacity, but upon keeping up or getting ahead in the quest for innovations that may alter the relative significance of existing weapons. In this setting, a static UN striking force, inherently vulnerable because of the impossibility of maintaining secrecy concerning its vital details, would soon become a negligible factor in the global political-military situation. The problem of keeping the UN force up to date, thus eliminating its tendency toward diminishing significance, brings us right back to the issue of the power base.

Moreover, the project of equipping the UN with a self-contained nuclear striking force involved imposing upon the organization all the difficulties and dilemmas associated with the doctrine of massive retaliation. It would be ironical if the United States escaped from the snares of reliance upon massive retaliation, only to saddle the UN with that strategic concept. It is hardly credible that such a political body as the UN would resort to thermonuclear attack whenever international aggression occurred or threatened—or desirable that it should do so. An international military establishment designed to maintain peace and security would require military versatility, the capacity for flexible and graduated response, to the same degree that a major national force requires it. To assert this is to deny that the problem of the power base can be circumvented by providing the UN with a stock of ready-made instruments of thermonuclear destruction, and to reaffirm the dependence of the UN upon its member states. A permanent UN military force for combating aggression is not a substitute for the willing collaboration of states, but simply one of the possible vehicles for such collaboration.

Thus far, my position regarding the possibilities of the use of military force by the UN has been essentially negative. I do not see the task of organizing an effective defense against Soviet aggression as one which can appropriately be assigned to the United Nations. This is a function of a coalition—and of institutions which comprise those states that are willing to associate themselves with the coalition and to contribute whatever they can to its strength. I am doubtful that there is a major role for the UN to play in mobilizing power—whether by pulling together national military contingents or by operating a permanent armed force under its direct authority—for the suppression of aggression outside the framework of the Cold War struggle. What then, if anything, is left as a military function for the UN?

We might find some clues in a perusal of the record of the organization. I think we can set aside the Korean case. Here, the UN endorsed and encouraged joint action against Communist aggression, and came to be clearly associated with one side in what was obviously a major episode of the East-West conflict. The initial enthusiasm for putting the UN into this kind of role, so sharply at variance with the original conception of the UN expressed in the Charter, quickly died away. By the end of the Korean War, the UN was being pushed—by the United States, among other members—into the position of a third party, disengaged from the conflict. It has been vigorously pulled in that direction in subsequent years, as its neutralist members have grown in numbers and matured in their understanding that their neutralism would be violated and endangered if they adhered to an international organization that entered—and brought them with it—into the vortex of Cold War disputes. Korea was an aberration, the expression of an ephemeral urge to make the UN an instrument of collective security in cases falling well within the scope of the Cold War. There is little sentiment among members of the organization for reviving this conception of the UN's function, and it is doubtful that the West can realistically expect or usefully attempt to bring about a development of the UN along these functional lines.

More promising clues are to be found in the string of cases which have involved the use of military personnel under UN auspices for purposes other than doing battle with aggressors—for supervising truces, patrolling borders or armistice lines, observing the degree to which rival parties respect agreed arrangements for stabilizing their relationships, and the like. These cases include UN interventions in the Palestine and Kashmir cases, in Lebanon, and—most notably—in the Suez and Congo crises. These are peace-stabilizing, or peace-keeping, or peace-restoring operations, efforts to aid disputant states in the implementation of political resolves to avoid the outbreak or the renewal of military conflict; they are not measures for the international defeat of determined acts of aggression. We may take UNEF and the military operation in the Congo as the outstanding instances of this sort of UN enterprise.

The late Secretary-General of the UN, Dag Hammarskjöld, functioned in this realm not only as a man of action but also as a man of thought. Having responded to critical needs and grasped opportunities for making the UN significantly useful in emergency situations, by creative improvisation of the UNEF and Congo forces, he turned to the articulation of a most perceptive theoretical analysis of the international political role which the UN had thus assumed. Hammarskjöld's classic statement of what he chose to call the concept of "preventive diplomacy" is contained in his Introduction to the Annual Report submitted to the Fifteenth Session of the General Assembly in 1960.[4]

In this essay, the Secretary-General brushed aside the idea that the UN could usefully or safely intervene in "problems which are clearly and definitely within the orbit of present day conflicts between power blocs." The effort to put the UN effectively into such situations would, he feared, be not only futile but dangerous as well—dangerous to the continuing usefulness of the organization in general and of its chief officer in particular. From this, he drew the conclusion

---

[4]Dag Hammarskjöld, "Introduction to the Annual Report of the Secretary-General on the Work of the Organization, 16 June 1959–15 June 1960," *General Assembly, Official Records: Fifteenth Session,* Supplement No. 1A, United Nations, New York, 1960.

that "the main field of useful activity of the United Nations in its efforts to prevent conflicts or to solve conflicts" should be defined as that of taking action to fill vacuums in areas of conflict outside of, or marginal to, the zones already clearly involved in the Cold War struggle, so as to minimize the tendency of—or to diminish the incentive for—great powers to move competitively into those situations. Thus, he hoped that the organization might prevent the widening and aggravation of the bloc conflicts. In these terms, the major political potentiality of the UN is to promote the stabilization of the Cold War, to help the great powers avoid or back away from confrontations that might have disastrous results for themselves and all the rest of the world. It is evident that Hammarskjöld was not engaging in armchair theorizing, but was stating an interpretation of what the UN had been doing, and was doing, in the Middle East and the Congo, and was projecting this same role into the future.

Two points are crucial to the theory of preventive diplomacy:

1. The kind of operation which is envisaged, designed to seal off a zone of trouble from the competitive intrusions of the East and the West, is dependent upon the active or the passive consent of both the major contestants in the Cold War. Hammarskjöld acknowledged this—perhaps not quite explicitly—when he described the UN's role as that of "providing for solutions whenever the interests of all parties in a localization of conflict can be mobilized in favour of its efforts." He hoped that the major powers would tolerate or even support UN ventures in preventive diplomacy because each would recognize its own interest in avoiding new confrontations that might disrupt their delicate relationships. The theory rests upon the assumption that conflict of interest breeds a limited community of interest, particularly in the thermonuclear era. Rival parties have a common interest in preventing their conflict from degenerating into uncontrollable violence. This common interest does not suggest that the conflict is unreal, or is not fundamental and deep-seated, or is diminishing in intensity. Quite to the contrary, it arises precisely because the conflict is a basic one; the community or mutuality of interest is a function of the intensity of the conflict of interest.

It is one thing to assert that the United States and the Soviet Union both *have* a stake in the avoidance of a military showdown, and thus in the encouragement of preventive diplomacy by the UN. It is another thing to assume that both great powers are *aware* of this common interest and prepared to act on the basis of that awareness. Putting Hammarskjöld's point negatively, we can say that the UN cannot hope to develop the function of preventive diplomacy successfully if the major powers do not share the conviction that their own interests would be served thereby. A UNEF or ONUC intervention is something that the UN can do *for* the great powers; it is not something that the UN can reliably do *against* the great powers, or either of them.

This immediately limits the field. It should be recalled that Hammarskjöld spoke of the possibilities of preventive diplomacy in areas *outside* of, or *marginal* to, the well-defined zones of the Cold War. He assumed, realistically, that neither of the major antagonists would look favorably upon UN intervention of the type under discussion within its own sphere of influence. Preventive diplomacy is applicable to the no-man's-land of the Cold War, the in-between area where both contestants may, on grounds of self-interest, give greater weight to the value of avoiding mutual confrontation than to the hope of winning a competitive encounter.

2. The function of preventive diplomacy is essentially *neutralist* in character. It does not involve neutral mediation in disputes and conflicts between the Cold War blocs—that is also an important political potentiality of the UN, but it falls under a different heading, and it calls for diplomatic or legal techniques rather than military or quasi-military instrumentalities. Rather, preventive diplomacy as such involves neutral interposition between contestants, using military personnel under UN direction as agents for achieving the neutralization of a trouble spot—i.e., for insulating the area against the intrusion of Cold War competition.

Preventive diplomacy is neutralist in method as well as design. It promises to fill a vacuum with forces contributed by relatively uncommitted states; note that the exclusion of military units from the major powers or the states most intimately aligned with them has been a cardinal principle in the constitution of UNEF and ONUC. Thus, it treats neutralist states as the members of the organization uniquely eligible for service as agents of the UN in the performance of its neutralizing function. Preventive diplomacy provides the relatively uncommitted states (I use the qualification in recognition that neutralism is never absolute) with an opportunity and a challenge to make their neutralism positive and constructive; it invites them to use their limited military forces, on behalf of the UN, to do something for the great powers that the latter could not do for themselves, and thereby to promote their own interest in the survival of civilization. Preventive diplomacy, in short, places the major active responsibility for the military function of the UN upon the smaller and less involved states. The great powers must *permit* the UN to play the neutral role; the states that stand most aloof from Cold War alignments must *enable* the UN to play that role.

It might be argued that the UN should develop, for the performance of this role, a standing international force, conceived as a continuously available UNEF, an instrument of preventive diplomacy rather than an army dedicated to the defeat of aggressors. Thus equipped, the organization would presumably be emancipated from dependence upon the uncertain willingness of neutralist states to provide units for exercises in preventive diplomacy. I am not convinced that such a development is either necessary or desirable. Thus far, the record indicates an impressive willingness on the part of the uncommitted states to do the jobs which preventive diplomacy requires of them. Moreover, there is substantial doubt that a standing international force would necessarily turn out to be the most appropriate or most acceptable instrument for dealing with particular cases that might arise; it may be that every case will be so distinctive as to require a tailor-made UN force. In practical terms, a permanent force might be inordinately expensive, given the budgetary realities of the UN. In any case, I suggest that the UN will be able to carry out successful operations of preventive diplomacy only if and when there is wide-spread willingness among its uncommitted members to undertake the military burden, and there is little point in attempting to evade the implications of this reality.

Up to this point, at least, the major difficulty has had to do not with the willingness of neutralist states to serve, but with the willingness of the great powers to be served. The problem of securing the necessary consent of the great antagonists is intimately connected with the issue of the neutral character of the UN in its practice of preventive diplomacy. The great powers will tolerate or support UN action in this realm only if they *want* the neutralization of a given trouble spot and if they *believe* in the neutral character of the UN's activity.

Let us look first at the question of the will of the great powers. In the major cases that have arisen–UNEF and ONUC–the United States has welcomed neutralization. The American stake in the avoidance of the new confrontations that might disturb the Cold War situation has been amply recognized. Nevertheless, it is not at all clear that either our public or our government is prepared to accept the general proposition that the UN can best serve us–or the world–by operating as a neutral force in global politics. We have valued the UN primarily as an instrument whereby Western victories have been won–or, at least, as a stage upon which Western triumphs have been enacted–and it is not easy to shift to the view that its value to us may be increased as our control over its operations diminishes. Yet, the point stands that the United States has approved and supported the neutralizing function of the UN in the Middle East and Congo cases.

The attitude of the Soviet Union has been different. In the case of UNEF, Soviet disapproval has taken the mild form of passive opposition–refusal to contribute financial support. One might make a case that this is really passive acquiescence. The Congo, of course, makes a much more interesting story. Why did the Soviet Union, after initially supporting the Congo operation, turn against it? A plausible answer is that the USSR did not want the UN to achieve the neutralization of the Congo, but preferred to have a free hand in undertaking to achieve the Communization of the Congo. The Soviet Union supported the UN initiative in the hope that it would contribute to the de-Westernization of the Congo–notably by ousting the Belgians–and then moved to enter its own Soviet elements into the situation. This analysis would suggest that the Soviets did not want to avoid the intrusion of the Cold War competition into the Congo, but welcomed such a competition in the expectation that they would win.

The second problem is that of great-power confidence in the impartial character of the UN: can the organization be trusted to function neutrally in the no-man's-land of the Cold War? The experience of the United States presents no difficulties for us. With considerable reason, we have normally regarded the UN as a pro-Western institution; at worst, it has appeared to function, or to be likely to function, neutrally. Again, the Soviet case is quite different. Starting with a deep-rooted conviction that it confronts a hostile world, the Soviet Union has had a virtually unrelieved experience as a perpetual minority in the UN; from the Soviet vantage point, the UN might, at best—but most improbably—function with genuine impartiality as between East and West. Note that the constant theme of the Soviet attack upon the conduct of the Congo operation is that ONUC is only spuriously neutral, that the whole affair represents the prostitution of the UN to the service of the Western powers. I am in no position to judge the sincerity of the Soviet assertions, although I must admit to some difficulty in believing that a Russian would not have serious doubts about the impartiality of the UN. We have not helped matters by our inveterate declarations that the UN does, and assertions that it should, serve the anti-Soviet cause—interspersed occasionally with appeals to the Soviets to recognize the "obvious" fact that the UN presides with majestic impartiality over the affairs of all the nations.

Indeed, the Soviets are not alone in interpreting the Congo operation as a move favorable to the West. Note what Ambassador Adlai Stevenson said in an address at Hofstra College on June 5, 1961:

> "The Belgian withdrawal was followed by anarchy with which on the one hand the Belgians stepped back and on the other the Russians began to step in. In these circumstances, any direct intervention by the West would have been interpreted as an attempt to reimpose colonialism. Local opinion would have swung over to support the Communists, and the West would have been left in the impossible position of fighting a guerrilla war against a background of implacable local hostility . . . direct Western interventions tend of their very nature to produce a revulsion of local feeling which threatens the effectiveness of the intervention. . . . The result is that in situations such as the Congo, the Western World would be almost powerless if there were no United Nations force available to restore order, [and] check a takeover by an outside power. . . . Direct Western action would only hasten a communist takeover."

Mr. Stevenson went on to say explicitly that the UN had frustrated the Soviet plan to establish control over the Congo, and that the UN is "the only instrument by which the end of the Western system of colonialism can be prevented from opening the doors to the new imperialism of the East."[5]

---

[5] Adlai E. Stevenson, "The United Nations First Step Toward a World Under Law," *Department of State Bulletin,* Vol. 45, 1961, p. 70.

I do not mean to be critical of the UN's giving the West a victory which, according to Mr. Stevenson, the West could not have won for itself. My point is that if an official American spokesman can regard the UN's Congo operation as an intervention justified less by its helping both blocs to avoid the dangers of a confrontation than by its helping the West to contain the expansionist thrust of the Communist bloc, it is plausible that a Soviet spokesman should regard the operation as an instance of unneutral, pro-Western, UN activity. Moreover, if we regard the Congo action as a defeat inflicted by the UN upon the Soviet Union, it hardly makes sense for us to expect that the Soviets will refrain from opposing the action, or will help to pay for it, or will be inspired to assist in equipping the UN to act similarly in future contingencies.

The Congo operation has not yet been concluded, although it now appears likely to be brought to a successful conclusion. This possibility might be taken as an indication that preventive diplomacy can, after all, be effectively performed in the face of great-power opposition. Perhaps the Soviet attack upon the operation was never as determined as it was made to appear, or the Soviet hostility was mollified by the alterations of UN policy and personnel which occurred in the course of the operation. In any event, the Soviet Union refrained from carrying out the threat to wreck the organization because of its activity in the Congo. While the outcome of the Congo case may suggest the wisdom of testing the limits of Soviet toleration for operations of this kind, rather than surrendering to announced opposition, it ought not to stimulate the confident assumption that the UN can be regularly used to carry out the function of preventive diplomacy, with or without the support or acquiescence of such a power as the Soviet Union. The extreme difficulties which the Soviet reaction against the Congo operation posed, and the grave risks which the UN encountered in conducting that operation under the political circumstances which developed, should be taken as a warning against adopting that assumption. Regardless of the outcome of the Congo case, it seems, on balance, to confirm the general proposition that the UN can effectively perform the quasi-military role attributed to it under the theory of preventive diplomacy only if, and insofar as, the major powers are impelled by their perceptions of their own interests to welcome UN interposition as a means of helping them to avoid dangerous confrontations, and are convinced that the UN can be relied upon to act in a neutral manner in the exercise of this function.

It appears that the only significant military function which may reasonably be attributed to the UN is that suggested by the theory of preventive diplomacy—the conduct of operations, analogous to UNEF and ONUC, designed to assist the great powers in keeping the Cold War cold. This can be done for the great powers only if they are agreed in wanting it to be done, and only if each of them is confident that the UN will genuinely promote the neutralization of trouble spots, not act in the interest of the other. The outlook for the continuation and development of this role by the UN is discouraging, primarily because of the disaffection of the USSR. If the Soviet Union is not persuaded that it has more to gain from the containment of the Cold War, the prevention of its spreading into new and dangerously explosive situations, than from the waging of the Cold War competition wherever it may spread—and if the Soviet Union is not persuaded that the UN is capable of serving with genuine neutrality as an agent of preventive diplomacy—then it seems to me that it is a major task of American policy, inside and outside of the UN, to promote these convictions on the part of the Soviet Union. If the United States and the Soviet Union can join in accepting and even in valuing the performance of this role by the UN, it seems to me that the organization may contribute significantly to the stabilization of the global situation. If they cannot, the UN may yet contribute valuable services in other realms, but I see no important role for it with respect to the use of military force under international auspices.

The Political and Philosophical Aspects of U.N. Security Forces

John W. Holmes

This is a conclave of pragmatists. Our concern is with a category of international mechanisms that have grown out of experience, which are known to work, however imperfectly. This is not a constitutional convention of philosophers composing utopias. The value of our subject matter is that it is related to the real world of conflict, confusion and cross-purposes. We must nevertheless try to see it in perspective, try to set it against what the political philosophers say is required and estimate in what ways it is wanting. We must examine how or whether it fulfils a function in men's progress to a governed world, and even ask whether we are on the right or wrong track. We shall no doubt address ourselves largely to the means by which U.N. peace-keeping practices can be functionally improved for the kind of purposes in which they are now engaged. We shall also have in mind how they might be developed to meet new situations, how they might ease us through the revolutionary upheavals ahead, and what if any relation they have to the international force prescribed for a disarming and disarmed world.

The purpose of this exercise in perspective is not only to assess the opportunities for development but also to rid ourselves of illusions. These illusions are often bred of the rhetoric inevitably–and often excusably–used about U.N.

John W. Holmes, "The Political and Philosophical Aspects of U.N. Security Forces," *International Journal,* Vol. 19, No. 3 (Summer 1964), pp. 292-307. Reprinted by permission of the author and of *International Journal.* John W. Holmes is President of the Canadian Institute of International Affairs. This article is a slightly amended version of a paper read at a conference on U.N. security forces at Oslo, February 20, 1964.

Emergency Force (UNEF), U.N. Operations in the Congo (ONUC) and the other gallant achievements of U.N. security forces. We need optimism to encourage us, but the optimist is usually the man who recognizes the limitation both of what has been attempted and what has been accomplished; the cynic who paralyzes our endeavours is often a man frustrated by visions of a dream world.

One is faced at the beginning with a problem of definition. Our principal interest is in the Gaza and Congo forces, but the product of U.N. experience has been not a single kind of international force but rather a variety of supervisory armies, observer corps, border patrols, ranging from small groups of officers to military units numbering thousands. Much of their virtue lies in their diversity. It is hard to identify what they have in common except that they are all "forces" which accomplish their missions not really by force at all but by the persuasion of their presence. As is known from the Congo experience, there is still need to limit the use of force to accord with varying situations. This kind of intervention is most effective when the military force is associated with a U.N. mediatory presence. It is more closely related in kind to the nonmilitary mediation of the United Nations between Cambodia and Thailand, for example, than to the United Nation's single effort at collective security action in Korea. This is not collective security action in the proper sense of the term at all. The force, as an instrument of the United Nations, armed or unarmed, interposes rather than enforces, develops the U.N. role neither as a policeman nor an avenging fury but as an objective entity. The United Nations accepts as inevitable the quarrelsomeness of its members and seeks in this way only to get them to agree. The pure objectivity of the force, however, is far from absolute. The United Nations often does not pretend to be neutral in these disputes. It may provide a force as in Yemen without any commitment on the merits of the case, and it may seek to be uncommitted in internal disputes as in Lebanon or the Congo. However, over Congo or Suez, U.N. bodies adopted moral positions on aspects of the issues at stake. In the light of U.N. opposition to certain parties in the Suez and Congo cases, some element of enforcement was implicit in the very U.N. presence, even if the military power was by no means adequate to impose a U.N. will.

There is no generalization which accurately fits all these things. The function of these bodies is adapted and adjusted to accord with the moral and military strength the United Nations musters in the particular situation and in the certainty of its convictions about the rights and wrong of the case. The certainty of its convictions, needless to say, is determined not just by the validity of the respective arguments of the disputants but also by the weight which their partisans can throw about in U.N. councils. The power and authority are affected by the degree of unanimity which exists in the United Nations–and particularly among the leading powers.

A perceptive explanation of the function of U.N. peace-keeping forces as now developed is given by Inis Claude in his *Power and International Relations:*

"This . . . is not a device for defeating aggressors—and certainly not for coercing great powers determined to expand the sphere of their control—but for assisting the major powers in avoiding the expansion and sharpening of their conflicts and the consequent degeneration of whatever stability they may have been able to achieve in their mutual relationships. The best hope for the United Nations is not that it may be able to develop a military establishment which will enable it to exercise coercive control over great powers, but that it may be able to continue the development of its capability to serve the interests of the great powers—and of the rest of the world—by helping them to contain their conflicts, to limit their competition, and to stabilize their relationships. The greatest political contribution of the United Nations in our time to the management of international power relationships lies not in implementing collective security or instituting world government, but in helping to improve and stabilize the working of the balance of power system, which is, for better or for worse, the operative mechanism of contemporary international politics. The immediate task, in short, is to make the world safe for the balance of power system, and the balance system safe for the world."[1]

Professor Claude's definition sets out U.N. security forces in their place in the history of international relations. We might at this point look at our accumulated U.N. peace-keeping experience in relation to two concepts of international forces: first, the persistent anticipation of an "international police force" capable of enforcing world law or agreed international decisions anywhere in the world; and secondly, the San Francisco plan embodied in the U.N. Charter for a security force composed of national contingents placed at the disposal of the United Nations and acting on the basis of great power consensus.

With the concept of an "international police force" this U.N. peace-keeping has little in common. It is generically different because it is based on a quite different view of the relations among peoples. The "international police force" assumes a delegation of supreme authority to a world federal government or at least to some authority with supreme security functions. Such a force, to exercise unquestioned power, would have to operate in a virtually disarmed world. Our kind of peace-keeping assumes the necessity of acting in a world in which military power is controlled by states, although the states may on occasions delegate military force for international assignments. That this is the kind of world we are going to live in for a long time to come—unless we expire in it—is the most prudent assumption. It is not likely to be changed merely by imprecations against the wickedness of national sovereignty, because the disorders which trouble us have their roots not in the petty stubbornness of nation states but in the disorderly contours of the earth's

---

[1] Inis L. Claude, Jr., *Power and International Relations* (New York; 1962), p. 285.

surface and the multiplicity of tribes who inhabit it. Inter-tribal conflicts would outlive the destruction or sublimation of national sovereignty. My own view is that for an inherently disorderly universe a flexible array of sovereign states of varying shapes and sizes is probably the safest system of government, and the world is less likely to blow up if we have a United Nations of a non-federal kind and peace-keeping methods which are essentially diplomatic in character. The difference between these two concepts—our peace-keeping and the international police force—seems to me so clear I hesitate to labour the obvious. The only real question is whether or not we should see in the Gaza and Congo forces the nucleus of an "international police force." One can be misled by seeing too much significance in what have been reasonably successful experiments with polyglot military units. It is not, however, the composition of the international force but the control of it which is crucial. We are not within far distant sight of an international authority capable of mounting and directing an international police. It is, in fact, too early to say whether the "international police force" is our goal at all. In the meantime, assuming that it is could lead us into experiments which are bound to fail and destroy with them the sound precedents which have been established.

Although it is customary to decry the illusions of the constitution-makers at Yalta, Dumbarton Oaks, and San Francisco, they were closer to earth than are those who dream of the "international police force." If we want to make progress from where we stand we might better set as our target the kind of force envisaged in Article 43, approaching it, however, enriched by the variety of experience we have had in U.N. peace-keeping by means never envisaged in 1945. The kind of peace-keeping we have developed did not, of course, have its roots in Article 43: it developed when the effort by the Military Staff Committee to implement Article 43 failed. The essence of the San Francisco principle of security was the delegation by member states, especially the great powers, of forces to serve the purposes of the U.N. Those purposes would be enforceable because they would be supported by the great powers—or if not supported by all of them, at least not actively opposed by any great power. The principle broke down, not because it was intrinsically unsound, but because the great powers moved rapidly away from consensus.

The kind of peace-keeping functions the United Nations has developed did not come as a conscious alternative to Article 43; they just evolved out of necessity. The experiment started before, and was resumed after, the Korean experience convinced most people that, although the Korean effort was by no means a failure, it was *sui generis* and did not provide a precedent for U.N. collective security action which could be followed again. The early experience of U.N. intervention in Greece, Indonesia, Kashmir, Palestine were steps on the way to the much bolder experiment of UNEF, and the remarkable success of UNEF set a pattern for the plunge into the Congo. These achievements were pragmatic. I don't believe anyone, scholar or bureaucrat, had articulated in advance this particular kind of middle power operation, although Mr. Trygve Lie certainly deserves credit for adumbrating, in his early proposals for a U.N. Guard Force, the concept of a limited U.N. body of a military kind capable of maintaining in troubled areas the agents of U.N. mediation. Now, of course, we have a great deal of theory being expounded about this kind of peace-keeping, but it is a codification of what has taken place and a projection of past experience into the future—and all the sounder for being that. There was never a deliberate intention in setting up U.N. forces as we know them to set the United Nations off on a different course from that which had been contemplated in the Charter. It was an effort to cope as well as possible with the dangerous situations which flared all over the world during a period of great power disunity. It was in fact the United Nations groping, with lessor powers as its agents, to take advantage of the elemental but tacit consensus which did exist among the great powers, the consensus of fear of uncontrollable conflict. That consensus was neither strong nor explicit enough for the great powers to act directly by combination of their own forces, but they were prepared to let others act. Some of the great powers viewed these events with, to say the least, very little enthusiasm, but their fear of conflict and their deference to a U.N. majority have held them back from bold enough opposition to wreck the operations.

The kind of U.N. security forces we are talking about, in which lesser rather than great powers make personnel available for U.N. purposes, is a great deal closer in kind to the San Francisco concept than to the idea of an "international police force." The difference, which is admittedly great, lies in the scope of action which can be envisaged without great power participation. We must be extremely wary of assuming that the rudimentary peace-keeping we have been able to develop could, in the absence of a far larger degree of great power consensus than now exists, be pushed to fulfil the collective security function which the framers of the Charter had in mind. It should not be forgotten, however, that it was not the intention of the great powers who drafted the essential principles of the Charter that the U.N. security provisions should be implemented against any of them; that denial was implicit in the provision for the veto on which they all insisted. It is the extent of great power consensus rather than any fundamental difference between the principle of Articles 42 and 43 on the one hand and the principle of UNEF or ONUC on the other which determines whether or not U.N. security forces can expand the area of their competence.

There is much reason for gratification with the results so far achieved. Fighting was stopped in Greece, Indonesia, Kashmir. Relative stability was established in the Middle East. The Congo has a chance. The fact that all this has been achieved to a considerable extent by diplomatic pressures of the great powers outside the United Nations is no reason for despondency about the U.N. role. The United Nations is essentially a broad framework. It is a purpose of U.N. peace-keeping to be associated with or to be an agent of the direct negotiation between disputants or their intermediaries. What it might be asked, is outside the United Nations if it contributes to a reasonable settlement of disputes? In addition to these specific achievements in various parts of the planet has been the experience of international collaboration. Brian Urquhart,[2] who should know, put it this way:

"The thousands of soldiers from some twenty countries who accepted the challenge in the Congo have begun to learn to apply the arts of war to the infinitely subtle and difficult problems of maintaining the peace—this may be a development of more lasting importance than what eventually does or does not happen in the Congo itself."[3]

The accomplishments of U.N. peace-keeping should not be underestimated; and yet they raise certain difficult questions not only about the future of U.N. peace-keeping but about the record.

The basic thesis of these enterprises is that our object is to stop the fighting to provide an opportunity for negotiated settlement. A settlement was achieved in Indonesia, although it may have set a precedent for a later U.N. role in West Irian that was more a face-saving than a peace-keeping operation. There is no settlement after fifteen years in Kashmir or Palestine. The U.N. Military Observer Group in India and Pakistan (UNMOPIG) and U.N. Truce Supervision Organization (UNTSO) look like being permanent establishments. UNEF has provided a framework for a temporary peace, but lasting peace seems no nearer. The U.N. Observer Group in Lebanon (UNOGIL) did help to make possible a transition of political power in Lebanon, although some might argue that this was achieved by the intervention of the U.S. Marines. A final verdict on the accomplishment of ONUC cannot yet be given with assurance. It is said, of course, that the cost of maintaining these establishments is relatively small in an armed world and well worth while. Fighting has been contained, although the aim of promoting settlement has all too seldom been achieved.

A more disturbing question is whether the intervention of the United Nations made a lasting settlement more difficult. We live in a world in the throes of violent change, of old discontents, new and unstable governments, empires in fission and drastic inequalities. Is the achievement of a new stability dependent on the completion of violent solutions whether they are in the abstract good or bad? Would the sub-continent, for instance, be more or less tranquil if the situation had been frozen after rather than before the Pakistanis secured a solution by

[2] Brian E. Urquhart is Principal Officer in the Office of the Under-Secretary for Special Political Affairs of the United Nations, and formerly Representative of the United Nations in Elisabethville.

[3] Brian E. Urquhart, "United Nations Peace Forces and the Changing United Nations: An International Perspective", *International Organization,* Vol. XVII, No. 2, Spring, 1963, p. 347.

force? Would there be less ferment in the Middle East if the Israelis had been able to consolidate their positions on the old borders of Palestine; or in Central Africa if some strongman had had a chance to establish his authority by force over the whole of the Congo before the United Nations arrived on the scene in 1960? Or consider the obverse argument: how happy would we be if the United Nations, in accordance with peace-keeping precedents, had established a U.N. presence with force to promote a peaceful settlement in Goa before the Indians took direct action? Without U.N. intervention in Palestine or Congo there would of course have been bitterness and continuing tension; but would the rough arbitrament of the violent solution have provided a better base for progress in the area than the perpetuation of uncertainty and the immobility imposed by the U.N. presence? And the cost of this is that the United Nations is involved indefinitely in financial drains which threaten its health and have led its major members into an impasse that could wreck the organization. Should we not at least have tied the continuing presence of a costly U.N. force to a commitment of the disputants to serious negotiation?

Of course, I think the answer to these questions is no. It seems to me that although the second and major half of our aim has not been accomplished, it was still worth while to stop the fighting. The fighting may not have spread, and the great powers may not have become involved as we feared, but the risk of these things happening was too great to be taken. History is long, and fifteen years is not an excessive period in which to wait for peace to come when the grudge is ancient. We ought to show the same patience with small cold wars as we are learning to show over the big one. This is how it appears to me but I have been too much involved in these things ever to see them objectively. Nor has my country ever been tranquillized or paralyzed by U.N. peace-keeping. We can never know what might have happened, and we dare not assume that the way history worked itself out was the right way. We have to keep these hypothetical but nasty questions before us if for no other reason than to recognize that we must be discriminating in the application of this kind of U.N. force. There is no generally valid answer. The intervention of U.N. forces may have been wrong in some past cases and right in others.

We tend too early to accept as categorical the distinctions between disputes in which the great powers are and those in which they are not directly involved. We tend to dismiss the Korean crisis of 1950 by explaining that it has nothing to do with our kind of peace-keeping. Well, it may not belong to this chapter of the book, but it was a very real crisis. There is no guarantee that there will not be more like it, and the United Nations will not be able simply to declare it out of bounds. On the other hand, would it have been better to try in Korea our more conventional kind of U.N. peace-keeping? Would it have been better for the United Nations to remain uncommitted as a belligerent and keep itself available for good offices in the settlement? If the United Nations had left the fighting to the immediate parties and their great and small power friends, might it have had a better chance to be the *deus ex machina* when the truce was in sight? Would we thereby have avoided the Chinese argument that the United Nations, as a belligerent, had forfeited any right to an arbitral role in the reunification of Korea? As one who was present at Lake Success in the summer of 1950, I do not see how we could have acted otherwise. We were still perhaps beguiled by the collective security concept of the United Nation's function, and this looked like a challenge to U.N. authority before which it would be fatal to fail. The implications of the balance of terror had not yet been absorbed. Nevertheless, the hypothetical questions about Korea we must ask ourselves in retrospect so that we shall calculate wisely in the next crisis.

A final and quite unrelated question is whether we may now be in danger of letting the United Nations become a mere service agency, hiring out policemen to maintain agreements in which it plays no part. In West Irian and Yemen the United Nations had no real say at all in the truces or settlements agreed on by the parties with the good offices or pressure of great powers; and yet it has organized the supervision. As I have suggested earlier, one must not under present circumstances reject reasonable settlements reached off the U.N. premises. However, the United Nations must be sure they are reasonable before it accepts responsibility for maintaining them. While avoiding the pretension to settle all disputes by its captious majorities, the United Nations must at the same time avoid the humiliation of being used by powers, great or small, for their private purposes.

Each of these questions could be exhaustively argued, and there is no final answer. However, we ought not to let our enthusiasm for accomplishments prevent us from keeping these doubts in the back of our minds.

We are confronted now, and particularly since July, 1960, with a conflict between political and practical realities. The United Nations has been conducting military operations which defy every rule of good soldiering. The world political situation, however, is such that another U.N. force is likely to be required at any time, but a direct attack on the military problems seems impossible.

The argument for a nucleus of a permanent force, at the very least a considerable military establishment in the Secretariat, the training of standby forces, perhaps even U.N. bases and a U.N. intelligence network seems to this layman incontrovertible. It is clear, however, that for international political reasons a standing U.N. force is out of the question. The consensus does not exist which would authorize us to go very far beyond Dag Hammarskjöld's recommendation of a force formed *ad hoc* from standby forces in contributing countries, and it is politically unwise for a westerner to push. The political advantages of spontaneous improvisation are great, and it is tempting for statesmen, diplomats, and theorists like me to be complacent, to say that it always has been worked out somehow and will the next time. But the history of ONUC provides too much proof of what a near thing it was—so much luck, so much depending on heroic improvisation and the availability of remarkable men. We must press hard and with as sound a diplomatic base as possible to achieve at least minimal improvements: extension of Secretariat functions, establishment of precedents and procedure, reliable financial provisions, training of experts—if not undertaken by the United Nations itself, possibly by some unofficial international institution growing out of this conference.

Aside from improving the machinery, is there any way we can extend the applicability of present procedures? The formal definition of bolder theories of peace-keeping by any U.N. sub-committee would be as futile as the attempt to define aggression. Every step forward has been taken in the pressure of necessity when the consensus enlarges. Still, we can in private think about the direction in which progress might move.

All plans for the future must be based on a recognition of the slender resources available—personnel and material, as well as financial. We shudder at the prospect of another crisis, because those in which we are still involved absorb all the people we can get. How could the Secretariat cope with another operation like ONUC? I hasten to recognize that I would have asked the same question before Congo, a challenge which revealed extraordinary resources from African states. Diplomats should not assume the United Nations cannot cope with another such challenge, but they should not forget that U.N. forces do not spring fully armed out of thin air.

Need we accept as permanently desirable that only middle and small powers—preferably uncommitted—should participate in U.N. security forces? The arguments for doing so are strong. Not only has this practice been good for the United Nations, it has been good for the middle powers. We of the middle powers have all felt that our contributions to U.N. forces have given us a purpose in the world which justified our existence. We have even been tempted into smugness *vis-a-vis* the quarrelsome and predatory great powers. It has been good, practical U.N. politics to emphasize the objectivity of the U.N. forces and attribute it to the chastity of the weak powers which manned them, forgetting that lesser powers can have even more vigorous special interests in disputes than remoter great powers. We have conveniently forgotten also the part the great powers have actually played in the operations. The U.S. role in UNEF and ONUC may have been confined to transport and general servicing, but it has been indispensable. Britain and the Soviet Union have also made facilities and transport available. I recognize of course, that the part the Soviet Union played may not be considered a contribution, and that it can be argued that the United States and Britain have pursued special interests. So have many of the lesser powers involved in the U.N. Force. Great powers can be neutral enough in some controversies. Consider, for instance, the role the United States is playing in the disputes involving Indonesia—and, I add hopefully, the role France might play in Asia.

In staffing international forces, we might be less absolute in our thinking. If we have to cope with new situations, we shall almost certainly have again to call on the Americans for help. If the trouble should come in the Western Hemisphere it would be better to ask the British and French. It would be much better, of course, if we could also make use of Soviet services. Despite the obvious disadvantages, the advantages of including the Russians could be much greater than merely helping with the logistics. It could assist in winning them from an attitude of mistrustful toleration of exercises in which no members of their camp participate to positive collaboration in U.N. peace-keeping. The extending U.S.-Soviet dialogue could conceivably make this possible. The inclusion of Soviet or Eastern European personnel in U.N. forces would be primarily a reflection of rather than a cause of changing great power relations. We should recognize, however, that the broadening of the composition of U.N. forces is something to be anticipated rather than avoided, even though the United Nations cannot safely move too far ahead of the great powers in a policy based on *détente*.

Only if there is collaboration among the great powers in peace-keeping can we ever hope to apply this U.N. function to the great issue of our time. I am not suggesting we could then enforce the principles of collective security on all powers. I am thinking only of peace-keeping roles extended, for instance, to Berlin. It would not be wise for the United Nations to venture in its councils to impose a settlement on Berlin, even if it were not prevented from doing so by Article 107. Nevertheless, if the great powers concerned were to reach an agreement which required neutral supervisions, it is conceivable that the United Nations could fulfil that function. There are strong cases for and against the occupying powers doing any such thing, or the United Nations accepting an assignment not of its own making. We must, however, contemplate the possibility that such a role for the United Nations might be found helpful. I do not want to argue here the case for and against zones of disengagement or nuclear disarmament in Europe or elsewhere, but these, too, are possibilities for U.N. service, possibilities which would be useful experiments in testing U.N. supervision of disarmament provisions. They would almost certainly require participation not only of uncommitted forces but also of forces committed to both East and West. It should be borne in mind also, that U.N. supervision was part of the formula on which President Kennedy and Premier Khrushchev found a way out of the impasse in Cuba, even though this was not carried out for reasons which did not seem to involve the validity of U.N. supervision in principle. It is not as certain as commonly stated that U.N. security forces as we know them have no role to play in controversies between the great powers.

It is usually forgotten that we have had for a decade in Indo-China a reasonably successful example of a peace-keeping operation comparable to U.N. missions, established by the great powers and operating in an area where their interests clash dangerously. This precedent is largely ignored by writers on this subject, presumably because it is outside the United Nations. Here we have an example of the great powers, faced in 1954 with the imminent catastrophe of uncontrollable conflict, negotiating a truce even though two of the great powers were not speaking to each other. Supervisory commissions for Viet-Nam, Laos and Cambodia were authorized on the troika principle of one communist country, Poland; one Western country, Canada; with a neutral chairman, India. These commissions were surprisingly effective in the disengagement of troops and populations in the first year or so of the truce and since then in serving as a reminder of international concern in its maintenance. It goes without saying that the troika arrangement often produced deadlock and has seemed more intractable than an entirely neutral body would have been. However, it does represent the real facts of power in the area in a way a neutral commission would not have done. It is fatuous to hanker after a supervisory commission homogeneous enough to reach agreement if such a commission has no influence on the disputants. The truces have been roughly maintained by the equilibrium of those external pressures which were represented in the commissions. It is unfortunate that the deterioration of the truces has diverted attention from a peacekeeping experiment which would be a pilot project for the United Nations—a pilot project which provides warnings as well as precedents. It was at least one step forward from the formula of two Communist states and two neutral states which the United Nations established to supervise the truce in Korea and which resulted in total deadlock. Whether it would have been more effective as a U.N. project rather than remaining responsible to a conference of powers is an argument with much significance for our discussion. Certainly the participants would have welcomed U.N. acceptance of the burden of logistics and administration. The lack too of an objective international entity like the U.N. Secretariat meant that the commissions were less coherent or singleminded. On the other hand, this inchoate international mechanism aptly reflected the minimal consensus among the powers. It reflected also the unwillingness of the great powers, even with their veto rights, to concede to a U.N. body the right to interfere in an area of such crucial importance to their vital interests. It was not merely the need to include the Peking government in the arrangements that kept this operation outside the United Nations. Even if the great powers in future are disposed to leave supervision of their settlements to the United Nations, they are likely to keep the United Nations as far removed as possible from the politics of the settlement.

For the time being we shall have to improve our U.N. peace-keeping forces on the accepted basis—with the Secretariat and the middle powers in the foreground and the great powers in the background. There are limitations, however, to what can be accomplished unless participation becomes more nearly universal and all the great powers are committed. Even if the fifth great power, sitting sullenly outside, shows no inclination to participate, and one of the lesser great powers holds such activities in contempt, concurrence of the other three would greatly extend the area of operation.

I do not think the kind of peace-keeping developed in Gaza and the Congo is incompatible with the basis of security envisaged at San Francisco. If we are working our way towards great power unanimity at least on fundamental attitudes to war and peace, then I think we should try to work our way back—or forward—to the basis of Article 43. If we do so, we could resume the effort to implement the Charter, a great deal wiser, on the one hand, from the United Nations' experience with collective security over Korea and, on the other hand, from its success with procedures of truce-keeping, tranquillization, and prevention adapted to the rudimentary state of international organization. It is to be hoped also that the great powers would have acquired a broader appreciation than they had in 1946 of the role lesser powers can play in the maintenance of peace.

It is only by this path that we could ever find our way to the international force which is expected to operate while the world disarms. How this international force would work I do not yet comprehend. That we cannot have disarmament without some kind of international force is a dogma now accepted by the two superpowers and most other people. The United States in its disarmament proposals of April, 1963, envisaged by the end of the disarming process a U.N. force with "sufficient armed forces and armaments so that no state could challenge it." Most students of international security measures discourage belief in the foreseeable possibility of such a force based on a monopoly of military powers under the control of a world authority responsible to the peoples of the world. Nevertheless, this utopian vision appears in the formal proposals of a hard-headed government. (The cynic could say that this is the American way of making sure that there will never be a state of total disarmament, but the cynic is never more than partly right when he talks about American policy.) On such a conception I remain agnostic. I cannot believe in it as a foreseeable goal, any more than I can believe that a federal state could ever be fitted safely to the jagged geography of this universe. At the same time I recognize that we cannot rule out the possibility of some day coming to these answers. I am inclined to think, however, that too many minds are frozen in the assumption that progress must be found in steps which lead towards the international police force and the world federation, thereby limiting the range of invention. It could lead us up constant blind alleys instead of more promising approaches.

In a recent report on *Disarmament and European Security* prepared for the Institute for Strategic Studies appears the following comment on the world authority required for a disarmed world:

"In the end, it is possible that such an authority might be created through the commitment of national forces to a unified command in the manner foreseen by paragraph 8 of the Nassau Agreement, for the more limited purposes of the North Atlantic Treaty Organization. This system allows countries such as the United States and the United Kingdom to take part in a unified system while remaining secure in the knowledge they have in the hands of their own officers weapons which can, if necessary, be used under the orders of their own chiefs of staff. To rely on a peace-keeping authority constituted on this basis (a system much closer to what the Russians are proposing than what the West appears to be proposing) is to give the appearance of disarmament without for many years abandoning the reality of national power. But with this security national military systems would erode away, like the methods of personal and local self-protection in the old American West. The political framework of a disarmed world could be created and could through custom and acceptance be relied on increasingly to carry the burden of security."

This kind of thinking seems to me more profitable than the concoction of constitutions for international armies rooted to no feasible political institution. It is closer to our U.N. experience and it is closer to the intentions of the Charter on which there was great power agreement in 1945. Apocalyptic pronouncements that a world moving fast to destruction requires drastic measures are hard to deny, but they don't get us over the steps to Utopia. We must rather keep our eyes on the world as it exists and the progress that has been made, hoping that the moderation of international relations because of the dread facts of power and growing habits of collaboration will enable us to keep the peace more effectively and more reliably.

In Search of a Thread: The UN In the Congo Labyrinth

Stanley Hoffmann

It is possible to distinguish roughly two periods in the history of the United Nations. During the first, which lasted until the middle nineteen fifties, the Western powers had a fairly secure majority in the General Assembly, and Cold War issues tended to dominate. The supreme test of that first phase was the Korean War. It showed both that the new International Organization refused to practice appeasement and that in a bipolar world whose main antagonists were engaged in an idealogical struggle and endowed with nuclear weapons, UN intervention in the conflicts between the blocs would either expose the Organization to a demonstration of impotence or submit the world to the risks of escalation. A second phase began when membership of the UN increased, and the newly-independent nations became the biggest group within the Assembly. Now, as Dag Hammarskjöld put it in his report to the fifteenth General Assembly, the main task in the area of peace and security shifted to "preventive diplomacy"—rushing to the scene of fires which break out "outside the sphere of bloc differences" before the arrival of the major contenders. The biggest challenge has been the Congo crisis. It has tested all the assumptions which had been made—by scholars as well as by the late Secretary-General—about the role of the UN, its possibilities and its limits, and about the relations between its principal organs and its main groups of members.

Stanley Hoffmann, "In Search of a Thread: The UN in the Congo Labyrinth," *International Organization,* Vol. 16, No. 2 (Spring 1962), pp. 331-361. Reprinted by permission of *International Organization.*

It is as if a malevolent historical force had thrown into one pot all the separate problems with which the Organization had dealt, *seriatim,* in previous crises, plus some enormous new ones as well. It is as if the UN had had to play, at once, the role of three mythological figures. Sisyphus, of course, and, as usual, three times already the crisis appeared "almost" over, and the Secretary-General reported that the circle had been closed, only to discover that it was a vicious one. The Congo has also behaved as a Sphinx to the UN Oedipus: the questions which the Organization has been asked to answer have become increasingly tougher. Finally, the complications have been so great, and the moves of the World Organization have been so laborious, that one is tempted to compare it to Theseus looking for the Minotaur in the labyrinth; but Theseus, here, had no reliable thread.

It is impossible, obviously, to deal with all the facets of the crisis. I will limit myself to the period from July 1960 to January 1962, and I will not discuss either the financial aspects of the crisis, or the civilian operation in the Congo. I will concentrate on the attempts made by the political organs of the UN to find a thread, and on the lessons which can be drawn from the experience; but it is not possible to write a detailed history of those attempts in an article, or to arrive at peremptory conclusions at this stage. The reader will have to be satisfied with highlights, and with questions.

I THE STORY

First phase; July 1960. In order not to lose our own way, we should keep in mind the distinction between the *end* of the UN mission in the Congo, and the *means* at the UN disposal. When the Congolese *force publique* revolted and Belgian troops intervened, a whole range of issues appeared: (a) the problem to which two cables signed by President Kasavubu and Prime Minister Lumumba referred: the presence of Belgian troops; (b) the breakdown of law and order, which had been the cause of their intervention; (c) the danger of intervention from third powers as well, should the UN fail to cope adequately with the crisis. Already, on July 12, Vice-Premier Gizenga had appealed to the United States. On July 13, one of the cables mentioned threatened the UN with an appeal by the Congo to the Bandung powers. On July 14, Messrs. Kasavubu and Lumumba cabled Mr. Khrushchev;[1] (d) the issue of the territorial integrity of the Congo—for on July 11 Mr. Tshombé had proclaimed the independence of Katanga.

[1]For the text of those cables, see *Chronique de Politique Etrangère,* July-November 1960 (Vol. 13, Nos. 4-6), pp. 668 and 696.

The two cables of the Congolese leaders requested UN aid exclusively on the first count—against what was termed Belgian aggression. The secession of Katanga was presented by them as an aspect of Belgium's conspiracy rather than as a separate issue. The "internal situation in Congo" was expressly ruled out from the request for aid.

Since the Republic of the Congo was not yet a member of the UN,[2] however, the Security Council met, not at the request of the Congolese leaders, but at the request of the Secretary-General, acting under Article 99 of the Charter. It is convenient, for the sake of analysis, to lump together the first two debates of the Security Council, the two statements made by Mr. Hammarskjöld on July 13 and 20, his first report of July 18, and the two resolutions of July 14 and 22.

As for the *nature* of the UN task, it became immediately clear that, contrary to the qualification given in the Congolese cables and to the terms of Soviet proposals, the UN action would not be an enforcement action under Articles 41 and 42, against an aggressor. It was not the Korean precedent that was being followed, but the precedents of all the other operations in which the UN had acted not as a soldier, but as a fireman. The precise legal basis of the UN intervention was not made clear (and remains in doubt), but the political nature was unmistakable.

As for the *objectives* of the UN, the situation was more complicated. One of the issues listed above was dealt with directly in both resolutions: the withdrawal of Belgian troops became the first objective. The restoration of law and order was the object of the key provision of the resolution of July 14—the one which authorized "the Secretary-General to take the necessary steps, in consultation with the Government of the Republic of the Congo, to provide the Government with such military assistance as may be necessary, until . . . the national security forces may be able, in the opinion of the Government, to meet fully their tasks." The goal of eliminating foreign interference was set in the second resolution, what foreign governments were asked not to do was "to impede the restoration of law and order and the exercise by the Government of the Congo of its authority"—not the only kind of interference, as one soon discovered. The issue of secession was alluded to obliquely—in the same sentence. Foreign governments were also asked to refrain from undermining the territorial integrity and the political independence of the Congo. Thus, for the time being, the emphasis was being put only on the other three objectives, of which two were quite familiar. For the withdrawal of the invader and the insulation of the troubled area had been precisely the objectives of the UN in the crises of Suez and Lebanon.

---

[1] Non-members can only appeal to the Security Council under Article 35, par. 2, i.e., in the framework of Chapter VI. See Michel Virally, "Les Nations Unies et l'affaire du Congo en 1960," *Annuaire francais de Droit International*, VI, 1960, pp. 557-559 and pp. 563-564.

As for the *means,* they consisted of the UN peace force created in accordance with the resolution of July 14. Here again, the thread suggested by Mr. Hammarskjöld was a familiar one; but here the trouble begins. On the one hand, the Secretary-General's statement of July 13 and report of July 18[3] defined the nature of the force as if the Congo were merely Suez and Lebanon revisited. Concerning the force's composition, troops from the permanent members of the Security Council would be ruled out. Concerning the mission of the force, it would "not be authorized to action beyond self-defence." It could not become a party to internal conflicts. It could not be used to enforce a solution of pending problems or to affect the outcome of political conflicts. On the other hand, however, the mission of the UN Operations in the Congo (ONUC) was not the same as that of the UN Emergency Force (UNEF) and the UN Observation Group in Lebanon (UNOGIL). In neither case had the UN been put in charge of assuring law and order within a nation. Mr. Hammarskjöld was applying to a particular set of objectives standards which had been effective in much narrower circumstances. Hence two problems arose, which were going to constitute the UN's main sources of trouble.

First, Mr. Hammarskjöld was raising a new issue—the role of the UN in the domestic disputes within the Congo. The settlement of those disputes was not to be a UN goal. It was indeed an issue which the two Congolese leaders had originally also ruled out of UN jurisdiction. But if those disputes were of no concern to the UN force, what was then the relation of the UN operation to the central government? During the months ahead, this would become one of the major bones of contention among the Members of the UN. Was the UN operation an arm of the central government? Did, on the contrary, the UN have the authority to tell the Congolese how they should govern themselves? The Secretary-General's very insistence on keeping the UN out of internal conflicts dictated his own answer, which was *no* to both questions. Secondly, by answering them in the negative, he was creating a crucial problem: the adequacy of the means to the end. Could a peace force whose activities were restricted by the principles derived from precedents really remedy the breakdown of law and order? The very terms of the agreement Mr. Hammarskjöld signed with the central government concerning ONUC showed that he realized that the precedents were not entirely valid. The Congo government stated that it would be guided by the fact that it had requested military assistance, and the UN affirmed that it intended to maintain its force "until such time as it deems the latter's task to have been fully accomplished."[4] If the restoration of law and order required a smaller degree of UN dependence on the consent of the host state (once consent to the force had

[3] S/PV.873, July 13/14, 1960, and Document S/4389.

[4] Addendum 5 to the Secretary-General's first report, Document S/4389.

been received), would it not require a revision of other principles as well—such as the defensive nature of the operation and its commitment to nonintervention?

Second phase: August 1960. The first test of Mr. Hammarskjöld's policy was the crisis over Katanga in August 1960. The doctrine which he developed in his report of August 6, in the addendum of August 12, and in his statements to the Security Council on August 8 and 21—and which the Council endorsed in the resolution of August 9—confirmed his original interpretation.[5]

The position of the Congolese government was simple. The objectives of the UN ought to be not only the withdrawal of the Belgians and the protection of lives and property, but also the maintenance of Congolese territorial integrity and the establishment of the central government's authority over all the country.[6] Those objectives could be met only if the UN force tried to reach them. What Mr. Lumumba was asking was that ONUC become the secular arm of his government, whose objectives would thus be recognized as those of the whole undertaking.

Mr. Hammarskjöld's interpretation was totally different. He continued to insist on a much narrower list of objectives. Relying heavily on the precedent of Lebanon, he distinguished between (a) the UN duty to prevent outsiders from affecting political developments in the area (hence the need to get the Belgians out of Katanga) and (b) the taking of a stand in internal political disputes. This amounted to saying that the two issues of political control in the Congo and of territorial integrity, both raised by political disputes among the Congolese, would not be among the concerns of the UN (except to the limited extent to which the resolution of July 22 had dealt with the latter). But if his interpretation of the objective was more restrictive than Mr. Lumumba's, his definition of the means rejected the Prime Minister's hierarchy. The UN force would not at all be at the disposal of the central government. It would enter Katanga to carry out the UN mandate, thus defined. But this definition also meant that the central government's authorities could not accompany or follow the UN forces, given Katanga's opposition to them. The combination of a mandate to preserve law and order throughout the Congo, and of a refusal to intervene in domestic disputes, insured that the "law and order" which would prevail in Katanga could only be that of the UN, but not that of the central government.[7] From the viewpoint of Mr. Lumumba, the UN was doing both too little and too much—too much, by reserving

[5]Document S/4417 and Add. 6.

[6]See Mr. Lumumba's letter of August 14 in Document S/4417, Add. 7.

[7]Addendum 6 to Document S/4417 states: (a) that the UN force cannot be used on behalf of the central government to subdue the provincial government; (b) that UN facilities cannot be used to transport civilian or military representatives under the authority of the central government to Katanga, beyond what follows from the general duty to maintain law and order; and (c) that the UN has no right to refuse the central government to take any action of its own in accordance with the principles and purposes of the Charter.

to itself a kind of monopoly of force; too little, by nevertheless refusing to use force itself and by sticking to a narrow definition of its objectives.

Mr. Hammarskjöld's conception was basically a prophylactic one: the role of the UN consists of extinguishing fires, of curtailing violence—both through insulation from outside interference and through elimination of civil war. But two fundamental questions can be raised about such an approach. First, does it not artificially separate the problem of the use of force (inside and outside) from the underlying substantive political issues? This distinction had already characterized the policy of the UN in the Middle East crisis of 1956.[8] There, UNEF intervened so as to get the British, French, and Israelis out of Egypt, but the settlement of the disputes which had led to the explosion was kept quite separate from, and was pursued less vigorously than, the action of the UN to restore peace. Here, the UN, under the Secretary-General's guidance, was putting a ban on violence once again. But it was also passing a self-denying ordinance on the domestic political issues whose very existence was responsible for the resort to force. Those issues were supposed to be resolved peacefully by the Congolese themselves, and ONUC could not intervene except to preserve law and order. This was a police rather than a political conception of the UN role. But, precisely because the policeman was asked to shoot only in self-defense, the success of his mission depended on his not having too much policing to do—i.e. on a rapid settlement of those underlying issues in which he was not supposed to meddle.

Secondly, however, the somewhat artificial separation between the policing mission and the conciliatory function which had ultimately worked in the case of Suez, and which also succeeded in Lebanon because of a quick solution of Lebanon's domestic crisis, was much less tenable in the Congo. In Suez, a restoration of the *status juris* could stabilize, if shakily, the area for some years. In Lebanon, there was no general breakdown of law and order, and no secession. The trouble with Mr. Hammarskjöld's application of the precedents was that it not merely avoided the underlying political issues; it also made much more difficult the accomplishment of those tasks which he himself accepted. For, despite *and* because of his emphasis on nonintervention in domestic conflicts, he was undermining the central government. His reasoning on the nature of Katanga's secession is interesting. The problem, he said, stemmed neither from the presence of Belgian troops there, nor from "a wish of the authorities of the province to secede from the Republic of the Congo. The question is a constitutional one with strong undercurrents of individual and collective political aims."[9] Whether he intended to or not, the Secretary-General was thus questioning the political legitimacy of the *loi fondamentale* and the authority of the central government

[8] See the author's "Sisyphus and the Avalanche," *International Organization*, Summer 1957 (Vol. 11, No. 3), pp. 446-469.

[9] Document S/4417.

established in accordance with that law. The implications were not merely a return to the *status juris* of July 4, but a questioning of this status. Now, if the very constitutional foundations of the Congo were thus put in question, the consequences could not be other than disastrous. For, on the one hand, there was the risk of a vacuum of authority—the central government's being challenged by the definition Mr. Hammarskjöld had given of ONUC's task, but ONUC being, also by definition, prevented from substituting itself for the central government as the supreme political authority in the Congo. And on the other hand, the UN was not seeing to it that this vacuum be filled rapidly, since the ban Mr. Hammarskjöld was putting on the use of force by all parties to domestic disputes threatened to freeze chaos. As a result, the objectives of the UN—law and order, noninterference, and the departure of the Belgians—would be much more difficult to achieve. More violence and chaos were inevitable just as the Secretary-General was prematurely stating that the objectives had been reached. The next stage, he added, would be up to the Congolese people.[10] It was reconciliation and compromise he expected, but total bedlam he got.

Third phase: September 1961-January 1962. The events which followed the Security Council debate of August 21 are well known. Mr. Lumumba, who in July had threatened to turn to the Soviets for help if the Belgians did not leave within a few hours,[11] now asked for and received Soviet help in preparation for a drive against Katanga. His action led to his dismissal by President Kasavubu. The Premier in turn ousted the President. A new government, headed by Mr. Ileo, never became more than a shadow, since parliament never approved it, and since Colonel Mobutu seized what can hardly be called power. The phase which lasted from September 1960 to February 1961 was by far the saddest in the history of the Congo crisis—the winter of everyone's discontent.

On the one hand, the disappearance of any central government, the collapse of all institutions except a President with sharply curtailed powers under the *loi fondamentale*, and a parliament which was both deadlocked and dispersed, made of prophylaxy a pretty hopeless task. Belgian military and paramilitary elements and political and economic advisers were coming back both in Leopoldville and in Elizabethville. Foreign interference was inevitable. It was so obvious that the political vacuum had to be filled, that most of the interested states—i.e. practically everyone, big powers and Afro-Asian nations—took sides in the Congolese political battles. Finally, with the mushrooming of *de facto* authorities all over the Congo, arrests of political rivals, roaming private armies, etc., civil war on political as well as on tribal lines broke out repeatedly. Meanwhile, the two issues which the UN had not tackled directly before—the settlement of political differences and territorial integrity—also remained in suspension.

---

[10] S/PV.887, August 21, 1960.

[11] See Mr. Kanza's statement before the Security Council, S/PV.877, July 20/21, 1960.

On the other hand, the United Nations did not revise its objectives and its means drastically. A few changes in the definition of the goals were made. Thus, in the first place, the General Assembly resolution of September 20 did, so to speak, make the connection between the prophylactic tasks and the domestic political situation. However, the barrage of nonintervention was not abandoned, and the Assembly, in conformity with a wish expressed in Mr. Hammarskjöld's fourth report to the Security Council,[12] merely called on the Congolese for a speedy solution by peaceful means of all internal conflicts, with the assistance of African and Asian representatives appointed by the Advisory Committee the Secretary-General had set up. Thus the Assembly was taking cognizance of the issue which had become the crucial one—the issue of government. But the role of the UN remained limited to conciliation and good offices. The principle that the vacuum of authority had to be filled by the Congolese themselves still stood. Indeed, the same resolution repeated the words, now meaningless, of the resolution of July 14: the Secretary-General's task was "to assist the central government of the Congo in the restoration and the maintenance of law and order." In the second place, the goal of noninterference was faced more realistically. It had not been enough to ask states to refrain from undermining the central government. It was also necessary, in order for "preventive diplomacy" to succeed, to ask states not to lend arms or military personnel to any of the Congolese factions—not even to those which claimed to be the legitimate authority. Thirdly, the same resolution stated, less obliquely than in July, that the territorial integrity of the Congo was one of the objectives of the UN. But here again, implementation remained up in the air. The passage of the resolution to which I refer simply asked the Secretary-General to safeguard the Congo's unity.

A UN operation whose ends and means had been inadequate while there still existed a central government proved even more weak once disintegration spread. Two sets of difficulties became apparent in the new circumstances of quasi-anarchy. First, the distinction among *objectives* to which the Secretary-General was clinging became practically untenable. He still insisted on "the duty . . . to observe strict neutrality in the domestic conflicts."[13] As long as he had been able to give top priority to the task of external prophylaxy—getting the Belgians out and preventing other kinds of meddling—the main consequence of his insistence on nonintervention had been a conflict with the central government. The principal and immediate victim had indeed been that government. Now that it had collapsed, the most urgent problem was one of internal prophylaxy—avoiding all-out civil war. But with the performance of this task, the objective of nonintervention seemed incompatible. To insist on nonintervention endangered the UN operation itself. The reports of Mr. Dayal made it clear that the line to

[12]Document S/4482.

[13]S/PV.896, September 9/10, 1960.

which his superior was clinging—that the UN force should do its best to preserve law and order, but should not intervene in domestic conflicts, even if it could be defended as an intellectual distinction or on purely legal grounds (as in the Secretary-General's statement to the Security Council on December 13)[14]—was of little operational value to the unfortunate UN authorities in the field. The only way to avoid political intervention in a civil war is to stay out completely—and the precedent of the Lebanese constitutional crisis was simply irrelevant. Once one steps into such a situation, one intervenes whatever one does, or does not.

On the one hand *actions* undertaken by ONUC, and justified by the need to safeguard law and order,[15] could not but have a political result, even if they had no political intent. The decision of UN representatives to close the radio station and the airports of Leopoldville early in September, justified as a way of preventing a popular uprising, resulted in destroying Mr. Lumumba's hopes of regaining power. Later, the decision to prevent Colonel Mobutu's men from arresting Mr. Lumumba was justified by the need to avoid violence but denounced as political interference by Lumumba's enemies. As the harassed Special Representative noted in his second report, "almost every significant measure taken by ONUC, in the impartial fulfillment of its mandate, has been interpreted by one faction or another as being directed against itself."[16]

On the other hand, damned if it acted, ONUC was bound to be damned if it did not act—and one of the dangers of Mr. Hammarskjöld's fine distinction was that precisely since it did not indicate clearly what actions could be undertaken for the protection of lives and property without stepping over the line, it incited authorities in the field to *inaction.*[17] The consequences of inaction on behalf of political neutrality were catastrophic: political splintering and slaughtering. *De facto* authorities appeared in various parts of the country, and as Mr. Van Bilsen has remarked,[18] nonintervention indirectly consolidated all such changes even though they were brought about by force. Mr. Dayal and Mr. Hammarskjöld were reduced to severe criticisms of the irresponsibility and brutality of such local tyrannies. Mr. Dayal, instead of putting the blame on the principle he was

---

[14]S/PV.920, December 13/14, 1960.

[15]Or by the need to avoid foreign interference, such as Mr. Hammarskjöld's request to Belgium not to send any technical or financial aid to the Congo except through the UN (October 9 and 19: see Mr. Dayal's second report, Document S/4557).

[16]*Ibid.*

[17]On this point, see Robert West, "The UN and the Congo Financial Crisis," *International Organization,* Autumn 1961 (Vol. 15, No. 4), pp. 603-617; and John Holmes, "The UN in the Congo," *International Affairs,* Winter 1960-61 (Vol. 16, No. 1), pp. 1-15.

[18]A. A. J. Van Bilsen, "Some Aspects of the Congo Problem," *International Affairs,* January 1962 (Vol. 38, No. 1), pp. 41-51.

trying to uphold, tended to use the Belgians as scapegoats in his reports.[19] As for violence resulting from UN inaction, the most spectacular example was the final arrest, deportation, and murder of Mr. Lumumba, whom the UN force considered to be beyond their protection once he escaped from Leopoldville. As long as there was no central government with wide authority, law and order could not be preserved. The Secretary-General was quite right when he told the Security Council on December 7 that the creation of such a government had never been one of the objectives of the UN, that it was left to the Congolese and that chaos was their fault.[20] But the combination of a narrow UN mandate and of an unprepared, insufficient, and disintegrated Congolese political class was a vacuum filled only by violence.

Secondly, even if the limited objectives of the UN operation could have been kept apart from the political disputes which the UN wanted to avoid, the *means* at the disposal of ONUC were inadequate. On the one hand, the size of the peace force remained too small to contain civil war in a country as large as the Congo, and the Secretary-General was right again to remind those who wanted to increase the role of the UN in the Congo that they would also have to increase the means at the disposal of the UN. On the other hand, even a larger force would still have been handicapped by its status as a peace force. Mr. Dayal noted the heavy strain put on the soldiers by the duty not to use force unless in self-defense and "not to resort to military initiative in situations which would normally call for a strong reaction from courageous and responsible troops."[21] The essential task of insuring law and order could have been accomplished only if the UN forces had been able to disarm the multiple armies which were on a rampage throughout the Congo and whose actions Mr. Hammarskjöld himself had equated with genocide.[22] However, not only would such a forceful act have blurred the line between political intervention and the protection of lives and property, it would also have required a change in the nature of the force. To disarm only Mobutu's forces would have been a political choice. To disarm all of the Congo's bands would have been a giant undertaking.

The effect of those difficulties, which were the inevitable result of the UN mandate applied to conditions of civil war, was a double political crisis. In the Congo, the UN authorities ended by being on bad terms with every faction: not only with Mr. Lumumba's supporters, because of the events of August and early

---

[19]One should also mention the contradictions between cases of UN action, such as the closing of Leopoldville's airports, and instances of inaction, such as the fact that Elizabethville airport was left open when Lumumba landed there as a prisoner (cf. President Nkrumah's speech to the General Assembly, March 7, 1961).

[20]S/PV.912, December 7, 1960.

[21]Document S/4531.

[22]S/PV.896, September 9/10, 1960.

September, and later of the circumstances of his death, but also with President Kasavubu, the College of Commissioners and Colonel Mobutu, because of Mr. Dayal's sharp criticism of their behavior, and later of the UN failure to stop pro-Lumumba bands from seizing power in various parts of the country; and of course also with Mr. Tshombé, because of the UN insistence on a withdrawal of the Belgians. In New York, a major crisis developed between the Secretary-General and a large number of African and Asian nations, whose representatives, pointing out the perils I have tried to analyze, suggested a strengthening of the mandate. The UN operation was in an impasse, and there appeared to be two ways of breaking out of it.

If the UN stuck to its mandate, and the pattern of violence continued, the only way of avoiding the disintegration both of the chaos and of the UN operation would have been a withdrawal of ONUC–this was indeed the conclusion developed (no doubt in part for tactical reasons) by the Secretary-General before the General Assembly on December 19. If the UN could neither stand aside in the midst of civil war nor take sides–and since it was impossible for the force to interpose itself on behalf of law and order without appearing actually to choose sides–withdrawal could at least safeguard the future of the UN itself.[23] The other way of breaking the deadlock consisted, on the contrary, of realizing that ONUC would be condemned to a disastrous outcome as long as the UN did not, so to speak, wrest from the squabbling Congolese the initiative of trying to solve the domestic conflicts and restore a central government, as well as prevent the Congolese from aggravating those conflicts by the use of force on a massive scale. The choice was between getting out of the political vacuum which the UN had not received the mandate to fill, and having the UN fill the vacuum through a change of mandate.

The second solution would have meant a shift from Mr. Hammarskjöld's basic distinction and a strengthening of the UN means. But the discussions among the UN Members throughout the fall and the first half of the winter revealed that bold action by the UN could be as disruptive as the relative inaction for which Mr. Hammarskjöld was being blamed. There would be no peace in the Congo without a return to more "normal" political life. The Congolese seemed incapable of moving in such a direction. But the Members of the UN clashed violently about the direction which they wanted such a political life to take. In the discussions of these months, arguments about the UN mandate concealed intentions and interventions about the future of the Congo. To stay out of present Congolese politics was impossible. To get into the politics of Congo's future was divisive. Both "solutions" were explosive for the UN.

The evolution of what one might call Mr. Hammarskjöld's parliamentary situation is significant. So long as there had been a central government, the

[23] A/PV.957, December 19, 1960.

Secretary-General had received the firm backing of the Security Council, the Soviet Union's arguments and proposals had been rejected, and the Soviets did not use the veto. The first sign of a breakdown in the consensus was Guinea's sharp criticism of the Council's policy on August 21. But it was only when the central government collapsed that the cleavages among the Africans and Asians became clear. The Soviets seized the opportunity to widen the breach and to further polarize the situation by using their veto on September 17, thus transferring the problem to the General Assembly. Three months later, the previous consensus in the Council had disappeared,[24] and the consensus which had still been manifest in the special Assembly session on September 20 had also evaporated: the difference with Suez and Lebanon in the field was resulting in another and major political difference in the "parliamentary" situation in New York.

President Nkrumah, in the general debate of the regular Assembly session, had criticized the UN for having remained neutral between the lawbreakers and the legal authorities.[25] But the point was precisely that UN Members disagreed for political reasons as to who were the legal authorities. There were three possible but highly different handles with which the political pot could be lifted from the Congo fire: the President of the Republic, Mr. Lumumba, and the Congo parliament (generally assumed to be favorable, in its majority, to the deposed Premier). To many nations of Asia and Africa, including some which had backed the Secretary-General's interpretation of the UN role (such as Ceylon and India), Mr. Lumumba represented the legitimate political leader of the Congo, whether for political or for more legalistic reasons.[26] The Western nations, however, chose to back Mr. Kasavubu, and the Assembly vote on the Credentials Committee's proposal to seat Mr. Kasavubu's representatives is an interesting one.[27] From then on, the conflict opposed two factions. On the one hand, there were those who, so as to bolster Mr. Kasavubu (who looked as if he needed time to win), argued for a restatement of the "Hammarskjöld line," and wanted it made clear that the initiative for a return to a normal political life would have to come from Mr. Kasavubu—meanwhile the UN mission would remain essentially the defense of

[24]On December 13, Ceylon and Tunisia gave up the idea of submitting a draft; the four-power draft (Argentina, Italy, United Kingdom, United States) would have been accepted except for a Soviet veto, but Tunisia abstained and Ceylon joined the Soviet Union and Poland in opposing it.

[25]See UN *Review,* November 1960 (Vol. 7, No. 5), pp. 33-35.

[26]On October 28, Ceylon, Ghana, Guinea, India, Indonesia, Mali, Morocco, and the UAR sponsored a draft resolution for the immediate seating of Mr. Lumumba's representatives (Document A/L.319/Rev. 2).

[27]The Assembly voted 53-24-19 in favor of seating Mr. Kasavubu. But among the 53 states there was only one of the members of the Conciliation Committee (Senegal); seven members were among the opponents (Ghana, Guinea, India, Indonesia, Mali, Morocco, the UAR); and six abstained (Ethiopia, Malaya, Libya, Pakistan, Sudan, Tunisia).

law and order. Those nations' views about *who* should fill the political vacuum in the Congo coincided with Mr. Hammarskjöld's view about *how* it should be filled. They hoped to reach their objectives through his procedure. On the other side stood those who realized that a blunt proposal to liberate Lumumba and to disarm Mobutu's forces (as pressed by the Soviets) had no chance of being adopted; they suggested more moderately, but unmistakably in the same direction, that all political prisoners be released, parliament be reconvened, and measures be taken to prevent armed units from interfering in political life. When the matter came to a head before the General Assembly on December 19-20, Mr. Hammarskjöld, who had quite lucidly analyzed before the Security Council a few days earlier the disadvantages of a narrow mandate, did not speak out for a broader one. Both draft resolutions failed to be adopted. As a consequence, the UN remained tied by the previous resolutions and interpretations, which had exposed its weakness. The vicious circle was made more cruel by a series of troop withdrawals decided on by the states most hostile to Mr. Kasavubu, and more evident by the gap among African and Asian states which the rival conferences of Brazzaville and Casablanca exposed.

Fourth Phase: February-August 1961. The first major change in the mandate of the UN was made by the Security Council in February 1961 (and confirmed by the General Assembly in April). The circumstances that led to it are highly significant. By the end of January, the situation of ONUC appeared pretty close to that brink of withdrawal about which the Secretary-General had been warning: Mr. Kasavubu was requesting Mr. Dayal's dismissal and summoning ONUC to help him subdue the pro-Lumumba forces in Stanleyville and Bakavu or threatening otherwise to seek help elsewhere.[28] The nations devoted to Mr. Lumumba were upset by his transfer to Katanga. Mr. Hammarskjöld's reaction was not to suggest that ONUC get out, but to advocate a stronger mandate. However even now it was only obliquely, or so to speak crabwise, that he was moving to let the UN deal with the political conflicts of the Congo. His approach remained a policing one. Thus, without advocating that the somewhat intangible barrier between "law and order" and political intervention be destroyed,[29] he preferred to operate through a change of his previous interpretation of the mandate to insure law and order. This objective, he now stated, did require a reorganization of the Congolese army which would take it out of politics. This was less than the "interposition" which he had rejected in December but more than the previous piece-meal protection of lives and property which left Congolese armed bands intact.

---

[28]Document S/4643.

[29]However (see Document S/4606), the Secretary-General had informed Mr. Kasavubu of the strong conviction of almost all the Members that parliament should be convened.

It meant no break from his previously stated determination to limit the duty of the UN to

"unburden the authorities of the immediate responsibility for the protection of life and security and to eliminate foreign military intervention so as . . . to create a framework within which the people of the Congo could find its way to a stable government, enjoying adequate nationwide authority."[30]

It simply equated such protection with the elimination of domestic military intervention as well. Nor did he propose a major change in the means of ONUC. He suggested that the army's reorganization (which, not being a disarmament would presumably not require the use of force) be done with the cooperation of the leaders concerned. Whether the scheme would have worked is hard to say.

Precisely, however, because this suggestion still seemed to respect artificial distinctions, those states which wanted the UN to fill the political vacuum in the only way which they accepted came forth with proposals for urgent measures to free Mr. Lumumba, reconvene parliament, and disarm Colonel Mobutu's forces. Once again, a deadlock seemed in the making, for the same reasons as in December. But one event drastically altered the picture: Lumumba's assassination. From now on, those who had been his champions had to choose between two alternatives. They could adopt the policy of vengeance advocated by the Soviet Union, which in a series of not very consistent proposals advocated on the one hand that the UN operation become a collective security enterprise, under Article 41, against Belgium, Mobutu, and Tshombé, and on the other hand that the operation be discontinued within a month. Or else they could keep pushing in the same direction as before—the return of parliament, the neutralization of Mobutu—even though the political results might well not be the same any longer. But from now on, those who had been most reluctant to move in such a direction because they felt that Lumumba would be the only beneficiary of these measures were far less unwilling to strengthen the UN mandate, as long at least as the objectives and means were not biased in favor of the murdered leader's partisans. Thus a rapprochement took place between the more moderate elements of the two camps into which the UN had been divided: the resolution of February 21, which had a close resemblance to the eight-power draft rejected by the General Assembly and opposed by the United States in December, was adopted in a vote in which the United States sided with Ceylon and the UAR; only the Soviet Union and France abstained. The seventeen-power draft endorsed on April 15 by the General Assembly, which incorporated the suggestions of the Conciliation Commission, and which did not differ much from the eight-power draft of December, received the support of three Asian states which had voted against the eight-power text, and of thirteen African and Asian states which had abstained previously. Of

[30] See footnote 14.

the seventeen African and Asian nations which had voted for the eight-power draft in December, six endorsed the new text in April, eleven abstained. Those shifts give evidence both of a rapprochement and of the traces left by past battles.[31] Indeed, those states which had most vigorously backed Mr. Lumumba tried, both in the Council and in the Assembly, to strengthen the mandate of the UN operation even beyond what the new consensus was willing to accept, and in such a way that the pro-Lumumba forces would gain from the UN intervention, but those attempts failed.[32] It is significant that the only states that voted against the seventeen-power draft on April 15 were, on the one hand, the Soviet bloc, and on the other, seven of France's former African colonies.

The resolution of February 21, 1961, and the two resolutions of April 15 defined the new UN mandate in the following fashion. First, as to the *objectives*, the issue which was, in a way, the oldest of all, Belgian withdrawal, was dealt with vigorously both by the Council and by the Assembly. Not only troops, but paramilitary personnel, political advisers, and mercenaries, were asked to withdraw. Noninterference by other states was also requested again, in sharp terms. The extension of the "law and order" mission of the UN to cover a reorganization of the Congo army, which Mr. Hammarskjöld had suggested, was endorsed by the Security Council. The touchy issue of domestic Congo politics was finally tackled by the UN. This time, the Council urged that parliament be convened, and the Assembly also asked for the immediate release of all parliamentarians. Secondly, as for the *means*, ONUC was empowered by the Security Council resolution to use force, if necessary, in the last resort in order to prevent civil war. The Secretary-General stated that the February resolution gave the UN a clearer and stronger framework but did not provide a new legal basis or new means of implementation. What he meant, one can assume, is that if there was a shift there was no mutation. On the one hand, UN meddling in Congolese political disputes remained limited to the suggestion of a procedure (the summoning of parliament). Thus the Secretary-General's distinction between law and order and UN responsibility for political settlement was theoretically still standing.[33] On the other hand, the transformation of the peace force into a shooting force

[31] The seventeen-power draft was endorsed by the Philippines, Thailand, and Japan which had voted against the eight-power draft on December 20; Cyprus, Burma, Lebanon, Jordan, Nepal, Pakistan, Iran, Malaya, Senegal, Somalia, Chad, Tunisia, and Liberia abstained in December, but voted for the draft in April; Ethiopia, Nigeria, Togo, Libya, Saudi Arabia, and Sudan voted for both texts; Ceylon, India, Indonesia, Iraq, the UAR, Ghana, Guinea, Morocco, Mali, Afghanistan, Yemen voted for the eight-power draft in December and abstained in April. The ex-Belgian Congo had voted against the eight-power draft in December and abstained in April.

[32] Draft by Ceylon, Liberia, and the UAR, Security Council, February 21 (Document S/4733); it dealt exclusively with incidents in Leopoldville, Katanga, and Kasai.

[33] Before Lumumba's death, the reconvening of parliament, supposed to be favorable to him, was a substantive move; now it became merely a procedure.

was doubly limited, not only by the condition of "last resort," but also to the accomplishment of only one part of *one* of the objectives: the "law and order" goal, insofar as the prevention of civil war (not the new task of reorganizing the army) was concerned.

If the Secretary-General was more willing to stress the continuity of UN action, Mr. Kasavubu was more struck by the shift. Not only was he being told how to restore political life, but he was also being asked to discipline and reorganize his army—and in this respect the line of separation between the UN task of preserving order and the UN refusal to intervene substantively in domestic affairs was really invisible to the naked eye. Not too surprisingly, the Congolese President reacted at first by trying to solve the political crisis in his own way (Tananarive Conference) and Mobutu's troops reacted by attacking ONUC. But at Tananarive Tshombé, not Kasavubu, won, and gradually the Congo President came to realize that he had more to gain by working with the UN than by opposing it, especially since many of its members were still willing to strengthen the mandate so as to favor the Lumumbist elements in the Congo. Reconciliation was made easier by Mr. Dayal's departure from the Congo in March, followed by his formal resignation on May 26. On May 17, Mr. Hammarskjöld and President Kasavubu signed an agreement which substituted cooperation for conflict. With the assistance of the Secretary-General's new representatives, the main Congo factions came to an understanding about a new session of parliament. After the tragi-comedy of his arrest at Coquilhatville, Mr. Tshombé appeared to be willing to join the proceedings, and early in August, a new Premier, Mr. Adoula, reported to Mr. Hammarskjöld that the constitutional crisis of the Congo was over. The Secretary-General replied that he agreed to deal exclusively with Mr. Adoula's government. The UN appeared, for the second time, to have closed the circle. There was a central government in which Mr. Gizenga, the heir of Lumumba, participated. The talks about the withdrawal of Belgian elements were going well (especially since there was a new Belgian government also). Law and order appeared assured. There remained only the issue which trouble at the center had overshadowed for almost a year: Katanga.

Fifth Phase: September 1961-(?). At the center, it was to the extent to which a temporary settlement of political conflicts had been negotiated that it became possible *both* to reduce the amount of violence committed by Congolese bands and factions and to avoid a UN resort to force in implementation of the February resolution. But the absence of any political settlement between Messrs. Kasavubu and Adoula on the one hand, and the Katanga authorities on the other, endangered everything that had been achieved. It seemed to make a solution by force inevitable, with all its consequences for law and order, and it also threatened to destroy the political compromise of Leopoldville, by providing Mr. Gizenga with a powerful nationalist weapon. Just as inevitably, the UN authorities in the Congo were being pushed into a corner. If they did nothing, their Herculean work of the past would perhaps be destroyed. Should they not use force first, before the Congolese were at it again?

Once more, the alternatives seemed to be either impotence or an enlargement of the mandate. For the UN mission had been neither broadened nor strengthened with respect to Katanga. As for the objective of territorial integrity, as we have seen, it had been approached rather obliquely by the various resolutions. The best lever at the disposal of the UN was the presence of Belgian and other foreign soldiers and advisers in Katanga. The way to the objective of territorial integrity seemed to pass through "objective No. I," although the Secretary-General had warned a year before that Katanga's dissidence was not merely a Belgian design. However, even that lever was not easy to manipulate, since the UN had not been allowed to use force in order to get to "objective No. I."

The UN moves against Katanga came in three phases. The first was that of August 28, when UN forces in Elizabethville proceeded to arrest more than 200 mercenaries. The legal basis of the UN action, in this writer's opinion, is exceedingly shaky. The officer-in-charge, Mr. Linner, noted that the UN had previously lacked authority to act, but that such authority was provided by a request from the Congo government for assistance in the execution of a decree passed by the government for the expulsion of non-Congolese men serving in the forces of Katanga.[34] It is true that under past resolutions of the Security Council, the UN was supposed to assist the central government in the restoration of law and order. But ONUC had been authorized to use force only to avert civil war. What prevented a major political explosion at the time was the fact that the UN, which acted by surprise, met with no resistance, and that Mr. Tshombé endorsed the move.

A second one came two weeks later, and this time a battle broke out: this was the series of events which led to Mr. Hammarskjöld's death. The report of Mr. Linner is extremely discreet about the basis and circumstances. The UN representative in Elizabethville, Mr. O'Brien, has been less discreet.[35] Whether his version is entirely correct—as in any battle, each combatant is likely to take what he saw for the whole thing—I cannot say; but it is an intriguing one. According to Mr. Linner, the UN forces, which found themselves in a most dangerous situation, in the midst of sporadic attacks and an ocean of hostile rumors, had to resort to "security precautions similar to those of Aug. 28." This implied that the UN was acting both in self-defense and on behalf of the central government—a point which raised the whole issue of the relations between the government and ONUC, i.e., reopened the whole question of intervention in domestic affairs. Mr. O'Brien's account is less defensive; according to him, he had suggested that the use of force be based on the resolution of February 21 which authorized

[34] Document S/4940.

[35] See his two articles in the *Observer,* December 10 and 17, 1961.

it to prevent civil war—but also that it be continued "until the secession of Katanga . . . had been ended." Mr. Khiari, the head of UN civilian operations, arrived in Elizabethville on September 10 and instructed the UN authorities in Katanga to proceed as Mr. O'Brien had indicated: not only were the mercenaries to be expelled, but three of Katanga's ministers were to be arrested under warrants signed by the central government; "Mr. Tshombé also was to be arrested if absolutely necessary." If this version is correct, then (a) it implies that there now existed between the central government and ONUC the very relationship which Mr. Hammarskjöld, precisely because of his emphasis on nonintervention in domestic conflicts, had constantly rejected;[36] (b) it suggests what the French call a *détournement de pouvoir:* the use of a power conferred with respect to one objective, so as to reach another goal for which no such power has been granted; (c) it reveals that the chain of command was quite extraordinarily lax; not only does Mr. O'Brien suspect that the Secretary-General never knew of Mr. Khiari's instructions, but Mr. O'Brien writes "it seemed entirely natural to accept verbal instructions from him (Mr. Khiari) in so important and secret a matter"! Mr. Hammarskjöld's reaction, reported by Mr. O'Brien as indicated by Lord Landsdowne who saw him in Leopoldville on September 16, and demonstrated by his message to Mr. Tshombé—in which he (a) repeated that conflicts had to be settled by negotiation, conciliation, and mediation, and (b) stressed the need for a cease-fire—can hardly be called endorsement of his subordinate's action.

But this action, in a way, was an anticipation of and an advance on the new mandate which marked the beginning of the third phase, in the Security Council resolution of November 24, 1961. The importance of the shift can hardly be exaggerated: the UN was doing now, under acting Secretary-General U Thant's leadership, what it had refused to do during the first Katanga crisis, in August 1960, under Mr. Hammarskjöld. The events which prompted the change were: the failure of Katangese authorities to carry out the February resolution concerning the mercenaries; the failure of efforts at reconciliation between Tshombé and the central government; the beginning of a new breakdown of law and order as a consequence of military operations by Generals Mobutu and Lundula against Katanga; and the fear of a collapse of the central government because of the failure to put an end to Katanga's secessions, in particular because of Mr. Gizenga's own behavior in Stanleyville. Fifteen months earlier, Mr. Hammarskjöld's use of preventive diplomacy had led both to more violence and to political chaos. This time, the UN redefined its mission in such a way that preventive diplomacy included both what can be called a preventive use of force and a clear-cut intervention in domestic disputes. It is ironical that the late Secretary-General's

[36] Lord Landsdowne reported that Mr. Hammarskjöld denied that the operation had been undertaken on behalf of the central government (*Observer,* December 10, 1961.)

thread should have been discarded so shortly after, in the introduction to his last annual report, he warned the Members of the UN that whatever mistakes had been made,

"it is to be hoped that they do not lead members to revise the basic rules which guide the UN activities in such situations, as laid down in the first report of the Secretary-General to the Security Council on the Congo question, which the Council, a year ago, found reason unanimously to commend."[37]

The resolution of November 24 repudiated Mr. Hammarskjöld's doctrine on two points. Concerning the *means,* the acting Secretary-General was now authorized to use force, not only as a last resort against civil war, but also for the apprehension of all foreign military and paramilitary personnel and political advisers. But it is about the *objectives* that the biggest change took place: the principle of nonintervention in domestic disputes was now dropped, precisely because it seemed to stand in the way, not only of the mission to insure law and order—always in question as long as the political disputes persisted—but also of the goal of territorial integrity, which the resolution squarely endorsed by condemning all secessionist activities. On the contrary, so as to preserve law and order as well as to eliminate secession, the Council "declared full and firm support for the Central Government of the Congo" and urged all Members to support it. Whereas Mr. Hammarskjöld's stand on domestic conflicts had led him, on the one hand, to analyze Katanga's position not essentially as either a Belgian maneuver or a desire for secession, but as a constitutional disagreement which was beyond UN jurisdiction, the new analysis backed the central government's stand on the *loi fondamentale* and treated Katanga's position as merely an obstacle to Belgian withdrawal and Congolese territorial integrity. Whereas Mr. Hammarskjöld's stand on domestic conflicts had led him to adopt toward the central government of Mr. Lumumba an attitude of reserve, even, at times, reproach and certainly noncooperation as to the suppression of Katanga, acting Secretary-General U Thant urged "a sympathetic attitude on the part of ONUC toward the efforts of the Government to suppress all armed activities against the central government and secessionist activities."[38]

The *combination* of the means now at the disposal of the UN and of the new objectives produced in turn a third and very important change. Under Mr. Hammarskjöld, the two limitations of the restriction of the objective of law and order by the principle of nonintervention and the restriction of the right to use force to the goal of preventing civil war had reduced the resort to force by ONUC to a very narrow range of possibilities. This was no longer the case. The Security Council resolution of November 24 restated that ONUC was to assist the central

---

[37] See *International Organization,* Autumn 1961 (Vol. 15, No. 4), p. 562.

[38] S/PV.982, November 24, 1961.

government in maintaining law and order, but now that the principle of nonintervention was dropped, this restatement meant a mutation. In accordance with Mr. O'Brien's anticipation, it meant that ONUC in the future could use force to assist the central government if the latter requested such aid so as to preserve law and order—an indirect, but considerable, revision of the mandate, as it actually added a whole new range of possibilities for the use of force.

Since the passage of the resolution the UN has used force twice. The most spectacular instance, of course, was the "second battle of Katanga," which raged for more than ten days in December 1961 and the political reverberations of which are well known. Both the officer-in-charge and the acting Secretary-General have presented the UN operation as one of the self-defense, both to restore law and order in Elizabethville and to regain liberty of movement.[39] As an indication of the change of policy since September, this time there was no negotiated cease-fire agreement. Less noticed, but in some ways even more interesting, has been U Thant's decision to let ONUC assist General Lundula's efforts in Stanleyville to disarm Gizenga's *gendarmerie.* U Thant accepted "within the framework of ONUC's mandate to assist the central government in the maintenance of law and order and in the prevention of civil war."[40] What made of this decision a peculiarly remarkable move was the fact that it was taken even though the Soviets on November 24 had vetoed an American amendment aimed at condemning secessionist activities other than Tshombé's, i.e., Gizenga's.

As a consequence, Mr. Gizenga's demise has consolidated the central government, and Mr. Tshombé's military defeat has led to the Kitona agreement with Mr. Adoula. However, events of recent weeks have shown that Katanga's secession continues. Against Mr. Tshombé, the UN has barely begun to use its new mandate. It could resort to force again—either so as to expel those hydra-like mercenaries; or as an adjunct of the central government, should the latter ask the UN to assist it in restoring law and order in Katanga; or under an equally broad interpretation of its rights to use force so as to prevent civil war. With the principle of nonintervention gone, such an objective as the maintenance of law and order (of which the avoidance of civil war is one facet) can be given a very, let us say, flexible interpretation. Nor is there any doubt that Katanga's continuing secession imperils all the present objectives of the UN—Belgian withdrawal, foreign noninterference, the maintenance of public order, a stable central government, and the Congo's territorial integrity.

---

[39]See UN *Review,* January 1962 (Vol. 9, No. 1), pp. 6-7 and 44 ff.

[40]See *ibid.,* February 1962 (Vol. 9, No. 2), p. 27.

II THE LESSONS

The Role of the UN. At this stage, a balance sheet of the UN operation in the Congo must begin by "accentuating the positive." Even if we leave aside the achievements in the field of technical assistance, we must list the following among the successes of the UN. (a) Considerable accomplishments have been made in the mission of "external prophylaxy." Even in Katanga, the presence of Belgian military and political defenders of Mr. Tshombé seems now limited to men whom their government condemns and who stay in Katanga as Tshombé's pretorians, not as Belgium's rearguard. The intervention of other nations has been either channeled through the UN (US help to ONUC in Katanga) or limited to political pressure. (b) Remarkable progress has been made in the solution of domestic problems: a large measure of law and order has been restored and a central government with wide authority has finally been established. Only Katanga's secession remains a major issue.

However, the undertaking has been a painful one, and the main lesson about the role of the UN may well be the following. On the one hand, just as events of recent years, including the Congo operation, have vindicated to a large extent the "Founding Fathers'" idea that the UN could not be effective unless there existed a concert of the big powers, the Congo crisis has shown that they were wise in assuming that the Organization's efficiency would also be imperiled if it intervened in the domestic affairs of states. On the other hand, the very nature of international politics condemns the UN to a choice between abdication, if it takes literally the warnings of the Charter, and turmoil accompanied by numerous remonstrations of embarrassment or impotence, if it disregards those caveats.

Mr. Hammarskjöld's policy was an attempt to find a middle way. There is a fascinating contrast between the fashion in which he used his own powers and the manner in which he interpreted the UN mission. Mr. Hammarskjöld was determined to have the Secretary-General play as large a role as conceivable. He used for the first time the power of initiative of Article 99. Secondly, as a result of the suggestions which he himself made to the Security Council and which the early resolutions embodied, he was given important mandates: to report on the military assistance provided by the UN, to act so as to obtain the Belgians' withdrawal, and (through the General Assembly resolution adopted in September 1960) to safeguard the unity of the Congo. Thirdly, he used with considerable imagination the power to interpret ambiguous resolutions and the power to carry out mandates, even though the political organs, paralyzed by dissension, failed to provide him with guidance. In this area, as he explained in his Oxford speech of 1961,[41] he was determined to act until and unless disavowed

[41] "The International Civil Servant in Law and in Fact," SG/1035, May 29, 1961.

by the political organs—and he was challenged at times, but never disavowed by any majority.[42]

However, where the role of the Organization itself was concerned, we have seen how subtly narrow the Secretary-General's concepts and interpretations were. Because of his insistence on a limitation of UN ends and means the Congo operation appeared to be plagued by three contradictions which I have discussed elsewhere.[43] There was a contradiction between the reality—one of civil war—and a principle which, even though it was derived from the Charter, nevertheless could only be a crippling fiction given the circumstances, i.e., the principle of nonintervention. There was another contradiction between the nature of the problem and the way in which the UN approached it, i.e., the concentration on the policing rather than on the political aspects, on the shibboleth of force rather than on the causes which led to its use. Such an emphasis resulted from the principle of nonintervention, but it had marked previous UN actions as well. It may have resulted from Mr. Hammarskjöld's own sense of priorities, but it can also be traced back to the Charter (where Chapter VII is informed by a sense of urgency entirely missing from Chapter VI). Finally, a contradiction existed between the stakes of the Congo conflict and the means at the disposal of the Organization.

I have tried earlier to show the inconveniences which resulted from the Secretary-General's approach. But it would be thoroughly unfair to condemn the effects without assessing the motives; and his reasons for his somewhat narrow and tortuous line cannot be dismissed lightly. Patrick O'Donovan has described him as a man who "compels himself to objectivity as priests do to prayer, and he binds himself by simply two laws: the UN Charter and the law of possibility."[44] By putting together various statements (and particularly those of the last annual report), I think one can derive the following arguments. First, the UN, in its mission, should respect its own basic principles; among those principles is that of nonintervention, which meant here that one had to let the Congolese "decide freely for themselves without any outside influences and with full knowledge of facts."[45] The implication clearly was drawn, in the Secretary-General's last two annual reports, that the Organization would destroy itself if it sacrificed its principles to expediency whenever it was not absolutely obliged to do so (as it was in areas, like Hungary, where it was quite without

[42] On April 15, 1961, a Guinean amendment aimed at deleting the words "by the Secretary-General" in one part of the Seventeen-power draft was defeated by a vote of 83-11-5.

[43] See "An Evaluation of the UN," *Ohio State Law Journal,* Summer 1961 (Vol. 22, No. 3), pp. 447-494.

[44] "The Precedent of the Congo," *International Affairs,* April 1961 (Vol. 37, No. 2), pp. 181-188.

[45] See *International Organization,* Autumn 1961 (Vol. 15, No. 4), p. 561.

influence): "any result bought at the price of a compromise with the principles or ideals of the Organization . . . is bought at too high a price."[46] If the UN wanted to preserve its authority, it simply could not become just the instrument of shifting majorities, for it would then lose the support of the minorities. An international organization, which is not a super-state, can deepen its authority and play its role only if it acts as an impartial force, not if it is merely a weapon in the hands of blocs. Secondly, the UN had to remain modest because, in the present conditions of the world, international organization is particularly fragile; it simply does not have the means to be very ambitious, and any policy which would expose the Organization beyond those means would backfire. Also, the more ambitious its operation, the more it risks becoming a stake in the power struggle. One can imagine how much UN resources would have been taxed if it had had to step, not merely through resolutions, into the Algerian war. These were precisely some of the reasons which had led most Members tacitly to discard the collective security function of the UN.[47] In an explosive world, few nations are willing to let an international soldier operate if they are not sure that this soldier fights their battles. As long as such is the case, it is wiser to have the UN play the role of honest broker, or of fireman. Dag Hammarskjöld's calculation was that, so to speak, a minimal operation would get maximum support.

The trouble was that a minimal operation produced what looked like maximum turmoil in the field, and that dissatisfaction with this state of affairs resulted in minimal support. Mr. Hammarskjöld had feared that a more daring approach would backfire. His cautious one backfired in three ways. First, the Secretary-General, who was so deeply convinced of the decisive importance of his office, exposed himself most dangerously. Any Secretary-General who tries to be the spokesman of a still only virtual international community runs a number of risks. If he defines the "international interest" in so impartial a way that it does not coincide with the interests of any group, there will be a glaring gap between his constituents and himself, and he will be performing a solitary tightrope walk too far over the ground; to change the metaphor, the "loneliness of the long-distance runner" is a melancholy one. If he defines the international interest in such a way that it coincides with the interests of some, this convergence of "supranational" and "international" calculations may destroy his usefulness on both levels, since the opponents of his constituents will accuse him of partiality. Finally, in both cases, any attempt at defining an international interest which differs from their own will bring down on him the wrath of the Soviets; they resent any chief executive who is more than a mere

[46]"Introduction to the fifteenth Annual Report of the Secretary-General to the General Assembly," *UN Review,* October 1960 (Vol. 7, No. 4) p. 27.

[47]See I. L. Claude, Jr., "The UN and the Use of Force," *International Conciliation* (No. 532), March 1961.

administrator, and less than their ally, and they deny the possibility of impartiality anyhow.[48] Now, Mr. Hammarskjöld's pitfalls were the first–isolation–and, inevitably, the third. While he isolated himself from a deadlocked melee of former constituents, some of whom attacked him bitterly, the operational weaknesses of his doctrine, which I have discussed, isolated him at crucial moments from his representatives in the field: in both directions the transmission links were strained.

Next, Mr. Hammarskjöld's approach backfired for the UN operation as well. In New York, discontent with the turn of events produced the very political polarization and paralysis which he probably thought a more aggressive policy would provoke. This revealed that in any major crisis, whatever its approach, the UN could not avoid becoming a stake. Moreover, the Secretary-General's line made it a stake, but prevented it from being a very impressive force on the spot. There, ONUC was caught in the dead end I have mentioned. Its legal status reveals the inadequacy of the thread: since it was not a collective security operation, it required the consent of the host state; but precisely because it had to restrict itself to a much smaller task than the one the government of the host state wanted it to accomplish, it had to be able to stay there and operate (or abstain from operation) despite that government's hostility. It was the very emphasis on modesty of ends and means which led to an assertion of independence from the central government. It could not be the latter's arm; it had to be autonomous so as to be able often to be much less. The Secretary-General, halfway, so to speak, between the Korean and Suez precedents, chose to find a legal shelter in Articles 39 and 40.[49] But at the same time as he was proclaiming the duty of nonintervention, he stated that the UN task consisted of saving a drowning man even without his authorization.[50] Ambassador Dayal found that it was not easy to be both neutral and at the service of the central government. Neither in New York nor in the Congo did the policy of Mr. Hammarskjöld provide the necessary cooperation of the Members and of the host.

Finally, only to the extent to which the original ends and means were violated or transcended has some progress appeared in the Congo. The ban on force and on UN political intervention resulted only in violence. It is the combination (a) of violence despite the ban (Lumumba's murder), (b) of UN local violence leading to or resulting from a lifting of the ban (against Katanga), and (c) of

[48]See Michel Virally, "Vers une Réforme du Secrétariat des Nations Unies?" *International Organization,* Spring, 1961 (Vol. 15, No. 2), pp. 236-255.

[49]Statement to the Security Council, December 13, 1960. On this issue, see E. M. Miller, "Legal Aspects of the UN Action in the Congo," *American Journal of International Law,* January 1961 (Vol. 55, No. 1), pp. 1-28; and Alan Karabus, "UN Activities in the Congo," *Proceedings of the American Society of International Law,* 1961, pp. 30 ff.

[50]A/PV.906, October 17, 1960.

political pressures exercised from the outside on the Congolese which have broken the deadlock of the first winter. Proudhon has written that force remains the law-maker in a whole series of cases, among which he listed the creation, absorption, and break-up of a nation.[51] Mr. Hammarskjöld's policy seemed to lead to an endless terror. The UN gradually opted for an end, even if mildly terrifying.

Good intentions, but results which disproved them—this is a harsh verdict. Indeed, it may well be too harsh. For we must consider now the *alternatives.* On the one hand, total UN abstention would probably have led to big power intervention at a much higher pitch of intensity, and possibly to another international brushfire conflict such as those of South East Asia, with incalculable effects on Africa. On the other hand, what could a stronger UN mandate have meant? In the first place, theoretically, it could have meant a genuine UN takeover, whether one called it trusteeship or full responsibility for law and order, as Ghana and Ceylon suggested it at times:[52] in other words, a finding that the Congo was not ready yet to use its premature independence. Thus it would have been the responsibility of the UN to exert that monopoly of the use of force which is the mark of sovereignty, to revive political life, and so on. But one sees at once that such a solution was a practical impossibility, not only because of the contradiction between such UN administration and the previous proclamation of Congo's independence, at a time when the winds of anticolonial change simply will not reverse themselves, but also because of a fundamental truth of which Mr. Hammarskjöld was deeply aware: the UN is not a kind of monolithic force capable of imposing its order on a domestic chaos. It is itself an arena and a stake. It is a battlefield of national and bloc forces. It is condemned to carry to the scene of domestic chaos its own chaos of individual interests and global incoherence, in General de Gaulle's words.[53] The relations between troubles in the Congo and troubles in the UN remind one of the complicated mirror games which embitter the two troupes of actors who perform, on two superposed levels, in Jean Genet's play, *The Blacks.* Mr. Hammarskjöld may have been wrong to believe that the more modest the mission, the more subdued the intra-UN clashes; but he was right to guess that the greater the responsibilities and the stakes, the bigger the peril. The definition by the UN of a Congo policy, at a time when Lumumba had split not only the Congo but the Organization itself, would have been practically impossible. Indeed, the deadlocks of the winter of 1960-1961 proved this.

In the second place, a stronger UN mandate could mean (and to a large extent means today) not a submission of the Congo to the UN, but a subordination of

---

[51] *LaGuerre et la Paix,* Vol. I. Paris, E. Dentu, 1861.

[52] Notably in the Security Council debates of February 1961.

[53] See his press conference of April 11, 1961.

the UN to the central government of the Congo. But here there are problems and contradictions just as formidable as those which plagued Mr. Hammarskjöld's policy of an independent but limited ONUC.

First, the new mandate allows the UN to use force to further certain political objectives–for the first time since the fateful General Assembly resolution of October 7, 1950, on the unification of Korea. If I may quote myself,[54] the reason for not encouraging such a trend is that when there is no well-defined and sufficiently broad consensus on those objectives, such a UN operation is likely to impair the future usefulness of the UN. It reduces the willingness of nations to let the UN be the *deus ex machina* in emergencies. Whereas Mr. Hammarskjöld's policy reduced the effectiveness of the UN as a force so much that its mission became a stake, the opposite line risks making of its mission so much of a stake in the big power struggle that its effectiveness would be impaired. For the big powers may keep a certain detachment about peace forces, but they can hardly fail to be more worried, and therefore more involved, about shooting forces. Political efficiency is thus not assured, nor is military efficiency. For the forces at the disposal of the UN remain pitifully weak, and the Members have shown no willingness to accept even a permanent peace force. Should a shooting UN force be defeated, one can imagine what a setback it would be; but should it win and reach its objectives, the UN itself could be rocked by dissents and withdrawals. The pitfall which the acting Secretary-General must avoid is the second one I have listed: the pitfall of partiality.

Thus, the use of force by the UN to reach political goals in a collective security operation such as Korea made trouble, and more trouble could be expected, should the Korean precedent be repeated in circumstances in which aggression was less clear and the UN objectives were more controversial. But, secondly, the conditions of a civil war are even more ambiguous and dangerous for the UN. The resort to violence by an international organization in such circumstances takes on a very different meaning; for the use of an international force as a police force at the service of a government is a highly questionable precedent. In a world in which so many regimes are shaky, so many borders artificial, so many unions arbitrary, can the UN afford to serve as the secular arm, say, of a future Mali complaining about another Senegal secession? Here is the strength of Mr. Hammarskjöld's position: if one starts poking in domestic conflicts, where does one stop? In a world of glass houses, not too many bricks ought to be thrown, so that the interior of the houses can remain unrevealed. Insofar as we are all murderers, let us not call each other criminals–this is the precept which any attempt at defining aggressive war violates. Insofar as we are all potential Congos, should we be so enthusiastic about letting a weak government use a world force as its constabulary?

---

[54] "Popularity and Power in the UN," *New Leader,* February 19, 1962, pp. 22-23.

Finally, the example of the Congo today shows that ONUC cannot be simply an arm of the central government for the restoration of law and order. For insofar as law and order are still threatened by the lack of discipline in the government army, as U Thant has recognized, some margin of independent action must be preserved.[55] Consequently the risk of new disagreements with the local authorities as well is not ruled out.

Thus, the final lesson about the UN mission is that the world is too explosive either to live without an impartial fireman, or to turn him into an additional pyromaniac. But in circumstances of civil war, the world at large and the scene of the fire simply will not let the fireman do his job easily. Mr. Hammarskjöld's "preventive diplomacy" required, in order to be successful, (a) firm support from his political constituents, i.e., both a tacit concert of the Great Powers and a consensus of those states which he saw as the main "clients" of the UN, and (b) the cooperation of authorities on the spot. These were the conditions which had prevailed in previous crises, but which the Congo circumstances made largely impossible. The opposite policy, however, puts the UN into the position of acting not so much as a help to states, as if it were a state using force to reach political goals when peaceful solutions have failed. Consequently, instead of removing causes of tension and eliminating violence, it adds more trouble. Instead of an international Red Cross, there is one more army at work. The very broad definition of self defense in the second Katanga operation, in December 1961, reminds one of Robert W. Tucker's analyses of nations' hypocrises or inconsistencies in the claim of self-defense.[56] Furthermore, since the UN is neither a nation, nor a supranational agency endowed with compelling authority and force over nations, its action cannot help reflecting the conflicts among its Members[57] and the frailty (political and administrative) of its executive.

I would therefore conclude that in the present world, civil wars will be rough on the UN whatever policy it adopts. Since however the UN can often stay away from them only at too great a peril to itself and the world, it seems condemned to muddle through, case by case, in search of an all-too-breakable thread. In other circumstances the late Secretary-General's

---

[55] See footnote 38.

[56] Robert W. Tucker, *The Just War*, Baltimore, Johns Hopkins University Press, 1960. The reports of the officer-in-charge of UN operations explained that among ONUC objectives there was a very broad range of objectives in and around Elizabethville [see *UN Review*, January 1962 (Vol. 9, No. 1), pp. 45 ff].

[57] One of the aspects of those conflicts is the slowness and heaviness of the procedure in New York: suggestions about good offices or any reorganization took weeks to mature. In the Security Council, invitations to non-members to present their viewpoints as interested parties also led to delays. As for the military and administrative weaknesses of the Secretariat, see the introduction to the fifteenth annual report, and my remarks above.

cautious policy is more appropriate to the present world.[58] Maybe he was too narrow in his policing, antiseptic, but not sufficiently political approach to disputes. For although he was willing to *send* a force to curb violence, he hesitated, as in the Suez crisis, to *use* a force to further certain political objectives. But he was, I think, justified in refusing to use *force* in order to reach them. Unfortunately, such a distinction is very hard to maintain in circumstances of civil chaos.

The Behavior of the Members. A few remarks should be made about the attitude of the UN Members during the Congo crisis. Once again, we find that their approach to the UN is a purely instrumental or tactical one. When they think that the Organization can promote their interests, they are quite willing to strengthen its mandate. When they think their interests require that the local status quo be left to take care of itself, they see to it that the mandate remains unobtrusive. Thus, the United States, long respectful of the Congolese right to settle their own disputes, nevertheless pressed for (and obtained) UN "recognition" of Mr. Kasavubu. When the local situation became disturbing to US interests, the US supported first the limited strengthening of the mandate in February 1961, then the considerable shift of November. The USSR, unable to get either in the Security Council or in the General Assembly a majority to support its own policy–which would have made of ONUC first Lumumba's arm, then his liberator, and finally his avenger–nevertheless opposed resolutions (such as the seventeen-power draft in April 1961) which would have somewhat strengthened the UN mandate but in a direction contrary to Soviet interests.[59] Most of the Casablanca powers, having failed to get the Assembly to strengthen ONUC according to their desires, weakened it deliberately, since it was not serving their interests, by withdrawing from ONUC and from the Conciliation Commission. A number of delegates, favorable to Lumumba and to UN pressure on the Congolese designed to bring out the re-emergence of Lumumba as the leader, opposed the seating of Mr. Kasavubu in November 1961 under the pretext that such a move would hurt the process of conciliation in the Congo. Similarly, sovereignty is a catchword which can be used by all, with very different tactical meanings. To some of the former French African colonies, respect of the Congo's sovereignty means a strict policy of nonintervention; to Ghana, Guinea, or Mali it means a thorough decolonization and the rejection of "fake" independence.

---

[58] See Michel Virally, L'ONU, Paris, Ed. du Seuil, 1961.

[59] Similarly in November 1961 the Soviets voted against a United States proposal which would have authorized the Secretary-General to assist the central government in the reorganization of Congolese armed units–the kind of measure which the Soviets advocated some months earlier.

If we turn to *the two main powers,* we reach certain conclusions which are mildly surprising. On the one hand, the Soviet Union has been, on the whole, rather isolated. In the Security Council, at first the Soviets did not dare to oppose an operation sponsored by Tunisia and Ceylon. When they used their veto against a draft which outlawed bilateral military aid to the central government, they found themselves alone in opposing the same text in the special session of the Assembly. The only draft they presented themselves in the Assembly (April 1961) not only did not go much beyond the seventeen-power draft which the Assembly endorsed, but even then received the support of only seventeen African and Asian states, while fifteen abstained and fourteen voted against it. They never submitted to the Assembly their plan of February 1961 for the dismissal of the Secretary-General and for termination of the UN operation within one month. In their suspicion of any UN undertaking which did not serve their own policy they were in a way closer to the more "conservative" states–such as those ex-French colonies which joined them in opposing the seventeen-power draft in April–than to the Casablanca powers, whose Congo policies largely coincided with Soviet desires but who would have liked the UN to turn over the responsibility for enforcing those policies to a kind of African command and peace force, with the exclusion of anyone else, particularly the Great Powers. In the Congo, the period of spectacular Soviet intervention was brief–the last two weeks of Mr. Lumumba's tenure as premier. Subsequently, Soviet activities were confined to recognition of, and political advice to, Mr. Gizenga.

On the other hand, the United States has, on the whole, succeeded rather well in either getting its own views endorsed by the General Assembly (e.g., the seating of Mr. Kasavubu) or reconciling its views and those of a large number of Africans and Asians. The only difficult period was the winter of 1960-1961. Such important steps as the original three resolutions, the seating of Mr. Kasavubu, the Security Council shift in February 1961, and the new policy of November 1961, were all endorsed by the United States. The Assembly votes of November and December 1960 showed a split between most of the Africans and Asians and the United States, but Lumumba's death narrowed the gap and produced the shifts in votes I have mentioned. Whether the US decision in November 1961 to support the resolution submitted by Ceylon, Liberia, and the UAR was ultimately in the US interest is a matter of domestic debate. What matters here is that it was not resisted by the United States, and that US policy makers decided it was in the national interest to support Mr. Adoula.[60]

Thus it is true that, at some of the crucial stages in the Security Council, the Soviets and the Americans found themselves either voting together (resolutions of July and August 1960 and November 1961) or not voting against one another

[60] See George W. Ball, "The Elements of Our Congo Policy," Department of State Publication 7326, December 1961.

(February 1961). This conjunction reflected the need for both superpowers to court and coax the "Third World" rather than to coerce and constrain it. But it is also true that, on the whole, and until now at least, it is the Soviet Union which has lost its gamble and the United States which has to a considerable extent succeeded. Of course, success has come precisely because US objectives were limited: a neutral Congo, not an ally. And, as shown by recent events, the creation of such a neutral Congo may even require the crushing of the most publicly pro-Western faction, in Katanga. However, Ambassador Stevenson's idea of the coincidence of US and UN interests,[61] and Mr. Ball's demonstration that "the UN is in the Congo with objectives that . . . parallel our own" are not false. To American right-wing critics, such a parallel only shows that the United States defines its objectives and interests in too "soft" a way. But to the Soviets, this seems little consolation for the emergency of a non-communist state, in which Lumumba is dead, Gizenga ousted, and Tshombé–indubitably a boon to extreme nationalists–something of an outcast. To the considerable extent to which Dag Hammarskjöld's definition of preventive diplomacy has facilitated such a conciliation of US and new nations' interests, the Soviets could not fail to see in the UN an American instrument and in the Secretary-General a Western stooge even though he was obviously moved more by principles than by "power bloc" calculations. Their frustrations in the Congo fed their attack on Mr. Hammarskjöld. As Daniel Cheever has suggested,[62] United States reliance on the Secretary-General to reach objectives consonant with US interests, flexibility defined, has seriously exposed the Secretary-General. It will be interesting to see whether Mr. Hammarskjöld's successor will be capable of acquiring at least Soviet neutrality, without supporting such policies as would reduce US enthusiasm for the UN and complicate US conciliation with the new states' interests.

For if we turn to the attitudes of *the new states,* we find that the so-called African-Asian bloc is so complex, and alignments within so un-frozen, that the way in which these states divide is far from determined. Much depends on the events, of course, but also on the kind of leadership provided both by the Secretary-General and by the United States. A fine analysis by Robert Good[63] has shown that, on the whole, the new states can be divided among "conservatives," "moderates," and "radicals." But two remarks must be added. First, one of those sub-groups has been monolithic. Thus, among the "conservatives," the vote of April 17, 1961, showed that some, like Senegal, were less conservative than others. Among

---

[61] Quoted by Alexander Dallin, "The Soviet View of the UN," *International Organization,* Winter 1962 (Vol. 16, No. 1), p. 36.

[62] See Andrew Gyorgy and Hubers S. Gibbs, eds., *Problems in International Relations,* revised edition, Prentice-Hall, New York, 1962.

[63] "Congo Crisis: The Role of the New States," in *Neutralism,* Washington, D.C., Center of Foreign Policy Research, 1961.

the moderates, some, like Ceylon and India, evolved in the direction of the radicals. Others, such as Tunisia, remained more favorable to a policy of non-intervention. Still others, such as Togo and Nigeria, passed through a "radical" phase during the winter, and left it when Lumumba disappeared.[64] Among the radicals, there remained throughout a difference between states such as Guinea or Mali, which not only withdrew their troops but also attacked the Secretary-General in violent terms, and Ghana, which criticized his policies and proposed an African substitute expedition but never broke with him nor withdrew its troops. Secondly, and consequently, it becomes obvious that the opportunities for political maneuver are considerable. In the circumstances of November-December 1960, too narrow an interpretation by the Secretary-General and too strong a United States support for one of the local contenders produced a deadlock in which a US and British resolution received the support of only eight African and Asian states.[65] In April 1961, a less restrictive interpretation, endorsed by the United States, was backed by 25 of the nations of Africa and Asia.[66] It is clear that no procolonial stand has a chance of being accepted either in the Security Council or in the General Assembly. But the gamut of possible anticolonialisms is still extremely wide.

If this is, in a way, a reassuring conclusion after too many depressing ones, there remains however one very dark spot. There is, almost everywhere, a widening gap between what nations expect the UN to do for them and what they are willing to do for the UN. It is true that they have tended to blame the Secretary-General for carrying out the mandate which they had either given him, or failed to modify. As he reminded them, "this is your operation, gentlemen."[67] But the financial difficulties of the UN, which result in so large a part from the Congo crisis, have pointed out more clearly and more cruelly than ever that international organization is an ambiguous half-way house which is asked to look as if it were a force of its own while embodying all the conflicts and inhibitions of a fragmented world. Consequently, whoever serves as such an organization's executive head is performing the thankless, indispensable, and suicidal task of a "Pope without a Church"[68] trying to realize as much of the Charter ideal as the nations will allow, in a world whose secular religions are locked in battle, whose realities turn ideals into weapons, and weapons into the most final of all final solutions.

---

[64] See footnote 31.

[65] The two-power draft, on December 20, 1960, received 43 votes in favor, among which were those of Malaya, Iran, Laos, China, Japan, the Philippines, Thailand, and Pakistan.

[66] See footnote 31.

[67] A/PV.871, September 26, 1960.

[68] Herbert Nicholas, "United Nations?" *Encounter*, January 1962, p. 8.

An Appraisal

Herbert Nicholas

I

It is sometimes instructive, as Holmes long ago pointed out to Watson, to begin by asking a few questions about dogs that do not bark in the night. Suez and the Congo are not the only major crises which have disturbed the United Nations. Yet they are the only ones to which it has responded by creating a true United Nations force. Why?

Consider the case of Hungary. Coincident with Suez, it provoked from the General Assembly stronger verbal denunciation. While the Anglo-French attack was described colorlessly as "military operations against Egyptian territory,"[1] the Soviet move in Hungary was denounced initially as "foreign," "armed intervention," and later as a "violation of the political independence of Hungary," a deprivation of "its liberty," and a "violation of the Charter,"[2] Yet the employment of a United Nations force of any kind was not even considered; it was left to the Secretary-General to "investigate" and "observe the situation directly through representatives named by him."[3]

[1] General Assembly Resolution 997 (ES-I), November 2, 1956.

[2] General Assembly Resolution 1131 (XI), December 12, 1956.

[3] General Assembly Resolution 1004 (ES-II), November 4, 1956.

Thus, though the United Nations' judgment was unequivocal, its actions were minimal. Vehemence stopped at words because everyone knew that to go further was to involve one's country in an outright clash with a great power in an area which the Soviet Union was obviously going to regard as vital. Nor in this regard was there any difference of degree among the critics of the Soviet Union—all, from the United States down to the smallest member of the General Assembly, drew back from any action stronger than words. It was not merely the defense of Hungary that was unthinkable; even the admission into the country of the mildest form of United Nations presence, the Secretary-General's representative, could not be insisted upon in the face of Soviet refusal, and was in fact never secured.

Five years after Hungary, India invaded Goa. The issue was brought before the Security Council by Portugal on December 18, 1961, with a request for an immediate cease-fire. A Western-sponsored resolution was not only defeated by a Soviet veto but was also opposed by all three Afro-Asian members of the Council. The "Uniting for Peace" mechanism was not invoked, it is generally understood, because there seemed no prospect of obtaining a two-thirds majority in the General Assembly for any resolution along the lines of that defeated in the Security Council. However, even the defeated resolution gave no hint of the possible employment of a United Nations force; it called only for an immediate cessation of hostilities, a withdrawal of Indian forces, a solution by peaceful means, and the provision of such assistance by the Secretary-General as might be appropriate. India announced the surrender of the Goan forces on the same day that the Security Council met.

In Goa, in contrast to Hungary, no great power was directly involved. Aggression, in most ordinary senses of the term, had clearly been committed. Nevertheless, any realistic observer of the reactions in Turtle Bay to India's action must recognize that, in the present UN context, there is one crime which in certain circumstances may be judged to outweigh the crime of aggression—namely, colonialism. The failure of the United Nations to register even a verbal protest against India's behavior in Goa was basically due to the fact that Portugal had put itself outside the pale by its actions in the same year on Angola. Since the UN can assist only those who at any rate initially can themselves resist, the sheer rapidity of the Indian operation would probably have deprived any United Nations resolution of more than academic effect. But, even if time had permitted the interposition of a UN force between Goa and its attackers, a sufficient number of impartial small powers would not have been willing to serve on it.

Lastly, let us consider Korea. Here the United Nations came nearest to establishing a fighting force. It did create a United Nations command and requested Members to make forces available to it, but this was a mere anointing of the existing United States Far East command, a sanctification, as it were, of its personnel and its commander, General MacArthur, and of whatever active units Member States might supply and place under his command. In an important sense, the action taken by MacArthur and his forces was United Nations action; this was its status in international law.[4] In terms of international politics and of international organization, however, it fell crucially short of being a real United Nations operation. It was not under the executive control of the United Nations; the Secretariat had no part in its organization or deployment; it was not financed by the United Nations, nor did the United Nations determine in any but the very broadest terms the conditions and objectives of its employment. The response to the appeal to all Member States to furnish assistance was generally poor. One Member, the United States, was the self-appointed Atlas of the operation, without whose broad shoulders all would have failed. By the end of 1950, the only foreign ground troops fighting by the Americans' side were from the United Kingdom, Australia, France, Greece, and Netherlands, the Philippines, Thailand, and Turkey.[5] South Koreans apart, the unified command in Korea consisted of about a quarter of a million Americans compared with only about 36,000 troops from all other Member States combined.

Of the three cases only Korea bears the slightest resemblance to Suez and the Congo in that here the United Nations response to a violation of the Charter took a forceful form. This was due in large part to a series of happy accidents. The fact of aggression could be quickly established, owing to the presence in Korea of the United Nations Commission on Korea. Resistance could be quickly organized, because a great power had its armed forces virtually *in situ* when the fighting broke out (and the other super power behind the aggression had made the mistake of walking out of the Security Council). Supplementary assistance was lent to the United States-United Nations command by countries who felt themselves already bound to support American action by virtue of other ties, most obviously by their common North Atlantic Treaty Organization (NATO) membership. And although the Soviet Union was wholly hostile to the United Nations action in Korea, it did not attempt to frustrate it in a manner that might cause a local police action to escalate into a direct clash between two super powers. Indeed, the Korean conflict occurred at a time when the American lead in nuclear weapons made it reasonable to suppose that the United States was, strictly speaking, the only super power.

Soon, however, countervailing considerations made themselves felt. The very predominance of United States strength which made the United Nations operation in Korea possible also diminished its United Nations appeal and reduced the crucial element of universality. This, in fact, accounted for what Mr. Lie

---

[4]See Guenter Weissberg, *The International Status of the United Nations* (New York: Oceana, 1961), pp. 78 ff.

[5]In 1951, ground troops were also furnished by Belgium, Canada, Colombia, Ethiopia, Luxembourg, and New Zealand.

called the "disappointing"[6] response to his appeal to Member States for further assistance. More seriously, the open intervention of Communist China transformed the nature of the conflict and greatly heightened the risks of its growing, if not into a conflict of super powers, at least into an interminable and costly war in which military advantages accruing to superior nuclear weapons would be offset by the political impossibility of using the weapon of Hiroshima in the service of the Charter. Support at the United Nations fell away from an operation which previously, however inadequate its United Nations character, was yet felt to serve United Nations objectives.

Subsequently, the emphasis fell increasingly on the search for a Korean settlement, reaching a point indeed where, in the behavior of many Members even outside the communist bloc, the United States and the North Koreans were treated as if both were in equal violation of the Charter and as if each needed in equal measure to be forced to keep the peace. Members differed in their degree of concern over the prolongation and extension of the war, but sooner or later all shared the conviction that to persist in using force, no matter how impeccable its United Nations credentials, was to frustrate the very purpose of the Organization. In this sense, as has frequently been observed, the moral of Korea is not that collective security under United Nations auspices can be made to work, but that not even United Nations auspices will persuade Member States to risk military action where no vital national interest, narrowly construed, is involved, and where United Nations action may lead to hostilities with a major power.

This brings us to the two clear occasions when the dogs did bark, and the police did turn out—Suez and the Congo. In neither case can one explain United Nations action by the operation of a single factor; in both, several desperate elements combined. Let us take them in order.

II

In the first place, the complex of military events which it is convenient to call "Suez" occurred in an area long the subject of continuous United Nations concern. At the time of the Israeli attack there was actually operating at Gaza the United Nations Truce Supervision Organization (UNTSO) under its Chief of Staff, General Burns. His presence in the area served something of the same purpose in relation to the organization of the United Nations Emergency Force (UNEF) that the United Nations Commission on Korea served in relation to the alerting of the United Nations in Korea.

Secondly, Suez lay outside the zones of direct great power confrontation. But at the time it was a key area strategically and economically which the West could

[6] Trygve Lie, *In the Cause of Peace* (New York: Macmillan, 1954), p. 338.

not afford to lose to the Soviet bloc and which the Soviet bloc was proportionately eager to acquire. Two permanent members of the Security Council, the United Kingdom and France, regarded Nasser's nationalization of the Canal as an assault upon a vital national interest, but they always claimed that their forceful action to protect this interest was intended only to fill the void created by United Nations impotence in the face of the Israeli attack. Whether true or not, the argument made it difficult for them to refuse a United Nations force when offered, and indeed, in the case of Britain at least, reflected a profound national schizophrenia on the propriety of her violent action. Furthermore, the joint strength of Britain and France, though overwhelming against Egypt, was not sufficient to put them in the great power class, as became apparent when pressure was put on them simultaneously by the United States and the Soviet Union. This pressure was strong and potentially irresistible. Yet it was not in the United States' interest to drive her closest allies into too humiliating a retreat, and the Soviet Union's "rocket-rattling" diplomacy certainly worked both ways–stiffening Anglo-French resistance at least as much as it accelerated compliance. Nor did Nasser want to exchange British and French occupation of the Canal for Soviet tutelage. Thus a complex of considerations all led to the acceptance of Lester Pearson's UNEF as a device which would enable all parties to return to the *status quo ante* with maximum speed and minimum loss of face.

It is perhaps true that the UNEF idea owed some of its immediate acceptance to the fact that it was imperfectly understood: Britain and France in particular hoped to see the force act as the agent of the United Nations in implementing the six-point recommendations on a Canal settlement announced by Mr. Hammarskjöld on October 12, 1956, while Israel hoped to see it remedy her grievances about transit through the Canal and the Gulf of Aqaba. If true, however, this remains a marginal consideration. UNEF was created basically because no interested power could impose a solution alone, and all powers, great and small alike, preferred an internationally contrived and controlled solution to a conflict which could develop dangerously into a wider war. Negative considerations pointed the same way; neither of the two alliances, the Warsaw Pact or NATO, felt their vital interests threatened (however much, briefly, Britain and France may have), and neither Israel nor Egypt, on reflection, wanted a fight *à outrance* then and there.

To see these as the underlying factors that made UNEF possible is not to depreciate the efforts of Lester Pearson and the other representatives who came to be known at the United Nations as the "fire brigade," or the role of the Secretary-General and the Secretariat. "Factors" by themselves do not stop wars; they have to be assessed and manipulated by human beings. If courage, perserverance, diplomatic skill, imagination, and personal prestige had not existed in the right quarters at the right moment in 1956, the resulting drift and confusion would have required more than a UNEF to remedy them.

The celebrated conditions of UNEF laid down by the Secretary-General in his two reports of November 4 and 6, 1956,[7] were the necessary preconditions of its existence and also set the limits to what it might achieve. No one except the Soviet bloc states and the convicted trio of Britain, France, and Israel was willing to enlist in a United Nations force with coercive powers; no one was willing to fight Egypt or Israel, or possibly both simultaneously, in order to impose a just settlement–whatever that would have been–on these old combatants. Once this was recognized, it followed inevitably that the United Nations force could have only the function of facilitating the invaders' withdrawal, of maintaining a minimum of order in the transitional phase from war to armistice, and, finally, of keeping the local combatants, Israel and Egypt, at arms' length. The element of force was, strictly speaking, minimal. It was military only in being composed of soldiers; its functions were fewer even than those of a normal civilian police corps. Police exist to prevent crime and enforce the law as well as to preserve the peace, but UNEF has no powers to prevent anything save the most blatant frontier violations. Its role is pacific and passive. It is essential interpository in character, a moral United Nations presence given physical embodiment on a scale sufficiently extensive to guarantee that neither side can aim the slightest blow at the other without involving itself by that very act in larger, international consequences. Ever since the cease-fire and withdrawals were effected, UNEF has been in fact a larger and more physically impenetrable UNTSO.

In this capacity its success is undoubted. It has not only achieved its immediate objectives; it has also kept the peace between Egypt and Israel ever since, both in the large and obvious sense and in that of reducing to a previously unknown level the number of incidents along the border. This has been due to many factors besides the efficiency and loyalty of the force. Though the basic local antagonisms remain, nothing has occurred to provoke another 1956 flare-up, while the great power outsiders have all for various reasons been tolerably content not to stoke up the fires of Egyptian-Israeli animosity.[8] Then again there has been a simplicity, a straightforwardness about UNEF's role, rare in international affairs, which has helped it greatly. Its task is only to patrol a strip of desert, for the most part totally uninhabited, where it can exercise its simple function with a minimum risk of offending the susceptibilities of its host country or of anyone else. To adapt Tacitus, "Because it is a solitude, they can keep it at peace." The

[7]UN Documents A/3289 and A/3302. The conditions were later codified in Document A/3943. In summary, these principles were: (1) no permanent member of the Security Council or any "interested" government should contribute contingents; (2) the force should not be used to affect the military or political outcome of the dispute; (3) its arms should only be used in self-defense; and (4) it should not be stationed on a state's territory except with that state's consent.

[8]Some would list the protective blanket of the Eisenhower Doctrine among the dampening influences on the Middle East, though this seems to me more disputable.

boundary it patrols is ideal for its purpose—open to view, clearly demarcated, uncomplicated by the presence of any human or economic factors more portentous than the occasional Bedouin herdsman and his flock.

Finally, the Arab-Israeli rivalry for all its intensity is basically parochial in scale. Outside the Moslem world few countries feel themselves deeply committed to one side or the other. This has made it comparatively easy to recruit for the force contingents whose nationality does not involve them in any serious risk of partisanship or even in accusations of partisanship. The Americas, Scandinavia, India—from this core it was not too difficult to construct a force which satisfied the criteria of geographical representativeness and detachment from local and great power conflicts.

In consequence, the difficulties of the force have been virtually confined to the familiar problems of finance. These, of course, reflect the fact that what was originally welcomed as a solution to an emergency has now become an apparent permanency. The fireman has turned into the lodger. The respite which UNEF provided for solving the Middle East problem has turned out to be the solution itself. It might even be argued that the existence of UNEF has relieved all the parties concerned of the need to find some other more lasting solution, but this argument would carry more force if anyone could suggest what such a solution might be. As it is, the forces of world politics and the circumstances of Middle East geography have made it possible to provide inveterate antagonisms with a mutually tolerable insulation. In so doing they have created a precedent and left a legacy of practical experience in the organizing and operating of a United Nations force.

When this legacy was drawn on in the Congo, it was in circumstances that soon made one wonder how far UNEF could properly be regarded as a precedent for the United Nations operation in the Congo (ONUC).[9] To take the simplest factor first, in place of the sealing off of a desert peninsula as in Suez, the Congo crisis required the insulation of an almost land-locked subcontinent, as well as the internal policing of that same huge area. Similarly, whereas UNEF had only to keep two organized and accountable states apart, ONUC had the double task of excluding outside intervention and creating internal viability. While UNEF could operate in an area physically free from complicating interests or inhabitants, no United Nations operation in the Congo could possibly avoid contact with Congolese life at every point—and in circumstances where any contact (or indeed no contact) inevitably involved interference. Finally, whereas it was relatively easy to construct a UNEF out of the contributions of disinterested states, disinterestedness was a much harder quality to command where the Congo

---

[9] In the interests of convenience I have used "ONUC" throughout to refer to the United Nations military force in the Congo, although strictly speaking, of course, it applies to the important civilian operation as well.

was concerned. (What is more, for reasons of incipient Pan-Africanism and color consciousness it was, when discovered, by no means so obviously welcome.) At the very outset all these complications presented a formidable challenge to ONUC; before it had been long in operation, others, and worse, arose for which there was no precedent in the annals of international organization or in the records of international law.

Paradoxically—and the whole Congo operation was a jungle of paradoxes—it was easier to get ONUC established than UNEF. The whole United Nations was intensely "Africa-conscious"; the Secretary-General, then at the height of his prestige, had already established a United Nations presence in Leopoldville in the person of Dr. Bunche; and the fact that, at least in one aspect, ONUC could be viewed as a technical aid operation made its initial acceptance easier. Again, the need for the force did not immediately proceed from any actual clash of major powers which might try to bargain and prevaricate before making way for it; only one power with modern armaments was involved, Belgium, and even it did not oppose the force in principle. The prize of the Congo was indeed a rich one, but no one in July 1960 was willing to be labeled a colonialist in order to win it, not even the Soviet Union. The United States in particular was content to see a neutral Congo established. The now classic rules of super-power diplomacy operated: neither side wanted to see the other gain control of the territory, but equally, neither wished to see a Congo civil war escalate into something more general. Each side no doubt gave different weight to different considerations, but initially the result was the same—a Security Council vote in which the United States and the Soviet Union voted on the same side and France, Britain, and Belgium abstained, ostensibly only because of reservations about the wording of the paragraph asking for Belgian troop withdrawals.

There was from the beginning an ambiguity about the authority and objectives of ONUC which reflected the anomalous position of the Congo itself, a state so newly independent that the *Loi Fondamentale* designed to authorize its constitution had not yet been ratified by the body appointed to do so, the Congolese parliament. In part, ONUC was a routine response to a routine request from a new state for technical assistance; what was novel was that it was for *military* assistance, a category hitherto unknown in United Nations technical aid circles. Simultaneously, however, it was an appeal for United Nations protection against the reintroduction of Belgian troops into the territory of an ex-colony now independent and also, from the United Nations point of view, a necessary safeguard against unilateral assistance pouring in from rival sides of the Cold War. ONUC's role from the outset was consequently a dual one—the provision of both internal and external security. Though the words "international peace and security" do not appear in the Security Council resolution[10] passed at its first meeting

---

[10]UN Document S/4387.

concerning the Congo on July 14, 1960, the Secretary-General later[11] stated that his authority to summon the meeting came from Article 99 of the Charter,[12] and any such verbal deficiency was quickly made good in the following resolution of July 22.[13] Thus the force had a role closely analogous to that of UNEF—to facilitate and accelerate the withdrawal of foreign troops and to remove by its presence the justification for any other powers' interference; but it could not assume, as UNEF did, that the host country would look after internal security. Indeed ONUC's ability to restore internal security was a practical (if not a legal) condition of the successful discharge of its obligations toward international peace and security.

Nevertheless the Secretary-General took the view that the principles which he had laid down for the UNEF were equally valid for ONUC. As he told the Security Council on July 13, 1960:

"The United Nations Force would not be authorized to action beyond self-defence[14] .... They may not take any action which would make them a party to internal conflicts.... The selection of personnel should be such as to avoid complications because of the nationalities used.... This does not ... exclude the use of units from African States, while ... it does exclude ... troops from any of the permanent members of the Security Council."[15]

In saying this, the Secretary-General could hardly have been unaware, even at this early stage of the operation, that the problems presented by the Congo were vastly different from those of Suez. His emphasis on UNEF principles in the Congo context must therefore have reflected, as was surely right, a concern for the context of international politics within which the problems of the Congo would have to find their solution, if at all.

---

[11] Security Council *Official Records* (15th year), 884th meeting, August 8, 1960, p. 5.

[12] To "bring to the attention of the Security Council any matter which in his opinion may threaten the maintenance of international security."

[13] UN Document S/4405.

[14] How strictly this was originally interpreted can be seen in the wording of the leaflet distributed by Dr. Bunche and General von Horn to all members of ONUC on their arrival in the Congo:

"You serve as members of an international force. It is a peace force, not a fighting force.

"The United Nations has asked you to come here in response to an appeal from the Government of the Republic of the Congo. Your task is to help in restoring order and calm in this country which has been so troubled recently. You are to be friendly to all the people of this country. Protection against acts of violence is to be given to *all* the people, white and black.

"You carry arms, but they are to be used *only* in self-defense. You are in the Congo to help *everyone,* to harm no one."

[15] Security Council *Official Records* (15th year), 873rd meeting, July 13, 1960, p. 5.

As every UN debate from the July 13 Security Council meeting onwards showed, the gravest differences of opinion existed among Member States as to what kind of settlement, what kind of Congo indeed, should be aimed at—differences, moreover, not merely between the Soviet bloc and the West but also within the West, within the Afro-Asian group, and even within the ranks of the Africans themselves. Even before Katanga's secession or the outright clash between Kasavubu and Lumumba, these differences were violent enough to guarantee that, if the United Nations attempted to formulate a positive policy for ONUC, it would not merely provoke a clash of opposites; it would reveal the lack of *any* clear majority consensus. (This was precisely what did happen in December 1960.) The only way to avert such a clash was to insist on the principle of non-interference and its corollary of no initiative in the use of force and to hope and work for conditions in which the empty formalism of the first and the acute frustrations of the second did not become too evident or impose too great a strain on those who had to apply them. Nor is it relevant to say that such a policy could not succeed unless it can be shown what other course of action would have been more successful.

Certainly, if a proving-ground for the Secretary-General's principles were desired, no more exacting one could be devised than the Congo. As might be expected, having regard to the conditions which provoked ONUC's presence, the first principle to come under strain was the ban on the use of armed force. In a country where the government was little more than an expression and where the army had no officers and was mutinous, any peace force was bound to find itself in a self-contradictory position. In Suez and Gaza there were always local police forces to whom UNEF could turn over any violators of the peace who came its way. In the Congo such entities hardly existed, yet ONUC itself had no powers to arrest or even disarm the mutineering elements of the *Force Publique.* Such a power eventually was given, and critics have argued that the biggest error of the whole Congo operation was not to have given it at the very beginning. This may be so, but two things have to be remembered. First, in a continent hypersensitive about "neo-colonialist" interference and in a country teetering on the edge of mass hysteria, it was important for the United Nations' long-term mission to preserve the image of itself as a pacific agent seeking only to help Africans to help themselves. Secondly, although some states that contributed to the force, e.g., Ghana, were willing, even eager to have their troops employed forcefully, others would have refused contributions to a force which was involved in the killing of Africans even in the best causes and even at the hands of other Africans. When, later on, resolute measures were taken, certain states did seek to withdraw in protest.

But, of course, more was involved than clashes with *Force Publique.* The issue of force or no force merged into the issue of interference or non-interference. Non-interference was even less possible in practice than abstention from force, because the mere presence of ONUC was interference. Non-interference, however, was also a more indispensable principle because there was no agreed alternative to put in its place. Even after the passage of the Security Council resolution of February 21, 1961,[16] authorizing "the use of force, if necessary, in the last resort," it was still the United Nations' position that it was not going to become a party to any internal conflict in the Congo. Similarly, when in September 1961 open fighting developed between ONUC and the Katangese forces, the United Nations' objectives (*pace* Mr. Conor C. O'Brien) were only the expulsion of "foreign mercenaries," the prevention of civil war, and the defense of its own positions. When finally, by the Security Council resolution of November 24, 1961,[17] the Secretary-General's authority was broadened to include "vigorous action, including the use of requisite measure of force if necessary," the object of this was still said to be the exclusion of foreign intruders.

It was also true that the United Nations accepted the unity of the Congo as axiomatic and secessionist activities as illegal. It explicitly rejected Katanga's claim to independence. Nevertheless, it never laid on ONUC the task of enforcing Congolese unity or ending Katangese independence. These objectives were to be secured by conciliation, moral pressure, or, at most and not until very late in the day, economic and financial sanction. Moreover, since ONUC had a positive obligation to prevent civil war, it was as opposed to the central government's forcible occupation of Katanga as to Katanga's forcible secession.

In all these senses the United Nations was impartial. Within the framework of Congolese unity it was for the Congolese to decide who should rule and how. But in almost all the actual power contests of Congo politics the United Nations could not avoid taking decisions which favored one side or the other. Seizing the radio station and closing the airports was a logical application of ONUC's duty to stop civil war and external interference, but it was also inescapably an act which, at the moment it was taken, tilted the scales in favor of Kasavubu and against Lumumba. The fact that this occurred in the Alice in Wonderland situation when the President claimed to have dismissed his prime minister and the prime minister claimed to have dismissed his President provided a further legal justification for the United Nations action but left its practical consequences unchanged.

In its external role as the United Nations' agent for relieving the Congo of Belgian interference and protecting it against all other non-UN intrusions, ONUC ran into comparable difficulties. Its early claims of success in effecting Belgian withdrawal turned out to be premature since Katanga remained a center of foreign influence and activity, hostile alike to the UN and to the central government, while ONUC's inability to restore order even in the rest of the Congo provided

[16] UN Document S/4741.

[17] UN Document S/5002.

Belgium with an excuse for retaining or reintroducing her forces. This in turn aggravated Congolese impatience and encouraged factional leaders to seek extra-UN assistance of a kind which was only too readily available, with the result that a month or so after ONUC had come into operation massive Soviet aid was placed at the disposal of Lumumba.

The Soviet assistance came by air and, to be countered, necessitated the closure by United Nations forces of all Congolese airports. No doubt this action hampered Soviet plans for further intervention, though its legal justification and its immediate purpose were to prevent Lumumba from using the troop-carrying Ilyushin planes to launch his forces against Kasai province. Nevertheless, it is almost certainly true to say that it was Mobutu's seizure of power and his ensuing expulsion of all Soviet bloc representatives rather than any direct ONUC action which put a stop to Soviet intervention. It was on this account that no direct on-the-spot clash between the Soviet interlopers and the ONUC command occurred. No doubt the Soviet Union, in the interests of its relations with the African powers, was glad not to have any such showdown. On the evidence available, however, it cannot be said that the mere presence of ONUC was adequate, as many hoped it would be, to deter great-power intervention. It is one thing to violate a clearly held United Nations patrol line; it is another thing to fly "volunteers" into a civilian airport with little or no show of military might. ONUC's experience here is a reminder that the third dimension of the air can make non-sense of the attractive concept of a United Nations buffer force whose mere physical presence on the ground serves as an adequate moral trip-wire or plate glass window.

The cross-currents set up by factional fighting inside the Congo and intervention from outside complicate the Congo operation in two other respects. In getting on to a decade of operation UNEF has had little difficulty in holding its national contingents together or in maintaining equable relations with its host government. ONUC speedily ran into trouble on both fronts. Dag Hammarskjöld's decision to make ONUC a predominantly African force was certainly a right one; no other course would have secured the indispensable moral backing in Africa or the African votes in the United Nations. But it was impossible for a force so composed to be completely disinterested. Each contributing state had strong views on every Congo issue, and every decision that ONUC had to make imposed a strain on its loyalties. Looking back over the fiercely troubled course of the Congo since July 1960 one is truly impressed to see how well in such circumstances the conglomerate ONUC held together. Nonetheless, it is instructive to notice how and where the bonds of loyalty chaffed.

Thus in September 1960 ONUC's denial to Lumumba of the use of the radio station and airports provoked Guinea, Ghana, and the United Arab Republic to threaten a withdrawal of their troops and claim a right to place them at Lumumba's disposal. This led the Secretary-General to elaborate the basic principles on which a composite UN force operated, as follows:

"Were a national contingent to leave the United Nations Force, they would have to be regarded as foreign troops introduced into the Congo, and the Security Council would have to consider their continued presence in the Congo, as well as its consequences for the United Nations operation, in this light."[18]

This important circumscription of the conditions under which withdrawal could take place was further sharpened the following January when Morocco ordered its brigade to "cease to perform its functions" while remaining in the Congo. The Secretary-General insisted that it could remain only "as an integral part of the United Nations force" and that any other position would be "untenable."[19] Morocco agreed to its troops remaining under the United Nations flag until repatriation could be arranged, "but if called upon to act against their conscience" they would feel bound not to accept any decision contrary to the interests of the Congo and of legality."[20] The Secretary-General's own inimitable blend of legal argument, moral authority, and diplomacy in fact prevented most of these threatening checks ever being presented for actual payment, but even so he could not eliminate the enervating effect which they had on the United Nations operation. Whereas UNEF was a force united in a common acceptance of a clearcut task, ONUC for long periods at a time lacked any agreed purpose, indeed at certain periods was sharply divided within itself. Even if the disagreements of participating governments were not fully reflected in the behavior of their contingents, they could not but impair their full cooperation.

To speak of a "host government" in the context of the anarchy which prevailed for most of 1960 and 1961 in the Congo is to bring out how remote were the realities of the United Nations operation from the language of law and diplomacy in which it had to be clothed. Repeatedly ONUC found itself not merely at odds but actually at blows with the agents of the government whom it was to "assist" and "consult with," to quote the language of repeated United Nations resolutions. Most of these incidents belong to that level of UN-Congolese relations which had more to do with bizarre bargaining and gang warfare than diplomacy, but some of them raised issues not only important at the time but having possible future significance for United Nations procedure and international law. This was conspicuously true of Kasavubu's attempts to impose impossible conditions on ONUC, particularly in connection with the use of the

---

[18]Security Council *Official Records* (15th year), 896th meeting, September 9, 1960, p. 20.

[19]UN Document S/4668.

[20]*Ibid.*

port of Matadi in March 1961. These led the Secretary-General to issue the following interpretation of their relations:

"The relation between the United Nations and the Government of the Republic of the Congo is not merely a contractual relationship in which the Republic can impose its conditions as host State and thereby determine the circumstances under which the United Nations operates. It is rather a relationship governed by mandatory decisions of the Security Council.... Only the Security Council can decide on the discontinuance of the operation and ... therefore conditions which, by their effect on the operation, would deprive it of its necessary basis, would require direct consideration of the Security Council. ..."[21]

Here, obviously, we have a potentially far-reaching modification of the 1956 doctrine requiring the consent of the host state as a necessary precondition of the presence of a United Nations force. Partly this reflects the shift in the source of the mandate from the General Assembly to the Security Council; partly it reflects the distinctive role of a United Nations force called in to provide internal aid as well as external protection. Yet even so, a word of caution must be added. It is in the Congo context that the Secretary-General is speaking–i.e., in a political hall of mirrors, where the reality and its reflections become swiftly indistinguishable and nothing is quite what it seems. For if one seeks to establish what sanctions the Secretary-General employed to secure the cooperation of the Congolese authorities or at least to curb their obstructiveness, one finds that they amounted to nothing more or less than the threat to withdraw the presence which offends. It was in these terms that Dag Hammarskjöld wrote to Kasavubu on December 21, 1960, warning him against behavior which would lead on to civil war:

"I sincerely trust that no situation will develop which would give me no choice but to recommend to the Security Council that it authorize the withdrawal of the United Nations Force ... thus throwing on the authorities of the Congo the full responsibility of maintaining law and order."[22]

We are back, not for the first time, in the world of the nursery where authority and prudence alike reinforce the wisdom of Hilaire Belloc's advice:

And always keep a hold of Nurse
For fear of finding something worse.

[21] UN Document S/4389/Add.5.

[22] UN Document S/4606.

III

Any lessons which one may draw from these events while the Congo operation is so recent must be tentative. Even so, something can be said.

First a *caveat.* It is often said that the Congo is *sui generis.* It certainly differs from any situation the United Nations has had to tackle before, but is it so different from what may arise in the future? As long as underdeveloped countries are in ferment and communist (or other) powers prefer subversion to open aggression, variations on the Congo theme are practically bound to occur. No doubt also it is true that the United Nations is not designed to cope with such situations; as an international organization it is built on the assumption that viable states are the entities with which it has to deal. This palliates failure, but it cannot excuse inaction. Future Congos cannot be ignored simply because they were not dreamed of in the philosophy of San Francisco. This is not to say that the United Nations ought to get into every situation where internal breakdowns occur; if such crises can be settled without such intervention, so much the better. But if they threaten international peace and security, the United Nations cannot side-step them on any narrowly legalistic ground.

But it is also probable in any foreseeable future that the balance of world politics, in particular the near-deadlock rivalries of East and West and the persistent floating votes of the nonaligned, will remain much as before. If so, Suez and the Congo suggest that there are limits to what any United Nations force can, at present, achieve. UNEF represents about as successful a buffer operation between states as can be imagined—in about as propitious a set of circumstances. Happy the UNEF of the future which has as easy a task. In the more likely case, however, in which external clashes are accompanied by internal breakdown, some if not all the problems of ONUC seem likely to recur. There may be fewer difficulties on the ground—there could hardly be more—but there are likely to be just as many in the council chambers of the United Nations. If this is so, it seems idle to press for a United Nations force which would discard the three principles of "force only in self-defense," "non-interference," and "entry only with the consent of the host country." Of course these principles are not adequate (whatever that may mean); they are merely in the present state of the world indispensable. They may be stretched, modified, even conceivably bypassed; they cannot within the framework of the present United Nations be replaced by any positive alternatives.

If this is true, it does not follow that no improvements on ONUC are possible or that no advance planning, even perhaps advance organization, for a United Nations force, can be contemplated. On the contrary, the peculiar strains which such a role imposes on a United Nations force and its leaders make it the more desirable that everything which is politically possible should be done to train it for the discharge of its very distinctive functions. It lies outside the scope of this paper to consider how this could best be done, but that it should be done is certainly in accordance with our conclusions.

Certain other conclusions also follows. If one asks why, despite all its difficulties, ONUC was able to function as well as it did, or—to concede everything to its critics—to function at all, the answers are threefold. First, because the West, and in particular the United States, has been willing to foot the financial bill. No doubt it is wrong—in terms of the Charter—that this burden should fall as unevenly as it does. But if, like Britain, any Member State is inclined to feel self-righteous when it pays its share or, like France, self-justified when it does not, let it pause to ask whether its national interest would be better served if the Soviet Union paid the whole. Piper-paying and tune-calling are not interchangeable terms in the United Nations—otherwise what would the Charter be for?—but they are connected. Certainly, no future ONUC can operate unless it has funds, and if it is to operate with higher efficiency than the present Congo force, it will need larger funds. These can only come from the well-to-do West—unless they are to come from the Soviet Union.

The second reasons for ONUC's survival is the general willingness of most of the states variously described as "nonaligned," "neutralist," or the "fire brigades," to support the operation by their votes and often by their contributions. In this the role of the Afro-Asians has been crucial not only because of their numbers but also because of their position on the spectrum of United Nations politics. They alone could supply the disinterestedness which comes from their relative impotence and the loyalty which reflects their own dependence upon the Organization.

This dependence has often seemed to be personified in their support of the Secretary-General and has even been ascribed to a personal confidence in Dag Hammarskjöld. But to see it entirely in these terms is to mistake the man for the institution. It is not by an accident of personality that the creation and functioning of UNEF and ONUC have been linked so closely with the office of the Secretary-General. It is because any sustained executive functions, however limited, can only be discharged in an organization like the United Nations by its Secretariat, a body which the Secretary-General at once leads and personifies. Only the Council and the Assembly are capable of authorizing a United Nations force, but if the history of Suez and the Congo demonstrates anything, it is that they are utterly incapable of running it. In this more than in anything else that the Secretary-General is called upon to do, the now familiar concept of "filling a vacuum of authority" manifests and justifies itself.

There is a logical connection between the Soviet opposition to ONUC and its advocacy of the "troika." An equivalent logic dictates that no future United Nations force is conceivable for which executive authority is not delegated to a Secretary-General willing and able to act when his "parliamentary" overlords are deadlocked. An advisory committee may abate his loneliness; it cannot relieve him of his responsibility and should not seek to curb his authority. If the office seems dangerously potent, as so developed by Dag Hammarskjöld and as apparently now operated by U Thant, the weapons of negation and frustration are at hand in the Security Council, the General Assembly and, behind both, in the financial deliberations of the Fifth Committee. Those who wish to use them, however, should do so with a full awareness of the consequences. Nothing in the experience of Suez and the Congo suggests that an international force is exempt from the workings of the inexorable rule that he who wills the end must will the means as well.

B. *The Decolonization Struggle*

The drive to independence of the new states of Africa and Asia has been one of the dominant features of the post-1950 international political scene. Although, until 1960, the principal arena of action in this drive was more often outside the confines of the United Nations, the United Nations, from its inception (following in the footsteps of the League), concerned itself with colonial problems. In Ernst B. Haas' article, we are given an analysis of the various contending forces that shaped the United Nations approach to these problems. Haas concludes that the United States proposals for a trusteeship system resulted from the interplay of humanitarian and strategic considerations, and from the urgings of allies, with the strategic considerations gaining important victories in the final proposal. At the San Francisco Conference, which drafted the United Nations Charter, a final compromise was arrived at between the contending pressures of the American, Soviet, Arab, British, French, Dutch, and South African positions. The compromise that was finally reached satisfied no one completely. However, the fact that the clashes took place at the international level between contending states prompts Haas to predict that at least the hope of an increased international supervisory role is possible.

Harold Jacobson, looking back on seventeen years of United Nations experience in dealing with colonial problems, assesses the impact of the United Nations on the decolonization process. In this field, the United Nations has performed essentially three tasks.

1. Through the mechanism of the trusteeship system and the Declaration on Non-Self-Governing Territories, the United Nations has provided some degree of international supervision of the colonial regimes.
2. The United Nations has legitimized the independence of the host of new nations that have gained their freedom since 1945.
3. The United Nations has provided an instrument for extending assistance to these new states in order to facilitate their participation in international politics.

In evaluating the impact of the United Nations on colonial problems, Jacobson carefully notes that in many cases the impetus for independence either predated the founding of the United Nations or clearly arose from sources outside of the Organization. On the other hand, it does appear that the constant concern of the United Nations with the manner in which the colonial powers conducted themselves was an important prod toward better rule and earlier independence of these territories. Jacobson also maintains that the colonial revolution was probably more peaceful because of the involvement of the United Nations.

The Attempt to Terminate Colonialism: Acceptance of the United Nations Trusteeship System

Ernst B. Haas

I THE LOGIC OF COMPROMISE

To the contemporary liberal humanitarian the acceptance of the League Mandate System by the world's chief colonial powers signified the advent of a New Deal for dependent areas in which the older and baser motives of empire were defeated even if not completely eliminated. To the contemporary mind impressed with the prevalence of power politics, however, the acceptance of the Mandate System signified nothing of the kind. It merely represented a new form of compromise between clashing imperial powers who sought to remove one source of friction by recourse to "internationalization".[1]

In terms of the motivations of the statesmen who accepted the supervisory machinery of the League for the areas seized from Germany and Turkey in 1918 neither explanation is wholly applicable.[2] Rather, the Mandate System found

Ernst B. Haas, "The Attempt to Terminate Colonialism: Acceptance of the United Nations Trusteeship System," *International Organization,* Vol. 7, No. 1 (February 1953), pp. 1-21. Reprinted by permission of *International Organization.* (The author gratefully acknowledges the valuable assistance given by Leonard C. Rowe in the preparation of this article.)

[1] See, *e.g.,* H. Duncan Hall, *Mandates, Dependencies and Trusteeship* (Washington, 1948) in which the power political interpretation of the acceptance of both the Mandate and Trusteeship Systems is used.

[2] These points are elaborated in some detail in my article "The Reconciliation of Conflicting Colonial Policy Aims: Acceptance of the League of Nations Mandate System", *International Organization,* Vol. VI, No. 4.

ready acceptance primarily because it served as a suitable compromise solution in four distinct motivational dilemmas faced by British and French leaders. Firstly, there existed the need, within the domestic British political picture, to reconcile the Liberal and Labor groups with the Conservatives on colonial policy. The former insisted on a policy of "no annexations" and urged that the British Empire was already too large for efficient administration, while the latter demanded annexation of the key African, Middle Eastern and Pacific areas. Secondly, the Mandate System managed to bridge the gap between wartime promises to the Arabs for independence and the Tory and French demand for unilateral control over the vital communications routes and oil fields of the Middle East. Thirdly, the granting of "C" Mandates to Australia, New Zealand and South Africa appeased the land hunger of these Dominions and saddled them with a minimum of international control while *pro forma* the British Empire was not expanded and the "no annexations" pledged honored. Thus harmony within the Commonwealth was maintained at the time when it was most needed, i.e., at the point in history when the Dominions achieved the right to conduct their own foreign relations. And fourthly, the Mandate System was an acceptable compromise between the liberal humanitarianism of Woodrow Wilson, who sought to strike a blow against further colonial expansion of any kind, and the strategic and economic motives of French and British groups which had historically been identified with expansion and who did not want to stop in 1919. Thus, rather than signifying the victory of one set of motives, the acceptance of the Mandate System was due to the necessity of finding compromises between clashing aspirations.

What were the chief motives which needed reconciliation? In the realm of ideology the chief impetus for acceptance came from the liberal humanitarians who identified service to native progress with international control; they were opposed by the conservative humanitarians who were most willing to admit the paramount duty of the metropolitan country to serve native interests first but without supervision by the League. The conservatives saw no inconsistency between native progress and special strategic and economic privileges for the metropolitan country. In the field of strategic bases and communications, by contrast, the two schools were in agreement on principle. Strategic areas were to be retained under national control. However, the liberal forces sought to utilize the Mandate principle for this purpose, while the conservatives preferred unfettered annexation. In the realm of economics, finally, the liberals sought to realize a measure of free trade through the introduction of the Open Door in colonies while the conservatives preferred annexation in order to maintain protectionism and national privileges in investment. These clashing aspirations were represented not only on the domestic political level but on the inter-Commonwealth and inter-allied levels as well. As indicated above, the acceptance of the Mandate System was due to the need for reconciliation between them.

It is the purpose of this article to explore the motivations which underlay the acceptance of the Trusteeship System in 1945. The analysis will proceed on the hypothesis that the motivational forces which existed in 1918 still prevailed at the time of the San Francisco Conference, though perhaps in modified form. Furthermore, an additional motivation must be considered in the contemporary setting of the problem: the aspirations and demands of areas which in 1919 were colonies but in which a lively sense of nationalism had come to the fore by 1945. The demands of erstwhile colonial nations may have called for more reconciliation than had been true of any of the motives prevalent in 1919.

II ACCEPTANCE AND LIBERALISM IN THE UNITED STATES

It was liberal opinion in the United Kingdom which took the lead in pressing for the "no annexations" policy in 1917 and it was again liberal opinion which insisted on a "New Deal" for colonies in 1942 and 1943. However, it was primarily American sources which furnished the impetus and they now demanded far more than merely international supervision over colonial administration. The issue raised during the second World War involved nothing short of emancipation of colonial peoples from foreign rule and the inauguration of an internationally controlled colonial policy aimed at preparing dependent areas for independence. Church groups, labor unions, and professional organizations hailed the section of the Atlantic Charter which declared that "they [the United States and the United Kingdom] respect the right of all peoples to choose the form of government under which they will live." Numerous spokesmen, including Henry Wallace, demanded the immediate liquidation of colonial empires, and the Commission to Study the Organization of Peace concluded that "the whole of the continent of Africa (apart from . . . the Union of South Africa) and the whole of the Polynesian Island group now under colonial administration, should cease to be regarded as projections of Western power interests and be placed under varying forms of international administration and supervision . . . ." A group of five hundred Protestant leaders pressed for the adoption of such a scheme at the San Francisco conference and urged the United States delegation that "we can find no moral grounds to support the acquisition of bases by a single nation, first, through forthright annexation, or, second, under the guise of trusteeship. Either procedure would violate a pledge made in the Atlantic Charter."[3]

---

[3]Commission to Study the Organization of Peace, *Preliminary Report and Monographs,* in *International Conciliation,* No. 369, April 1941, p. 201, p. 519. Also National Conference of Christians and Jews, *Uncio Memos,* No. 3, May 16, 1945.

With the condemnation of colonialism on moral grounds President Roosevelt and Secretary of State Hull had no quarrel. Both men, but especially Hull, were in the forefront of those who pleaded for the inauguration of a colonial New Deal. Thus Hull said on July 23, 1942:

"We have always believed–and we believe today–that all peoples, without distinction of race, color or religion, who are prepared and willing to accept the responsibilities of liberty, are entitled to its enjoyment. We have always sought–and we seek today–to encourage and aid all who aspire to freedom to establish their right to it by preparing themselves to assume its obligations. . . . It has been our purpose in the past–and will remain our purpose in the future–to use the full measure of our influence to support attainment of freedom by all peoples, who by their acts, show themselves worthy of it and ready for it."[4]

At the same time a committee was created within the Department of State to prepare recommendations for American policy along these lines. While opposing the immediate granting of independence to all dependent areas, Hull nevertheless favored an international administrative organ with jurisdiction over *all* colonies to prepare them for independence. Hull soon retreated from this position but both he and Roosevelt were adamant in insisting that the Atlantic Charter be applied to colonies as well as to states conquered by the Axis, despite British objections to this interpretation.[5] Liberal humanitarianism again found expression in the first official policy recommendations on trusteeship, submitted by Hull to Roosevelt on March 9, 1943:

". . . it is the duty and purpose of the United Nations which have, owing to past events become charged with responsibilities for the future of colonial areas to cooperate fully with the peoples of such areas toward their becoming qualified for independent national status."

Regional organs, on the model of the Caribbean Commission, composed of the imperial states, other interested states and representatives of the natives, were set to dates for full independence and prepare the populations for this status. Furthermore, some areas occupied by enemy forces and torn from their former rulers were not to be restored to their European masters after the war, but speedily prepared for independence by an International Trusteeship Administration.[6]

---

[4] *Postwar Foreign Policy Preparation, 1939-1945,* Department of State, Publication 3580 (Washington, 1950), hereafter cited as Notter, p. 109.

[5] *Ibid.,* p. 110. Cordell Hull, *Memoirs* (New York, 1948), Vol. II, pp. 1598-1599.

[6] Notter, *op. cit.,* pp. 470-472; Hull, *op. cit.,* pp. 1236-1237.

III TRUSTEESHIP AS A NON-IDEALOGICAL COMPROMISE FORMULA IN THE UNITED STATES

Liberal humanitarianism thus took the initiative in the creation of the postwar Trusteeship System. But even though Hull and Roosevelt shared these convictions, they constitute by no means the only motivations underlying American policy. Roosevelt considered world peace unattainable unless colonial nationalism was appeased in time and future areas of conflict thus reduced. Hull, always preoccupied with free trade, saw in the independence of colonies an excellent wedge for the ending of imperial preference systems. Nor were these the only economic and security considerations which commended the trusteeship principle to the Roosevelt Administration. Roosevelt thought of trusteeship in terms of a device to accommodate a variety of international troubles not necessarily related to encouraging the independence of colonial peoples. "The area he mentioned," noted Cordell Hull, "ranged from the Baltic to Ascension Island . . . and to Hong Kong." Indo-China was to be a trust area primarily in order to keep future French Governments from giving military privileges to Japan, as the Vichy regime had done after 1940. Hong Kong was to be a free port under trusteeship in order to satisfy Chinese claims and British interests. Similarly, the Kuriles, Dakar, "some points" in Liberia and the Netherlands Indies might be internationalized because of their general importance. Korea was to become a trust area apparently to forestall the establishment of a Soviet regime, which Harriman feared if Korea were to become independent.[7] That United States security considerations were never lacking in these motivations is made plain by Hull's conclusion that American trusteeship responsibilities should be confined to the Western Hemisphere and the Pacific.[8]

And, of course, the issue of Pacific bases soon gained prominence in Roosevelt's thinking. Like Hull, he thought that American need for the mandated islands should not find expression through outright annexation. He feared that such American action would set a bad precedent for the Russians and Hull noted that "our acquisition of these islands stopped us from objecting to similar acquisitions by other nations." But Roosevelt never denied the need for keeping the islands under United States control. As early as July 10, 1944 he wrote to the Joint Chiefs that:

"I am working on the idea that the United Nations will ask the United States to act as a Trustee for the Japanese mandated islands."[9]

---

[7]Hull, *op. cit.,* p. 1304, pp. 1596-1597, James V. Forrestal, *Diaries* (New York, 1951), p. 56.

[8]Hull, *op. cit.,* pp. 1599-1600, 1638-1639.

[9]*Ibid.,* p. 1466; Notter, *op. cit.,* p. 387; Forrestal, *op. cit.,* p. 33. Also see George H. Blakeslee, "Japan's Mandates Islands," Department of State, *Bulletin,* December 17, 1944, p. 764, in which the strategic value of the islands is expounded, Huntington Gilchrist, in *Foreign Affairs,* 1943-1944, demanding an American trusteeship over the Islands for security reasons.

And in March of 1945 Roosevelt made it clear that though sovereignty over the islands would be vested in the United Nations, "we would be requested by them to exercise complete trusteeship for the purpose of world security." While he objected to Australian demands to annex New Guinea outright, he favored the establishment of American bases in New Caledonia under trusteeship principles. Clearly, the humanitarian motivation was not the only one. To the United States, the trusteeship principle afforded a convenient tool for acquiring control over strategically desirable areas without seeming to violate the pledges of the Atlantic Charter.

Whether these non-humanitarian considerations or British coolness toward the first drastic American trusteeship proposals brought about a changed approach cannot be ascertained. Certain it is that the Department of State advocated "self-government" and not "independence" for trust areas after July of 1943 and reduced the power of the proposed international colonial authority.[10] In the "Possible Plan" for international organization, prepared for the Dumbarton Oaks Conference, the retreat is in full evidence. International supervision "might be extended to any territories" but *a priori* it was to apply only to mandates and areas detached from enemy states. With the exception of the "strategic trust" provisions the plan here submitted was almost identical with the one finally submitted to UNCIO.[11]

But to the War and Navy departments this compromise was unacceptable. Forrestal opposed even the mild trusteeship proposals of the Possible Plan and on the eve of the Dumbarton Oaks Conference informed Stettinius that "it seems to me *sine qua non* of any postwar arrangements that there should be no debate as to who ran the Mandated Islands." Consequently, as the Joint Chiefs strongly supported Forrestal's objections and as Henry L. Stimson added his doubts of the wisdom of the proposed arrangements, the United States delegation at Dumbarton Oaks refrained from submitting its trusteeship scheme to the Soviet and British delegates. The deep division of opinion within the U.S. Government prevented the assertion of the Hull-Roosevelt outlook.[12] Nor was this rift healed by the time of UNCIO. Determined to iron out domestic differences of opinion, the President instructed the warring cabinet members to agree on a joint formula by means of inter-departmental consultations on trusteeship. Consultations took place during the winter of 1944-1945 but on March 13, 1945, Stimson could still "repeat his concern about the trusteeship concept and he told the Secretary of State he thought he would in due course have to get rid of the gentleman in his Department who was the sponsor of this idea."[13] Stimson called the

[10]Notter, *op. cit.*, pp. 481-482.

[11]Notter, *op. cit.*, pp. 245, 606.

[12]Forrestal, *op. cit.*, p. 8; Hull, *op. cit.*, pp. 1706-1707.

[13]Forrestal, *op. cit.*, p. 36

trusteeship idea a "quixotic gesture" and at the time of Yalta argued against raising the issue at all until the Soviet Union had committed itself to entering the Pacific War. And on the eve of UNCIO he and Forrestal presented a memorandum to the President—with which Stettinius had refused to associate himself—urging that the Pacific Islands were of primary importance to the security of the world and that therefore "we propose not only to keep them but to exercise our ownership as a trust on behalf of world security, not for any national advantage. . . ."[14] Notwithstanding the inconsistency of speaking of "ownership as a trust" the clamor of Army and Navy succeeded in preventing the Conference at San Francisco from discussing any concrete areas to be placed under the Trusteeship System.

Traditional isolationist sentiment in the United States closely identified itself with the Army-Navy outlook. Senator Harry F. Byrd demanded that "we should control all the mandated islands and Japanese owned islands that the Army and Navy think we should control" and the Hearst press, in May of 1945, followed up by arguing that:

"The American military and naval authorities know what islands in the Pacific must be permanent strongholds. . . . American military and naval opinion and judgment should prevail in this matter. . . . It is no part of the business of the United Nations Conference of San Francisco. It is not the business of any nation in the world except the United States of America."[15]

Clearly, the division of opinion within and outside the government was bound to change the last proposals of the Possible Plan and change them even more toward unilateralism.

IV THE VICTORY OF STRATEGIC MOTIVATIONS IN THE UNITED STATES

Accordingly, the instructions the American delegation carried with it to Yalta were studiously vague on the topic of trusteeship. Trusteeship principles were to apply to the administration of all colonies but only such areas as were voluntarily submitted by colonial powers should be placed under direct international supervision. The Sponsoring Powers were to draft trusteeship proposals, but "these proposals should deal only with the principles and the mechanism which should govern these trusteeship arrangements. They should not be concerned at this

[14] *Ibid.*, p. 28, pp. 37-38.

[15] National Conference of Christians and Jews, *Uncio Memos,* No. 2, May 9, 1945.

stage with specific territories to be placed under trusteeship or with the disposition or allocation of particular territories." Thus the door was left open for the later realization of Stimson's and Forrestal's demands.[16] Since the two Secretaries continued to insist on a clear American statement of the need to acquire outright control over the Pacific Islands prior to UNCIO, no draft trusteeship proposals could be submitted until a few days after the opening of the Conference. The United States Working Paper which contained these proposals is the expression of the compromise between these clashing domestic motivations.[17]

The Working Paper sought to realize a portion of the liberal humanitarian motives establishing general rules of administration for all colonies, i.e., the Declaration Regarding Non-Self-Governing Territories. It sought to apply these demands to specific trust areas to be placed under the Trusteeship Council's supervision though only self-government was to be the ultimate destiny of such territories. Submission of colonies to the System would be voluntary, the United States delegate emphasized, but since it was taken for granted that enemy colonies and dependencies would be so disposed of the Rooseveltian motive of using the System as a means for internationalizing any vital area could be met. Hull's free trade philosophy was to be met through the establishment of the open door in trusts. But while Roosevelt's strategic thinking welcomed the trusteeship device as making control easier, the Armed Services opposition to this approach carried the day at UNCIO. Not only were no specific colonies to be placed under the System discussed at San Francisco, but the introduction of the "strategic trust" idea went a long way toward making internationalization meaningless for the veto-bound Security Council was to exercise supervision over strategic trust areas. Thus appeased, the Army and Navy approved the Working Paper. In the effort to accommodate all motivations, the simple trusteeship proposal of 1942, dictated by liberal humanitarianism and applicable equally to all colonies, was weakened by providing three types of colonial status: strategic trusts with conditional responsibility to the United Nations, ordinary trusts with full United Nations rights of supervision, and the remaining colonial territories over which the United Nations would exercise no jurisdiction directly, though protected by a general declaration of administrative principles.

In fact, it was the strategic motivation which was stressed by the first statement of the United States delegate, in which it was declared that international peace and security and the welfare of the dependent peoples constituted twin objectives which could not be separated. This seemed to justify the special provision made for strategic trust areas and permission to use general trusts for military purposes. In fact, the United States delegation insisted that the first basic objective of the Trusteeship System was "to further international peace and

[16]Notter, *op. cit.*, pp. 387-390, 662-663.

[17]*Ibid.*, pp. 428-434; Forrestal, *op. cit.*, pp. 44-45.

security." Emphasis was now placed on security and not on freedom for colonial peoples. Only on the non-controversial issues of respect for human rights and freedom from discrimination did the Americans welcome the amendment of the Working Paper. The new approach was symbolized best, perhaps, in the joint Anglo-American declaration appended to the Rapporteur's Report of Chapter XII, dealing with the problem of an administering state's withdrawal from the organization or committing an act of aggression. The two delegations declared "that the action to be taken in such a case can only be decided upon at the time and in the light of all relevant circumstances" and they saw no reason why a state's withdrawal from the United Nations should in any way affect its role as a trustee so long as it continued to fulfill its Charter obligations otherwise.[18]

Thus established the Trusteeship System seemed innocuous enough to staisfy the sentiments of the most hardened isolationist. When the Senate took up the ratification of the Charter, its Foreign Relations Committee received letters from Stimson and Forrestal explaining that the document met all United States military and strategic needs. Forrestal insisted, however, that the Navy be consulted before the Pacific Islands be placed under the System and he wanted it understood that:

"... our agreement that this Charter is in accord with the military interests of this country is conditioned by our understanding that the United States is not committed by this Charter or any provision thereof to place under trusteeship any territories of any character, and that if this country hereafter determines to place any territory under trusteeship this will be done only on such terms as it may then voluntarily agree to."[19]

When questioned on the same point by Senator Johnson of California, the Chairman, Senator Connally, confirmed that "under our conception, all we have to do is to hold on to them [the Pacific Islands] until such time as we need to give them up. I do not think that we would want to give them up if they are in strategic areas. If we did we would give them up with strings on them ...." Mr. Pasvolsky then confirmed this interpretation.[20] The final American formula

[18]The voluntary nature of the System was clearly expressed by Leo Pasvolsky in his testimony before the Senate Foreign Relations Committee. See *The Charter of the United Nations,* Hearings before the Committee on Foreign Relations, United States Senate, 79th Cong., 1st Sess. (Washington, 1945), p. 316. The United States stand is described in United Nations Conference on International Organization, *Documents,* Vol. X (London and New York, 1945), hereafter cited as UNCIO. See especially Documents 310, pp. 439-440; 552, pp. 477-478; 877, pp. 513-514; 1018, pp. 543-544; and Annex C of Document 1091, p. 620.

[19]Hearings, *op. cit.,* Letter to the Committee, July 9, 1945, pp. 313-314.

[20]*Ibid.,* pp. 314-316.

succeeded in satisfying both the strategic and the humanitarian motivation, though it was the latter which had to pay the greater price.

V ACCEPTANCE AND THE CHALLENGE TO EMPIRE

It was the United States which took the initiative in advocating an expanded principle of trusteeship after the war but the aspirations of the dependent areas provided the chorus which produced the underlying demand for such a system. The State Department was made particularly conscious of the need to meet the ever-growing force of colonial nationalism by the situation in the former Dutch East Indies. As the reconquest of this area was undertaken, the United States government refrained from making an agreement with the Netherlands government in order not to prejudice the future independence of Indonesia.[21] But similar demands were heard elsewhere. The Congress Party in India, on the threshold of independence, was clamoring for the elimination of colonialism everywhere through international action. The Philippine government and the Chinese government agreed. Egypt, Iraq, Syria and many Latin American states, especially Mexico, went on record in their desire for an international supervisory system which would guide all dependent areas to independence. The very nations which had until recently been ruled from Europe and Washington were the chief advocates of a firm anti-colonial policy to be adopted by the new United Nations Organization. It was not surprising therefore that the chief criticism of the American Working Paper at San Francisco came from this camp.

National independence, then, was the watchword for the Asian and Arab delegations. Australia and New Zealand were quick to identify themselves with this group, though their motivations were by no means entirely due to humanitarian considerations. While Evatt demanded the obligatory submission of all colonies to United Nations supervision and pressed for a far more detailed statement of administrative principles by which colonial powers were to guide themselves than provided in the American draft, a persistent emphasis on strategic factors emerged as well. Thus the Australians were quite as consistent as the American delegation in urging the primacy of security considerations and the need to free "C" Mandates from restrictions as to fortification. Nor did Evatt or New Zealand's Peter Frazer challenge the strategic trust proposal. It appears that this Dominion attitude was dictated, first, by the desire to appease the clamor of the nationalist movements to the north in order to live in harmony with these emergent national communities, and secondly by the desire to consolidate control over strategic

---

[21] Hull, *op. cit.,* p. 1599.

outposts under the guise of disinterested trusteeships. Nevertheless, the effect of these motivations was a union of forces between the young nations at UNCIO and the Dominion demands in challenging the American compromise.[22]

The Arab and Asian states themselves differed in their substantive proposals despite their united opposition to the Working Paper. China demanded "self-government *or* independence" as the aim for trust areas and the creation of legislative assemblies in them. The immunity of strategic trusts from United Nations supervision was to be minimized, trust administration was to be in United Nations hands and infractions of trusteeship obligations were to be considered matters of international concern. While China's motivations did not seem to include immediate colonial emancipation the Chinese delegate nevertheless was quoted as saying that:

"For the United States to annex or lay permanent claim to single trusteeships of Pacific Islands would be unfortunate indeed. This would constitute a dangerous precedent for England and Russia to do likewise with territories they have torn from the enemy.... Single-nation controls are dangerous–dependent people must be assured of economic assistance and eventual independence...."[23]

Similar restraint was not displayed by Egypt, the Philippines, Syria, Mexico and Iraq. Preparation of all colonies for independence by the United Nations was demanded in emphatic terms, and the Philippines' Carlos Romulo insisted that "self-government" really meant independence. Mexico stressed the primacy of native welfare over security and called attention to what was considered the parallel situation of 1919. Egypt wanted trusts assigned, transferred and terminated by action of the General Assembly and mandates included in the System by definition rather than by voluntary submission. Strategic trusts were to be minimized and the administering state was not to possess unlimited rights to make use of trusts for security purposes. Rights of existing mandatory states were to be weakened and the privileges of indigenous populations enhanced in what seemed an Egyptian attempt to use the Trusteeship System to change British policy in Palestine and Jordan. The demand that native populations were to be rejected by the colonial powers who countered that the "voluntary basis" of the system would be destroyed by these amendments to the Working Paper.[24]

---

[22]UNCIO, *op. cit.,* Documents 230, pp. 641-655; 241, pp. 428-429; and 1018, p. 543; Herbert V. Evatt, *Australia in World Affairs* (Sydney, 1946), pp. 28-30, 50, 111-112, 133, 166, 184. Also see Evatt's contribution to K. M. Panikkar (ed.), *Regionalism and Security* (New Delhi, 1948).

[23]National Conference of Christians and Jews, *Uncio Memos,* No. 3, May 16, 1945.

[24]UNCIO, *op. cit.,* Documents 364, pp. 446-447; 404, pp. 452-454; 448, pp. 459-460; 512, pp. 468-470; 552, pp. 475-478; 580, pp. 485-488; 712, pp. 496-500; 735, pp. 506-507; 877, pp. 513-518; and 1018, pp. 543-544.

These aspirations, to be sure, were not met in anything like their entirety. But the mere assertion of colonial nationalist demands made the creation of some new trusteeship arrangement a foregone conclusion. Unlike the situation in 1919, international accountability on basic human rights, on freedom from discrimination and economic exploitation and even a limited amount of political development was not seriously challenged at all in 1945. While the total motivation of the former colonial areas was not realized at UNCIO the acceptance of the expanded Trusteeship System itself constituted a recognition of the demands of the new nationalism.

VI ACCEPTANCE AND SOVIET MOTIVATIONS

Moreover, the forces working toward the acceptance of the trusteeship principle derived a good deal of support from sources outside the former colonial areas. Not only was much private and public sentiment in the United States in favor of a New Deal but similar pressure was exerted by the Soviet Union and to a lesser extent by Labor opinion in the United Kingdom. The Soviet Union raised the issue of trusteeship as early as the Dumbarton Oaks Conference and pressed the United States for a definite commitment. Molotov had expressed an interest in it at the Moscow Meeting of the Foreign Ministers in 1943, while Eden was not prepared to discuss it then. At Yalta the Soviet spokesmen took no exception to the United States proposals but they brought their own scheme to San Francisco, a scheme which departed in some essential respects from the United States plan. Thus while the Soviet plan accepted the distinction between trust areas and the general declaration for other colonial territories, the Russians specified that full national independence was to be the aim for trusts and that United Nations supervision was to ensure progress toward full independence. The Trusteeship Council was to possess full powers of direct inspection and investigation in trust areas, a point on which the United States plan had been less definite. And finally, the Soviet Union demanded a permanent seat for itself on the Council. These points were insisted upon by the Soviet delegation at UNCIO and they also demanded that colonial powers assume responsibility for developing all dependent people toward *political* progress, though independence was not directly called for. Naturally enough, the Soviets insisted that the term "states directly concerned" be defined in detail, since the Soviet Union later claimed to be one of those states.[25] Furthermore, it appears that Soviet readiness to accede to the strategic

[25]Notter, *op. cit.*, pp. 660-661; Hull, *op. cit.*, pp. 1304-1305; and UNCIO, *op. cit.*, Documents 241, pp. 428; 310, pp. 441; 404, pp. 453; 230, pp. 641-655.

aspects of the United States plan was motivated by the desire of acquiring a similar trust for the Soviet Union, expressed by Molotov to Stettinius at UNCIO. This desire took on concrete form at the Potsdam Conference, at which Stalin made it plain that the Soviet Union was interested in obtaining a trusteeship over Libya, thus meeting the United States Navy's strategic claims in the Pacific with corresponding claims in the Mediterranean.[26] Whatever Soviet motivations in 1945 may have been, it is clear that Soviet support for the adoption of a trusteeship principle was a powerful force making for the acceptance of the System by the colonial powers.

VII ACCEPTANCE AND THE POSITION OF BRITISH LABOR

Nor was the position of the British Labor Party a factor to be ignored. Participating in the wartime coalition government and readying itself for the general election of 1945, the party was in an excellent position to force some of its policies on the Conservatives. Thus the party's colonial platform in 1943 had called for the development of political self-government "and the attainment of political rights not less than those enjoyed or claimed by those of British democracy." It also demanded "the application of Socialist policy in the economic organization of the colonies and the acceptance of the principle of international supervision and accountability." In 1944, the Annual Conference of the party declared:

"In all colonial territories the first aims of the administration must be the well-being and education of the native inhabitants; their standards of life and health; and their preparation for self-government without delay. . . . There must be a sincere determination on the part of those responsible for colonial administration on the part of those responsible for colonial administration to put native interests first in the priorities they organize. . . . In regions such as Africa, South-East Asia and the South-West Pacific, where neighboring colonies are administered by different Governments, we strongly recommend the early creation of Regional Councils to coordinate economic policy–trade, transport, etc.–with a view to making the interests of the colonial peoples primary beyond all doubt."

Not only was the administering authority to publish regular and full reports on its work, but the regional councils to be created were to be given facilities for

---

[26] James F. Byrnes, *Speaking Frankly* (New York, 1947), pp. 76-77, 92-96. E. Zhukov, writing in *New Times,* No. 14, 1945, claims that Soviet policy was motivated by the desire immediately to end colonial imperialism and to acquire a strategic trust area.

direct inspection in all colonies. It was the party's left wing, however, which tended to make the anti-imperialism issue one of the mainstays of the program, while the party leadership had no such overriding interest in it.[27] To a much greater degree than is true of the anti-imperialist pressure exerted by the Australian and New Zealand Labor Parties, this program must be attributed to the liberal humanitarian motivation. To the British workingman the development of a strong Indonesian or Indian nationalism was not a matter of direct concern, to be appeased in time. British Labor's colonial program in 1945, while by no means as rigidly socialist as in 1918, nevertheless espoused international accountability as a progressive principle rather than as a diplomatic concession, in contrast to Conservative coolness toward the whole approach. But it must be admitted that Labor's program could easily consider itself satisfied with the Declaration Regarding Non-Self-Governing Territories and did not have to hold out for the more liberal demands.

VIII ACCEPTANCE AND THE OPPOSITION TO TRUSTEESHIP

Despite American proposals, Soviet Pressure, Arab assertions and Socialist declarations the governments of Britain, France, Belgium, the Netherlands and South Africa yielded only slowly and exacted a large toll from the original demands for a colonial New Deal. During the last two years of the war, while preparations for the System were being made, the government of General Charles de Gaulle gave no evidence of any interest in these developments. In fact, the Free French Government's record seems to suggest that a tightening of the French Empire through the French Union was contemplated rather than an increase of international supervisory jurisdiction. After having been invited to become one of the sponsoring governments, the French delegation at San Francisco generally associated itself with the United States Working Paper, but proposed a number of changes. Thus, instead of mentioning self-government or independence among the goals of the Trusteeship System, the French plan merely called for the "progressive development of political institutions." The System, moreover, was to be limited to mandates and enemy colonies and the necessity for securing the submission of such areas with the consent of the mandatories was stressed. And finally, the French plan made no mention of the power of the Trusteeship Council to investigate conditions or receive petitions. During the discussions in the Committee the French expressed the hope that the debate would proceed within "precise limits" and called attention to the fact that the Dumbarton Oaks Draft

[27] Labor Party, *Report of the 43rd Annual Conference,* 1944, p. 9, and *Report of the 42nd Annual Conference,* 1943, pp. 4, 207-208.

expressly forbade intervention in the domestic affairs of member states. Again taking refuge behind the non-intervention doctrine, the French delegation declared in an annex to the Rapporteur's Report that "none of the provisions submitted for the approval of this Committee implies total or partial renunciation by the French Government" of this principle. French lack of enthusiasm for the System was thus not left in doubt, and French acceptance, as in 1919, must be attributed to considerable outside pressure.[28]

The French were not alone in their opposition. South Africa declared herself unable to accept any changes in the existing mandate terms and opposed the extension of the trusteeship principle to territories within the metropolitan area of member states, i.e., to South-West Africa after the Union was ready to annex it.[29] The trusteeship principle, urged the Netherlands delegation, was an admirable device for dealing with enemy areas, but it would hinder rather than help the development toward self-government if applied to colonies, since the European possessions would naturally progress toward free association with the metropolitan area. Specifically, it was pointed out that in areas in which the prerequisites for independence existed such a status would be achieved with or without the activities of the United Nations. Instead the Dutch wanted the international system to assure protection of native land rights, abolish forced labor and end racial discrimination. They were distinctly not interested in the political features of the United States Working Paper.[30] Dutch acquiescence in the System can thus be explained primarily as resulting from the nonapplication of its operative features to the Dutch possessions.

It was the attitude adopted by the United Kingdom, however, which was of focal importance not primarily at San Francisco but during the preceding two years when the United States developed its trusteeship proposals. At first, the Foreign Office seemed to follow a policy of studied indifference. Cordell Hull relates that he mentioned the American trusteeship scheme of 1943 no less than three times to Anthony Eden at Quebec before the Foreign Secretary decided to acknowledge it. And, continues Hull, "the Foreign Secretary said that, to be perfectly frank, he had to say he did not like our draft very much. He said it was the word 'independence' that troubled him. He had to think of the British Empire System, which was built on the basis of Dominion and colonial status."[31] Eden again refused to consider the trusteeship problem at the Moscow Conference and no particular interest in the matter was expressed by the British delegation at Dumbarton Oaks. Just before Yalta, Colonel Oliver Stanley, Colonial

---

[28]UNCIO, *op. cit.,* Document 230, pp. 641-655; 260, p. 433; and Annex D to Document 1115, p. 622.

[29]*Ibid.,* Document 260, p. 434; 310, p. 439.

[30]*Ibid.,* Document 260, pp. 433-434; 1090, pp. 561-562.

[31]Hull, *op. cit.,* pp. 1237-1238.

Secretary, suggested to Washington that the other colonial powers be consulted before further talks were conducted, but the State Department refused to comply because it was feared that the British merely wanted to bolster the anti-trusteeship camp through this procedure. At this stage, the British suggested international supervision through Regional Commissions composed only of colonial powers, and again the State Department turned this suggestion down as inadequate.[32] Obviously, no progress toward a strong Trusteeship System could be made without the cooperation of the principal colonial power, and this British attitude was sufficient in itself to induce the United States to weaken its original sweeping proposals, even without the further impetus of domestic American opposition to trusteeship.

At San Francisco, the British delegation presented a mixture of conservative humanitarian, economic and strategic motivations in the effort of minimize international control. The British draft trusteeship scheme stipulated self-government as the aim of the System and provided for the submission of any territory to it through the voluntary action of the metropolitan country. Mandates and ex-enemy colonies were to be put under it as well, again through voluntary submission only. Moreover, the administering powers were to be "advanced nations . . . who are best fitted to undertake this responsibility and who are willing to accept it." In their strategic and military portions the British proposals were identical with the American, but unlike them, the Trusteeship Council was to function under the Economic and Social Council and not as a "principal organ" of the United Nations, apparently an attempt to deprive the Council of importance and publicity. And finally, the British draft made no mention of the Council's right to visit trust areas or to receive petitions. Existing mandatory rights, the British insisted, could be changed only with the consent of the Mandatory state. Like the French and Dutch, they warned against the introduction of independence by fiat and advised to await its arrival through "natural development."[33] In the final analysis, therefore, the British conceded only the very qualified "independence" phrase for trusts and the Trusteeship Council's right to visit trusts and receive petitions. This, to be sure, they would scarcely have admitted had it not been for American and Arab pressure. But, as was implied in statements later made in the House of Commons, it was considered wise to sacrifice the façade of control and retain the essence.

Prime Minister Attlee, in presenting the Charter to the House, discussed the Trusteeship System as no more than the main principle of colonial administration which the United Kingdom had followed for decades. Like the State Department, he stressed the role of trust territories in the maintenance of international peace and security and like Senator Connally he assured the House that the Charter did not *ipso facto* place any territories under international supervision

[32] Notter, *op. cit.,* pp. 662-663.

[33] UNCIO, *op. cit.,* Document 310, p. 440; 230, pp. 641-655.

"or take any decision as to future of such territories, nor by passing this motion will the House be entering into any commitment." A Labor member thereupon asked the government to place voluntarily some of the mandates under the System as a gesture of British faith in the new arrangements. Colonel Stanley, now speaking for the opposition, did not view matters in the same light. He demanded assurances of the government that it did not intend to relinquish control over any mandates then held and furthermore that the Government refrain from placing any British possessions under the System. He advised caution "until it [the government] had had much more experience of the working of the present system, and until we could see much more clearly that it would be to our advantage and the advantage of the Colonial Empire." Mr. Bevin, in answering, was able to reassure the opposition on both counts and there the matter ended.[34] Labor's motivations and those of the Conservatives seemed quite reconciled by the Trusteeship System as adopted.

Britain's acceptance, therefore, can be attributed first to the need of meeting the demands of her American, Soviet and Dominion allies, and secondly to the fact that acceptance would cost nothing in terms of effective control and perhaps gain something in terms of Arab and Indian good will. Certainly, a policy of unmitigated opposition, such as that adopted by France and The Netherlands, was impossible to a Britain committed to freeing India, Burma and Ceylon and cooperating with Australia and New Zealand. Conflicting inter-Empire and inter-Commonwealth motivations, though far less pronounced in 1945 than in 1919, still prevented the government in London from following the French course.

IX SUMMATION OF REASONS FOR ACCEPTANCE

It thus appears that neither a progressive spirit of disinterestedness nor a strong humanitarianism can claim sole credit for the acceptance of the Trusteeship System in 1945. Furthermore, the situation of 1945 offers no evidence that the System was readily accepted because it was to serve as a device to cushion rivalries between imperial powers. Roosevelt, it is true, did consider this aspect. But the fact that the System was applied voluntarily by powers not divided by such rivalries in recent decades should disprove this explanation.

International trusteeship in 1919 owed its acceptance to the necessity of finding a compromise solution to a series of clashing colonial policy motivations. It owed its continuation in 1945 to precisely the same kind of situation. However, the motivations had changed not only in content but, more significantly, in terms

[34] *Hansard,* Vol. 413, August 23, 1945, col. 667-669, 703-704, 929-935, 940.

of the groups now identified with them. The area of disagreement had tended to shift from the domestic and inter-Commonwealth levels to the inter-allied plane. The protagonists of a colonial New Deal were identified with the new Asian and Arab states and with Latin America, receiving only sporadic support from groups in the United States, while the established colonial powers showed a consistent unity in their opposition to a new colonial policy to be conducted under the auspices of an international organization.

The aspirations of the anti-colonial groups, then, called first and foremost for the realization of the liberal ideology, the elimination of foreign rule and the speedy progress of colonial peoples—all colonial peoples—toward a measure of independent status. Social, cultural and economic progress were not enough. National independence was demanded at the earliest possible moment, to be achieved through the supervision of the United Nations. In the forefront of those who argued in these terms were, of course, the Arab, Asian and Latin American spokesmen. Liberal opinion in the United States at first favored and supported these demands but at least on the governmental level this support slackened by 1945 under the influence of a different type of motivation. And liberal opinion in the United Kingdom, Australia and New Zealand, while in theory sympathetic to these aspirations, was a poor third in the actual support given to this motivation. A further motive favorable to the colonial New Deal was that represented by the groups and individuals who welcomed international rule as a device for acquiring strategic bases without seeming to resort to renewed imperial expansion. As in 1919, the members of this group saw no inconsistency between paramount regard for native advancement and the utilization of the areas in question for unilateral military purposes. President Roosevelt and the Department of State as well as the governments of Australia and New Zealand were the typical exponents of this aspiration. The primary motive of the Soviet government in arguing for a strong United Nations Trusteeship System seems to have been the same. A final body of opinion of some moment which supported the colonial New Deal was a group of free traders, symbolized by Cordell Hull, who saw in trusteeship over all colonies a way to combat protectionism. Support for this aspiration was in the main limited to opinion in the United States.

The opposition to the New Deal for colonies, however, was equally strong and was furthermore favored by the fact that it had existing international law and actual control over dependent areas on its side. In the realm of ideology, the conservative humanitarian position was its point of departure. International supervision, said the spokesmen for the British, French and Netherlands governments, was unnecessary if not harmful for the gradual development of colonies toward self-government and free association with the metropolitan country. Similarly, the colonial powers were agreed that the Open Door should be minimized and national prerogatives in investment and trade policies continued. And on the key issue of international or unrestrained unilateral control over strategic bases the spokesmen of the colonial powers agreed with the position of the United States armed services in urging the minimization of supervision. Aspirations, in short, were such as to make the introduction of international controls feared and opposed.

In the dialectric of E. H. Carr, the process of policy formulation in international relations is held to be a synthesis of two antithetical forces: the demands of power politics, usually identified with conservatism, and the demands of utopian idealism, as put forward by liberals and socialists.[35] If we apply these concepts to the evolution and acceptance of the trusteeship principle in 1919 and 1945 we may identify the "realist" thesis with those who opposed trusteeship on grounds of national power or those who favored it because it facilitated power compromises. Power in either case is the key criterion of conduct. The "utopian" antithesis, by contrast, would then be represented by those who urged the adoption of trusteeship on grounds of humanitarianism, economic liberalism and devotion to principles of national self-determination. The foregoing analysis should provide ample material for the rejection of this type of categorization of motives.

Thus in the realm of the humanitarian ideology, the "realist" no less than the "Utopian" can claim his share in the acceptance of the new principle. Regard for the economic, social, cultural and even political development of dependent peoples has long ceased to be the monopoly of the socialist and liberal strands of opinion whom Carr considers to be the utopians. While it remains true that in 1919 and 1945 conservatives tended to oppose international supervision while liberals generally argued for it, the difference in outlook is to be explained in terms of varying conceptions of "reality". Similarly, the issue of strategic bases cannot be treated simply by claiming that realists sought to prevent international supervision or limit it to insignificant areas because they desired unilateral military control while utopians were indifferent to this power political aspect of colonies. Again the issue between the proponents and the foes of international supervision involved different interpretation of reality rather than the antithesis suggested by Carr. Nor can the economic factor in colonialism be easily fitted into the scheme. To be sure, protectionism and opposition to trusteeship tended to go hand in hand while the principle of the Open Door was generally identified with those who argued for international supervision. But while the interplay between the two forces was a vital factor in facilitating the acceptance of the principle only a value judgment would entitle us to brand the Open Door as "utopian", even in the Mannheimian sense.

---

[35] E. H. Carr, *The Twenty Years Crisis* (London, Macmillan and Co., 1948).

X IMPLICATIONS FOR THE FUTURE

The fact that the United Nations Charter was able to synthesize these clashing aims should not obscure the equally important fact that the "synthesis" was somewhat artificial. To be sure, liberal humanitarianism received its satisfaction in the Declaration Regarding Non-Self-Governing Territories but conservative humanitarianism was made content by the limited application of the Trusteeship System proper. Military opponents of international rule were reconciled through the strategic trust provisions but those who saw in trusteeship a means for internationalizing future trouble spots received satisfaction through the possibility of the submission of any colonial area to the System. Economic liberals could take comfort in the Open Door provision and economic protectionists in the corresponding escape clauses. Colonial nationalism was temporarily appeased but colonial empires seemed also to remain intact. How a "reconciliation" of this type would work in practice was soon demonstrated by the stormy sessions of the Trusteeship Council and especially by the Fourth Committee of the General Assembly, in which the colonial powers consistently oppose the unceasing demands of India and the Moslem states for speedier progress toward colonial independence.

Clearly, no single motivation was satisfied with the compromise at UNCIO. And the developmental potentialities of the Trusteeship System are in sore danger of suffering atrophy because of the superficial nature of the compromise. Only the fact that clashes in colonial policy have today shifted from the domestic and inter-Commonwealth levels to the inter-Allied plane may provide us with hope that international supervision will continue as a force of some moment. In a very real sense, the success of the Trusteeship System is intimately tied up with the ability of western statesmanship to adopt the long-range view of concession to the Arab-Asian demands instead of the short-range policy, notably represented by France at the moment, to "hold on" at all cost and defy the United Nations in the process, if necessary.

Keeping the Arab and Asian states favorably disposed toward the West has emerged as one of the chief tasks of NATO diplomacy. Obviously this requires a modicum of concession to their aspirations which happen to include the desire to make use of the Trusteeship System for the elimination of colonialism. Long-range benefits for the West, it would seem, could be obtained by giving the Arab-Asian bloc the satisfaction of seeing further withdrawals from colonial possessions. And the forum of the United Nations could provide the mechanism whereby this interest would be served at a minimum of expense in terms of prestige lost by the old colonial powers. Instead of the short-range course of meeting Indian or Egyptian complaints with compromise resolution after compromise resolution, the implementation of which is always open to considerable doubt, the colonial powers might regard the United Nations as a useful agency for giving the champions of anti-colonialism—defeated in 1945—an opportunity to express their preferences *and* for giving them the further satisfaction of seeing their demands carried out.

The South-West and North African situations as well as the unwillingness shown by the administering authorities of regular trusts to expedite their own withdrawal, however, seem to confirm the victory of the short-range view. If this trend is to continue the surface synthesis achieved at San Francisco will become increasingly artificial and not even the Cold War will act as a catalyst toward the progress of international supervision.

The United Nations and Colonialism: A Tentative Appraisal

Harold Karan Jacobson

I

Colonialism, at least as it is generally defined in the United Nations as Western rule of non-metropolitan areas, is rapidly being brought to a close. As a consequence, within a few years some of the activities of the United Nations will be reduced to almost insignificant proportions. Seven of the eleven territories that were once included within the trusteeship system have already achieved self-government or independence,[1] and another, Ruanda-Urundi, will soon attain that goal. Unless new territories are added, only Nauru, New Guinea, and the Pacific Islands will remain under trusteeship. The list of territories which according to the General Assembly are subject to the provisions of Chapter XI of the Charter has not been cut as drastically, but in terms of the number of people involved, the reduction is equally impressive. Even with the high rate of population growth and the addition of the Spanish and Portuguese dependencies, the number of

---

Harold Karan Jacobson, "The United Nations and Colonialism: A Tentative Appraisal," *International Organization,* Vol. 16, No. 1 (Winter 1962), pp. 37-56. Reprinted by permission of *International Organization.*

[1] British Togoland elected to join Ghana, which became independent in 1957. The French Cameroons, French Togoland, and Italian Somaliland attained independence in 1960. The trusteeship for the British Cameroons was terminated in 1961 when the Northern Cameroons became part of the Federation of Nigeria on June 1 and the Southern Cameroons joined the Republic of Cameroun on October 1. Tanganyika became independent December 9, 1961. Western Samoa gained that status January 1, 1962.

people living in such areas is about one-fifth of the 1946 figure of 215,000,000. With a few important exceptions such as Kenya, Uganda, Nyasaland and the Rhodesias, and Angola and Mozambique, the territories which in the UN's view "have not yet attained a full measure of self-government" are small and have populations of less than one million. It has already been recommended that the future of the Department of Trusteeship and Information from Non-Self-Governing Territories[2] and the possibility of allocating its duties to other departments be reviewed in the light of these developments. Although colonial disputes will probably continue to occupy prominent places on the agendas of the Security Council and the General Assembly for a time, the number of possible controversies of this nature is quickly diminishing. On the other hand, the passing of colonialism has also confronted the United Nations with new problems and tasks, as the Congo dramatically illustrates. Thus, an important chapter in the history of international organization is almost concluded, while another is just beginning.

It may be an appropriate time therefore to attempt a tentative appraisal of the work of the United Nations with regard to colonialism: to consider the manner in which the UN has performed its tasks and to ponder the effects of its actions. Since there is a definite connection between earlier events and some of the problems of the post-colonial era, an analysis of the UN's work in this field just necessarily extend beyond the actual period of colonial rule; to a limited extent a review of the last chapter must also include a preview of the next.

II

Before examining the substantive aspects of the UN's activities with regard to colonialism, it may be useful to consider the institutional and political framework within which these activities have been carried on. From reading the Charter, one might expect that most of these functions would have been conducted within the Trusteeship Council, and, in the case of colonial disputes, within the Security Council. This has not been the case. The General Assembly, for reasons which are common to nearly all aspects of the UN's work and others which are especially related to this field, has overshadowed both organs. The Assembly has set up its own subordinate bodies to deal with colonial problems: the Committee on Information from Non-Self-Governing Territories and the Committee on South West Africa. It has belabored the Trusteeship Council and has in a sense reversed some of that organ's decisions and recommendations. It has considered

[2] See the report of the Committee of Experts on the Activities and Organization of the Secretariat: Document A/4776, pp. 61-62.

colonial disputes which the Security Council has refused to view and has acted when that body would not.

Since the broad reasons for the development and enhancement of the General Assembly's role are well known, we need only consider those which are especially related to colonial problems. Here, the basic reason for the Assembly's becoming the most important center of activity is that the advocates of change—the side really interested in involving the UN—have been in a stronger position in this body. Mustering support for anticolonial actions has always been easier in the Assembly than in either the Trusteeship Council or the Security Council. In terms of the UN's total membership, the colonial powers have constantly been overrepresented on the two Councils, and as the membership has grown, so has the disparity between the political composition of these organs and the Assembly. Moreover, the two most important colonial powers have held veto rights in the Security Council, and while they have seldom used this privilege, it no doubt has had a deterrent effect. Another important factor, given the nature of the power of the United Nations, is that the Assembly has been more productive of world headlines and a world-wide audience.

There are also other explanations for the Assembly's prominence. Had South West Africa been put under trusteeship, the Assembly probably would not have become so deeply and persistently involved in that question. Had the colonial powers given meaning to the provisions of Article 77c of the Charter by voluntarily putting some of their colonies under trusteeship, the pressure to develop the Committee on Information might not have been so great. To be sure, the movement to develop Chapter XI began before it was certain that this subparagraph would be a dead letter, and it would have been a potent force as long as any dependent territories remained outside of the trusteeship system. Perhaps few, if any, seriously expected that the colonial powers would make extensive use of Article 77c. As it was, however, the anticolonial forces could take the position, trenchantly expressed by the study group which analyzed India's role in the UN, that:

> ". . . the division of dependent areas into non-self-governing territories and trust territories was merely an accident of history; the former were the possessions of the victors of the two world wars and the latter those of the defeated."[3]

This attitude nourished the already existent desire to provide the same degree of international supervision for both types of territories.

---

[3] *India and the United Nations* (New York: Manhattan, 1957), p. 101.

Nor would one gain a sense of the importance of the Secretariat in this phase of the United Nations work from reading the Charter. Nevertheless, in routine matters, although not in crises, the Secretariat has been extremely influential. The Secretariat's expert knowledge concerning some of the more technical issues in the colonial field has caused many delegates to rely heavily on it as a source of advice. They have also been willing to allow it considerable discretion in handling day-to-day colonial issues. Moreover, the UN's procedures for dealing with such matters have enhanced the Secretariat's influence. Reports have figured prominently in this phase of the UN's work. Members of the Secretariat usually draft these reports, and then the delegates amend and approve them. When the pressure of time is great and little national staff assistance is available, as in the case of visiting missions, the power to draft verges on the power to commit. By and large, the Secretariat's influence has benefited the anticolonial forces. For one thing, although the Secretariat's knowledge has been available to all, it has been more useful to these delegations, for their national staffs could hardly match those of the colonial powers. More importantly, the sympathies of the UN Secretariat appear generally to have tended in this direction.

Turning from international institutions to states, we find that both major protagonists in the Cold War have played distinctive roles in the UN's activities concerning colonialism.

Many commentators have attributed an obstreperous and obstructive quality to the Soviet Union's participation in this phase of the UN's work.[4] Without question the USSR and the Soviet bloc have been the most outspoken critics of colonialism in the United Nations. Vyacheslav M. Molotov, in a press conference at San Francisco, gave a forecast of this when he stated: "We must first of all see to it that dependent territories are enabled as soon as possible to take the path of national independence."[5] Soviet policy has not deviated from this line; it has granted the colonial powers no quarter.

One effect of this has been to encourage the development of more extreme positions on both sides and thus to constrict the possibilities of agreement. In this sense, the adjective "obstructive" can accurately be applied to the USSR's conduct. Soviet behavior has had a demonstrably inflationary effect on the actions of the anticolonial forces.[6] Extreme

---

[4]See for example: Annette Baker Fox, "International Organization for Colonial Development," *World Politics*, April 1951 (Vol. 3, No. 3) pp. 340-368, pp. 353-354; and, Sherman S. Hayden, "The Trusteeship Council: Its First Three Years," *Political Science Quarterly*, June 1951 (Vol. 66, No. 2), pp. 226-247, pp. 229-230.

[5]*New York Times*, May 8, 1945.

[6]For a few examples see Elliot R. Goodman, "The Cry of National Liberation: Recent Soviet Attitudes Toward National Self-Determination," *International Organization*, Winter 1960 (Vol. 14, No. 1), pp. 92-106.

Soviet proposals could not be ignored. The advocates of change have been forced either to support them, or to introduce alternative proposals. Then too, the Soviet bloc has usually supported anticolonial initiative made by others. Western commentators have sometimes characterized this Soviet support as a "mixed blessing," but the record gives little indication that the beneficiaries have been seriously bothered. To the contrary, in parliamentary situations support is generally welcomed, regardless of the source, and by taking the most extreme positions, the USSR has allowed others to appear fairly moderate in comparison. On the other side, the colonial powers have recoiled before the Soviet accusations, becoming more and more defensive and less willing to submit their colonial affairs to international scrutiny. One unfortunate consequence of all this has been the occasional tendency of the administering authorities summarily to dismiss as propaganda any criticism voiced by the USSR. As a result, valid points have sometimes been obscured.

Viewed in a somewhat different perspective, it is striking how little the Soviet bloc has been involved in the UN's activities relating to colonialism. By virtue of Article 86 the USSR has always held a seat on the Trusteeship Council, but no member of the Soviet bloc has ever been elected to this organ. The Soviet Union has always been a member of the Standing Committee on Petitions, but beyond that it has held few positions on the Trusteeship Council's subsidiary organs. No Soviet national has ever been a member of a visiting mission or of a plebiscite or election inspection team.[7] Soviet bloc representation on the body now known as the Committee on Information has been limited to the membership of the USSR from 1946 through 1952.[8] No member of the Soviet bloc has ever been a member of the Committee on South West Africa or of any of the *ad hoc* bodies concerned with this territory. One of the most important factors in the decisions concerning the Italian colonies was a desire to preclude Soviet influence. The Soviet bloc (although not Yugoslavia after its break with the bloc) has been excluded from all of the committees and commissions which have been established to deal with colonial disputes. Despite its determined efforts,

[7] On the one occasion when the question of the USSR's participating in a visiting mission was formally raised, the Soviet representative immediately replied that "his delegation would be unable to take part . . ." (Trusteeship Council *Official Records* [5th session], p. 257). The discussion occurred in July, 1949. It concerned the composition of the mission which would visit the trust territories in the Pacific in the late spring and early summer of 1950.

[8] In the 1952 election the USSR was defeated by China, 27-24, on the second ballot. In 1955 China won a place over the USSR again, this time on the first ballot. Three years later, the Soviet Union again seriously offered its candidacy, but withdrew at the last moment in favor of Ghana so as not to split the vote against China. Tactically the move was successful as China was not elected.

the USSR was unable to gain a seat on the Economic Commission for Africa (ECA), a body of potential importance for the immediate post-colonial era.[9]

These facts give some point to the Soviet Unions' insistence at San Francisco that the Charter should require that the five Great Powers be represented on the Trusteeship Council. Indeed, it might be argued that one of the central themes running through all of the activities of the United Nations with regard to colonialism has been an attempt to minimize possibilities for Soviet influence in the process of decolonization and to exclude the USSR from the colonial settlement. Sometimes this has been done under the guise of keeping the Cold War out. It should be remembered, however, that excluding the two major protagonists, as in ECA or the United Nations Emergency Force, or even the members of the two alliance systems, does not necessarily exclude Western influence. Interestingly, hardly any non-communist states have objected to the Soviet bloc's exclusion, except in the case of the Economic Commission for Africa.

These comments are not made to pass judgment on the justice of the situation. The Soviet bloc generally did not have historical interests in or connections with the areas which were the object of this aspect of the UN's work. From the point of view of the West, there have been sufficient reasons for excluding the USSR and its allies. Nor are these comments intended to indicate that the USSR's participation has been unimportant or without influence. Their purpose is merely to delineate more precisely the impact of Soviet policy.

In contrast to the USSR, the United States has been deeply involved in most aspects of the UN's work concerning colonialism, and it has been extremely influential. The United States has occupied a key position in the Trusteeship Council and consequently has often been able to mold this body's actions. American proposals have provided the basis for much of the work of the Committee on Information. Countless General Assembly resolutions have been shaped so that they could gain American approval. In crisis situations, such as that involving Indonesia, the United States has frequently exercised a determining role.

[9] The Sudanese draft resolution defining the terms of reference of the Economic Commission for Africa (Document E/L.780 and Rev. 1) gave membership to both the United States and the USSR. The African states which were then in the UN strongly supported this provision. The USSR was eager to serve on the Commission. The United States, however, argued that membership on the Commission should be limited to the states of Africa and the relevant metropolitan powers. The Council finally rejected the paragraph in question by a vote of 5 (Indonesia, Poland, Sudan, USSR, and Yugoslavia) to 12 (Brazil, Canada, Chile, China, Costa Rica, France, Greece, Mexico, Netherlands, Pakistan, United Kingdom, and the United States) with one abstention (Finland) (ECOSOC *Official Records* [25th session], p. 86). ECOSOC Resolution 671 (XXV) April 29, 1958, provides that membership on the Commission is open to independent states in Africa and to states which have responsibilities for territories in Africa as long as these responsibilities continue.

The UN has been a useful instrument in this respect for the United States. It has provided an access to problems which might otherwise have been beyond the realm of American influence.[10] For one thing, the United States had few intrinsic reasons for becoming involved in unextraordinary developments in Africa. Furthermore, advice from an international organization is sometimes more acceptable and more effective than advice from an ally.

Of course, membership in the United Nations has also forced the United States to take stands when it might have preferred to remain silent. In short-range and tactical terms, actions in the UN obviously have often placed the United States in a difficult dilemma.[11] If the United States were to side with the anticolonial majority in the UN, it would anger the colonial powers, several of which were important allies of the United States.[12] On the other hand, if the United States were to support the colonial powers, it would violate the much vaunted American tradition of anticolonialism, disappoint the anticolonial group, and leave the field open for the Soviet Union. Moreover, the problem which the United States has faced has not simply been a matter of deciding which side to support. Americans too frequently forget that the United States is a colonial power, of however modest proportions, and that it has been unwilling to take some of the actions which have been demanded by the anticolonial forces.[13] Further, at times the anticolonial pressures have almost taken the form of a campaign against foreign investment, which has definitely put the United States on the defensive. Military considerations have also posed problems for the United States, and it has been hesitant to support independence for territories which might not be able to maintain internal stability or be impervious to communist pressures. Some, of anticolonial persuasion, regard the United States as the foremost neocolonial power.

Frequently the United States has sought to resolve its dilemma through refuge in a kind of neutralism, and the record contains a large number of

---

[10] Annette Baker Fox foresaw this at an early date and urged the United States to take advantage of it. See "International Organization for Colonial Development," *World Politics*, Vol. 3, April 1951, pp. 340-341.

[11] The best treatment of the way in which the United States has met this dilemma is Robert C. Good, "The United States and the Colonial Debate," in Arnold Wolfers (ed.), *Alliance Policy in the Cold War* (Baltimore: The Johns Hopkins Press, 1959), pp. 224-270.

[12] For a detailed description of several instances in which allies put pressure on the United States see Senator Wayne Morse's supplementary report of the Committee on Foreign Relations on his experiences as a delegate at the fifteenth session of the Assembly: *The United States in the United Nations: 1960–A Turning Point* (Washington, D.C.: Government Printing Office, 1961).

[13] See Harold Karan Jacobson, "Our 'Colonial' Problem in the Pacific," *Foreign Affairs*, October 1960 (Vol. 29, No. 1), pp. 56-66.

American abstentions on colonial issues. However, neither side has regarded abstention as a neutral course, and in fact it has not been without political significance. Among other things, it has affected the number of votes required to achieve a majority, since according to the UN's rules of procedure, abstentions are not included within the meaning of the phrase "Members present and voting."

But even in these short-range terms "the dilemma" has not been the only aspect. The United States position as a "progressive" administering power, which it sometimes flaunts to the discomfort of its allies, has had its compensations. Although being placed in the middle may have been painful, it has also frequently resulted in unusual opportunities to influence the outcome: for instance, in the Indonesian and Suez crises and in the decisions relating to the Committee on Information. Whether one emphasizes the problems which the UN has created for the United States by its actions in this field or the opportunities that it has offered depends at least partially on one's estimate of the inevitability of the changes which have occurred in the colonial field during the past two decades.

There is some justification for dividing the remaining Members of the UN into two groups; for putting the western European states, the older members of the Commonwealth, Iceland, and Israel in one category, and the Latin American, African, and Asian states (often including Nationalist China) in another. In broad terms, the activities of the United Nations concerning colonialism have been characterized by a struggle of the latter group—the anticolonial forces or the advocates of change—against the former. On this level the Soviet bloc must be added to the anticolonial forces, and the United States to the West. However, a division on exactly these lines has prevailed only occasionally, on such issues of principle as the question of including the right of self-determination in the draft covenants on human rights and the passage of Resolution 637 (VII) of December 16, 1952, "The Right of Peoples and Nations to Self-Determination." Thus, although this gross distinction may describe the tenor of the UN's proceedings, it has little meaning beyond that. Even on general issues the two groups have not been completely unified, and on more specific questions their internal divisions have been pronounced.

Within the West, the states which are, or previously were, responsible for dependent territories have formed a special subcategory. The colonial powers have often felt beleaguered in the United Nations. Several of them have charged that the United Nations has exceeded its proper jurisdiction in this sphere. As a group, they have felt that the UN has unfairly scrutinized their colonial practices in detail, while it has given much less attention to what they have considered the more serious offenses of others in different areas. They have resented criticisms of conditions in their dependent territories by delegates from states which may not have had even equal standards of economic, political, and social life. They have often regarded the UN's recommendations as utopian schemes, untempered by concern for reality.[14]

However, there have been differences among the colonial powers. The Union of South Africa, Portugal, and Belgium have been the least sympathetic to the United Nations activities concerning colonialism. The Union of South Africa has refused to place South West Africa under trusteeship. It has bitterly criticized the UN's work with regard to this territory, and on occasion has boycotted the Assembly in protest. Portugal has refused to admit that it is a colonial power and to transmit data to the Committee on Information. Belgium ceased participating in the Committee on Information in 1953. If a continuum were drawn with these three states, in the order listed, at one extreme, moving toward the other end, an appropriate rank order would be: France, Spain, Italy, the United Kingdom, the Netherlands, Australia (after the Liberal-Country Party gained power in December 1949) and, close together, the United States, New Zealand, and Denmark. There have been occasions, though, when this ranking would not apply. For example, during the early years France submitted political information on Morocco and Tunisia as well as the required economic, educational, and social data, and from time to time France has voted for resolutions concerning non-self-governing territories which the United Kingdom opposed.

The other Western countries, particularly the Scandinavian states, Greece, Turkey, Iceland, Ireland, and Israel, have been much more willing to go along with, or at least not to oppose, the Assembly's anticolonial majority.

On the anticolonial side, there has been a basic distinction between the Latin American states and the African-Asian group. The Latin American states have usually supported and have sometimes even led the anticolonial forces. However, this group has contained a wide range of views.[15] Some Latin American states, such as the Dominican Republic, have consistently taken positions which were very close to those of the colonial powers, while others, for example, Haiti, Mexico, and Guatemala, have been among the UN's most rabid anticolonialists. Furthermore, as a group, the Latin American states have generally been somewhat

---

[14]For a sample of this opinion see Sir Alan Burns, *In Defense of Colonies: British Territories in International Affairs* (London: George Allen and Unwin, 1956). Sir Alan Served as the delegate of the United Kingdom to the Trusteeship Council for nine years and also participated in the General Assembly. Even Sir Alan's more moderate successor, Sir Andrew Cohen, has occasionally shown signs of similar feelings. See his *British Policy in Changing Africa* (Evanston: Northwestern University Press, 1959).

[15]This has been graphically illustrated by two statistical analyses: Thomas Hovet, Jr. *Bloc Politics in the United Nations* (Cambridge: Harvard University Press, 1960), p. 141; and, Leroy N. Rieselbach, "Quantitative Techniques for Studying Voting Behavior in the UN General Assembly," *International Organization*, Spring 1960 (Vol. 14, No. 2), pp. 291-306, pp. 300-306. For a more detailed analysis of the position of the Latin American states see: John A. Houston, *Latin America in the United Nations* (New York: Carnegie Endowment for International Peace, 1956), pp. 162-221.

less extreme than the African-Asian group. Since they had few direct ethnic and cultural ties with the peoples of the dependent territories, and since their own colonial experiences and revolutions were different from those being considered by the UN, the anticolonialism of the Latin American states has not had quite the same emotional content as that of the African and Asian states. At times the Latin American states have even acted as if they felt closer ties with the metropolitan powers.[16] Perhaps because of their own emphasis on the doctrine of nonintervention, some Latin American states have paid greater attention than the African and Asian countries to the legal niceties which were involved in colonial issues. The Latin American states have generally been more sensitive to the Cold War implications of the UN's actions in this field and more responsive to United States leadership. Since the Latin American states were not uniformly and unalterably committed to the most extreme anticolonial position, and because of the political composition of the United Nations, this group has occupied a key role in the UN's decisions concerning colonialism. The support of some members of this group has been a virtual requirement for the adoption of any resolution, and this has frequently served as a moderating influence.

Although the African-Asian group has generally taken a more extreme anticolonial position, this group has not been a solid unit either. Among the Asian states, those which have alliances with the West have often taken a somewhat less demanding stand. The African group has also been divided.[17] The relatively moderate position of several of the former French sub-Saharan territories has been well documented.

Just as many in the West have become critical of the UN's activities concerning colonialism, and some have even grown embittered; similar reactions, although with different content, have developed among the anticolonial states. On this side, the criticism is not that the United Nations has violated the terms of Article 2, paragraph 7, by intervening in essentially domestic matters, but rather that this article has illegitimately been used to frustrate the Organization and to preclude constructive action. The anticolonial forces have been as distressed about the slowness with which the United Nations has become involved in colonial disputes and the limited extent of this involvement as the colonial powers have

---

[16] Latin American concern for Italy was an important ingredient in the decisions relating to the Italian colonies. The sympathy which some of these states felt for France appears to have been a major factor in the General Assembly's decision, at its sixth session in Paris in 1951, not to discuss the Moroccan dispute. In 1956 the Latin American relationship with Spain and Portugal apparently was the key factor in the General Assembly's reinstitution of the requirement that certain categories of decisions regarding non-self-governing territories required a two-thirds majority for adoption.

[17] See the interesting analysis of the reactions of the African states to the UN's actions concerning the Congo: Robert C. Good, "Four African Views of the Congo Crisis," *Africa Report,* June 1961 (Vol. 6, No. 6), pp. 3-4, 6, 12, 15.

about the fact of the UN's involvement. To those of anticolonial persuasion, Chapter XI has been "given meaning" through the activities of the Committee on Information, not "amended." This view has it that the colonial powers, rather than having magnanimously cooperated with an enterprise of dubious legality, have dragged their feet and have violated the spirit, if not the letter, of Article 73 by not supporting the work of the Committee on Information more fully.

III

The first task of the United Nations in this field was that of providing a measure of international supervision of colonial regimes. Chapters XII and XIII of the Charter gave the UN an elaborate mechanism for this work. With provision for annual reports from the administering authorities, petitions from the indigenous inhabitants, and visiting missions to the field, the system was well designed to maintain a close relationship between the World Organization and dependent territories. Its application, however, was limited to the eleven territories which were voluntarily put under trusteeship. Counting the dependencies of Portugal and Spain, there were more than eight times as many non-self-governing territories outside the trusteeship system, and they contained over ten times as many people. For these, with the exception of South West Africa which was given special treatment, the UN's machinery was the much looser and less substantial structure derived from Chapter XI.

The differences between the two principal systems have been analyzed in detail elsewhere.[18] The continual drive of the anticolonial forces to endow the Committee on Information with the attributes of the Trusteeship Council is proof that these differences exist and are significant. Granting this, it is important not to become so engrossed in the legal and formal distinctions that decisive similarities between the two systems are obscured.

Probably the most significant procedural difference between the two main sets of machinery has been that through the acceptance of petitions, the dispatch of visiting missions, and the attendance of special representatives from the territorial administrations at Trusteeship Council sessions, the United Nations has been able to have direct contact with the trust territories. This has not been the case with the other territories, or in UN parlance, the non-self-governing territories.

---

[18] See James N. Murray, Jr., *The United Nations Trusteeship System* (Urbana: University of Illinois Press, 1957); Emil J. Sady, "The United Nations and Dependent Peoples," in Robert E. Asher and others, *The United Nations and the Promotion to the General Welfare* (Washington, D. C.: The Brookings Institution, 1957), pp. 815-1017; and Chairman Edwards Toussaint, *The Trusteeship System of the United Nations* (New York: Frederick A. Praeger, 1956).

Governments are required to supply more data to the Trusteeship Council, but there is a relationship between the Council's Questionnaire and the Committee on Information's Standard Form. Although Article 73e does not require political information, five of the ten (if Portugal and Spain are included in the total list) administering powers have transmitted such data regularly. In addition, as mentioned above, France also did this for a limited time with respect to two territories, and in 1961 the United Kingdom announced that it would henceforth submit political information for all dependent territories which remained under its administration. Moreover, at one of the most important points, the termination of dependent status, the United Nations has required and obtained political data concerning non-self-governing territories.

The Committee on Information is not formally authorized to make recommendations concerning political matters, but as one delegate with strong anti-colonial views put it in private conversation, "we have gotten around that." To some extent he was right. There is a difference between recommending that the number of unofficial representatives on the Tanganyikan Legislative Council should be increased and recommending that there should be greater participation by indigenous populations in the formulation of economic plans in non-self-governing territories, but the difference is not one of kind. Perhaps the most important distinction is in the degree of specificity. This probably accounts for the intense opposition of the colonial powers to the suggestion, which was made in 1955, that the Committee on Information should be given the right to make recommendations concerning regional groups of territories.[19]

The substantive recommendations of the Trusteeship Council and the Committee on Information have been strikingly similar. Because of its composition and method of operation the Trusteeship Council could generally only pass judgment on actions which had already been taken and adopt exhortations.[20] This is also what the Committee on Information has done, albeit in more general terms. Both bodies have advocated the same things: increased educational facilities for the indigenous inhabitants; enlarged social welfare programs with emphasis on community development; more extensive and comprehensive economic programs which would aim at diversification; and, greater opportunity for the indigenous inhabitants to participate in decision-making. Although the colonial

[19]The United Kingdom threatened to withdraw from participation in the committee if it were given this power (General Assembly *Official Records,* Fourth Committee [10th session], pp. 108-109). The UK and other colonial powers have also used this threat to block proposals that the committee be given permanent status.

[20]Or as Annette Baker Fox put it: "The Trusteeship Council tends to ventilate existing practices rather than to analyze alternative solutions for problems perplexing conscientious administrators." ("International Organization for Colonial Development," p. 347.) One wonders, though, whether the administering authorities would have been willing to accept a different role for the Council.

powers have been asked to take steps to preserve (or discover) traditional cultural values in the dependent territories, basically the UN's recommendations have been directed toward encouraging social, economic, and political change. When the General Assembly has adopted resolutions concerning colonial practices it has underscored these themes. In the case of the trust territories the basic themes have been embroidered with such things as expressions of hope that the administering authority would take steps to develop a national consciousness in the territory under scrutiny. But at their core the recommendations concerning trust territories and non-self-governing territories have been the same.

The most salient motive force underlying the UN's recommendations seems to have been a feeling that all racial discrimination should cease and that the indigenous inhabitants of dependent territories are entitled to a position of full equality.[21] The anticolonial forces appear to have been convinced that in almost all instances logically, and as a practical matter, full equality could be achieved only through independence.

They have also taken the position that "good government is no substitute for self-government." Thus, most of the UN's recommendations have been aimed, directly or indirectly, at hastening the transfer of power to the indigenous inhabitants. The opponents of colonialism have rejected the thesis that certain minimum economic and social standards are a prerequisite to independence. They have buttressed their case by citing data submitted to the UN showing the slow pace of progress by dependent territories in these fields. They have argued that progress will be accelerated when the indigenous population has control. However, they have never allowed this contention to be scrutinized. After a brief attempt, the Secretariat was in effect forbidden to compare conditions in non-self-governing territories with those in neighboring independent states.[22]

It is not going too far to state that the majority in the United Nations has viewed the task of supervising colonial administrations principally in terms of bringing these regimes to a close. Nowhere is this more evident than in the long-standing and acrimonious debate concerning the establishment of intermediate and final target dates. In this sense, General Assembly Resolution 1514 (XV) of

---

[21] It can be expected that the anticolonial forces will continue to advance similar demands even after colonialism as such passes. The resolution that the International Labor Organization adopted in the summer of 1961, on the prompting of Nigeria, which recommended that the Union of South Africa withdraw from membership (ILO Conference, *Provisional Record*, 1961 [45th session], No. 38, p. vi. The resolution was adopted by a vote of 163 to 0, with 89 abstentions), and the actions against this country at the sixteenth session of the General Assembly are surely an indication of things to come. To the anticolonial forces, it will be a continuation of the same battle.

[22] General Assembly Resolution 447 (V), December 12, 1950.

December 14, 1960, The Declaration on Colonialism, could well be read as a capstone to the UN's attempt to supervise colonial regimes.

There is little reason for believing that this conception will change with the contraction of colonialism. On the contrary, the anticolonial powers seem determined to push for the final liquidation of colonialism in the shortest possible time. With their strength augmented by the UN's new Members, they are in a better position to advance their cause. Now the African, Asian, and Latin American states by themselves constitute a two-thirds majority. Further, the states which have been admitted to the UN since 1959 have not tempered the position of the anticolonial forces. Indeed, some of them–Mali for instance–seem to favor even more extreme stands.

Since the majority in the United Nations has taken this view, it is inappropriate to compare the work of the Trusteeship Council and the Committee on Information with that of the Permanent Mandates Commission, for the League defined its role in quite different terms. The League was chiefly concerned with improving standards of colonial rule, while the UN's aim has been to liquidate colonialism. Political bodies, like the Trusteeship Council and the Committee on Information, are probably better suited for the latter task than groups of experts, such as the Permanent Mandates Commission. The two concepts also call for different types of recommendations.

In the UN's drive to liquidate colonialism the nature of the post-colonial political regimes has largely been ignored. This has been true even with regard to trust territories where there have been no constitutional barriers to the discussion of political issues. The UN has championed a few democratic precepts, such as universal suffrage and majority rule, but in practice this has generally amounted to urging that a plebiscite should be held to accept or decide the method of terminating dependent status and to approve the successor government. Illiteracy has been held to be no barrier to the right of suffrage.

Assessing the effects of the UN's attempt at supervision is difficult. In the case of the trust territories, there appear to have been a few instances when UN recommendations had a direct and immediate effect. The UN's involvement was apparently a factor in New Zealand's revision of its regime in Western Samoa in 1947.[23] To meet Council criticisms, Australia changed certain provisions in the law which provided for the administrative union of Papua and New Guinea.[24] But it is hard to find many cases in which the correlation between UN

[23]See Lawrence S. Finkelstein, "Trusteeship in Action: The United Nations Mission to Western Samoa," *International Organization,* May 1948 (Vol. 2, No. 2), pp. 268-282.

[24]See Norman Harper and David Sissions, *Australia and the United Nations* (New York: Manhattan, 1959), pp. 193-196.

recommendation and action by the administering authority was so clear-cut.[25] More often, the UN's function, lacking all but moral sanctions, seems to have been to affect the climate of opinion: to create the support attitudes favoring change.[26] It has exposed the actions of the administering authorities and has made colonial officials more aware of the implications of their actions. Progressive forces have sometimes used the UN to buttress their case in arguing for liberal colonial policies. In these respects the World Organization has occasionally been a counterbalance to settlers and old-style imperialists. The UN has also been used as a scapegoat for actions which were unpalatable to certain groups. Finally, the UN has provided a measure of support and protection for indigenous nationalists by focusing attention upon them and by giving them a forum in which to expound their views.[27]

The UN's general proclamations concerning self-determination and its actions with regard to South West Africa and other non-self-governing territories have obviously been designed with the hope of achieving the same effects. The difference has been that in the case of the trust territories the UN has had immediate access to both colonial administrators and the indigenous population. Since the issues involved generally have not commanded wide public attention, this access has been extremely important. No doubt, this explains why the anti-colonial forces have argued so persistently that the administering powers on the Committee on Information should include in their delegations representatives of the indigenous population and functional specialists.

A system of the type that the United Nations has developed for supervising colonial regimes depends for its effectiveness in large part on a fundamental agreement on values: those affected by recommendations must concede the premises on which they are based. That the UN's system has had as much

[25]For analyses of this issue see the Secretariat study concerning the implementation of UN recommendations concerning trust territories (Document A/1903 and Adds. 1 and 2); Margaret L. Bates, "Tanganyika: The Development of a Trust Territory," *International Organization,* February 1955 (Vol. 9, No. 1), pp. 32-51; and B. T. G. Chidzero, *Tanganyika and International Trusteeship* (London: Oxford University Press, 1961).

[26]See the interesting discussion of this matter in Annette Baker Fox, "The United Nations and Colonial Development," *International Organization,* May 1950 (Vol. 4, No. 2), pp. 199-218.

[27]Certainly the 1954 visiting mission to East Africa which suggested, *inter alia,* that Tanganyika should become self-governing or independent in less than 20 years (Trusteeship Council *Official Records* [15th session], Supplement No. 3, "Report on Tanganyika," pp. 67-68) had a profound effect on the Tanganyika African National Union (see Thomas R. Adam, "Trusteeship and Non-Self-Governing Territories," in Clyde Eagleton and Richard N. Swift (ed.) *Annual Review of United Nations Affairs,* 1955-1956, New York: [New York University Press, 1957], pp. 117-140, pp. 125 ff.).

success as it has reflects the fact that the anticolonial and nationalist demands were derived mainly from the intellectual transition of the West.[28]

The UN's system of supervision has also had secondary effects and byproducts which so far remain largely unexplored.[29] Developments in one territory have probably affected other areas. One writer (a British official in Tanganyika) has speculated that the greatest impact of the trusteeship system "is likely to flow from its progressive disintegration."[30] So far as byproducts are concerned, observers have noted that some petitioners seem to have used their opportunity to appear before the United Nations primarily to advance their political fortunes at home, and that certain states have tried to structure internal political developments in trust territories to the advantage of more or less radical forces.[31] The Soviet Union has sought to use its position on the Trusteeship Council's Standing Committee on Petitions to create the impression that it alone fully supported the demands of the downtrodden in the trust territories. One suspects that fear of neocolonialism was not the only factor which prompted Ghana and several Latin American States to press for studies of the effects of the European Economic Community on the trust and non-self-governing territories; their own commercial interests were deeply involved. Nor is it overly Machiavellian to think that some offers of scholarships and fellowships for students in dependent territories have been made in the hope that this would be a way of molding future elites. It is far from clear, however, what these efforts have achieved.

IV

A second task of the United Nations has been that of officiating at the liquidation of colonialism. In most instances this has meant participating in the birth of states. Articles 83 and 85 of the Charter made it clear that the Organization

---

[28] See Rupert Emerson, *From Empire to Nation: The Rise to Self-Assertion of Asian and African Peoples* (Cambridge: Harvard University Press, 1960).

[29] Among other things we know very little about the reactions of the inhabitants of dependent territories to the United Nations. The only detailed analysis of this question is: Camilla Wedgwood, "Attitudes of the Native Peoples of Papua and New Guinea to the United Nations 1945-1954," Appendix D in *Australia and the United Nations*, pp. 384-400.

[30] John Fletcher-Cooke, "Some Reflections on the International Trusteeship System, With Particular Reference to its Impact on the Governments and Peoples of the Trust Territories," *International Organization*, Summer 1959 (Vol. 13, No. 3), pp. 422-430, p. 430.

[31] See *ibid.*, p. 427; and Ernst B. Haas, "Dynamic Environment and Static System: Revolutionary Regimes in the United Nations" (paper read at the 1961 Convention of the American Political Science Association), note 47.

would have this function with respect to trust territories. Article 73e has been interpreted as giving the United Nations a similar role with regard to non-self-governing territories; the majority has asserted that the UN has the right to determine whether or not a colonial power is justified in deciding to cease transmitting data concerning the economic, educational, and social conditions in a given territory. In the case of the Italian colonies, the United Nations became involved by default when the Great Powers could not agree. Finally, despite the protestations of several colonial powers, the UN has assumed a role in colonial disputes, such as those involving Indonesia, the French North African colonies, Cyprus, and Angola.

In performing this task the United Nations has first of all provided support for nationalist forces. It did this by demanding and supervising elections at crucial points in French Togoland and Ruanda-Urundi. When the Assembly decided in 1949 that Libya should become independent no later than January 1, 1952, and that Somaliland should also gain that status by the end of 1960, it must have given encouragement, as the French feared that it would,[32] to nationalist forces everywhere and especially in the neighboring territories. Probably these decisions relating to the former Italian colonies were among the most significant of the UN's actions in this field.

In the case of Indonesia the support was more direct and tangible. At several key points in the struggle the United Nation's role was decisive, and its influence generally redounded to the benefit of the Republicans.[33] It might be argued that the United States played the crucial role—for example, its decision to cut off Marshall Plan aid to the Netherlands East Indies and apparent willingness to go even farther had a telling effect—but it is hard to see how the United States could have become as aroused as it did or as involved as it was without the UN. The point is not that traditional forces ceased to be operative, but rather that the United Nations became an important new ingredient.

The United Nations has played the same role, although with much less intensity, in the cases of Morocco, Tunisia, Cyprus, Algeria, and Angola. Although brief, ambiguous, and sometimes innocuous resolutions may seem to be of minor importance, the strenuous efforts of both sides to influence the outcome provide evidence that at least the parties which are most immediately concerned think that they are significant. An interesting pattern of events has developed over the years with respect to the UN's discussions of the French North African colonies. First there is increased tension and violence; next, a new French proposal for

---

[32]See Peter Calvocoressi, *Survey of International Affairs,* 1949-1950 (London: Oxford University Press, 1953), p. 545.

[33]See the fascinating study by Alastair M. Taylor, *Indonesian Independence and the United Nations* (Ithaca: Cornell University Press, 1960).

settlement; and finally, the Assembly debate. The same sequence was repeated when Cyprus was considered. Rupert Emerson explained it this way:

> "At least until the unlikely event of the creation of an international organization empowered to decide when and how each colony should attain self-government, the dependent peoples who receive an international hearing will usually be those who have resorted to self-help."[34]

Those who allege that action by the United Nations has complicated negotiations are in a sense correct in that UN support has probably made nationalist elements more potent and demanding. On the other hand, when the UN failed to support the nationalists, the colonial powers occasionally became more intransigent.[35] The broader point, though, is that the United Nations has provided an arena which has been used to mobilize pressure and in that way has contributed to the liquidation of colonialism.

Secondly, the United Nations has performed a validating function. UN membership has become an important symbol of national independence.[36] Each time that a new state is admitted to membership, the World Organization acknowledges that the colonial tie has been broken. Presumably, this action also endows that state with a degree of legitimacy and enhances its status as an entity. Further, UN membership has importance for the domestic prestige of the new governing elite. In many cases this is all that the United Nations has done.

In others, however, its involvement has been more extensive. By approving the termination of the trusteeship agreements for the French Cameroons and Tanganyika, the United Nations formally sanctioned the grant of independence. In the Indonesian case, its involvement was even deeper, for the UN played a major part in shaping the settlement. It has also done this, although not to the same degree, with respect to French Togoland and Western Samoa by its supervision of plebiscites or elections which will have immediately preceded independence, and it will have performed the same role in the case of Ruanda-Urundi. With regard to Somaliland, the United Nations helped to keep a messy border situation from becoming explosive by providing a mechanism for settlement and meanwhile more or less endorsing the provisional line.

---

[34] *From Empire to Nation,* p. 399. The nationalist forces clearly recognized this. In 1952 the French censorship disclosed two letters which were allegedly written by Dr. Habib Bourguiba in 1950 (*Le Figaro,* April 7, 1952). In them Dr. Bourguiba told Mr. Abed Bouhafa, a representative of the Arab League in the United States, among other things, that violence alone would force the United Nations to consider Tunisian affairs.

[35] France certainly acted this way in 1952. See Richard P. Stebbins, *The United States in World Affairs,* 1952 (New York: Harper, 1963), p. 362.

[36] See the place accorded to it in General Assembly Resolution 742 (VIII), November 27, 1953, "Factors Which Should Be Taken Into Account in Deciding Whether a Territory Is or Is Not a Territory Whose People Have Not Yet Attained a Full Measure of Self-Government."

The UN's validation may have been even more important when colonial status was ended through the union of a dependent territory with an independent state. In Eritrea, British Togoland, and the British Cameroons, the UN-supervised plebiscites were essential elements in the solutions. However much one might deplore the gyrations of the Assembly in the last two instances,[37] the plebiscites did provide acceptable solutions to what otherwise might have been very troublesome issues.

The United Nations has also given its approval when a non-self-governing territory became fully integrated into the political structure of the metropolitan state. While this action with regard to Greenland and Alaska and Hawaii may not have had too much significance, it established a standard. Having granted approval, the Assembly presumably could refuse to do so in other cases. Given these precedents, the United Nations may well be in a better position to dispute the Portuguese contention that its "overseas provinces" are not non-self-governing territories.

The United Nations also gave its approval to the status of Puerto Rico and to that of Surinam and the Netherlands Antilles. But in these cases it did something beyond validating the liquidation of colonialism. Here, in the discussions of the "factors," and in the debates which occurred in 1956 and 1957 concerning the future of French Togoland, the UN began to explore ways of ending colonial rule which involved neither full independence nor full integration with an independent state. In the case of French Togoland, the United Nation's involvement was clearly a factor in the alteration of the territory's status, and the subsequent grant of full independence. The UN's action may also have had some impact on the formulation of the constitutional provisions for Surinam and the Netherlands Antilles.[38] What the UN has done in these cases is to attempt to define a new and internationally approved status to substitute for colonial rule when it was impossible to apply either of the two more obvious solutions. Such a status is not easy to construct, and the skepticism which was expressed in the debates is warranted, at least in general terms if not in the cases which were discussed. On the other hand, many of the remaining dependent territories will probably require such a solution. Many of them are relatively minute and have small populations; they are hardly economically viable in modern terms. Independence, therefore, is not a realistic alternative, unless the concept is changed.[39] Nor will the metropolitan

---

[37] For a detailed description of the UN's involvement in one of these cases see James S. Coleman, "Togoland," *International Conciliation,* No. 509, September 1956, pp. 1-91.

[38] See Emil J. Sady, "The United Nations and Dependent Peoples," p. 914.

[39] It may well be though if Western Samoa is a harbinger. Certainly independence does not mean the same thing for Western Samoa–an area with 1,130 square miles of land and a population of about 106,000–as it does for larger and more populous territories, such as Tanganyika.

states be willing–rightly or wrongly–to integrate all of these territories into their own political structures on equal terms.

Clearly the United Nations has not progressed very far in defining this new status. The relevant part of the List of Factors contained in General Assembly Resolution 742 (VIII) is far from an adequate set of criteria for it.[40] However, a start has been made, and the concrete cases have provided some experience with the problems of the practical application of broad principles. As the fate of the major dependent territories becomes more and more clear, it may be easier to consider this issue again in the UN. Since precedent will not be so important, the anticolonial powers may be less doctrinaire. On the other side, the colonial powers will have no ulterior motives, if they ever did have.

V

The third task of the United Nations has consisted of providing assistance to newly independent states and facilitating their participation in the world community. This task has been regarded as a logical and necessary extension of the UN's activities concerning colonialism. One reason for this view is the awareness that the liquidation of colonialism inevitably left a void which had to be filled. Whatever its faults, colonialism performed a number of useful functions.[41] It frequently provided the motive force for processes of social, economic, and political change. It was always a source of some technical assistance, and it was often a source of financial aid as well. Colonialism provided a system for managing relationships both between the dependent territories and metropolitan states and among the dependent territories themselves. Another reason is the general recognition that not all of the newly independent states have been as well prepared for their new status as might have been desirable. The nature of this third task is still evolving; much will depend on the outcome of the UN's involvement in the Congo. Although it is therefore far too early for a detailed appraisal of the

---

[40] For example, the list mentions eligibility for UN membership as one criterion. It is hard to believe, however, that full membership would be appropriate. More thinking needs to be done along the lines of Lincoln P. Bloomfield's suggestion of associate membership. See *The United Nations and U.S. Foreign Policy: A New Look at the National Interest* (Boston: Little, Brown, 1960), pp. 199-200).

[41] See Rupert Emerson, *From Empire to Nation;* Max F. Millikan and Donald L. M. Blackmer, *The Emerging Nations: Their Growth and United States Policy* (Boston: Little, Brown, 1961); and Reinhold Niebuhr, *The Structure of Nations and Empires* (New York: Schribner's 1959).

UN's performance of this third task, the record of events so far is not without significance.

The United Nations has helped the newly independent states in developing their economies. In most instances, however, the Organization's greatest contribution has not been in directly providing concrete aid; the UN has been more important as a catalytic agent. It has provided means of publicizing the needs of the newly independent states and of the less developed countries generally. It has also provided a mechanism which could be used to put pressure on the more wealthy countries. This pressure appears to have been a factor in the expansion of both multilateral and bilateral aid programs.[42] The Economic Commission for Asia and the Far East has served as a catalytic agent in a different fashion. Through its advocacy and support of the Mekong River Project it has provided an important stimulus for national development efforts and cooperative endeavors. In time, the Economic Commission for Africa may also perform this function.

The United Nations has recognized an obligation to provide concrete assistance to newly independent states. This was first done in the case of Libya in 1950. Since 1959, both the General Assembly and the Economic and Social Council (ECOSOC) have proclaimed that the UN has a special responsibility with respect to former trust territories and a more general obligation to all newly independent states.[43] ECOSOC has completed a study of the available international assistance, and both the Council and the Assembly have urged that this be supplemented. However, on the basis of results thus far, the outlook is not promising. Libya's experience gives little reason for optimism, and although the general aid programs of the UN and the specialized agencies have been enlarged in response to the process of decolonization, they are still greatly overshadowed by programs which are conducted bilaterally or through agencies with restricted membership. Realistically, there is little reason to expect that the liquidation of colonialism will make either the West or the Soviet bloc significantly more willing to channel their aid to underdeveloped countries through the UN and the specialized agencies. Also, the debates on the resolutions which have been adopted in the Assembly and ECOSOC indicate that if too much preference is given to newly independent states, other underdeveloped countries will certainly object.

There is, of course, one extremely important exception to these generalizations. In the Congo the United Nations has launched an unprecedented program

---

[42]See John G. Hadwen and Johan Kaufmann, *How United Nations Decisions are Made* (Leyden: A. W. Sythoff, 1960), pp. 109-111.

[43]See particularly General Assembly Resolutions 1414 (XIV) and 1415 (XIV), December 5, 1959.

of technical and financial assistance.[44] As of June 30, 1961, the Civilian Operations of the United Nations in the Congo had an international staff of 750. There were 100 medical specialists alone. In addition, the United Nations had granted the government of the Republic of the Congo $15,000,000 to meet its urgent requirements for foreign exchange. However, the circumstances which led to a program of this magnitude were also without parallel. Few states have been as ill-prepared for independence as the Republic of the Congo, and the situation there could easily have sparked a major conflagration. Even if an analogous case were to arise in the future, in view of the difficulties which the United Nations is having in financing its activities in the Congo, it is an open question whether such extensive operations could be undertaken again.

The UN's task of aiding newly independent states has also included significant political functions. So far the UN has done three things in this realm.

First, it has played a role in the relations among the new states. The liquidation of colonialism can result in difficult and explosive situations, as it did when the British rule was ended in India and Palestine. The UN's peacekeeping activities with respect to Kashmir and the Arab-Israeli dispute are well known; presumably they could be repeated. Moreover, imperialistic desires are found not only in the West. By its actions with regard to Lebanon and Jordan, Cambodia and Thailand (the Beck-Friis mission), the Sudanese-Egyptian border, Laos, and Kuwait, the United Nations has attempted to provide security for newly independent states. The existence of the UN may well have been a deterrent in other cases. The United Nations has also facilitated contacts among the representatives of the new states. This is a significant, natural outcome of the processes of parliamentary diplomacy.

Secondly, the United Nations has played an important role in the relations between the new states and their former metropoles. The debates concerning West Irian, Suez, and the Tunisian-French imbroglios are examples. Wherever justice may lie in the controversy between Indonesia and the Netherlands over West Irian (or the Netherlands New Guinea), the UN has provided a channel for airing the dispute peacefully. Whatever views may be in the West, the UN's role in the Suez case was widely interpreted by anticolonial forces as the frustration of an attempt to reassert colonial rule. Similarly, Tunisia has regarded its appeals to the UN as efforts to protect its sovereignty. It can be expected that the new states will continue to attempt to enlist the assistance of the United Nations in cases of this nature. Given the almost paranoic fear of neocolonialism

[44] For general descriptions of the UN's Civilian Operations in the Congo see General Assembly *Official Records* (16th session), Supplement No. 1, "Annual Report of the Secretary-General on the Work of the Organization, 16 June 1960–15 June 1961," pp. 47-51; and "Chaos Averted in the Congo," *United Nations Review,* September 1961 (Vol. 8, No. 9), pp. 29-31.

in many of the newly independent states, the colonial powers might find it useful to involve the UN frequently in their relationships with their former dependencies.

Finally, in the Congo, the UN's role has been to buttress the internal structure of the state and to bring some stability to a chaotic political situation.[45] Although it is impossible to tell how successful this endeavor will ultimately be, even the achievements so far are significant. However, the difficulties involved in the UN's playing this role are also apparent. Efforts to achieve internal stability cannot be neutral, for they inevitably have far-reaching domestic and international consequences. Moreover, since the United Nations was created with international disputes primarily in mind, it has been difficult to define the basis for the Organization's actions in the Congo. Initially, there appears to have been some hope that such Western concepts as federalism and parliamentary rule would provide helpful guidelines for the UN's operations,[46] but the inapplicability of these principles soon became apparent. Thus far the United Nations has successfully surmounted these obstacles, and hopefully, it will continue to do so. It would be rash, however, to expect that the UN could again easily undertake political responsibilities similar to those which it has assumed in the Congo.

The record is mixed, but it indicates that serious attempts have been made in the United Nations to deal with many of the problems of the post-colonial era, and at this stage, a summing up would show relative success in several areas.

VI

Evaluations of the activities of the United Nations with regard to colonialism will vary, depending as they do on personal values. Final judgments will be impossible until the outcome of events still in process is clearly known. Nevertheless, some conclusions can be stated without entering the debate over the merits of UN's role and without going beyond the bounds imposed by the available evidence.

---

[45] See Inis L. Claude, Jr., "The United Nations and the Use of Force." *International Conciliation,* No. 532, March 1961, pp. 325-384, pp. 376-379; and John Holmes, "The United Nations in the Congo," *International Journal,* Winter 1960-61 (Vol. 16, No. 1), pp. 1-16. For a discussion of some of the legal aspects of the UN's playing this role see E. M. Miller, "Legal Aspects of the United Nations Action in the Congo," *The American Journal of International Law,* January 1961 (Vol. 55, No. 1), pp. 1-28.

[46] See especially Document S/4417, "Second Report by the Secretary-General on the Implementation of Security Council Resolutions S/4387 of 14 July 1960 and S/4405 of 22 July 1960."

It is clear that the UN's part in the revolution which has occurred in the colonial system in the last two decades was modest. Many of the most important motive forces were at work before the Organization was established. The British Parliament adopted the Colonial Development and Welfare Act in 1940, and the independence movement in such places as the Indian subcontinent and Indonesia was already under way by the end of the Second World War. Even after it was established, the UN played no part in some important developments concerning colonialism—for instance the settlement in Indo-China—and was only peripherally involved in others.

It is equally evident, though, that the United Nations has contributed to raising standards of colonial rule and to hastening the liquidation of colonialism. For various reasons, the UN was constitutionally committed to become involved in the struggle.[47] Once engaged, it inevitably altered the balance of forces and thereby affected the outcome. On balance, the colonial revolution has probably been more peaceful because of the UN's involvement. A case can also be made to the effect that the UN has contributed to international stability through its activities at the time of the accession of dependent territories to self-government or independence and in the post-colonial era. It would be going too far to state that the United Nations has provided adequate substitutes for the colonial system or that it has devised wholly effective measures for bringing what some have termed "teen-age states" to responsible maturity, but the Organization has made significant progress in these areas.

Establishing a connection between the activities of the United Nations and the nature of the emerging states is more difficult. The UN has generally favored modernizing over traditional elements. It has upheld the goal of racial equality and advanced the concept of the plebiscite, but beyond that it has done little to implant concepts of democratic rule. This is understandable. There is certainly no agreement among the UN's Member States that democracy as practiced in the West is the most desirable form of government. Moreover, democratic concepts (again as understood in the West) may have little applicability in primitive contexts where national unity is not even established.[48]

Some scholars and statesmen have decried the fact that in its activities concerning colonialism, the United Nations has been more an arena for combat than a focal point for international cooperation. Perhaps this view overstates the facts. But even if the allegation were correct, it would not necessarily be a cause for despair. Peaceful cooperation requires consensus, which was clearly

---

[47] See Inis L. Claude, Jr., *Swords into Plowshares: The Problems and Progress of International Organization* (New York: Random House, 1959, 2d ed.), pp. 341-371; and, Ernst B. Haas, "The Attempts to Terminate Colonialism: Acceptance of the United Nations Trusteeship System," *International Organization*, February 1953 (Vol. 7, No. 1), pp. 1-21.

[48] See Rupert Emerson, *From Empire to Nation*, pp. 272-292; and Max. F. Millikan and Donald L. M. Blackmer, *The Emerging Nations*, pp. 68-90.

lacking in this case. Any observer of the San Francisco proceedings could see the deep dichotomy between the views expressed by Lord Cranborne of the United Kingdom on one side and those voiced by Fadhil Al-Jamali of Iraq, Carlos Romulo of the Philippines, and Professor Awad of Egypt on the other.[49] Lord Cranborne argued the necessity of empire; he maintained that liberty could not have been preserved in the Second World War without it. He regarded independence as an appropriate goal for only a few territories, and even for these, he felt that it was a distant objective. To the others, imperialism was an evil which should be terminated with haste. In their view, the best solution, almost without exception, was national independence. What is significant is the extent to which such a deep and important struggle has been carried on within an international organization.

From the perspective of those of anticolonial persuasion and of those whose prime interest is the achievement of a combination of international stability and orderly processes of change—including most Americans—the results of the UN's involvement in this struggle have generally been beneficial. In the end, probably even many of the colonialist critics of the United Nations will admit that the outcome was in their best long-run interests.

[49] UNCIO *Documents* (Vol. 8), pp. 143-146 (see also the milder revision, pp. 155-159), 133-134, 137-142, and 147-149, respectively.

C. Economic Aid and Development

In terms of money and personnel, by far the largest concern of the United Nations system is in the area of economic and social problems. As noted by J. N. Reedman, the focus of this concern, during the first twenty years of the United Nations, shifted primarily from the rehabilitation of the war-torn areas of Europe to the problems of the underdeveloped areas of the world. According to Reedman, this shift is not unrelated to the sharply rising number of underdeveloped states in the Organization after 1955. In general, United Nations activity in the economic area is of three types: action aimed at the study of a particular problem; action aimed at getting governments to take measures designed to deal with a problem; and operational activities carried on by the United Nations in order to assist governments in dealing with a problem.

Probably the most important example of United Nations action, aimed at the study of a particular problem, is the United Nations Conference on Trade and Development (UNCTAD), which first met in the spring of 1964. As Sidney Weintraub points out, this was the largest international conference in history, with approximately 2000 delegates. It was agreed by the states represented at this conference that UNCTAD should become a continuing subsidiary organ of the United Nations with the purpose of reviewing all issues that relate to the trade and development of the underdeveloped states. Because of the continuing nature of UNCTAD, Weintraub believes that it is vital to understand the politics of the first conference in order to understand the most likely course of this organ in the future. The overriding impression of the conference was the strong desire of the underdeveloped states for a change in the international economic system which they felt was depriving them of a just distribution of economic rewards. Weintraub emphasizes the potentialities for future trouble if this desire for change elicits only a defense of the status quo by those states now enjoying the benefits of the present distribution. Future negotiations may also be jeopardized if the developing countries continue to advance a triple standard according to which (1) no developing state makes demands on any other developing state, (2) demands on Communist states are not insisted upon if the Communist states balk at them, and (3) uncompromising demands are made on the Western states. The question remains: How will these political strategies, used at the first UNCTAD, influence the course of action taken by this vital organ in dealing with the problems of the less-developed states?

Nina Heathcote examines the activities of the United Nations in the economic field in order to determine its contribution to international stability. Particularly after the Congo crisis in 1960, all of us have become more aware that domestic instability in the new states, growing out of economic and social problems, can lead to serious international political crises. United Nations activity to mitigate these social and economic ills before they flare into violence contributes to the maintenance of international peace and security as surely (if somewhat less glamorously) as does a United Nations military force. Heathcote examines the extremely difficult job faced by the Organization in trying to perform the task of nation-building in the Congo after violence had begun. As she convincingly demonstrates, the record of United Nations economic activity under less trying circumstances than those of the Congo has not been entirely successful. The same circumstances that make the extension of economic assistance necessary also make its effective utilization by the less-developed states a problem. Are there any reasons for believing that the United Nations is a better instrument for the task of nation-building than other instruments?

The United Nations and Economic Development

J. N. Reedman

Since its beginning, the United Nations has been deeply involved in questions of economic development of less-developed areas. The Charter of the United Nations, signed in San Francisco in 1945, foreshadowed this preoccupation without laying down any precise lines of action. One of the aims of the United Nations laid down in the Charter is "to promote social progress and better standards of life and larger freedom" and one of its functions is "to employ international machinery for the promotion of the economic and social advancement of all peoples". Article 66, Paragraph 2 states that the Economic and Social Council "may, with the approval of the General Assembly, perform services at the request of the Specialised Agencies." In pursuit of these general aims and on the basis of the authority thus defined, the United Nations, together with the related Agencies, has developed a variety of activities and procedures, not all of which could have been foreseen in the confused, if hopeful, days of 1945.

Looking back after more than 15 years, the increasing preoccupation with the problems of economic development seems natural enough. After all, the signatories of the Charter saw the importance of these problems, even at a time when for many of them the rehabilitation and restoration of normal life after years of dislocation and destruction by war were the most immediate concern: while during their earliest meetings, the General Assembly and the Economic and Social Council were much exercised by problems of the aftermath of war, attention was focused sharply on questions relating to under-developed areas.

J. N. Reedman, "The United Nations and Economic Development," *International Relations,* Vol. 2, No. 3 (April 1961), pp. 125-134. Reprinted by permission of *International Relations.*

This fact is partly the reflection of the numerical weight of the less-developed countries among the United Nations–a weight which has enormously increased with the growth of membership from an original 50 to 99 in 1960, almost all the newer members being countries whose major economic concern is for their own rapid economic development. Partly, however, it is a measure of the importance with which, from the first days of the United Nations, the more highly-industrialised countries have regarded the growth of less-developed countries. For, despite wide differences of view which have sometimes been evident on specific questions, on methods and on procedures, a perusal of debates in the Economic Committee of the General Assembly or in the Economic and Social Council, reveals a common acceptance, both of the general objective and of the need to pursue it with urgency.

An early expression of this sense of urgency may be seen in the establishment by ECOSOC of the regional economic commissions which have provided a means by which the consideration of many aspects of economic development could be undertaken far more extensively and more effectively than could have been done by the direct action of the Council itself. Through the commissions, regional groupings of members of the U.N. are able jointly to take practical action for economic development within the general framework of U.N. policies and to complement the work of local organs in this field. It is true that in March 1947, when the Economic Commission for Europe and the Economic Commission for Asia and the Far East were established, problems of rehabilitation of economies devastated by war were uppermost in respect of most regions. But in the case of ECAFE, at least, furtherance of the economic development of the region was a main aim and longer-term questions of economic growth from low levels of national income immediately seized the attention as the characteristic problems common to most of the region. When, in the following year, the Economic Commission for Latin America was established, the accent was unequivocally on economic development and in the intervening years, these commissions, assisted by the permanent Secretariat, have been deeply involved in problems of basic economic development of common interest to the countries of their respective regions. The Economic Commission for Africa, brought into being only in 1958, comes into this heritage and finds itself in a congenial atmosphere in responding to the obvious development needs of Africa.

The activities of the U.N. bearing directly on the problem of economic development stretch to a much longer list of topics than can be adequately covered, or even intelligently itemised within the compass of a short paper. It is possible, however, to obtain some measure of their scope and significance by grouping them under three heads, according to the nature of the actions involved.

The three types of action thus distinguished are first, actions by which the study of a problem or problems is the immediate and chief aim; second, action by which governments are called upon or invited to take certain measures, whether jointly or separately, and thirdly, action by which the U.N. and or the specialised agencies are empowered to undertake operative programmes of direct assistance to governments. This is an arbitrary classification but its convenience for our present purpose of obtaining a general picture of U.N. action in the field of economic development may outweigh the inconvenience of its arbitrariness, so long as it is recognized that it has no particular merit other than its utility for this purpose. It will, of course, be recognised at once that there may be a very close connection between all three lines of action, that one may be intended to lead to another, and that a classification by the substance of matters dealt with (which for some purposes would be more useful, even essential) would frequently cut across them.

A large number of studies, both general and specific, in the field of economic development have emanated from the U.N., which in consequence has made its own considerable contribution to the flood of such studies coming in in recent years from many sources. These studies are all, in one way or another, produced in implementation of resolutions of the General Assembly, the Economic and Social Council or the regional Economic Commissions. That is to say, they are either undertaken with the regular work programme of the Secretariat operating under general directives, or they are produced in response to ad hoc and specific requests prepared by the regular Secretariat or are reports produced and published under the responsibility of experts specifically appointed for the task.

A very wide range of problems is encompassed in this outpouring of official publications. In general, however, as is to be expected from their basic motivation, U.N. studies are aimed ultimately at some sort of practical action by governments, and thus belong to a particular segment of the total stream of literature dealing with the problems of economic development. Nevertheless, a considerable number of U.N. studies are concerned with the broader and more general aspects of economic development, such as, for example, the report of the nine experts on "Measures for Economic Development of Under-Developed Countries", the ECLA study on "Theoretical and Practical Problems of Economic Growth" and "Processes and Problems of Industrialisation in Under-Developed Countries" to mention only three at random. It is indeed the need for such analytical studies as a basis for the formulation of recommendations for action which brought them into being.

Some brief examples will illustrate the point. First, in regard to the regional economic commissions, the major tasks of which are to give special attention to the problems of economic development and to assist in the formulation and development of co-ordinated policies in promoting economic development among the members in their respective regions. The Economic Commission for Asia and the Far East and the Economic Commission for Latin America were faced with a great lack of basic economic data in most of the countries in their regions. Therefore, before very much progress could be made towards effective co-operation in regard to development problems common to countries in the region, it was necessary to study and analyse more completely their basic development problems. Much attention had also to be given to improving the collection and dissemination of the basic statistics required for economic and social analysis and policy making. Thus, in the case of each of these regions, the Commissions necessarily became involved in basic studies, and in addition to producing regular surveys of economic conditions in their regions, both ECAFE and ECLA embarked on a number of basic analytical studies, dealing both with general and specific aspects of economic development. Thus, for example, ECLA has produced a series of macroeconomic studies relating to the region. ECAFE, in addition to producing a number of basic studies on specific aspects of economic development, has also undertaken through the establishment of an intergovernmental working party, studies on economic development and planning. These studies have included a systematic analysis of various national economic development plans carried out in co-operation with the governments concerned and a recently published report of a group of experts on programming techniques for economic development, with specific reference to Asia and the Far East.

The recently established Economic Commission for Africa has only just begun its programme of studies, in which is stressed problems of the collection, evaluation and dissemination of technological, economic and statistical information, the investigation or study of development problems and studies of the social aspects of economic development. In the years before the establishment of the Commission, the U.N. Department of Economic and Social Affairs, in response to resolutions of the Economic and Social Council, not only prepared an annual review of economic conditions in Africa, but also produced a number of studies analysing the basic structure of certain economies of the region, with a view to elucidating their characteristic development problems.

In more specific fields also the need for basic studies has been felt. Thus, in regard to the problems of industrialisation, the General Assembly in a resolution of 12th January, 1952, requested the Economic and Social Council to promote studies of a programme for the rapid industrialisation of under-developed countries, including the economic, social, fiscal, technical and organisational problems involved. Further debates in the Council and a Secretariat study on the "Processes and Problems of Industrialisation in Under-developed Countries" published in 1955 were followed in 1956 and 1957 by the Council's endorsement of a programme of work in the field of industrialisation and productivity proposed by the Secretary-General. The programme of work outlined a number of broad areas relating to industrialisation in which studies should be pursued. These included problems relating to the structure, operation and development of the industrial sector; to the relationship between the process of industrialisation and the development of other sectors, such as agriculture, power and transport; and to the social and demographic aspects of industrialisation. As a part of the implementation of this programme, the United Nations Department of Economic and Social Affairs now publishes a bulletin which appears periodically on "Industrialisation and Productivity" and which includes, among other things, the results of studies undertaken in this field.

A similar sequence of events is to be seen in regard to the conservation and utilisation of non-agricultural resources. The Economic and Social Council in 1951 requested the Secretary-General to initiate a systematic survey and inventory of such resources. As a part result of the work undertaken in implementation of this and other related resolutions, a number of studies of basic aspects of natural resources and their utilisation have been published among which, for example, are the "Survey of World Ore Resources–Occurrence, Appraisal and Use," "Non-Ferrous Metals in Under-Developed Countries," "Economic Applications of Atomic Energy," "New Sources of Energy and Economic Development," and "Integrated River Basin Development".

It has been widely recognised by the United Nations that for their rapid progress under-developed countries have need, in one way or another, of assistance which can for the most part be provided only by the more developed countries. In particular, they need capital to enable them to achieve a rate of investment greater than they could achieve from their own resources. They also need technical advice and expert skills and assistance in training. It is for the provision of these needs that the various operational programmes under the aegis of the U.N. have been established. The financing of economic development has been the subject of much discussion in the Economic and Social Council and in the General Assembly, but apart from the activities of the International Bank for Reconstruction and Development, the U.N. has not itself hitherto been a source of investment capital for economic development. Even the loans made by the World Bank for this purpose are a realtively small proportion of the total flow of capital towards under-developed countries. It has been estimated, for example, that in 1958, World Bank disbursements were about one-tenth of the total international flow of capital to under-developed countries, and about one quarter of the flow from public sources.

A further step in the provision of capital lending institutions on an international basis was taken when, in 1956, the International Finance Corporation was set up to provide directly and without government guarantees loans to private productive industry in developing countries. Compared with the World Bank, the volume of capital available for investment through the International Finance Corporation is realtively small, and by the end of September 1960, it had invested 45,000,000 dollars in 36 enterprises in 17 countries.

A more considerable step was taken in 1960 in the establishment of the International Development Association, which is intended to provide investment funds for under-developed countries in basic facilities, which may not themselves directly yield a return which would justify borrowing at ordinary market rates of interest. The I.D.A., which is an affiliate of the World Bank, has for its purpose "to promote economic development, increase productivity and thus raise standards of living in the less-developed areas of the world within the Association's membership, in particular by providing finance to meet their important development requirements on terms which are more flexible and bear less heavily on the balance of payments than those of conventional loans, thereby furthering the development objectives of the International Bank for Reconstruction and Development and supplementing its activities." The initial resources proposed for the Association are 1,000 million U.S. dollars.

The establishment of the International Development Association is an outcome, but not necessarily the conclusion, of the debates which have taken place over several years in ECOSOC for the establishment of a Special United Nations Fund for Economic Development (SUNFED) to make grants and loans on easy terms to less developed countries for investment in economic and social facilities essential to economic development but not in themselves directly remunerative. While the new Association certainly approaches the concept of SUNFED in the scale on which its operations are visualised and in its emphasis on loans on easier terms than for conventional loans, its close ties with the International Bank are a disappointment to many of the sponsors of SUNFED who apparently fear that the lending policy of the new Association may follow too closely normal banking practice. As the Association has not yet started operations no more can be said of it at this time.

Apart from these three institutions for the provision of investment of capital, the direct assistance provided through the U.N. and the specialised agencies for economic development of under-developed countries falls within the category of technical assistance. From the beginning, it had been recognised that the U.N. and the specialised agencies in their particular fields might, on request of member countries, give assistance in the form of technical advice on specific problems, and some early resolutions of the Economic and Social Council provided for modest programmes for such technical assistance in regard to social welfare and economic development. It soon became evident, however, that such assistance furnished as part of the regular work programmes of the Secretariat, and financed out of the regular budgets of the various organisations, would be quite inadequate to meet the demands for technical assistance which were becoming more clearly seen. Hence in 1949 the Expanded Programme of Technical Assistance, financed by voluntary annual contributions of member states additional to their assessed contributions to the regular budget was launched.

By 1955 the total programme cost of this expanded programme of Technical Assistance had reached 26 million dollars and in 1959 had risen to 53 million dollars. Technical Assistance is also provided under regular programmes by the organisations participating in the expanded programme and in 1959 thirteen and a half million dollars were expended in this way. In 1959, too, the U.N. Special

Fund completed its first full year of operation and by the end of the year had approved projects involving an expenditure of nearly 32 million dollars to be spent over a period of several years. The implementation of these programmes engages a very substantial proportion of the total activities of the secretariats of the various organisations concerned, especially in the case of certain of the Specialised Agencies and increasingly so in the case of the U.N. Department of Economic and Social Affairs and the regional economic commissions. Nevertheless, the total expenditure on all technical aid provided by the U.N. family is small compared with the total of expenditures on international technical assistance from all sources and it represents a very modest amount of a world-wide programme which is spread over one hundred recipient territories.

Perhaps the most significant aspect of these U.N. programmes of technical aid is that they are multilateral and world-wide in scope. As such, they have an obvious appeal to many recipient countries which, as members of the U.N., have a share in the formulation of general policies by which the programmes are set up and operated. The fact that all members are eligible to request technical aid and all members may also contribute to the aid available through the programme is no doubt psychologically and politically of great importance. But apart from these more general considerations there are certain other factors of the world-wide multilateral programme of technical assistance which are worthy of note. By far the greater part of expenditures under the United Nations Technical Assistance programmes is either for the provision of experts or for training fellowships and in respect of both these services a multilateral programme has obvious advantages over bilateral programmes.

In relation to the demand for technical assistance, the supply of suitable experts is scarce and as the technical assistance programmes increase in size the difficulties of the recruitment of experts become more acute. It is, therefore, increasingly important to match scarce resources to the largest possible number of demands and a multilateral approach offers the best opportunity of doing this, not only in regard to initial recruitment but also to the possible subsequent reassignment of experts to posts in other countries for which their qualifications may fit them. In a similar way, opportunities for the placement of fellows and trainees under a fellowship programme are in general greater under a multilateral than under a bilateral programme. The significance of these general conclusions is perhaps seen in better perspective if it is recalled that the United Nations Expanded Programme of Technical Assistance in 1959 provided assistance to no fewer than one hundred and two territories. The 2,291 experts employed in this programme in that year were chosen from sixty-four countries, many of the countries which were recipients of assistance in certain fields providing experts themselves in others.

On the other hand, the organisation of this world-wide system of technical assistance presents some problems which either do not arise in the case of bilateral programmes or else arise in a less acute form. One such problem is that of contributions in unconvertible currencies. While the greater part of the contributions to the Expanded Programme of Technical Assistance of the United Nations is in currencies which are freely expendable, some important contributions have been limited to expenditure within specific countries or currency zones and in some cases special arrangements are needed in order to relate requests for assistance to these restricted contributions and avoid the accumulation of unspent balances. Another problem lies in the need to organise recruitment and placement services on a world-wide basis. Extensive geographical range of recruitment is certainly one of the most important advantages of the programme but it calls for a very far-reaching web of contacts through which a regular flow of information may be obtained and hundreds of detailed contractual arrangements can be concluded. These have been made possible very largely through the co-operation of national committees of technical assistance and of comparable institutions in countries where national committees set up by the national governments do not exist.

Yet a third problem is that of co-ordinating the activities of the various participating international organisations of which there are now nine. This problem of co-ordination is indeed crucial. When the Expanded Programme of Technical Assistance was established it was finally decided after much discussion in the Economic and Social Council and in the General Assembly that the contributions of member states though made to the programme as a whole would be allocated to each of the organisations participating in the programme and that each organisation would administer its own programme of technical assistance in its specific field of activity. At the same time, measures were adopted to co-ordinate the activities of the various agencies concerned, both to secure unity in the general structure of the programme and co-ordinated action at the operative level.

Co-ordination in the structure of the programme was achieved through the Technical Assistance Committee, consisting of the members of the Economic and Social Council together with six additional members, which lays down the general policies under which the programme is operated. The Technical Assistance Board on which each of the participating Organisations is represented and which has a permanent Executive Chairman and a small Secretariat is responsible for the allocation of contributions to each of the participating agencies and for the co-ordination of the activities of the agencies in the programme as a whole. The Technical Assistance Board reviews and approves the requests of Governments which constitute their annual programmes. At the operating level the two most important instruments of co-ordination which have been developed under the Technical Assistance Board are the country programmes and the resident Technical Assistance Board representatives. Under the system of country programming, Member States submit their request for United Nations Technical Assistance in the form of an annual (as from 1961, two-yearly) programme comprising all the specific requests to the individual participating organisations. The appointment of resident representatives as field officers of the Technical Assistance Board in countries where the programme is sufficiently large to justify it is almost the necessary corollary to the system of country programming. These representatives as the chief officers in areas of assignment for the Technical Assistance Programme are able amongst other things to secure a proper co-ordination between the various agencies on the spot and also to assist the Governments in the drawing up of the country programmes constituting the requests by Governments, as well as to deal with some of the problems which may arise between the parties concerned in carrying them out. The important part played by the Technical Assistance representatives in discharging such tasks was underlined by a resolution of the General Assembly which provided that the Executive Chairman of the Technical Assistance Board and the Managing Director of the Special Fund enter into an agreement whereby the resident representative would normally serve as the channel of communication between the government concerned and the Special fund, particularly in regard to applications for assistance from the Fund. At the present time (1961), there are altogether some 48 Technical Assistance resident representatives covering some 70 countries and territories which between them are receiving well over 90% of the field programme.

In 1958, at its 12th session, the General Assembly greatly extended the activities of the United Nations in the field of technical aid to underdeveloped countries when it decided to establish "as an expansion of the existing Technical Assistance and development activities of the United Nations and the specialised agencies a separate Special Fund to provide systematic and sustained assistance in fields essential to the integrated technical, economic and social development of the less developed countries."

Several features of the Special Fund distinguish it from the Expanded Programme of Technical Assistance. In the first place its management and administration are centered in a Managing Director assisted by an Executive Board consisting of the Secretary-General of the United Nations, the President of the International Bank for Reconstruction and Development and the Executive Chairman of the Technical Assistance Board. Secondly, although wide discretion is left to the management of the Board in approving requests, its activities are broadly limited to so-called preinvestment projects in the form of surveys of resources, research and training and demonstrations which are calculated to create conditions making new capital investment feasible or more effective. Thirdly, projects to be approved by the Fund should be neither so large as to constitute a major investment nor so small as to lose the impact which is to be expected from a well organised and integrated project. Fourthly, projects are approved as a whole and may extend by stages over a number of years, the average duration of projects so far approved being approximately three and a half years. Nevertheless, both because of the nature of the projects which the Special Fund is designed to promote and because of the modest scale of its operations, it belongs within the category of technical assistance rather than of normal investment. In its emphasis on pre-investment and its concentration on fairly large and integrated projects it represents nevertheless a most significant addition to the technical assistance activities of the United Nations.

Nothing is said in this article of the third line of action distinguished above—namely direct recommendations of political organs of the United Nations for action, at the governmental and inter-governmental level, conferences, consultations, working parties and the like. There has been a great deal of action directly relating to economic development under this head through resolutions of the General Assembly and ECOSOC, especially within the regional economic commissions. It is, however, a subject of so considerable a scope and complexity that it should receive a separate treatment.

After the U.N. Trade Conference: Lessons and Portents

Sidney Weintraub

The United Nations Conference on Trade and Development—UNCTAD—was not only the biggest trade conference in history, it was the biggest international conference in history on any subject, numbering upwards of 2,000 delegates. It is worth repeating what Isaiah Frank noted in his article in the January 1964 issue of this journal, that the developing countries viewed the conference as the single most important event for them since the founding of the U.N. The formal findings and recommendations of the conference, which lasted for 12 weeks ending in mid-June, are embodied in its Final Act. That governments consider this an important document is clear from the long hours and occasional bitter debate that went into its formulation. But it is also clear that the official record of the conference at best can give only official conclusions and that these alone are not the stuff of which future policy is made.

The official conclusions are important. The preamble of the Final Act contains the "message" the developing countries want the world to have about the conference and why it was called. The Final Act states flatly: "The United Nations Conference on Trade and Development was convened in order to provide, by means of international coöperation, appropriate solutions to the problems of world trade in the interests of all peoples and particularly to the urgent trade and development problems of the developing countries."

The "findings" listed in the Final Act contain an excellent catalogue of what the developing countries see as their trade problems. These include the

Reprinted by special permission from *Foreign Affairs,* Vol. 43, No. 1 (October 1964), pp. 37-50.

disproportionately small share of developing countries in the more than doubling of world trade since 1950 and the resultant insufficiency of their foreign exchange earnings—hence, as they see it, the adverse effect this has had on their development. Developing countries contend that their terms of trade have deteriorated seriously in the last decade; that is, that there has been a marked decline in prices for many commodities which developing countries sell, and some increase in prices for the manufactured goods they must buy for their development process. This combination of price movements is cited as an important factor aggravating the difficulties of the developing countries. The Final Act enshrines the concept of a "gap" between import requirements and export earnings of developing countries, and even embodies an estimate made by the U.N. secretariat that the "gap" could be around $20 billion a year in 1970, given the 5 percent-a-year rate of growth which is the target of the U.N. Development Decade, and assuming that the future will be a replica of the recent past.

The use of the $20 billion figure illustrates that "facts" are not necessarily factual but may merely be a reflection of the views of the majority. The findings in the Final Act cite various policies of developed countries as contributing to the sluggishness of the export growth of developing countries, including tariffs, price support programs, the accumulation of surpluses and their depressive effect on world commodity prices, and the like.

The Final Act contains all the recommendations approved by the conference. UNCTAD was conducted in five main committees of the whole—the whole being 119 countries—dealing with primary commodity trade, trade in manufactures, finance and invisibles, institutional issues, and then a catchall committee for all other issues but which focused largely on attempting to formulate a set of principles which could guide the world in its future trade relationships. The Final Act contains recommendations in all these fields—in some cases the same recommendations that emerged from the committees; in other important instances, compromise recommendations which were reached in plenary only after the committees completed their work.

The Final Act is thus a vital document. It reflects the aspirations of the developing countries going into the conference, the issues deemed central coming out of it, the recommendations the conference was able to agree on by at least a two-thirds majority vote, and the observations of countries either concurring in these recommendations or indicating why full concurrence was not possible.

What the Final Act is not is perhaps more important to keep in mind. It is not necessarily a guide to what was in the minds of men—and of countries, since the men were official representatives—as the conference proceeded to its final, cliff-hanging agreements. The cliché sounded by almost all speakers as the conference closed was that this was just the beginning—this was only UNCTAD-1. The cliché, in this case, was true.

What governments must now focus on is where they, and the world, go from here in meeting the aspirations of the developing countries as set forth in the Final Act.

II

This is the first lesson, and a crucial one: that UNCTAD, or some variant of it, is now with us for the foreseeable future. The "continuing machinery," as the phrase went at the conference, could be important, or it could be futile. (The Swiss national exposition held every 25 years was going on at Lausanne concurrently with the conference. One of the exhibits at the exposition was a piece of machinery that moved its parts a lot, made a lot of noise, but served no other purpose. Some conference delegates referred to it as the "continuing machinery.") there is no easy *a priori* answer as to what the machinery will turn out to be—this depends on its secretariat and on governments, both of developed and of developing countries.

The approved recommendation on the continuing machinery calls: for future conferences at least every three years, and the next early in 1966, only two years hence; for a Trade and Development Board of 55 countries, almost half the participants, to meet normally twice a year between conferences, for which it is also to prepare; for the Trade and Development Board to have at least three committees, to deal with primary commodity trade, trade in manufactures, and with invisible issues (debt servicing, tourism, etc.), including shipping, and finance related to trade; and for all of this machinery to have its own secretariat in the U.N. structure, headed by a secretary general of the conference to be appointed by the Secretary-General of the United Nations and confirmed by the General Assembly.

What is significant is that the U.N. now will have machinery to review systematically, over time and in depth, all issues related to the trade and development of the developing countries. This, above all, was what the developing countries wanted. It is this that governments must now prepare for. And it is this that makes it important to understand the conduct at the first conference, and to seek to understand, also, the motivations for that conduct.

At the conference, the developing countries—the so-called Group of 75, since slightly expanded to 77—operated as a cohesive bloc. In a joint declaration of the developing countries read at the final plenary session and incorporated in full in the Final Act, this unity of the 75 was called by them "the outstanding feature of the entire conference and an event of historic significance." The developing countries clearly consider this unity as a portent of great significance.

How one looks at this unity depends on whether it will serve to generate reasonable or extreme positions. As the 75 rolled up inevitable majorities on resolution after resolution in the main committees, and even in the drafting committee where the factual record of the conference was assembled, there was some doubt as to its desirability. But it is a fact, and an important one, that the developing countries concluded that in unity there is strength.

At times this unity led to extremes and to majority votes on issues on which the developed countries were being asked to take actions but which tended to ignore their views. At other times, the unity of the 75 made compromise resolutions possible.

Fostered by this cohesiveness of the 75, the conference took on the air of a North-South confrontation, of the rich against the poor. There has been much talk in recent years that the division of the world, if one can talk of such a thing, should be along North-South economic lines rather than along the East-West lines of the cold war. UNCTAD was the first major conference where this was in fact the case. East-West issues arose, but secondarily. The Soviet Union generally was deemed to be a developed country and tended to be lumped together by the 75 with other developed countries. It would be utopian to hope that East-West divisions will be totally absent from the continuing machinery, but it can realistically be expected that these will be secondary to the North-South alignment.

But to call this a North-South "division" also would involve over-simplification. What the conference called for, as the developing countries themselves stated, was "international co-operation," not an international adversary proceeding. If there is to be a successful Development Decade, there will have to be a "joining" of interests between the North and the South. This, certainly, is an important lesson.

The developed countries, whether of the market or centrally planned type, as the U.N. parlance goes, were not monolithic. On many substantive issues of fundamental importance the industrialized countries of the West, plus Japan, New Zealand and Australia, were often widely divided. The Soviet bloc sometimes split on important votes when Poland or Rumania went in a direction different from that of the U.S.S.R. Divide and conquer took peculiar turns—turns which may well become the norm in the continuing machinery.

III

By trying to understand the motivations which led to the various decisions at this first conference, we may find it possible to understand also how governments are likely to act at future meetings.

In international bodies, governments don't like to talk too much about what they themselves should do; they prefer instead to place the emphasis on what others should do. This made for a sort of continuing refrain at UNCTAD and is likely to be the same in the continuing machinery. The theme of the conference—and this is reflected in the Final Act—was on what the developed countries must do to foster the economic development of the developing countries. The assumption under which the developing countries operated was that they already were doing what was possible in their own behalf and what the conference was all about was to examine what others, the developed countries, must do to help them. The following sentence from the final declaration of the 75 is illustrative of this mode of thinking: "The efforts of developing countries to raise the living standards of their peoples, which are now being made under adverse external conditions, should be supplemented and strengthened by constructive international action."

The developed countries argued that the crucial factor in economic development is self-help, and that if the conference was all about development, it should focus on the responsibilities of the developing countries. The latter were willing to accept this, in the abstract. This idea is even reflected in the Final Act. For example: "The developing countries recognize that they have the primary responsibility to raise the living standards of their peoples; *but* their national exertions to this end will be greatly impaired if not supplemented and strengthened by constructive international action based on respect for national sovereignty." The italics are supplied; there was always a "but" in the thinking of the developing countries. It was the phrase after the "but" that the conference focused on.

The tendency to want to talk about the shortcomings of others is a normal one. No country wants to spend its time at an international conference with a *mea culpa.* And yet, it will be appropriate for the continuing machinery to focus on both aspects of the development problem, the internal action and the external coöperation. They must go together if the aspirations of the developing countries are to be met. The job of governments, and of the secretariat of the continuing machinery, is to bring this mutuality of interest into focus without alienating either side.

There are issues on both sides in which sensitivities run deep. Some of these were highlighted at the conference and are likely to come to the fore again in the continuing machinery. By taking account of the depth of feeling, it may prove possible to minimize the acrimony.

Perhaps the most sensitive of all issues, especially to the most recently independent of the developing countries, is the concept of one country, one vote. This is wrapped up closely with the feeling for national sovereignty. On the other side, that of the developed countries, the feeling runs deep that the countries which will be principally responsible for taking actions in the trade and development field in the interest of the developing countries cannot subject themselves to the tyranny of the majority—in short, that one country, one vote is meaningless when automatic majorities are rolled up by countries which do not have to take any action in response to the votes. The conduct of the 75 in rolling up just such majorities on certain issues heightened this feeling of the developed countries.

As the conference negotiated itself to a close, this voting issue stood athwart all other issues and its resolution was required before all other compromises could become effective, and before the conference could close "successfully" or end in "failure." What could be done in the continuing machinery to protect the minority which was being asked to act, and at the same time recognize the deep feeling that national sovereignty should be preserved in the form of one country, one vote? This was, and is, the issue. The issue was side-stepped in the final compromise. The Secretary-General of U.N. was asked to appoint a special committee to report to the General Assembly, and to prepare proposals for procedures in the continuing machinery which work to establish a process of conciliation before voting, and to provide safeguards in the adoption of recommendations for action which might substantially affect "the economic or financial interests of particular countries." The resolution states that proposals of the special committee should not imply "any departure from the principle that each country has one vote."

In their final joint declaration, the 75 phrased their viewpoint on this issue as follows: ". . . it is their view [i.e., of the 75] that there should be ample scope for reaching workable agreement on substantial issues. But they categorically declare that no arrangements designed for this purpose should derogate from the ultimate right of the proposed Board and the Conference to adopt the recommendations on any point of substance by a simple majority vote in the case of the Board and two-thirds majority vote in the case of the Conference. The developing countries attach cardinal importance to democratic procedures which afford no position of privilege in the economic and financial, no less than in the political sphere." To the developing countries, "democracy" in U.N. parlance means that the vote of any one country is as good as that of any other country, the Security Council and several other bodies excepted.

This remains an unresolved problem. Its solution, in a way satisfactory to both groups, is probably a *sine qua non* to an effective continuing machinery. This is one of the cardinal lessons that delegates must have taken home with them.

Organizational questions also aroused deep feelings in other ways. The developing countries showed resentment, in varying degree, against various bodies in which their voice is not controlling. Some of these bodies are the U.N. Economic and Social Council, the General Agreement on Tariffs and Trade (GATT), and to a lesser degree the International Monetary Fund and the International Bank for Reconstruction and Development. The resentment often takes the form of lashing out at important bodies dealing with trade and development problems which have not been solved. Yet world food problems have not been solved, and the Food and Agriculture Organization is spared the resentment that devolves on the other institutions cited above. World health problems have not been solved but the World Health Organization is also spared sharp criticism.

Resentment seems to stem from a combination of important but unsolved problems (great problems are rarely "solved"; they are worked at), plus a less than controlling voice in the organization by the developing countries. As GATT grows in the number of its contracting parties, the majority of which already are developing countries, the feeling of developing countries toward it is changing. GATT operates under a one-country, one-vote rule, but voting is infrequent. If the U.N.'s Economic and Social Council is enlarged to increase the representation of developing countries, their feeling toward this may alter. But, of course. there may be a countervailing feeling. When developing countries control organizations, as they are likely to control the continuing machinery of UNCTAD, resentment may begin to build up on the side of the developed countries.

IV

Feelings run deep, too, on many substantive issues. Here there are vast differences in emphasis among the 75, and it was on these issues that logrolling among them was most effective; some important compromises took place among them, permitting the 75 to remain a cohesive whole.

The issues of the conference ran the gamut of international and domestic economic affairs. They included removing barriers to trade in primary commodities; examining the possibility of using commodity arrangements to expand export earnings of developing countries; removing barriers to trade in manufactured goods; the coming Kennedy Round of trade negotiations; building an export potential in the industrial field in the developing countries, and then of export promotion; giving trade preferences to developing countries for their manufactured products; improving the terms and conditions of aid; improving the procedures of the International Monetary Fund for compensatory financing to mitigate short-term fluctuations in export earnings; providing some form of long-term supplementary financing when the trend of export earnings of a developing country is declining; mitigating debt-servicing burdens of developing countries; examining the world shipping problem; making greater use of the world's money markets for financing development; promoting private investment; fostering greater regional coöperation among developing countries; providing adequate rules for access to ports for the score or more of landlocked countries in the world; and a host of others. Space is too limited to discuss all of them. It may be helpful, as a guide to the future, to highlight a few of these substantive issues—particularly those which are likely to be the focus of attention in the continuing machinery.

Terms of trade, and their deterioration for primary commodity exporters over the last decade, were an issue which had been highlighted by the secretariat in advance of the conference. Raúl Prebisch, the secretary general of the conference, and formerly the executive secretary of the Economic Commission for Latin America, has been stressing terms-of-trade problems for many years. Even those developing countries whose terms of trade had not worsened, or had even improved, felt obliged to refer to deteriorating terms of trade.

All developing countries, and for that matter most developed countries, agreed that some corrective action must be taken to prevent sharp fluctuations and declines in primary commodity prices. Where it may not be feasible to hold the price line for commodities, e.g. where doing so might merely invite natural or synthetic substitutes, some form of compensatory or supplementary financing was suggested in order that development programs not suffer from declining export receipts. This is perhaps the key substantive issue with which the continuing machinery must deal. It cuts across commodity policy; and primary commodities still make up some 85 to 90 percent of the export earnings of the developing countries. And it cuts across financial policy and the nature of aid to developing countries. Many of the resolutions at the conference dealt with some facet of this issue, which will be with the world for a long time.

The developing countries felt deeply that a new set of trade principles must be developed to govern future international trade relations. These principles are to be the Magna Carta of the world's "new international division of labor." Principles were drafted at the conference, some labeled general and others special, although it is hard to distinguish between the two groups. These principles were adopted by virtue of the developing countries voting yes, while the developed countries frequently abstained or voted no. In short, what UNCTAD adopted was a set of principles which does not have general agreement. It was agreed before the conference broke up that a major task is to reëxamine these trade principles, seek to shape them into a coherent whole, and to achieve more general agreement.

One other substantive issue should be noted—that dealing with preferential treatment for the manufactured products of developing countries when exported to developed countries. Among the developing countries, some of the more advanced might benefit from trade preferences. Those which are less advanced, and have practically no industry, would not benefit from preferences on goods they do not even produce as yet; on the other hand, they would, for the most part, have nothing to lose either. Some countries in Africa, however, now enjoy preferential trade treatment in the European Economic Community and might be in a worse position if they had to share these on an equal basis with other developing countries. Here, therefore, the interests of developing countries diverged. And here effective compromising was done at the committee level. It was agreed that preferences which involved discrimination against developing countries should be eliminated only along with "the effective application of measures . . . providing at least equivalent advantages . . ." for the countries losing these exclusive preferences. What these "equivalent advantages" should be were hinted at but never really spelled out in detail.

A similar, and perhaps even more important, compromise was worked out among the 75 to deal with the problem of the African countries which might lose their preferential entry into the European Common Market for such products as coffee and cocoa, on which the Europeans maintain tariffs for the express purpose of favoring their former colonies.

These were important compromises on issues on which feeling runs deep among the developing countries. Latin America, for example, has long resented the discrimination it faces in marketing its coffee in the European Common Market. But the fact that a compromise was possible was a tribute to the power both of logrolling and of the desire of the 75 to maintain unity.

V

There are other important lessons to be derived from the discussions at the conference. One is that the developing countries want change. They want a "new" international division of labor, which implies that the present one is bad. They want and have a "new" trade forum. They want "new" trade principles. They want new and different techniques of aid, not necessarily at the sacrifice of the old, but in addition to what is now being done. They want new trade rules to replace the most-favored-nation concept and instead deliberately to favor the developing countries.

There was some nervousness on the part of many developing countries in much of this. If aid techniques are to be altered, what about those countries doing fairly well in aid receipts? The other side of the trade-preference coin is trade discrimination. Some of the more advanced of the developing countries. those on the borderline and uncertain of their proper classification, were privately concerned that they might not be among the countries receiving preference and that they would therefore be discriminated against. These misgivings were not publicly aired, but were privately expressed. The unity of the 75 was too precious for public doubts.

However, the key fact is that the world's poorer countries want change. To the extent that their proposals are not accepted, this is often interpreted as a desire to maintain the status quo and is resented.

The developing countries are irritated by what they sometimes believe is the patronizing air adopted by the representatives of developed countries. The lesson of avoiding condescension must be learned and relearned. The press in the developed countries often reported that one important function of UNCTAD was education, and by this was meant the education of representatives from developing countries. The fact that education might also work in the other direction tended to be ignored.

It is hard to state which way the education went in this instance. People who attend such conferences, whether from developed or developing countries, are never quite the same, 12 weeks and hundreds of thousands of words afterwards. Something of the other fellow's viewpoint does come through. Presumably, open-minded and inquiring delegates from both developed and developing countries learned something, and closed-minded ones learned nothing, no matter what their national origin or the level of development of their country.

Insensitivity to the emotions and viewpoint of other people is not unique to representatives of developed countries. It also works the other way. Representatives of developed countries did not relish it when they were accused of being negative, or of being advocates of the status quo, only because they did not accept proposals of developing countries in precisely the words in which they were offered. Also, the running up on inevitable majorities by the developing countries, asking the other fellow to do something, was a technique which inevitably irritated the representatives of developed countries.

These same delegates were also struck by what often seemed to them to be a double, or even triple, standard on the part of the developing countries. The standard went something as follows: no developing country would make demands on any other developing country, on the assumption that they already were doing all that was possible; developing countries would make demands on what the U.N. calls the centrally planned economies, i.e. the Communist countries, but would not be insistent when the Communists balked or wished to rephrase these demands in their own language; finally, developing countries would make uncompromising demands on what the U.N. calls the market economies, i.e. the Western industrialized countries, and would not only reject the latter's attempts at modification, but would even express dissatisfaction when demands were not accepted precisely as made.

As an example, one of the demands made at the conference was that developed free-market countries should eliminate internal taxes levied on such tropical beverages as coffee and cocoa, on the grounds that these taxes impede consumption. In some European countries, the elimination of these long-standing taxes, while desirable, is also difficult since alternative sources of revenue must be found. Nevertheless, the developing countries continued to insist on the elimination of these taxes, and properly so.

A device in Communist countries comparable in effect if not in purpose is the large margin between import and retail prices for tropical products. These, too, impede consumption. It was suggested that these margins in the centrally planned economies should reflect only normal distribution costs and profit. The representatives of centrally planned economies objected to this, and quite vociferously. They said that retail prices were immaterial in a planned economy. They implied that the only purpose of retail prices was to act as a market-clearing mechanism. They argued that anyone advocating a reduced import-retail price margin in order to stimulate imports just did not understand what a planned economy was all about. The issue, of course, is important to the Communist countries in that it raises the issue of consumer sovereignty; but the argument that limiting the margin between import and retail price is impossible for a planned economy is not more convincing than the argument that a free-market economy cannot control its internal taxes.[1]

The important point that delegates noticed was that the developing countries, while they did bargain hard with the Communist countries, did not insist on maintaining their demands in the final resolutions, but instead accepted expressions of good intent, using language drafted by the Communist countries saying that they would increase their imports from developing countries.

It is hard to state why the demands placed on the Western industrialized countries and Japan tend to be greater than those placed on the Soviet Union. The reason given by most representatives at the conference was that the free-market economies tend to be more responsive to such pressure, and the Communist countries less so. In other words, the developing countries presumably exert pressure against the industrialized market countries because they hit pay-dirt; they exert less pressure against the developed Communist countries because their demands tend more easily to be sloughed off. Also, of course, the Western countries represent far more significant markets. Another reason might be that the developing countries are only now beginning to get used to treating the Soviet Union as a developed country, and their demands on it may increase as time passes. This is a portent for Moscow to ponder.

---

[1]At about the time this discussion was taking place, an article appeared in the Summer 1964 issue of *The New Hungarian Quarterly,* written by Róbert Hardi, an economist at the Karl Marx University of Economics in Budapest and Deputy Manager of KONSUMEX (Commodity Trading Enterprise). Mr. Hardi wrote that the socialist countries could undertake internal actions to stimulate imports from the developing countries. First among these, he wrote, "would be a decrease in the prices of tropical products on the home markets, resulting in increased demand. Price decreases of this type have recently taken place in a number of socialist countries. In Hungary a decrease in the price of coffee has, for instance, brought about a 100 percent increase in the volume of sales."

Perhaps the greatest danger that can come from these mutual irritations is that each side loses its appreciation of the aspirations and sensitivities of the other side. This is a lesson both sides must learn.

On the part of the developing countries, closing statement after closing statement reflected disappointment that UNCTAD, after only 12 weeks, had not solved all of the problems of economic development. For example, the final declaration of the 75 countries notes: "They [the 75] do not consider that the progress that has been registered in each of the major fields of economic development has been adequate or commensurate with their essential requirements."

A great danger is that in the developed countries a plague-on-your-house feeling will develop, prompted by the seeming insensitivity of developing countries to the viewpoint of others, the rolling up of majority votes, and the double and triple standard referred to earlier. Such a reaction could be tragic, in that it could result in the developed countries losing sight of the very real problems which the developing countries have in achieving adequate economic growth.

There was much talk in the closing days as to whether the conference was a "success" or "failure," but it was never quite clear what these words meant. To some developing countries, success meant stating all their demands in unvarnished form, without any alteration in wording, in order that these might serve as a charter for what the developing countries thought must be done. To most developing countries, it seemed more important to arrive at some agreed resolutions "in recognition of the need for a cooperative effort in the international field."

If one conceives of UNCTAD as a start, then if it made a good start, it was successful. One would assume that from the viewpoint of the developing countries a good start was made. The developing countries will have a forum in which to examine their problems systematically and to seek remedies to what they consider are now the defects in the world's trading system. From their viewpoint, this must be considered a major achievement.

From the viewpoint of the developed countries, the real issue certainly must be the extent to which international action can be taken to help the developing countries solve the real problems which they face. Economic development is a complex process, possibly the most complex process of human endeavor. Certainly, there is agreement among all men that greater prosperity for each is desirable for all.

The issue for the United States, therefore, must be: What can be done by all countries–developed and developing–to help achieve this greater prosperity? Viewed in this way, "failure" is to permit conditions to develop in the world which would prevent these cooperative international actions from being taken to achieve higher living standards throughout the world. "Success" will be measurable as greater prosperity is achieved.

United Nations and Nation-Building

Nina Heathcote

Is "nation-building" an effective new technique for maintaining stability in international politics?

After the last war nationalism appeared to be in decline. The resurgence of the two superpowers and the accompanying decrease of importance of the European states (for long, *the* nation states of the modern world), led many, particularly in the West, to believe that the end of nationalism was at hand. There was also moral revulsion against the nation state, which was credited with an essentially evil character–responsible, it was supposed, for two world wars and bound to cause more. As a more viable alternative to the post-war polarization of power, which had been reflected in such alliances as NATO and the Warsaw Pact, it was thought that the number of states should best be reduced so as to form larger units, i.e. regional rather than national groupings. The European Economic Community (EEC) was a striking expression of this sort of thinking.[1]

The United Nations somewhat mitigated such general denigration of the nation state. The Charter, for example, Articles 39 (Chapter VII) and 99 (Chapter XV) seems to assume that all the world's populated territories

---

Nina Heathcote, "United Nations and Nation-Building," *International Journal,* Vol. 20, No. 1 (Winter 1964-65), pp. 20-33. Reprinted by permission of the author and *International Journal.*

---

[1]Cf. the views of Walter Hallstein, *Economic Integration and Political Unity in Europe,* a speech made before a joint meeting of Harvard University and the Massachusetts Institute of Technology, May 22, 1961, Information Service of the European Communities (London), p. 6.

are (or will come to be) divided amongst sovereign nation states.[2] Moreover, as Hammarskjöld pointed out, it lays down "some basic rules of international ethics by which all Member States have committed themselves to be guided." In this sense, according to Hammarskjöld, the Charter takes a first step "in the direction of an organized international community, and this independently of the organs set up for international co-operation."[3]

By guaranteeing the territorial integrity of states and their other rights and by setting them up as guardians of international peace, the U.N. Charter had revived the idea of a "moral state." But in reality the United Nations did not, until the 1960's, escape the consequences of polarization of power, and was in effect dominated by the United States. This hegemony was challenged in the 1960's. Is the present decade then likely to be characterized by a re-emergence of the nation state?

It seems fashionable to think that this will be so, and that for stability's sake a multiplicity of sovereign states is to be desired, at least in some areas. The implication is not, of course, that this stability would then be maintained by re-establishing the balance of power. In Europe, partly thanks to the resources of the EEC, France has been able to reassert some of the influence lost since the Second World War. But the new nations of Asia and Africa, the main objects of the enthusiasm for nation-building, can by themselves project little power. In the post colonial period, especially 1960-61, they emerged rapidly, sometimes after much bloodshed and with the entanglement of other powers in the conflict. Few of them were stable or viable, or promised to become so in the near future. In the Congo Hammarskjöld set a precedent according to which U.N. intervention to minimize conflict at the birth of such a state need not contradict the Charter. Through this action he involved the United Nations very directly in nation-building–an experiment which proved hazardous to the future of the Organization.

After the present decade there should be few new nations requiring the type of assistance extended by Hammarskjöld to the Congo, unless some existing states undergo fragmentation. But as the new units are basically weak and unstable, fear of a world-wide conflagration or at any rate of some major international upheaval could inspire the United Nations to participate in "building up" the nations recently come into existence. This would be all the more likely if the Organization should be encouraged to do so by a great power such as the United States.

---

[2] A. L. Burns and Nina Heathcote, *Peacekeeping by UN Forces from Suez to the Congo* (New York, 1963), p. 23.

[3] *U.N. General Assembly. Official Records Sixteenth Session. Supplement No. 1A. Introduction to the Annual Report of the Secretary General on the Work of the Organization 16 June 1960–15 June 1961.* (Doc. A/4800/Add. 1), p. 1.

It is interesting that when Hammarskjöld organized the U.N. Security Council into endorsing his plan for the Congo action, he did so chiefly on the grounds that instability within that country might invite external intervention and so threaten world peace. This was not a universally accepted view of the impact the new states might have on international peace and security. Although all of the new states of Asia and Africa were economically under-privileged, and–but for India, Pakistan and China–militarily weak, the weight of their opinion expressed in the Assembly, where numbers count, was felt throughout the United Nations. For a while this gave colour to the possibility of a third, "moral" force in world affairs, which was to offset the "immoral" competition between the great powers. Thus they were at first represented as essentially peaceful. Conversely, peacefulness was often equated with non-alignment. Yet fear of violence as a result of creation of the unstable new states has partly motivated a new enterprise–nation-building–of which the Congo operation was to be an example.

It could perhaps be argued that the rise of the new states had somewhat reduced the cold war conflict, and had had a peaceful effect to that extent. The recovery of Europe and the rise of China, Indonesia and others, has led some to believe that the relative power of Russia and America, though not of course their absolute capacities, was declining. The U.S. proposal for a NATO multilateral force, France's uninhibited pursuit of its atomic policies and its recognition of Communist China, the Sino-Soviet rift and the Chinese attack on India are among the familiar examples cited in support of the view that there has been an apparent depolarization of power. Perhaps the present supposed *détente* is partly due to the fact that more *notice* is being taken of peripheral crises, occasioned by the states recently come into being, that do not necessarily involve the cold war issues–Indonesia's dispute with Malaysia, and the conflict in Cyprus.

The United Nations was not called upon to participate in nation-building until the Congo crisis erupted; so it is not surprising that, at least in its earlier stages, Hammarskjöld–the real author of the Congo operation–had no comprehensive guide to offer the Organization in its nation-building capacity, similar to his "Summary study" which had concerned itself with proper conduct of U.N. military and observer forces. The "Summary study," of course, was written as a kind of conclusion to the Suez and Lebanon operations and was based on experience, whereas in the Congo Hammarskjöld improvised while the U.N. action was in progress. Nevertheless, some of his thinking, episodic though it was, derived from ideas he had had in mind before the operation started.

As Secretary-General Hammarskjöld could hardly fly full in the face of the Charter, which plainly referred to sovereign nation states as its basic units. Nevertheless, although Hammarskjöld wished to temper some of what he regarded as the more dangerous aspects of sovereignty, he certainly did not think it possible in the present era to build up the United Nations into a superstate.

"We undoubtedly need world organization, but we are far from ripe for world government. . . ."[4] The United Nations was primarily "a dynamic instrument of *Governments.*"[5] Hammarskjöld's intention here had been to emphasize the word "dynamic," but he undoubtedly meant that at the present stage of evolution of individual states. These might eventually, through mutual co-operation, create amongst themselves a law-abiding community, but while this development could be kept fruitfully in mind, it was in too distant a future for the exact form to be predicted.[6] However, in the restrictions which the atomic age imposed on even the most powerful nation states, Hammarskjöld saw a unique opportunity for a first step in the direction of such co-operation. "Sovereign national States in armed competition of which the most that may be expected in the international field is that they achieve a peaceful co-existence" would no longer meet "the needs of the present and of the future in a world of ever-closer international interdependence where nations have at their disposal armaments of hitherto unknown destructive strength." The time had come for "intergovernmental action overriding such a philosophy" which would make possible "more developed and increasingly effective forms of constructive international co-operation."[7]

These were persistent elements in Hammarskjöld's view of the continuing world situation. But in February 1960 he came back from a tour of Africa obviously impressed with a newly emergent feature: the opportunities that the new nations of Africa presented for furthering his projects for the evolution of the United Nations; and in particular with the problems "of personnel . . . money . . . education and . . . moral support [required] in the reshaping of or the shaping of a nation."[8] It was probably at this point that Hammarskjöld began to consider seriously directing the resources of the United Nations towards nation-building in the new continent. He had thought for long that much could be accomplished in new countries; conversely, he expected that the new states would do a great deal for the Organization because "It is natural for old and well-established countries to see in the United Nations a limitation on their sovereignty. It is just as natural that a young country, a country emerging on the world stage, should find in the United Nations an addition to its sovereignty, an added means

[4] Dag Hammarskjöld, "The World and the Nation," *Three University Addresses on Service to the Community of Nations* (United Nations, N.Y., June 1955), p. 12.

[5] *Introduction to the Annual Report of the Secretary General,* p. 1 (my italics).

[6] Wilder Foote (ed.), *Dag Hammarskjöld. The Servant of the Peace* (London, 1962), pp. 251-252, 255.

[7] *Introduction to the Annual Report of the Secretary General,* p. 1.

[8] Foote, *Dag Hammarskjöld,* p. 236.

of speaking to the world."[9] In May 1959 he had explicitly excluded that "civilian tasks for the United Nations that would place an ultimate constitutional responsibility on any one of the main organs of the Organization exceeding what they are equipped or ready for. This excludes the imposition in this case of executive authority on the United Nations for administrative tasks which require political decisions."[10]

But in Africa, Hammarskjöld thought that the Organization, even if not directly involved in administrative tasks for the new nations, could "without pushing, without . . . becoming a party in their development . . . through proper means, even on the basis of fairly small amounts of money, come into the picture in such a way as to help considerably in *the framing of their political life* after independence and in the building up of the national state." This help the United Nations could provide, in the form of "technical assistance."[11] Having pledged itself to self-government and to independence as part of the human rights spelled out in the Charter[12] the United Nations alone could provide this sort of assistance.[13]

Hammarskjöld began by isolating two elements of the Charter as crucial to nation-building: the rights, firstly, to self-determination, and secondly, to equal economic opportunity, regardless of the member country's relative strength.[14] This concept of "equality" is important since, as Hammarskjöld had already indicated, the United Nations was to "build nations" primarily amongst states that were militarily weak, economically under-privileged and politically disorganized. Accordingly he treated economic and technical aid as "closely related to a policy aiming at self-government and independence for all . . . especially during the first years of independence on a new Member State."[15] These principles he tried to develop in the course of the Congo action, which was to be a precedent for the conduct of future U.N. operations concerned with nation-building.

The United Nations early struck difficulties with the principle of self-determination in dealing with the problem of Katanga's secession. The Congo's territorial boundaries had been defined by the act of independence from Belgium and not by the United Nations, which was called in only subsequently. On this basis the United Nations would not "recognize" Katanga as an independent

---

[9] *Ibid.*, p. 134.

[10] *Ibid.*, p. 206.

[11] *Ibid.*, p. 240 (my italics).

[12] *Ibid.*, pp. 237-8.

[13] *Ibid.*, p. 240.

[14] *Introduction to the Annual Report of the Secretary General*, p. 1.

[15] *Ibid.*, p. 8.

state. Though the United Nations proceeded no further against it while Hammarskjöld was the Secretary-General, later under U Thant the military forces of the Organization subdued the secession. Until November 1961 no resolution officially condemned the secession beyond reiterating U.N. support for the Congo's territorial integrity; and none thereafter authorized force to end the secession. However, in practice, the U.N. military intervention united Katanga with the Congo in January 1963.

Hammarskjöld had been unable to establish adequate criteria for nation-building by the United Nations. He had made it clear that the United Nations could only "establish . . . sovereign States for peoples who have expressed in democratic forms their wish for such a status,"[16] so that the initiative must always remain with the peoples concerned; but he did not indicate which territories might be incapable of becoming states, or of expressing self-determination, or how the United Nations should decide on the boundaries of a new state. Since in his opinion the United Nations would have particular scope for nation-building "in relation to countries under colonial rule or in other ways under foreign domination . . .,"[17] this omission was significant: U.N. experience in post-colonial countries so far has not been very encouraging. The United Nations had no means of deciding whether boundaries as defined by the outgoing colonial powers corresponded to the affiliations of the peoples concerned. Nor is it always meaningful to talk about "the democratic will" of all inhabitants in such new states as the Congo. In West New Guinea and in Malaysia on the other hand, the United Nations was over-ruled by power politics. In West New Guinea, the United Nations seems unable to ensure compliance with the agreement guaranteeing that Indonesia would effectively consult the wishes of the inhabitants; in Malaysia, findings of a U.N. report on the outcome of the elections have been rejected by Indonesia. These examples, along with that of Katanga already cited, show that the principle of self-determination is not explicit enough to guide policy. No one has defined generally acceptable criteria for deciding what units might form viable nation states.

Finally, the United Nations had not only to maintain the shaky boundaries of the Congo but also to restore its government. It is doubtful whether Hammarskjöld in sending the peace-keeping mission to the Congo had either purpose in mind. He had been ready to terminate the military aspect of the operation after the Belgian troops withdrew, and had foreshadowed this in August 1960.[18] But when the central government collapsed, the United Nations could hardly withdraw without exposing the Congo to even more outside interference than had been threatening at the start of the operation. Hammarskjöld at

[16] *Ibid.*, p. 2.

[17] *Ibid.*, p. 2.

[18] Burns and Heathcote, *Peacekeeping*, p. 46.

first defined the mission to the Congo as "technical assistance," although by military means. The involvement in the constitutional issues arose as a consequence of the United Nation's armed forces being for the first time deployed *inside* the territory of the state. Hammarskjöld was aware of the dangers and temptations to various power blocs presented by the United Nation's military presence within a new state, and had sought to safeguard the Congo from the dictation of a U.N. majority as well as from manipulation by the power blocs. He ruled that the United Nations must not dominate the assisted state politically through economic aid: "There should never be any suspicion that the world community would wish or indeed could ever wish to maintain for itself, through the United Nations a position of power or control in a member country."[19] That is, the United Nations must remain neutral in the country's domestic conflicts. In this task the Organization soon found itself in difficulties with various bloc interests, and the policy itself paradoxically involved the United Nations in constitutional problems of the country. As Hammarskjöld pointed out, it is a thankless and easily misunderstood role for the Organization to remain neutral in relation to a situation of domestic conflict and to provide active assistance only by protecting the rights and possibilities of the people to find their own way, but it remains the only manner in which the Organization can serve its proclaimed purpose of furthering the full independence of the people in the true and unqualified sense of the word.[20] The policy of non-intervention failed when (partly as its consequence) the Lumumba Government—which had been responsible for inviting the United Nations into the Congo—was overthrown. Hammarskjöld was now violently attacked by the Russians, who demanded that he should resign, refused to contribute to the costs of the Congo operation and proposed to reform the Secretariat on the Troika principle. After the news of Lumumba's assassination, in the winter of 1960-61, a number of influential Afro-Asians also seemed to have lost faith in his policies, and threatened to withdraw contingents from the U.N. forces. Thus the non-intervention policy failed to win for the United Nations a reputation for non-partisanship, yet it prevented the Organization from ensuring the political stability needed in the Congo in order to discourage unilateral intervention.[21]

Did Hammarskjöld see a unique opportunity for the entire world community to participate through the United Nations in nation-building? He seemed to think that there was an important division between the Communists who regarded the United Nations as static conference machinery, and the others, who saw in it (as Hammarskjöld did) a dynamic instrument of action which through a strong

---

[19]*Introduction to the Annual Report of the Secretary General,* p. 8.

[20]*Ibid.,* p. 7.

[21]Nina Heathcote, "American Policy Towards the U.N. Operation in the Congo," *Australian Outlook,* April 1964, pp. 84-85.

executive might make possible U.N. initiatives, as in the Congo. He then further distinguished the "different bloc interests" from those nations with "aims natural especially for those which recently have been under colonial rule,"[22] again implying that the Organization's nation-building ideals harmonized best with the aspirations of that group. Here one might disagree, and point out that while the last mentioned group was in fact the most immediate beneficiary of such policies, and was least equipped to play power politics on a world scale, the disinterestedness that Hammarskjöld appeared to impute to it has not been displayed in all cases. For instance, Ghana's activities in the Congo went beyond reasserting the United Nation's authority.

The United Nations as an international peace-keeping organization could not become party to such recognized mechanisms for maintaining international stability as balance of power or balance of terror, all of which presuppose retention of the nation states but do not rule out war. Hammarskjöld seemed to be interested in nation states as a presently necessary but perhaps a transient element in the process of developing world order. In the immediate future, he did look to nation states as potentially stabilizing agents, and in this sense he took into the account the traditional mechanisms mentioned above for maintaining a *precarious* peace. On this view the United Nations nation-building served that purpose as well as benefiting individual nation states.

What are the problems of nation building? Is it a meaningful and definite concept? Can it be a practicable policy? If the United Nations is to function properly as a world body effectively concerned with maintaining peace, then so long as the Charter remains unamended, it should ideally encourage the formation of free nation states so that recognized and popular authorities may shoulder responsibility for international actions. So long as the United Nations is confined to lending technical and economic assistance to states already formed, or to safeguarding their borders, the task of nation-building is merely difficult in practice. On the other hand, as soon as military or police action is taken, especially under conditions of domestic conflict, such as in the Congo, the Organization needs criteria as to what constitutes a nation.

The enthusiasm generated by recent efforts at nation-building gives ground for hope that a great deal might be learned from that enterprise about the nature of statehood. Yet the findings are often elementary and haphazard. The outstanding modern nation-builders have been of course, the colonial powers, and they had not in many cases set out with that end in view. Thus they left no uniform designs for the construction of nations. The marks of statehood usually accepted in diplomatic practice are: establishment of a *de facto* government; recognition by some other nation-states; and willingness to accept its predecessor's debts.

[22] *Introduction to the Annual Report of the Secretary General*, p. 7.

As the case of the Congo showed, all central authority may collapse, and recognition of a state by other nations may not always exactly coincide with self-determination by its nationals.

Self-determination is a principle which though often grounded in essential requirements of modern nationhood is not easily assessed in practice (as for instance in Malaysia); or it may be fatuous (as perhaps in the present situation of West New Guinea). Sometimes it obscures or conflicts with other considerations. Given the idealistic basis of the United Nations Charter–should it be the will of the people, or economic viability, or perhaps some other consideration that determines whose writ shall run? And in the light of experience in the Congo, Malaysia and Cyprus, may we not conclude that acts of self-determination by a new state may perhaps create as many problems related to self-determination as there were before?

Closely related to the ideal of self-determination is the ideal of a "moral state" which likens the worth of individual nations to the rights of individual men. The United Nations might be called upon to assist almost any state, viable or not, that manages to obtain admission to the world today. Hammarskjöld had hoped to substitute "right for might" after statehood was attained, and to make the "Organization the natural protector of rights which countries without it might find it more difficult to assert and to get respected."[23] International protection of small states, for purposes other than the maintenance of the balance of power, is a concept which belongs distinctly to our own era, beginning with Woodrow Wilson's early vision. But whether assuring the continued existence of small and weak states contributes to international stability is at least questionable.

In Europe, a nation state such as Britain even today may exercise quite a remarkable political influence in foreign affairs although in a global war it could perhaps do little more militarily than act as a trip wire. The new nations (apart from India and China) are not even in this category, let alone that of the leading European states in the nineteenth century. They project little power, and most of them present an international danger only in so far as they afford temptations for other powers to intervene. This was the rationale behind the U.N. action in the Congo. Conversely, when countries become stronger they do not always display peaceable tendencies. Indonesia is an example. There is an hiatus in all reasoning to the effect that a world of nation-states, provided they were benevolent in outlook and internally stable, would necessarily exhibit international harmony. Not every national interest coincides with such common interests as world peace. Nor do various nations share a common view as to what would contribute to such a peace. One may well fear that the present multiplication of nation states may result in an increase of problems derived from the correspondingly growing number of relationships.

---

[23] *Ibid.*, p. 2.

What can be done by nation states or by supra-national organizations that deserves the name of nation-building? No one, not even the United Nations, has the authority to create nations; nationhood is rarely imposed from without. The colonial powers had at times effectively welded tribes into nations, but then nationalism would frequently emerge in opposition to the continued presence of the colonial power. Other forms of nation-building such as technical or economic aid of instruction in public administration and security matters can operate only within already established nation states. Thus the would-be nation-builder may at times be open to charges of interference in internal affairs of the assisted state. This makes planning of aid by the donor well nigh impossible; and, as we know, its results are often fragmentary and not entirely successful. Whether massive economic or technical aid has the capacity to produce nations out of a chaos of political anarchy and backward economic conditions is thus at least questionable. The emergence of Afro-Asian states should not be regarded as returning us to an era of nationalism on the European scale. In Europe nations evolved slowly: the hurried attempts at building up new states have often endowed them with no more than the paraphernalia of government, producing what Hugh Tinker described as the broken-backed states.[24] That, under certain conditions, may be an acceptable form of national existence (as he argues), but characteristically it is not adapted to massive foreign aid operations of international authority such as, say, an international police force.

To Hammarskjöld, nation-building appeared primarily as a means of fostering international co-operation: that is, more than mere stability; rather, a sense of responsibility on the part of all members for the well-being and harmonious functioning of the entire world system. The United Nations, with no national interest of its own to serve, need not be distracted from the task by conflicting claims of interests, as may be a nation state. To the latter, the appearance of new states on the map, or the growing strength of established powers, may not prove an unmixed blessing. For that reason, the Communist countries always, and the Western ones most of the time, prefer to administer their own foreign aid, particularly in areas where they have an outstanding strategic interest. On the other hand, Western countries such as the United States found they could at times conveniently give aid to uncommitted nations through the United Nations. The prestige of the Organization makes such aid more acceptable to the recipients, as being without strings. The cynics would say that the United Nations in this role might serve as convenient camouflage for nationally interested policies, particularly since in its task of military and technical assistance for nation-building, the United Nations had to rely upon support of great powers, amongst whom the United States is by far the most prominent. The total American

---

[24] Hugh Tinker, "Broken-Backed States," *New Society,* January 30, 1964, No. 70, pp. 6-7.

contribution to the U.N. budget has been 47 per cent of all contributions,[25] and it has given more than its assessment, far more than any other country, to U.N. voluntary funds such as refugee work, relief, UNICEF and technical assistance.[26] The recent cut in U.S. foreign aid was said to have considerably reduced several U.N. programmes. The United States involvement in the United Nations' military and political effort in the Congo may not have helped the United Nations' reputation for impartiality, but it enabled the Organization to win battles and pay many of its bills. Thus it must appear that the U.S. role has been decisive, and that American policies towards nation-building must affect the capacities of the United Nations.

To conclude: U.N. efforts at nation-building have been mainly directed to the under-developed territories liberated from colonial rule. The policing action in the Congo was only partially successful: it failed to eliminate divisive influences, and fighting has continued even after the departure of the U.N. troops. The task of giving economic and technical aid to under-developed countries was inhibited by recipient government's lack of experience, and likewise has not been entirely successful.

Perhaps the term nation-building is somewhat too affirmative and dramatic, considering how limited is its scope. Colonial rule alone may deserve the name of nation-building, though often it proved neither altruistic nor systematic. The United Nations is probably the only body which can be credited with sufficient impartiality to protect the interests of weaker states. But it has little means to do so without support from some great power, particularly when undertaking military or police actions.

A further and more fundamental objection is that in the past nation states were reared by tradition. In spite of various well-known techniques for fostering patriotism, such as mass propaganda, concepts like national consciousness, the drive for self-determination, and other intangibles pertaining to modern states are not readily definable for nation-building purposes. In theory the United Nations may bolster governments by guaranteeing new states against aggression, by providing funds for their economic development and by teaching administrative skills; but it cannot of itself engage in arousing national spirit. In the Congo, it was left (paradoxically) to Tshombé, and perhaps his successors to try and deal in the traditional manner with the problem of unifying tribes into a nation: by warlike means, without the U.N. presence and possibly with assistance of foreign arms.

It seems unwarranted to hope that mere proliferation of states would contribute to international stability. Building up of neutral states might appeal as a

---

[25]Norman J. Padelford, "Financial Crisis and the Future of the United Nations," *World Politics,* Vol. XV, No. 4, July 1963, p. 536.

[26]*Ibid.,* pp. 533, 534.

sort of compromise device during the cold war for the allocation of no-man's land. But the military weakness of the new states makes it unlikely that they will soon be able to defend themselves, nor do they always refrain from exploiting cold war conflicts and dissensions within the power blocs. Nevertheless the United Nations' technical assistance ought not to be interrupted or abandoned: for purely humanitarian reasons, even intermittent attempts to relieve poverty and distress are worthwhile. Furthermore, through its nation-building activities, the U.N. initiative might be strengthened in the larger matter of preserving peace.

V THE UNITED NATIONS–PERSPECTIVES AND PROSPECTS

Because the aims of the United Nations represent the highest moral aspirations of individuals and political communities, it often has been considered by its friends as a paragon of virtue, whose only defect is that it is usually spurned in the rough-and-tumble world of politics. This moralizing attitude obscures the fact that the United Nations, in the contemporary international political system, is only one among several instruments through which states conduct their international relations. This conflict between the aspirations of the Organization and the realities of international political competition in a multisovereign world can lead both to cynicism and to disillusionment in analyzing the United Nations.

Louis Henkin examines this phenomenon with regard to American supporters of the United Nations. He traces much of this disillusionment concerning the United Nations' role in United States foreign policy to a failure to remember that the character of the United Nations has been changed fundamentally by the inability of the great power unity (which won the Second World War) to survive the shock of peace. It should not be too surprising, in a world of fundamental conflict between the great powers, that the Organization has a different role than that envisaged for a world of great-power cooperation. Henkin examines the relation between the purposes of the United Nations and the purposes of its members. He asserts that the "United Nations has no purposes other than those of its members, and is only the means of achieving those purposes." What is the aim of the Organization likely to be when its members have divergent purposes that they are attempting to accomplish through it? One probable result is that states will turn to other instruments of foreign policy to accomplish the purposes that cannot be fulfilled through the United Nations. The Cuban missile crisis of 1962 illustrates the subtle blending of various instruments of foreign policy in one crisis decision and its implications for the future of the United Nations.

When the United Nations celebrated its twentieth birthday in 1965 it was faced with a political crisis masquerading as a financial crisis that had already deadlocked the nineteenth session of the General Assembly and was menacing its continued existence. H. G. Nicholas, at that time, analyzed the factors underlying that crisis and their implications for the United Nations. His discussion of the various tactical considerations of the United States, the Soviet Union, and the Afro-Asian states in the crisis is particularly intriguing. Politics in the United Nations is a shifting mixture of short-run and long-run objectives involving legal and political questions, and the Article 19 crisis well illustrates this point. The question that generated the crisis (that is, what the role of the United Nations should be in the maintenance of international peace and security and, specifically, who should determine that role) has not yet been conclusively settled.

In the final selection, Stanley Hoffmann analyzes the potential role of international organizations in the international system and the factors that limit this role. He contends that there are no sudden mutations in international politics and consequently that the nation-state will continue as the fundamental unit of action. If this is true, what role is left for international organizations such as the United Nations?

1. The United Nations can play a valuable role in keeping before its members the purposes that it proclaims.
2. It can also develop new means to solve the growing array of problems that transcend the borders of any one country.
3. Finally, emphasis should be placed on the United Nations' role as a center for harmonizing the actions of states in those areas in which they have a common interest.

If Hoffmann is correct that in the long run the more important contribution of the United Nations is in building bridges of cooperation between states, what does this hold in store for its short-run activities directed at keeping the Cold War cold? If these short-run activities involve contention and conflict, are they not likely to hinder (if not completely block) the efforts toward long-run cooperation? On the other hand, if the United Nations can make a real contribution toward mitigating the Cold War, does it not have an obligation to do so? In view of the nature of conflict in the nuclear age, survival in the short-run is necessary before we can reap the benefits of long-run cooperation.

The United Nations and Its Supporters: A Self-Examination

Louis Henkin

Everyone born into the world alive, we know, is either a little liberal or a little conservative. But in the United States liberal and conservative, even as those terms continue to lose and acquire meanings, connote primarily domestic attitudes. For Americans as we look out beyond our borders, every child born into today's worldly travail would be, more aptly, either a little internationalist or a little isolationist. (Or, since the contrary of internationalism is no longer isolationism, perhaps a "unilateralist" or a large-sized "nationalist.")

It is to "internationalists" that this is written, in candid family discussion. I do not stop to identify them; for the most part they will recognize themselves, or be recognized, if only by their opponents. Nor does any definition promise to convey "internationalism." Internationalism, as I use it, is not a philosophy, political or moral. It is not a principle, although it is frequently involved with "principle." Internationalism is an attitude or a tangle of attitudes, part moral, part political; part idealism, part self-interest, more or less enlightened. They add up to a way of looking at the world and at the place and role of the United States in it. In the main, with ample allowance for individual differences, internationalists share particular and predictable attitudes on important issues of foreign policy: on war and peace; on national security; on disarmament and arms control; on the cold war; on neutralism; on colonialism; on foreign aid; on trade and tariffs; on unilateralism, bilateralism, multilateralism, in actions or

This paper was written to serve as the basis for discussion at Consultation No. 14, "Moral and Political Limits of Internationalism," sponsored by the Council on Religion and International Affairs, in Washington, D. C., November 1962. Reprinted with permission from the *Political Science Quarterly,* December 1963, Vol. LXXVII, No. 4.

institutions; on NATO and the European Community; on Cuba and China; on the Congo; on international order and international law; on the Bricker Amendment and the Connally Reservation.

The epitome, and a principal focus, of much that is meant by "internationalism" has been the United Nations. It is with the United Nations, and with the attitudes of American internationalists toward the United Nations, that we are concerned here. American supporters of the United Nations, it must be admitted, appear in need of renewing their strength. Their support for the United Nations needs re-examination, notably self-examination. We have fallen far from the easy grace that was our monopoly in "the last days" brought by victory in World War II; even erstwhile supporters have fallen away and begun to question. We have lost, too, the easy certainties of those days; it is not always clear to us how far our support for the United Nations goes, what it entails or requires, how it is reconciled with other desirable policies, with national or individual self-interest, with sophistication and realism. Uncertainty has seeped even into our attitudes toward the bible of the United Nations, the principles of the United Nations Charter.

The increasing uncertainties of supporters of the United Nations suggest the need to reason why. They suggest that it may be time to ask why we feel as we feel and propose what we propose, to re-examine our attitudes to assure that they have not become frozen in yesterday's context and encrusted with positions no longer relevant. It may help, also, to re-educate ourselves in a few respects about the character of the United Nations which we support, and about its place in the policy of the United States.

I SUPPORTING THE UNITED NATIONS

Internationalists are themselves a variegated species, but in their differing ways they have, generally, "supported the United Nations" since its conception during the Second World War; they have continued to support it through major transformations in its character, and in the face of radical changes in the policy of the United States toward the United Nations.

The story is familiar. It was so brief, and now so long ago, that many forget the shattered dream of Big Power amity and cooperation that brought major disillusionment, the frustration of the plans for a relaxed world order under the United Nations, surely the disappointment of those who planned yet stronger international institutions. With disappointed hopes came popular and Congressional skepticism, if not cynicism; "realism" took the forefront, "idealism" had to lie lower. The United Nations was early demoted from "*the* cornerstone" to "*a* cornerstone" of American foreign policy, and support for specific United Nations programs faltered if they did not seem to contribute to national security or to U.S. "victory" in the cold war. Multilateral efforts subsided in favor of traditional bilateral diplomacy. Disarmament efforts continued, but soon even became suspect in some eyes. The progress of international order was reversed: efforts to transform political questions into legal ones, to achieve additional accepted norms, and perhaps impartial adjudication, largely subsided; instead, even what had seemed to have qualities of law became uncertain, international law was subordinated to national foreign policy, and every nation did that which was right in its own eyes. Americans have continued to support the United Nations but in many cases without conviction, even grudgingly.

Some internationalists sometimes still appear amazed that American enthusiasm for the United Nations is not what it was even less long ago than 1945, that programs which seem so eminently reasonable meet growing resistance and rejection, that even pro-United Nations victories are increasingly narrow. This amazement itself may suggest inadequate appreciation by United Nations supporters of the forces shaping the reactions of citizens and leaders: the traditional isolationism of the American people, the wish to avoid "foreign entanglements"; the hopes and disappointments, the costs without obvious return, that have accompanied American commitments to the world before and since the United Nations—the world wars, Korea, Communist expansion. The cold war, in particular, has engendered a war vocabulary and war attitudes more conducive to nationalism, even chauvinism, and emotion, to "art thou for us, or for our adversaries," than to attitudes of rationality and recognition of common interests that inspire devoted support for the United Nations.

But while it is important to recognize these reasons for the increasing obstacles faced by United Nations supporters, it is not with the beam from the eye of others that the internationalist kingdom can be built. Examination may suggest that there is fault, too, in our own attitudes, some of them showing deposits of early postwar days, already too infrequently recalled. We were reluctant to shed the original conception of the United Nations, although the world not being what was thought, the United Nations could not be what was planned. We were reluctant to admit the failure of Big Power cooperation, to recognize the conflicting views of the United States, the Soviet Union, and Communist China as to how the world ought to be. We were reluctant to recognize the facts of power and the needs of national security which ran counter to the early assumptions and the original dream.

Most of us have learned, but in a measure, for some internationalists at least, similar or related faults are still too much with us. We have tended to be reluctant to recognize national interest, as though ours was profane but that of others, sacred. We have tended to idealize the United Nations as though it were an article of faith, rather than an essential political institution with essential, practical purposes. We have tended to romanticize–hoping that we are not patronizing–about others, about new nations, about "neutrals."

If one would generalize, the faults of the internationalist–in his attitudes toward the United Nations as on some other issues–are kin to the virtues of his positions. Being far-seeing, he tends to be romantic and sometimes spills over into sentimentalism. Seeing the other fellow's point of view, and having to defend it to the chauvinist, he sometimes identifies with it. Concerned with assuring that others do not reduce moral questions to differences of taste or judgment, he sometimes elevates his own opinion or preference to principle. Pressing for decency, fairness, and rationality in international affairs, he is reluctant to recognize the lack of these in others. Concerned with recognizing the interests and views of others, he may give them more than their due, and the United States less than it deserves.

Internationalists recognize that it is essential to avoid major war and to strive for peace, even–or especially–with Russia. Nothing in internationalism requires that we avoid recognizing that it is the Soviet Union, far more than the United States, that is responsible for the early inadequacies of the United Nations, for tension in Berlin, for lack of substantial progress in disarmament. Internationalists recognize that aid to new nations is practical as well as moral, essential to U.S. economic welfare as well as to U.S. interests in the cold war. Nothing in internationalism requires that we continue to give aid to nations without taking heed that they are able and willing to use it effectively. Internationalists recognize the importance of the United Nations. Nothing in internationalism requires that we support or accept irresponsible action by nations when that irresponsibility is reflected within the United Nations. The virtues of cooperation do not, *ipso facto*, render desirable every alliance, every integration, every submersion of nations into some larger unit.

Disappointment–and reluctance to admit and accept it–idealization, romanticism, are not immoral; but they are not solid foundations for national policy or a sturdy platform from which to influence national policy. Internationalism and support for the United Nations are surely no less essential now than they were in 1945; but to be relevant and effective, they must be built on an understanding of nations and the United Nations in today's world.

II UNDERSTANDING THE UNITED NATIONS

Misunderstandings of the United Nations by its friends have not been the most egregious, but they are misunderstandings to be particularly dispelled if intelligent support for the United Nations in U.S. foreign policy is to be maintained.

To articulate the obvious but sometimes forgotten, the nation is and will continue to be the current political unit. The United Nations is built on it, as is clear from its very name and from every frequent reference to matters "international." Old societies adhere to it, new ones aspire to it and insist on it, even if they must simultaneously seek new, "less sovereign" arrangements for their survival and development. Little is as universally accepted in the international arena as notions of sovereign equality, territorial integrity, and independence. Even "international communism" has not eliminated national boundaries and conceptions. The nation, one may assume, will figure in world politics for a long time. The persistence of nations does not mean, of course, the inevitability of virulent nationalism.

The internationalist, too, begins with a society of nations, however much some may deplore it or dream of the day when they will wither away. The foreign policy he would influence is that of our own nation, the United States. And nations, not unlike individuals, act in their own interests as they see their interests. They cooperate not from self-sacrifice, but for a common good to all.

National self-interest is a difficult concept in international relations, and internationalists, no less than ultra-nationalists, sometimes stumble over it. Metaphors which deal with the society of nations as though it were a society of men do not always add clarity; they inject values which are only speciously appropriate between nations, and confuse concepts of international morality, playing into the hands of those who reject morality between nations when they really mean that morality takes different forms and makes different requirements of nations.

Failure to understand national interest can be fatal to any internationalist position. We do not decry or eschew patriotism even when we flush scoundrels from its refuge. We are against chauvinistic nationalism, not merely from morality or taste, but because we do not think it serves the interest of the United States. To the internationalist no less than to the most extreme nationalist, U.S. foreign policy must be determined by U.S. interests. Internationalism does not need to insist on "morality", on idealism, on altruism, or cooperation per se; internationalism recognizes that policies which may look like or reflect any of these are frequently in the true interest of the United States.

The internationalist, then, must not be trapped into accepting even the appearance of a dichotomy between "U.S. interests" and "UN interests." The question for U.S. policy is not what can the United States do for the United Nations; it is, more clearly, what can the United Nations do for the United States. Nor must we be deceived by fears that the United States is "using" the United Nations for its own interests. The United Nations has no purposes other than those of its members, and is only the means of achieving those purposes. Whatever may be true for other nations, the purposes of the United Nations are, in the long run at least—and for the middle run, too—the purposes of American foreign policy. The United States is concerned to help achieve a world of nations at peace, enjoying independence with diversity, providing their peoples a decent share of the world's goods and opportunities; it can work to these ends through the United Nations. Peace, security—our own and that of others—effective control of armaments, improvement of the general economic and social welfare, are principal goals of American foreign policy as well as purposes of the United Nations. Even the immediate goals of the United States in the cold war (unlike those of the U.S.S.R.) are not far from those of the United Nations—support for the independence of nations, stability with peaceful change, foreign aid, and intelligent trade patterns. The need is to recognize, identify, even tailor U.S. interests common to those of the mass of United Nations members.

The internationalist must recognize also that the United Nations is not the only means for achieving United States goals, even the goals it has in common with the United Nations and with its members. Security against other big powers was one risk for which the United Nations was not—and could not—be equipped; the United Nations can only support national and allied defense efforts. Defending the democratic institutions of other countries against subversion may require national effort, with only ancillary support from the United Nations. The internationalist must also recognize that encouraging other forms of cooperation, whether in Europe or in the Americas, with appropriate degrees of U.S. participation, may contribute to United Nations goals directly, and build as well internationalist attitudes which will carry over into U.S. relations with the United Nations.

It is essential to recognize, too, that the United Nations has changed in basic ways; the changes reflect realization of initial error as well as adjustment to changes in the world which the United Nations represents.

The evolution of the United Nations may be epitomized in terms of its Secretaries General—from Lie to Hammarskjöld to Thant. Mr. Lie of Norway came to office with the original conception, and—as in Korea—dared to use the Charter and the institution even in support of one big power against another. Under Hammarskjöld of Sweden, and his adroit personal diplomacy, the United Nations did not take sides in the cold war, but rather mediated and moderated. The United Nations was for the interests of the small powers, including their interest in tempering the cold war. In the United Nations the big powers might even be made to support the interests of small powers. U Thant of Burma continues the process: the United Nations is almost universal; small and new nations are the large majority; the center of political gravity has moved to Asia, perhaps on the way to Africa. The cold war is of little interest except that it must be kept in check; colonialism and racism are the political targets, economic development the principal objective.

Slowness to recognize the evolution of the United Nations has troubled internationalism all along, but it did so particularly at the beginning. In the after-glow of World War II, we have suggested, some—including some in very high places—seemed to have the impression that with the United Nations would come the end of national power and its politics. But the United Nations did not abolish national power; it assumed and built on it. It also assumed that the allies of World War II would cooperate and join their power, adjusting or subordinating any conflicting interests, or at least sublimating them to a plane of political and economic competition. But while the principles were to apply to all, the Charter made no provision and intended no provision for protecting big powers against each other and small nations against big ones by enforcement action. Inevitably when the Soviet Union appeared to threaten other nations, small or big, provision had to be made outside the United Nations for the contingencies for which it did not (and could not) provide.

Isolationists and skeptics, of course, saw sooner the failure of the dream; they, in turn, failed to see what the United Nations could do or could be made to do. For some years, they went along, enjoying the hope that the United Nations might constitute a coalition against the Soviet Union. That hope terminated when the changing complexion of United Nations membership, combined with increasing Soviet sophistication, put an end to commonplace, overwhelming majorities against Russia. Too eager to reject the United Nations, isolationists and ultranationalists refused to see the interests of the United States which the new United Nations could serve. They were far less perceptive than the Russians who, recognizing the importance and potential of the United Nations, paid it the homage of attempting to frustrate or control it by *Troikas* and otherwise. The internationalist, on the other hand, reluctant to admit disappointment, was also slow to exploit the realistic potential of the United Nations. More serious still, he was reluctant to turn elsewhere to supply what the United Nations could not. In particular, he took too long to accept NATO. Failing to recognize early that NATO was not an inconsistent alternative to the United Nations, he helped others into that error; thinking they had to choose, they inevitably chose NATO, and turned from the United Nations.

The consequences of this error are still with us, and the internationalist must continue to fight it. As far as one can see, and regardless of test bans and other thaws in the cold war, there will be need for some defensive alliance against Soviet threat. Combined with this need, other forces have drawn our allies together and are exercising vague centripetal forces on the United States. One need not exaggerate the probability of radical political readjustments in an Atlantic Community to accept the likelihood of continued and extended relationships between the United States and western Europe. NATO itself may change radically in response to the changes since its creation, in the focus and character of the Soviet threat, in military weapons and strategy, in the condition of our allies. But the Atlantic area will surely remain an area of major concentration for U.S. policy.

The internationalist will welcome these policies. He will seek to promote attitudes and policies reflecting equality, cooperation, joint deliberation, and interest. But he will be alert to assure that the Atlantic Community and its variations should not become an alternative to the United Nations in U.S. foreign policy; it must be a complement to the United Nations and indeed a center for cooperation in making the United Nations effective for the important tasks which it can do now and in the future.

Recognizing that the United Nations is something different from what was once thought, the internationalist will be able to lead in constructive use of the United Nations for what it can do. If the United Nations is not capable of defending the United States or other nations against a major power, it can help deter such attacks. If the United Nations cannot prevent Soviet subversion, it can help deter such subversion as well as strengthen states and governments to render subversion less likely. The United Nations can play a big role in preventing hostilities not directly involving the United States and the Soviet Union. It can even help temper the cold war. It promises, perhaps, new United Nations roles, as in the Congo, in New Guinea, or in Malaysia. It can act as midwife for peaceful political and economic change, and itself administer programs of social and economic development. It can concentrate the policies of the powers of the world to influence the policies of one nation or another. For our conflict with communism, the United Nations can be more meaningful and more effective now that its membership is nearly universal and more variegated. While the United States (like the Soviet Union) gains little from blatant cold war propaganda and cold war skirmishes, the United States can gain considerably from action in the United Nations which supports peace, independence, and economic development.

The United Nations is an Instrument of International Politics. Perhaps the greatest confusion about the United Nations is common to its friends and foes. Foes point to cold war and world tension, to the spread of communism, to more-or-less patent international hostilities, and conclude that the United Nations has failed. This, of course, is old error. The United Nations reflects the interests and conflicts of the world. It can seek to accommodate these interests, prevent their irruption into active hostility, but it has no magic wand to make conflicting interests cease to conflict, and no force to enforce judgments. If the magic wand could be made, it is not clear that we would entrust it to anyone or any body; if the force could be created, it is not clear that any nation—including the United States—would agree to accept and submit to it.

The internationalist makes an analogous error. One hears periodic accusations by "friends" of the United Nations that it is being "by-passed" if some important issue between nations is not laid in its bosom. Of course, if resort to the United Nations is avoided even when other measures to deal peacefully with crises are not successful, the United Nations and its Charter may be reduced to neglected pieties. It is a very different matter, however, to insist that every issue arising between nations must come to the United Nations. Important international issues generally do come into its purview; it is not essential that they get there in any particular manner, at some particular time, or at all. Already it is a commonplace that it is no contribution to the growth of the United Nations to bring to it matters which are beyond its capabilities to improve. While it may be desirable occasionally to record a moral or political judgment, it does not help the United Nations if it takes action which will prove vain, either because it is irresponsible or because it so vitally affects some nation's interests that it could not comply. What is fundamental, the United Nations needs no "business." Like a national police or judicial system, the United Nations, ideally, should have no business at all. And the Charter itself makes it the primary duty of nations to settle their disputes themselves, provided they do it by peaceful means. Negotiation between the parties, if it leads to resolution, is, then, the first, the best, perhaps the only way for giving effect to the United Nations Charter and its system of order and law. Crises need not be prolonged, settlements need not be postponed or jeopardized, merely to give the United Nations a "role," or to build its record.

A special manifestation of this error, or of a similar error, may be found in the quest for disarmament. Here, too, the faults of the internationalist are not the most serious obstacles to a rational disarmament policy in the national interest. The isolationist and the ultra-nationalist are still reluctant to explore with open mind the possibility that agreed controls or limitations on armaments may contribute to U.S. security and other national interests more than can the uncertainties of the arms race. Some insist on more inspection than is necessary, instead of admitting that they oppose a particular—or any—disarmament agreement. Others have seized on real need for inducing and verifying compliance with a proposed agreement to make a principle of "inspection." Perhaps because they seek inspection for other purposes, they often fail to recognize that what is usually considered "inspection" is merely one way of verifying compliance with an agreement, that there may be other means of verification—perhaps less unacceptable to both the United States and the Soviet Union—that will deter violations and supply the necessary information as to whether a nation is complying. But if these are the errors of others, the internationalist, too, has contributed error. If he has not made a principle of inspection, he tends to make a principle of international inspection. He would like to use disarmament to help build the United Nations and auxiliary international institutions. But international inspection tied to the United Nations may not be the most effective detection system in all circumstances, and may not be acceptable to negotiating nations. Agreement on some disarmament measures may be more easy to achieve if inspection is left to reciprocal national verification—as in the Test Ban Agreement. Successful disarmament agreements may contribute measurably to international order, to strengthening the United Nations and other international institutions. Surely, quixotic insistance on international institutions should not become an obstacle to agreement on arms control or disarmament where it is otherwise in the national interest.

A related and perhaps even more serious misapprehension of the United Nations is that one can bring matters to it "for solution." The United Nations is not a judicial body before which two or more parties may seek an impartial decision in the light of accepted norms or principles. The United Nations is an instrument of international politics and diplomacy, a complicated, delicate, sometimes erratic instrument. It can do wonders, sometimes–in presenting varying interests and attitudes, focusing them on a given issue, making them available for adjustment and compromise, bringing other political influences to bear upon them.

With regard to issues of peace and security, the United Nations can be invoked in different ways, for different purposes, by different parties. In regard to those in which the Big Powers have major interest, the United Nations is an organism for concentrating political influence to contain and relax tensions. It is a forum for negotiations; it affords a means whereby other nations, with less involvement, can suggest adjustments and focus influence on parties who have not been able to resolve their differences. The United Nations might be used to gain support for a position which a party to a controversy seeks to maintain, or to compel concession from the other side. It might, on the other hand, be used by a state to let itself be "compelled" to make a concession or compromise that it is not prepared to make on its own. United Nations action, or the threat of United Nations action, might also be a means to bring about negotiations between parties or to affect the timing, progress, or outcome of negotiations.

In short, the United Nations is a political organization; the Security Council and the General Assembly are political bodies. They consist of representatives of nations. The United Nations can act on any issue only through the initiative of some members and the support of more, usually the vote of majorities. For the United States to bring a matter to the United Nations, wash its hands, and hope that some magic answer will come out would be reckless and irresponsible. What will come out will be influenced by what is put in, and what is done with it within the United Nations. And what the United Nations will do depends in large measure on what the United States proposes that it do, what policies it seeks, and what consultations, adjustments, and compromises can achieve. Taking an issue to the United Nations is not itself a "policy." It must not be a substitute for a policy; it should be a step in a policy and an instrument of a policy. The United States can bring an issue–whether Berlin, or Cuba, or Laos–to the United Nations, but it must know what it seeks, what policies consistent with the Charter and with the character of the organization it will ask for–as well as what is likely to come out.

III THE DIFFERENT FACES OF THE UNITED NATIONS

We have asserted that the United Nations is a political body. It needs also to be stressed, however, that there is another face to the United Nations—the law of the Charter; that the different faces—the law and the United Nations institution—are to be distinguished, as well as seen together in a total conception.

The UN Charter consists of two distinct elements. It is first a treaty in which adherents accept fundamental obligations, principally that (except in self-defense against armed attack) members must refrain from the threat or use of force against the territorial integrity or political independence of other states. (An ancillary requirement that members "settle their disputes by peaceful means" has not achieved affirmative significance, and in practice has seemed to mean only that members may not resort to force.) Other undertakings by members—for example, "to take joint and separate action in cooperation with" the United Nations to promote economic and social ends—are primarily hortatory, vague, and difficult to enforce. The bulk of the Charter, on the other hand, does not consist of obligations at all. It is a constituent document establishing institutions and defining their purpose, authority, and limitations. The Charter establishes various organs to maintain peace and to promote social and economic welfare; it distributes responsibility to various organs and calls for cooperation by the members.

The law of the Charter forbidding unilateral force is, of course, intertwined with the institutional pattern created by the Charter. One may say, indeed, that the primary purpose of the institution was to implement and enforce the law of the Charter against war. Unlike national self-help, the United Nations organs may authorize force when there is a threat to the peace even before armed attack has taken place. (At least as originally conceived there was no suggestion in the language or history of the Charter that the United Nations might authorize force for purposes other than maintaining peace, for example, to vindicate the principle of self-determination or the observance of human rights.)

The relation of the law to the institution, however, is more complicated than merely that of law to law enforcement. Authority to enforce includes the power not to enforce (as in Goa). In order to decide whether and how to enforce, moreover, the Security Council and the General Assembly must first sit in judgment on the action of member nations. And in the process of judgment and enforcement, inevitably the Council, and particularly the Assembly, exercise also legislative influence modifying the law of the Charter. In the first instance, of course, the actions of members, and the reactions of other members, have the effect of interpreting what the Charter obligations mean. Then, deliberations, recommendations, resolutions, and actions in the Council or Assembly inevitably determine what the law of the Charter means or may be held to mean in the future. That nations used and justified force at Suez, for example, inevitably entailed interpretation of the law of the Charter and an effort to persuade others to accept it. That the United States and other members held that this force was not justified constituted their different interpretation of the Charter. That the organs of the United Nations acted to have the use of force undone reinforced the meaning of the Charter as the majority interpreted it. Failure by the organs to take this action might, of course, have had important legislative consequences for the law of the Charter on the circumstances in which unilateral force may be used. Even little Goa—the action of India, its support by some members and its condemnation by others, the failure of any action by organs of the United Nations—has affected the meaning of the principle of the Charter against unilateral use of force, although it may be viewed by some as a special exception for attacks on colonialism (or even a smaller exception based on Goa's territorial relation to India) which hopefully will be limited there.

This built-in legislative, "amending" power, by nations and by the UN organs, may allow for changes in the law which have proved necessary in the experience of nations. It is of course a dangerous power, for passion and politics of the time may result in far-reaching, immature "amendment" of the original constitution. It was perhaps inevitable, and generally desirable, that the Charter be read to enhance the authority of various organs of the United Nations. Unhappily, other "amendments" to the Charter to date, and more that are threatened, would also erode the law of the Charter by increasing the circumstances in which nations may use self-help. But the law and the institutions are two faces of the United Nations profoundly interrelated. Supporters of the United Nations must remember, and remind others, that both faces exist; in particular, that there exists a fundamental legal obligation not to use force quite apart from anything the UN organs do, that the outlawing of unilateral force is a fundamental aspect of "the United Nations." Without the law against self-help, the institution lacks its principle purpose; indeed, one might question whether the United Nations could survive merely as a "legislature" without a "Constitution," without the basic principle of "order"—the prohibition of national force in self-help. Neither the law nor the institution may exert decisive influence in the determination of national policies; both exert appreciable, variable weight in support of international order. It is far from clear that the Charter, universally accepted and paid even the homage of hypocrisy, exerts a lesser deterrent effect than institutional majorities. Together, law and institution promise substantial hope for substantial order.

The law is essential, and the institution's primary purpose is to enforce that law. But the institution is a political body, not a court of law invoked by an agency dedicated to law enforcement. Even where it is agreed that the law has been violated, what shall be done about it is determined by the organs of the United Nations and these, we emphasize, are political institutions of international diplomacy. The United Nations, and United States policy in the United Nations, should support Charter observance, but they must also take into account the context of relations which led to the Charter violation, the character of the

United Nations, and the attitudes of the nations that compose it. One may applaud the leadership of the United States in bringing the United Nations to the aid of the Republic of Korea. One need not blame the United States for dropping the question of Goa in the circumstances of the case. Surely, the United States cannot raise the question of the incursions of Communist China against India so long as India for its own reasons does not seek the assistance of the United Nations or of its members in that forum.

At Suez, on the other hand, one may well ask whether the United States acted with proper understanding of the relation of the law of the Charter to the political institutions that constitute the United Nations. The attacks at Suez and Sinai were unlawful, but they had been provoked by Egyptian actions which were also not wholly consistent with the spirit of the Charter. Other violations of international law were charged, other national interests were claimed to have been violated. In the circumstances, even a judicial body might well have issued a decree which would have dealt both with the violation and its causes. Surely the General Assembly—a political body—might have dealt with the causes, with the seizure of the Canal, with the basic issues between Egypt and Israel, when it sought to undo the violations of the Charter.

Parliamentary Diplomacy. When we think about U.S. policy toward and in the United Nations, we think, usually, not of the obligations to refrain from force, but about U.S. attitudes toward the institutions established by the Charter, particularly the General Assembly. The deliberations and resolutions of these organs of the United Nations are political; the procedures, the motivations, the influences governing them are political.

I do not propose to draw sharp lines between commands (by the Security Council) and recommendations (usually by the General Assembly). In view of the veto, the Security Council cannot usually command an unwilling United States. For present purposes, whether the United States should exercise a veto in the Security Council raises many of the issues involved in the question whether the United States should disregard a recommendation of the Assembly. When the Assembly seeks to maintain international peace and security, moreover, its recommendations are in support of legal obligations in the Charter and deserve and command the highest compliance and support. Nor do I insist that legal obligations are very different from political incentives. In international affairs, in particular, the violation of legal obligations may be more offensive to morality, but its consequences are also largely "political"; and while most nations are—and should be—more reluctant to breach an obligation than to disregard a recommendation, all states will do the one or the other in some circumstances, with the political consequences the principal deterrent to non-compliance in either case.

Still, for whatever difference it may make, the "decisions" of the United Nations which concern us here are not legal adjudications or determinations, but political recommendations. The principal "recommender"—the General Assembly—is a special kind of political body. The United Nations now has 111 members and all are represented equally in the General Assembly. Equal vote suggests a body based not on the realities of power or any other selected qualities deemed relevant, but on a concept of equality of all nation-states. And decision by majority suggests another a priori concept—the right to make political judgments and decisions by majority of these nations acting as a parliament.

All of us are tempted, of course, to translate the familiar to the necessary. Americans think of institutions as democratic, to be run by a majority vote. And other nations, even those who do not know democracy or parliamentary majority vote at home, seek or accept it in the organs of the United Nations. The result is a body applying parliamentary practices to representatives, not of individuals, but of nations and governments. But it is far from clear that if the nation is a "natural unit" for some purposes, it is the proper unit for this purpose. If we recognize the right of nations to discuss any matter of international concern, one may yet ask whether issues arising in the discussion should be "decided" by majority vote of the nations. (In international conferences generally, nations are bound only by what they themselves agree to.) The "parliamentary body," moreover, represents a world which is not a unit with common agreed interests. The nations do not constitute a commonwealth dedicated to a common weal in all areas; the constitution to which they are committed is not universal or all-embracing; the issues that come before the United Nations include matters of divergent interest not covered by Charter commitment or other clear, agreed guiding principles.

Again, one might distinguish between questions. We lay aside internal questions of organization—whether membership, representation, or the selection of a Secretary-General. These must, of course, be decided by majority, as the Charter contemplated, and outvoted nations must acquiesce. In regard to substantive matters, issues of war and peace perhaps affect all nations sufficiently to suggest that, in a world of nations, the views of a majority of nations ought generally to prevail. Many economic and social issues, on the other hand, affect different nations differently, even if not always along the lines of "have" or "have-not." Other issues—colonialism, human rights—surely affect different nations differently, and have different importance for the "world community."

One must distinguish, too, among the different characters and roles played by the United Nations and the different kinds of action taken or recommended. The "majority vote" has different significance when two nations are urged to stop fighting and accept UN machinery to keep the peace (Gaza, for instance); when it recommends a guide to national policy for all nations (as in the Declaration of Human Rights); when it calls for specific political action by a particular nation (say, South Africa); when it establishes an economic program (like the United Nations Special Fund).

I would not favor changing the voting system; equality is the hallmark of prestige and sovereignty, particularly for the new nations, and its rigors are modified by influence enjoyed and exerted by advantaged nations. I am not suggesting that one nation-one vote should apply to issues of war and peace only, or to some issues and not to others. That is no longer feasible, and efforts to achieve it would be fraught with difficulty and danger to the United Nations. What is suggested is that the members of the General Assembly in their debates and in their recommendations must recognize the "artifical" character of their role. They must recognize, in particular, that their interest, their right to judge and recommend is very different in regard to sending police to help maintain the peace, from what it is when they recommend that a few nations contribute large sums to a development fund, or even that they disarm in ways which they believe may seriously affect their security. Internationalists surely must judge differently the different actions and the respect they deserve.

In our context, the United Nations is a voice of conscience, of world opinion and influence. If the voice is firm and clear and responsible, and represents a largely united United Nations membership, it will frequently be heard and heeded. Smaller nations will be more obedient (unless, as in the case of Communist satellites, a bigger one offers protection). *In extremis*, any nation will disregard the voice of the United Nations if important self-interests are believed at stake. In general, the West is more sensitive, more reluctant to face the guilt and the political cost of disregarding it. The Communist countries have frequently flouted it, but even they must pay it some respect. The point is that the issues that may come before the United Nations because they are now of international concern, require of all member nations maturity, self-restraint, responsibility. And it may be that whether other nations–say, the United States–should be obliged to listen and to follow majority decisions, may depend exactly on the issue involved, the responsibility with which it was considered and the decision voted–as well as how deeply it cuts into vital U.S. interests. The opinion of the International Court of Justice, which apparently recognizes as a legal obligation financial assessments by the General Assembly for any purpose, only underscores the need for responsibility in majority action.

There may be some occasions when irresponsible action on the part of United Nations members will compel the United States to refuse to go along. There may be occasions when vital U.S. interests are jeopardized by some call from a UN majority. They will be rare. Internationalists will recognize that UN majorities are also not infallible or irresistible, and that ultimately the United States may have to act as in its own enlightened judgment its security dictates. But internationalists will scrutinize sharply every suggestion that the United States disregard a UN resolution, and conclude reluctantly that it must do so in a particular, rare case. They must not allow every "violation" to become a rejection of the United Nations, or a precedent for further non-compliance.

To admit that UN actions are political and that there may be instances when the United States may feel compelled not to comply is hardly to adopt the recent suggestion that the United States pays too much attention to the United Nations or cares too much for so-called world opinion, at expense to its own interests. The relation, in general, of U.S. interests to UN interests has been considered. In regard to "world opinion," both proponents and opponents in recent exchanges seem to be aiming beside the point. Of course, we have said, the United States must look to its own interest; but may not its true interest lie in working through the United Nations, in seeking to mobilize its resources and its influence for a desired policy? May not true U.S. interest lie in giving substantial respect to UN resolutions so that it can build the influence of the United Nations and of such resolutions? Attention to world opinion is not a duty; it may only be a necessity when we are engaged in a struggle much of which is a struggle for men's opinions. As the United Nations is a particular focus of "world opinion," we can disregard it only with acute awareness of the need to do so. It is surprising that the "realists" so alert to the realities of the politics of national power are so insensitive to the realities of the politics of multinational power, focused at the United Nations.

IV THE CASE OF CUBA

One ought not end this self-examination without some words about Cuba. Recent developments there afford hard lessons for supporters of the United Nations. They suggest, first, that it is sometimes as difficult to define the "internationalist position" on an issue as it is to indicate the "liberal position" on domestic questions involving sharply competing values. Perhaps one must conclude that in extreme situations involving the national security, internationalist positions differ less markedly from those of ultra-nationalists, though their tone and their procedures may be very different. Cuba also stirs echoes of *inter arma silent leges*, or, at least, of Mr. Justice Holmes' comment that hard cases make bad law; some internationalists and *soi-disant* supporters of the United Nations have seemed prepared to accept and even promote some very bad law. In fact, the hardest lesson may be that, in crisis, internationalists must guard against the temptation to be or appear to be more nationalist than the ultra-nationalists.

The U.S. action in the Cuban incident, its apparent "success," and its acceptance by the U.S.S.R., promise important if yet uncertain consequences for international relations and for U.S. foreign policy. Their impact on the United Nations is less clear. Perhaps the consequences may be very different for the two different faces of the United Nations—the UN institution and the law of the Charter. The UN institution proved important as an available forum or context for negotiation and, perhaps–in the person of the Secretary-General–of good offices and impartiality. (To the United States it also afforded an important political forum to prove its case and disarm critical international political opinion.) For the authority of the organs of the United Nations to control the use of force, and for the law of the Charter, the consequences are less cheerful. Most distressing are the lengths to which even United Nations supporters have felt obliged to go to justify the action of the United States.

United States relations with Castro's Cuba have been a trial for internationalism almost from the beginning. Internationalists were particularly unhappy about the abortive invasion in April 1961. If, as appears, there was substantial involvement by the United States, the action was unilateral, and its failure, and events since, have helped to belie any justification for the action in "necessity," as well as the need to act alone. Although the United States was supporting an action by "rebel" Cubans, a major role by the United States was probably illegal, violating the less ambiguous principles of international law–the charters of the United Nations and the Organization of American States. The "quarantine" imposed in October 1962, also disturbed internationalists, but with different and more complex cause. Some were reluctant to conclude that developments in Cuba so imperiled U.S. security as to require measures which created a serious danger of nuclear war. Some–probably a small minority, even among internationalists–also had doubts about the steps taken. Accepting the facts as alleged, they wondered whether Soviet missile bases in Cuba would substantially increase the danger to the United States since–they had been led to believe–the Soviet Union had adequate missiles elsewhere which could destroy–hence deter–the United States. If the Cuban bases had primarily political rather than military objectives, these critics were more disposed to question the need for the blockade, and particularly its precipitateness and its unilateral aspects. They raised questions also about the legality of the measures taken, both as concerned Cuba and the nations whose vessels might be affected. A blockade is a violation of "the freedom of the seas," a "warlike" act and–they argued–a use of force contrary to the UN Charter. If at all, such measures could be justified only pursuant to UN resolution; at least nothing should have been done until after attempts in and through the United Nations to resolve the difficulties by negotiation and good offices.

These critical views were expressed, but most internationalists apparently did not share them. They, too, perhaps, were uncertain about the military importance of Cuban bases; but it was probable, they thought, that although the Soviet Union supposedly had short-range missiles in plenty, it had only a few intercontinental missiles at home (and not many submarines which could launch shorter-range missiles at the U.S.). Hitherto, then, Europe had been the principle target of Soviet missiles, and the hostage for the West; Cuban bases would bring the United States and the Latin American countries within reach of missiles of shorter range. That would complicate the theory and politics of deterrence, render less credible our commitment to risk destruction at home in behalf of the defense of Europe, and jeopardize the present international stability; it would also seriously unsettle the peace of this hemisphere.

Those who accepted the desirability of the quarantine also sought to justify it as consistent with the obligations of the United States to the United Nations and the UN Charter. Of course, they said, self-help should be avoided; in principle it might have been preferable to take measures (even the quarantine) only pursuant to authorization by the United Nations, after attempts to determine impartially the facts charged by the United States and to achieve the voluntary elimination by Cuba and the U.S.S.R. of the threatening weapons. But while this might have been preferable in principle, it was not realistic to demand it, and might have seriously jeopardized the success of the move. It was important to stop further missiles from coming into Cuba as well as to prevent the completion of the missile sites. Also, UN action might have been futile; it is most unlikely that the United Nations would have authorized the quarantine in the face of Soviet and Cuban denials and opposition; and unilateral action by the United States after failure to obtain UN approval would have been more difficult and even more violative of "internationalism" and the spirit of the Charter.

That the United States acted without authorization by the United Nations may reflect adversely on the institution. Even more likely, it will affect the law of the Charter. Clearly, the United States asserted the right to take action involving military power against the interests of other nations–Cuba, the Soviet Union, as well as others whose vessels plied to Cuba–without the authorization of an appropriate organ of the United Nations. Still, sober examination, with due concern for both the immediate interests and the ultimate importance of preserving the Charter, does not leave the United States without a case. The U.S. quarantine was new to international relations and to international law. Apart from the UN Charter, international law has no certain rule barring this kind of action in these circumstances. (Under traditional international law, the United States could presumably have rendered even a full blockade lawful by declaring war against Cuba.) The "freedom of the seas"–so far as it subsumes legal rules rather than a political slogan–was perhaps not seriously compromised by a limited blockade barring delivery of weapons of special character to one country in the novel context of "balance of terror." Under the UN Charter, it may be that the U.S. action was not clearly authorized; but, of course, major Soviet military buildup in Cuba, with purposes and effects far beyond the defense of Cuba, and deeply disturbing to stability in the hemisphere as well as to East-West relations, is even more likely a violation of the spirit–if not of some letter–of the Charter.

The legal issues under the Charter have also been less than clearly conceived. The principal issue of law, properly, is whether in the circumstances the blockade was a "threat or use of force against the territorial integrity or political independence" of Cuba or of other nations, or "in any other manner inconsistent with the purposes of the United Nations" (Article 2, §4). One may argue that the blockade, strictly speaking, involved no "use of force" within the meaning of the Charter, and that even the threats of force in the background, conditioned on legitimate demands, were minimal. One may argue, too, that any force involved was not against the territorial integrity or political independence of Cuba, or of Russia, or of the nations whose vessels were affected. Nor, it may be urged, was any force involved "inconsistent with the purposes of the United Nations." The action taken had no aggressive purpose, but was designed, rather, to eliminate a potential threat to peace. Moreover, while not authorized by any organ of the United Nations, it was not unilateral either; it was taken pursuant to a resolution of the Organization of American States, a regional arrangement under Chapter VIII of the Charter. This kind of regional organization furthers the purposes of the United Nations. Its interests and actions conform to the UN Charter, even if in the instant case the weapons and the vessels in question belonged to powers outside the region. The action here authorized was not inconsistent with what was contemplated for regional organizations; only "enforcement action"–a term suggesting something more than this limited blockade[1]–requires the prior authorization of the Security Council (Article 53).

Not wholly to the point has been the discussion of Article 51: "Nothing in the present Charter shall impair the inherent right of . . . self-defense if an armed attack occurs against a member of the United Nations. . . ." This article does not become relevant unless it is concluded that the U.S. action was contrary to Article 2(4) or some other provision of the Charter. Only then need one ask whether, despite such *prima facie* violation, the action of the United States is permissible under the exception provided by Article 51. Recognizing that Article 51 intended to reaffirm Article 2 and provide only a narrow exception permitting the use of military force if an armed attack occurs, one might say that, like Article 2, neither Article 51 nor any invisible radiations from it necessarily bar lesser action than actual fighting (for example, the quarantine) against threats of armed attack, against hostile, offensive armed preparations, against new strategic deployments disturbing to peace and stability. The "self-help" indulged by the United States was moderate: it involved no invasion of Cuban territory and no destruction; it was easy to terminate and undo; it was not unilateral, but done only after authorization by all the nations primarily concerned in a regional arrangement dedicated to the principles of the United Nations.

Some such argument can respectably be made. It would claim that the United States did not violate the Charter, but acted in accordance with an interpretation and necessary development of it in support of its basic principles. It might draw

---

[1]One may make something, perhaps, of the fact that another use in the Charter of the phrase "enforcement action" seems to distinguish it from "preventive action" (Article 2[5]); the blockade, in the circumstances, may be said to be more "preventive" than "enforcement."

a line in the definition of "force" in Article 2 in the light of the new technology and the delicate balance of terror which it has wrought; in that context, beyond the powers of UN organs to improve, states might be permitted to take minimal, non-destructive, revocable measures–measures short of war, short of actual shooting, and therefore not likely to "escalate"–in order to preserve the defensive balance and to contribute to international stability. And even such moderate steps might be permissible, perhaps, only when authorized by a regional organization like the OAS, the special character of which was recognized, and special authority for it contemplated, when the Charter was being drafted. This might, also, draw a line in the definition of "enforcement action," permitting the OAS the kind of moderate measures taken in Cuba even without authorization of the Security Council.

Such development of the Charter is in the spirit of constitutional growth. And the acquiescence of the Soviet Union will help confirm this development. Some may think this justification, too, not warranted by the principles relevant to the interpretation of the Charter today; some may find even this justification dangerous, opening loopholes of unknown dimension. Nations, however, must justify their actions; and it is desirable that international law receive at least that homage, even if some will consider it the homage of hypocrisy. But it matters very much which justification is offered. In my view, the one suggested is intellectually respectable, and need not prove destructive of the fundamental principles and purposes of the Charter. Unfortunately, even some staunch supporters of the United Nations have seen fit, instead, to suggest new readings of the Charter which threaten to stretch it until it bursts. They have announced a doctrine in interpretation of Article 51 which would permit use of total force, unilaterally, in "anticipatory self-defense," or perhaps even as "reprisal" in "protection of vital interests."

The issue is not new. Already, in regard to Suez, voices were heard urging the need to recognize the right to use self-help in response to hostile array of force, to action against "vital" national interests, to violations of international law and justice. Otherwise, it was said, since international law is still primitive, international adjudication minimal, international enforcement of law non-existent, injustice would be rampant and go unrectified. At that time, however, most students of the Charter saw no basis for any such additional exceptions permitting the unilateral use of force. Now, in the case of Cuba, even erstwhile supporters of the Charter principle, when France, Great Britain, and Israel felt compelled to act to vindicate important national interests, seem prepared to abandon it to justify U.S. action in protection of important national interests.

Few would suggest that the Charter can mean only what it once meant. The Charter is a constituent document and cannot be read only in the light of what was said, or intended, or foreseen, even by the most gifted of its begetters. It "is a Constitution we are expounding," and it must be read in the light of what has happened and what the world has become since the Charter was written. The law, like the institutions of the United Nations, must grow to reflect changes in nations, in relations between nations, in the force available to affect relations between nations. But reinterpretation of the Charter is a dangerous and delicate process. It is hardly constructive "interpretation" to "develop" the Charter by eviscerating its fundamental principle—the prohibition of unilateral force. A lawyer wishing to justify tearing up article 2(4)—the heart of the Charter—could even argue that it was intended to apply only in circumstances which have not in fact remained: that self-help was outlawed only on the assumption that, in accordance with the original conception, the Big Powers would keep and maintain the peace; that it was not intended to apply at all to the Big Powers *inter se*; that the provisions against self-help were not intended to apply when Big Powers today (and smaller ones tomorrow) can launch sudden devastating attacks with obliterating weapons. The notion of *rebus sic stantibus*—that agreements are binding only so long as circumstances are as they existed or were contemplated at the time of the agreement—is a classic attempt at avoiding treaty obligations; maybe it can apply even to a treaty like the United Nations Charter. But the question is not whether some argument can be made in justification if one wishes to tear up the Charter. The question is rather whether the Charter principle against force is still relevant in the new circumstances.

Of course, there may be some who think that outlawing force in today's world is unrealistic, undesirable, even dangerous and immoral. Others may think this international law, or all international law, an idle irrelevance. If law makes no difference, it makes no difference what the law says. Specifically, many may question whether the law against the use of force has any political significance, whether it has really deterred or prevented any nation from the use of force. Though we must give to the new weapons the major credit for deterring war, it is not irrelevant to suggest that refraining from force which begins in fear may yet become a principle of behavior. In fact, situations not involving directly, or necessarily, the big powers and their big weapons, also have not irrupted into war. In fact, nations generally seem to have been acquiring the attitude that war "is not done"; surely, with notable but few exceptions, traditional war has ceased to figure in the diplomatic planning of nations. (The new substitutes—subversion, insurrection, civil war—also present serious problems, but not the scourge of war; what, if anything, law can do about them is a different and difficult inquiry.)

The United Nations supporter, in any event—even if partly as an act of faith—has believed in the importance of putting the prohibitions on war into the law of the United Nations. If, then, even in cold war and among terrible weapons, the law of the United Nations matters, the United Nations supporter who thinks the Charter had better be read differently than we read it before Cuba must see where his reading leads. Surely they misconceive both international law and the interests of the United States who say that international law and the UN Charter are all right, but they cannot stand in the way of important national interests. (They, too, would do well to attend, at least, to the uses of law even in the politics of power, and the importance of legality in Soviet policies.) They misconceive both the significance of the United Nations and the character of new war who suggest that the basic concept of the Charter—outlawing unilateral use of force—cannot apply in the day of modern weapons. It was that mild, old-fashioned Second World War which persuaded all nations that for the future national interests will have to be vindicated, or necessary change achieved, as well as can be by political means, but not by war and military self-help. They recognized the exception of self-defense in emergency, but limited to actual armed attack, which is clear, unambiguous, subject to proof, and not easily open to misinterpretation or fabrication. Surely today's weapons render it even more important that nations should not be allowed to cry "vital interests" or "anticipatory self-defense" and unleash the fury. It is precisely in the age of the major deterrent that nations should be encouraged to strike first under pretext of prevention or preemption.

The argument that "anticipatory self-defense" is essential to United States defense is fallacious. The United States relies for its security on its retaliatory power, and primarily on its second strike capability. It does not expect that it would be able to anticipate an attack and it could not afford to be mistaken, to bring about total war by a "pre-emptive strike," if the Soviet Union were not in fact striking or preparing to strike. In all probability, then, only an actual take-off by Soviet planes or missiles would cause the United States to strike, and in that case the United States is not "anticipating" an armed attack, for the attack would have begun.

In fact, of course, for determining what the Charter means or should mean, the nuclear attack and the pre-emptive strike are not the relevant concerns. A nation planning all-out attack will not be deterred by the Charter, though it may well talk "anticipatory self-defense" to any left to listen. Nor does one prescribe rules for the nation threatened with such an attack. If a nation is satisfied that another is about to obliterate it, it will not wait. But it has to make that decision on its own awesome responsibility. Anticipation in that case may have to be practiced; it need not be preached. The Charter need not make a principle of it; the law need not authorize or encourage it. But surely that extreme hypothetical case beyond the realm of law should not be used to justify new rules for situations that do not involve the impending mortal thrust. Anticipatory self-defense as a rule of law has meaning only in less extreme cases. There, anticipatory self-defense, it should be clear, is a euphemism for "preventive war." The UN Charter does not authorize it. Nothing in international relations, including the new weapons, suggests that international society would be better if the Charter were changed—or read—to authorize it.

In any event, it should be clear, Cuba was not a case of "beating to the punch" someone who was about to strike. To say that whoever sets up "offensive weapons" justifies pre-emptive use of force would justify force by everyone everywhere. All nations are now faced by someone with power to strike them. Most weapons are "offensive" and could be used offensively. "Anticipatory self-defense," to be a meaningful extension, rather than a total rejection of any limitation on force, must surely entail some clear, present expectation of attack. Even a hundred years before the Charter, when war was legal, the right of self-defense was–said Secretary Webster in the *Caroline* case–limited to cases in which the "necessity of that self-defense is instant, overwhelming, and leaving no choice of means, and no moment for deliberation." And Webster's words were reaffirmed at Nürnberg.

If there were no other possible justification of the U.S. action than this destruction of the basic law of the Charter, one might do better, in effect, to plead "peccavimus," make some lame statement virtually admitting a violation, rather than to claim this new interpretation of the Charter. Indeed, lawyers who would justify military actions, whether in Suez, Goa, or Cuba, by exaggerated readings of Article 2 or of Article 51 may deal more serious blows to the United Nations and to the Charter than did these and other military actions themselves. One may recall, *mutatis mutandis,* what was said by the late Mr. Justice Jackson when the Supreme Court of the United States was asked to uphold the validity of a different military action:

"A military order, however unconstitutional, is not apt to last longer than the military emergency. . . . But once a judicial opinion rationalizes such an order to show that it conforms to the Constitution, or rather rationalizes the Constitution to show that the Constitution sanctions such an order, the Court for all time has validated the principle. . . . The principle then lies about like a loaded weapon ready for the hand of any authority that can bring forward a plausible claim of an urgent need. Every repetition imbeds that principle more deeply in our law and thinking and expands it to new purposes. All . . . are familiar with what Judge Cardozo described as 'the tendency of a principle to expand itself to the limit of its logic.' A military commander may overstep the bounds of constitutionality, and it is an incident. But if we review and approve, that passing incident becomes the doctrine of the Constitution. There it has a generative power of its own, and all that it creates will be in its own image."

In fact, as we have seen, what the United States actually did does not require emasculation of the Charter to justify it. President Kennedy and his advisers had a better understanding, even of the legal issues, than have some international lawyers and some "friends" of the United Nations who have sought to justify the action. The President recognized, apparently, that to read Article 51 as permitting the unilateral use of force merely because another nation achieves some capacity to strike would jeopardize the Charter. His action claimed only the right, in order to preserve international stability, to take moderate, non-destructible, revocable measures; and these (and even the limited, more active force which he threatened) he justified because they were taken following authorization by the Organization of American States.

United Nations supporters might still differ about Cuba. Most of them will probably follow President Kennedy's lead including his small extension of the Charter. But no one ought delude himself into thinking that one can "support the United Nations" while jeopardizing its basic advance in international law and the chief purpose of the UN Charter—the outlawing of war for national purposes. The obligation of nations to settle disputes peacefully, and the role of the United Nations in seeing that they do so, must inevitably decline if we expand the right of nations to use force in self-help. One does not support the United Nations by bringing back the day of "defensive" wars and "just" wars as each nation sees its needs of defense, its claim of justice.

Doubtless, internationalism—is no longer open to question, and internationalist policies will inevitably permeate U.S. foreign relations. The wisdom of many internationalist attitudes will continue to be recognized; some of them are inevitable, as even skeptics have learned when they took on the responsibilities of government. In addition, the engagement of U.S. interests and prestige in the cold war, and the passionate desire of ultra-nationalists, even of isolationists, for some undefined "victory"—which might well consist of maintaining or converting attitudes of other nations—will assure substantial internationalism in the years ahead. That other unexplored phenomenon of American politics—isolationism combined with vehement paternalism in the Pacific—will also help assure a more general internationalism, as supporters of action in the Pacific bargain for the support of internationalists.

So far as one can foresee, American internationalism will continue to include support for the United Nations. This support has survived radical transformations in the Organization, and in relations between nations; it will probably not be seriously jeopardized by further change, even emotionally laden events like the seating of Chinese Communist representatives. But the place of the United Nations in U.S. foreign policy is not the article of faith it was in 1945, or even a firm habit acquired since. For those who see in the United Nations an important means toward the major ends of American foreign policy, there are lessons to be learned and applied. We must recognize that internationalism, as reflected in the United Nations, is hardly the common faith of the American citizen; that while he may have the hopes and aspirations and ideals of internationalism, he is not in the habit of its attitudes and is not adjusted to its frustrations. We will have to persuade increasing numbers of citizens that supporting the United Nations is not soft-headed, wild-eyed, long-haired; that it may or may not be idealistic, but is eminently realistic; that it may be principled, but is wholly practical; that it is not a subtle form of near-treason, but, on the contrary, the most effective way of promoting American national interest. And we may not be able to count heavily on general "support for the United Nations," but will have to sell every particular measure and program on its merits.

To persuade others we will have to persuade ourselves. To be persuaded we will have to be accurate. In sum, we must understand the United Nations. We will ourselves have to recognize–and insist on–the basic principle of order on which the United Nations rests: force must not be used unilaterally for national purposes except in the extreme, defined, provable emergency of an armed attack. This principle reflects a recognition that war is no longer tolerable, and that other means must be found or developed to adjust relations between states. This obligation is fundamental. On it depend the United Nations, internationalism, world peace, the interests and survival of this nation and of other nations. It is the cornerstone of any rule of law. It cannot be observed by some nations or on some days. If this principle is destroyed or eroded, all hopes for international order will be destroyed or eroded. We will have to understand, too, the United Nations institution, not as it was, but as it is. We will have to judge it not by some faith or theory, but in the acid of national interest, enlightened, in a context of other national interests both common and competing. We will have to see political interests (like those of the United States) and institutions (like the United Nations) not with the eyes of romance and nostalgia, but with the eyes of sober citizens seeking in a real world a society we can contemplate, not with a shudder, but with hope.

The United Nations in Crisis

H. G. Nicholas

The twentieth birthday of the United Nations finds the Organization in a state of crisis. There is nothing so very surprising in this; the UN lives in a crisis-ridden world. But unlike most previous UN crises this one has largely eluded the awareness of British public opinion. Coming to a head at a time when the public mind was concentrating on the election of a new government and its subsequent battle for the pound, the impasse at the 19th General Assembly received often cursory or unobtrusive treatment at the hands of the British Press, while the emphasis of British official pronouncements fell, perhaps inevitably, upon the more reassuring aspects of the situation. The impression given was similar to that induced by a series of optimistic medical bulletins upon the victim of a stroke–only one side of the patient is affected, his speech is only partially impaired, with rest and care there is no reason why a normal life should not be resumed, etc. The result has been to deaden public awareness about the gravity of the UN's malady, while leaving the public mind confused about its causes. In particular, there has been a failure to distinguish between the short- and long-term causes, between those which have their roots in topical political disputes and those which arise from permanent changes in the political structure of the organisation.

It is, of course, obvious that the crisis is only in the most superficial sense a financial one. The UN finds itself short of money only because rich and powerful states have decided that it is in their interests to reduce it to such pecuniary embarrassment. And the reasons for their decision have very little to do with pressures from national treasuries; they reflect in all cases reasons of state elaborated in foreign ministries. That is why efforts to devise self-sustaining sources

H. G. Nicholas, "The United Nations in Crisis," *International Affairs*, Vol. 41, No. 3 (July 1965), pp. 441-450. Reprinted by permission of the author.

of revenue for the UN, like licence fees for the use of outer space or mineral rights in Antarctica, are merely exercises in misplaced ingenuity. Whatever the intrinsic desirability of such UN instrumentalities may be, their invocation in this context is misplaced. They confuse cash with authorisation, the right to own with the right to spend, the means with the ends. Basically the dispute is over what the UN should do, not over what it should spend in doing it.

In 1961, in the introduction to his last annual report to the General Assembly, Dag Hammarskjöld drew a now celebrated distinction between two concepts of the character of the UN then current amongst its membership.

"Certain members conceive of the Organisation as a static conference machinery for resolving conflicts of interests and ideologies with a view to peaceful coexistence within the Charter, to be served by a Secretariat which is to be regarded not as fully international but as representing within its ranks those very interests and ideas.

"Other members have made it clear that they conceive of the Organisation primarily as a dynamic instrument of governments through which they, jointly and for the same purpose, should seek such reconciliation but through which they should also try to develop forms of executive action, undertaken on behalf of all members, and aiming at forestalling conflicts and resolving them, once they have arisen, by appropriate diplomatic or political means, in a spirit of objectivity and in implementation of the principles and purposes of the Charter."

With a high degree of consistency the U.S.S.R. has led forth the Communist bloc as the champions of the first view, while the U.S.A. as the initiator of the Uniting for Peace resolution and the principal underwriter of such operations as Suez and the Congo has been the most notable advocate of the second.

Until at least the Cuba clash in the autumn of 1962 the gulf between these two concepts could be seen to be widening. It was dramatised in the clash over the succession to the Secretary-Generalship, the *troika* concept of calculated immobility being trotted out to check the development of the political potentialities of the office; it ran through all the East-West debates about the UN's proper role in the Congo. If the dispute over Congo and Suez financing had come to a head at that time it would have been natural to have seen it as the surface manifestation of this deeper dissension over the nature and functions of the organisation. It had been after all in relation to these peculiarly dynamic and, in the most literal sense, extraordinary manifestations of UN executive capacity that the financial issue had first arisen. For the Soviet Union, once its veto had been by-passed, the organisation of a financial stranglehold offered the best alternative method of getting the organisation away from its executive role and back to its conference function.

In an important sense this still remains the essence of the disagreement which has focused itself in the dispute over Article 19. For the Soviet Union indeed it may be the whole of what is at issue; a thorough-going Soviet victory which reversed the opinion of the UNEF and the ONUC were *not* expenses of the organisation and so were not legally chargeable to members, would go far to invalidate the legality of the Suez and Congo operations and would substantially erase them as precedents for comparable peace-keeping operations in the future.

But although an outright voting victory in the General Assembly would thus uphold the Soviet strict constructionist approach to the Charter, the reverse did not, and still does not necessarily hold. Those who, with the United States, advocated the broader, more elastic interpretation of the Charter and the General Assembly's and Secretary-General's roles within it, did not and do not require a rigid application of Article 19 in order to sustain their contention. While a refusal to pay, if sustained, can be used to knock out any peace-keeping operation past or prospective, it is not true that an insistence on payment is a *sine qua non* for such operations either now or subsequently. It would, after all, as a matter of practical expediency, have been perfectly possible for the expenses to be apportioned so that they were payable only by those who wished to pay them. To take an extreme case, the U.S.A. and her closest supporters could have paid them all, as they did in Korea. Why then, was it decided to draw the lines in such a way as to risk a confrontation? A confrontation, moreover, in which the West would stand to lose more by a defeat than to gain by a victory? Before establishing exactly what is at stake in the present crisis it is necessary to find an answer to these questions.

American support, both official and private, for the UN has been strong and, in the main, consistent over the 20 years since San Francisco. That the organisation exists and functions at all is due more to the United States than to any single nation. But there is a haunting paradox about the American role in the organisation, the paradox of the rich member in the poor man's club. The disparity between the U.S.A.'s economic strength and that of any other member is reflected in the 32 percent assessment levied on the United States in respect of the regular UN budget.[1] This creates problems; there is the problem for the other members of taking care, in the interests of the corporate health of the organisation, that they do not become too dependent on American generosity, too reluctant to pay their own share of the dues. There is also a problem for the United States, the nagging concern that Uncle Sam will be treated as a sugar-plum daddy and played for a sucker, his generosity mistaken for simple-mindedness, his wealth used to subsidize others' indolence. Hence the sustained campaign in the General Assembly's Fifth Committee to get the original United States assessment of 40

[1] For the total annual budget of all UN activities the U.S.A.'s contribution, assessed and voluntary, is even greater–almost $200m. out of $500m.

percent scaled down to its present 32 percent (and even greater proportionate reductions in respect of some other special UN assessments). At one time in respect of the UNEF and the ONUC the United States was paying almost half the cost. That the U.S.S.R., in addition to vilifying American policy in the forum of the UN, should be able to evade altogether its own, considerably smaller, assessments in respect of both operations has been a sharp thorn in the American side. That France, a NATO ally, should do the same in respect of the ONUC was in some respects more galling. That poorer countries should also at the same time be agitating for a capital development programme which would impose further charges on the "well-to-do" was yet another reason for the United States to see that outstanding arrears were paid up all around.

The officials in the International Organisation Bureau of the State Department, who had the task of justifying the United States UN contributions before Congress, could not fail to have these considerations always before their eyes. The amount in dollar totals, or as a percentage of total U.S. Government expenditure, was minute. This, however, was little help; the need remained to prove that the American taxpayer was not being cozened. For if he were cozened over this, what new burdens would be laid on him in the future?

That American policy on an issue of crucial importance for the country's foreign relations should be determined by the budgetary anxieties of a bureau of the State Department will surprise only those who are strangers to the Washington rituals of executive-legislation relations. Of course there were not wanting other arguments than the financial to bolster the decision. The "fiscal and constitutional integrity" of the organisation was frequently invoked, the old analogy of club membership and club dues was employed, appeal was made to the "inescapable" obligation laid on all the membership to apply Article 19 once the decision of the World Court had pointed to it. None of these arguments was devoid of foundation; some of them had a good deal of point. But it is hard to resist the feeling that their invocation was primarily due to the presumed need to avert congressional wrath, to "stand up" to the U.S.S.R. and to serve notice on all who might seek to board "the gravy train".

For, after all, there was another side to the penny, another set of arguments which might equally have been invoked. It might have been asked whether the national interests of the U.S.A. had not been served by the UNEF and the ONUC and, in particular, by the virtual exclusion of the Soviet Union from participation in these operations; whether the inescapable leverage which the United States enjoyed by virtue of its financial and logistical contributions to these forces had not been of inestimable value to American policy. To ask such questions is, at any rate from a Western point of view, to imply no criticism; we have all[2] benefited

[2]Yes, in the long run all, even the shareholders in the Suez Canal and in the *Union Minière du Haut-Katanga;* even Israel, even Belgium.

from these American actions in the UN—which is, of course, why (with the conspicuous and perverse exception of France) we have supported them. But to ask such questions is inevitably to invite another—whether he who so enjoys the tune is not singularly privileged in being allowed to pay the piper? Or, in more direct terms, whether the United States ought not to count itself uncommonly fortunate that the Soviet Union has not wanted to pay the whole bill—and, of course, in return to exercise a comparable degree of control over the operations? Or again, to put the question from another angle, was it not a bit extravagant to suppose that a Great Power member could be induced not only to tolerate operations which it has opposed, but also to be made to help pay for them?

It was no doubt assumed by those who planned the very rigid tactics of the United States delegation in the U.N. that distasteful though the American doctrine on Article 19 might be the Russians would eventually accept it. Had they not, after all, eventually accepted defeat on the *troika* issue, for all their emphatic campaign against the concept of a single Secretary-General? The analogy, in 1962, was fresh and appealing. It was, nonethless, erroneous.

The principal reason for the Russian abandonment of the *troika* proposal was their belated discovery that it was unpopular amongst that very element in the membership which it was largely designed to attract—the "neutrals". Dag Hammarskjöld's rival concept of his office, despite all the rough water which it encountered, had a special appeal for the Afro-Asians whose particular champion he had avowed himself to be. Once it became apparent that his successor would be an Asiatic from a neutral state there was no good reason why any of the non-aligned membership should abandon the unified, one-man, concept of the Secretary-Generalship. The Russians were on a losing wicket.

When, however, the issue was one of the payment of dues for operations, one of which had little relevance to most Afro-Asian aspirations (UNEF), and the other (ONUC) had become a source of bitter intra-African and, to some extent, intra-Asian dissension, the shoe was on the other foot. Here the Russians could play upon the rivalries between the "haves" and the "have-nots"; even if it was difficult to pass the U.S.S.R. off as a have-not it was comparatively easy (especially when the U.S.A. had wielded its threat about withholding contributions to the technical assistance programme and Congress was slashing foreign aid appropriations) to present the U.S.A. as a rich landlord trying to squeeze the wages of the night watchman out of the pennies of the poor, a pseudophilanthropist whose charity was conditional upon the poor's punctiliousness in paying their bills. This could be seen in the shift of sentiment in the 19th General Assembly; at the opening there was good reason to think that the U.S.A. had a majority of the membership on its side; by the adjournment this majority seemed to have swung the other way.

As the debate proceeded, it became increasingly apparent that there was an even more fundamental weakness in the American tactics—the Americans did not really want *at any price* the victory or principle on which they averred their hearts were set. A voting victory which would have resulted in the U.S.S.R.'s loss of voting rights in the General Assembly with whatever Soviet boycott of other UN organs this would have entailed—this would have meant a falling of the heavens which, it soon became apparent, even the State Department's passion for justice was not prepared to risk. Hence the undignified and threadbare succession of devices to avoid a "confrontation". In such a situation all the tactical advantages passed to the Russians. They had only to sit tight and refuse to pay while all the onus for the Assembly's frustration fell upon their opponents. Thus it came about that the same Western diplomacy which had promoted the appeal to the World Court and its acceptance by the General Assembly had now to shoulder the task of finding a way out of the impasse it had in large part created. Those who seek an epitaph upon this unhappy sequence of events will find it most succinctly expressed in one of those glyptic injunctions of the Ministry of Transport, erected as it happens by the side of the American Embassy in Grosvenor Square; it reads, "DO NOT ENTER BOX UNLESS YOUR EXIT IS CLEAR".

To heighten the paradox, the campaign to secure payment for the two big operations, illegally run, as the Russians insist, by the General Assembly, has gathered momentum at the very time when enthusiasm for this system of General Assembly peace-keeping has gone into a general decline. The root cause of this lies in changes in the composition and functioning of the United Nations which, in the long run, are of far more importance than the dispute over Article 19. Explicit recognition of them has been obscured by the polemics of the dispute, but it is almost certain that a resolution of present disagreements will involve a recognition by both the United States and the U.S.S.R. of certain common interests in the face of new challenges. The moment when the Americans are ostensibly most concerned to hold the Russians over a barrel until they pay for the UNEF and the Congo is in fact the moment when the Americans have become convinced that a new machinery must be constructed for launching future UNEFs and handling future Congos.

In 1950 the Americans tilted the balance of power among the UN organs in favour of the General Assembly. But this was an Assembly in which, unless the Latin Americans inexplicably defaulted, the Americans were sure of the necessary majority. With the head-long rush of decolonisation and the accompanying flood of new members this has ceased to be true. The basic characteristic of that half of the present membership which is African and Asian is its reluctance to be involved in the East-West dispute, its conviction that there are many other causes with higher priorities than the Cold war; indeed, its refusal to regard the Cold War as any of its business save in so far as it is everyone's business to keep it cold. This membership sees the UN as a forum to be used for the continuing struggle against colonialism and racialism, and as a lever to promote economic development and diminish the impotence of the Third World. A General Assembly largely so composed can no longer be relied upon to support American (or British, or French) policies as such; indeed it might even pursue a militant anti-colonialism which the Russians and Chinese could use as a bandwagon, as at one moment they looked like doing in the Congo.

Moreover, this same membership gives a priority to its economic betterment which will always be ahead of what the economically developed Powers, however enlightened and generous their policies, will be willing to concede. In the eternal rivalry between the poor and the rich, the poor will always ask for more than the rich will be willing to concede–just as, in the process of decolonisation, the demand for independence always kept ahead of the will to emancipate. The force which the UN has lent to such pressures, as a funnel intensifies a flood, has been well exemplified in Dr. Raul Prebisch's success in extracting even from the impotent 19th Assembly the power to establish as a permanent UN organ the Trade and Development Board and a substantial secretariat to service it. As a result of this the "75" who come within sniffing distance of being a two-thirds majority in the General Assembly enjoy also all the advantages which come of having a large pressure group built permanently into the UN structure. A cursory acquaintance with the history of the Trusteeship Council will attest to the potency of that. This intensive exploitation of the UN's potentialities as an economic institution has formidable implications. As M. Philippe de Seynes has put it:

> "A new channel–or circuit–is being established through which gradually all problems are being routed, even those whose consideration was previously reserved for more antiseptic and reassuring forums; a channel characterised by a different combination of forces and a special ideology, one in which new criteria are applied to national policies and through which the world community is constantly confronted with proposals which the major centres of economic decision-making cannot indefinitely overlook."[3]

This poses for the United States–and no less for its allies, in NATO and the UN–a problem. On what terms should they seek to live with a General Assembly so composed, so minded and so equipped? On the spectrum of possible responses the present U.S. doctrine on Article 19 would place her in an impossibly vulnerable wing. It would imply that whenever a two-thirds majority of the General Assembly carried a resolution recommending executive action, in the peace-keeping and, no less, the economic field, and by an equivalent majority assessed the

---

[3] *The Quest for Peace,* ed. by Andrew W. Cordier and Wilder Foote (New York, London: Columbia University Press, 1965), p. 189.

membership to meet the expenses thereof, that assessment would become legally binding, even though participation in the operation itself would remain voluntary. The oft-proclaimed recommendatory limitation on the powers of the Assembly is thus suddenly seen to shrink; a body which can impose taxation, with the sanction of de-representation, is something very different from a mere mouthpiece of the collective sentiments of mankind. In dissenting from such an interpretation of Article 19 the Russians and the French will not long stand alone; no Great Power, and few minor Powers, will accept the implications of such a doctrine when it is their ox which is being gored. Thus whatever outcome, dignified or otherwise, is devised for the present dispute over arrears, it is certain that the U.S.A. and the U.S.S.R.—and a train of other countries too—have a common interest in curbing the tax-collecting potentialities of the General Assembly in both the peace-keeping and the economic development fields.

The Security Council has already benefited from the West's fear of an over-developed General Assembly. It is not only the Assembly's procedural deadlock which has led the Council to be the preferred forum for the handling of Cyprus and the Yemen and even the Congo issue in its latest stages. The Council has, in fact, proved itself to be both reasonably representative and reasonably flexible in all these contexts. So there is a general disposition to envisage a greater reliance on it for the future. America and Russia have both accepted the need to enlarge the Council in order to prevent a repetition of those tiresome deadlocks in which too many voting blocs compete for too few elective seats. A Council thus enlarged will certainly be able to represent more bands in the Assembly spectrum. But it will still be dominated by the veto. Of course it may happen, in that era of American-Soviet *rapprochement* which we are always being told is just around the corner, that the super-powers will find a new harmony which will enable the veto to rust unused. I doubt it. To believe this is to confuse a *rapprochement* which is essentially negative—a resolve *not* to pursue certain mutually perilous policies—with an agreement on positive action from the UN, "placing greater reliance" on the Council is likely to mean little more than using it as a court of first instance. And this is especially true where any question of executive action, of a peace-keeping kind, is involved.

Nor is the need for such peace-keeping action likely to diminish. Every time a UN force finds itself in an embarrasing position, or treads on the corns of some local interest, the cry goes up that it is misconceived and should either be demobilised or turned into a military government, according to the taste of the critic. But the recurrent invocation of such blue-helmeted fire brigades shows that they meet a real need, the need which in varying degrees most member states recognise most of the time, of dampening down conflicts which would otherwise flare into open war. The same British Government which was so free with its criticisms of the UN force in the Congo was clamant in its eagerness to see a similar body established in Cyprus. There will be other Congos, other Cypruses. The West would indeed be foolish to deny itself the use of a practical device for insulating, sometimes even extinguishing, such conflicts. Nor, at least, as far as Britain is concerned, is any such course in contemplation. The government's recent offer of logistic support for a UN force of up to six battalions obviously envisages a strengthening of the UN's peace-keeping potentialities.

The problem is, then, to preserve the flexibility which the Council's veto denies without being committed to the potential tyranny of the Assembly's majority. One solution–Cyprus and Yemen point that way–is to make the financing of peace forces as voluntary as participation in them. But this is to lease out the UN emblem to whomever is able and willing to pay the wages of those who wear it. An army of such mercenary soldiers might, in particularly favourable circumstances, hold the sky suspended while the diplomats worked out a settlement, but in most situations it would lack the only weapon which is any use–the moral authority of the organisation. If the UN flag is on sale to any group in the membership which can pay for it, it is entitled to as much, or as little, respect, as its paymaster can command. The currency is debased and what is bought with it is a benefit of very dubious durability.

Another solution is one which has already been given semi-official currency by the Americans. This is to retain the power of compulsory assessment, but to trim the Assembly of its present control over it, for example, by providing that such assessments would have to be recommended to the Assembly by a committee in which the Great and Middle Powers would count for more. This, if realisable, has much to recommend it from the Western point of view. It retains the concept of universality, but relates it to the realities of power and responsibility. But it is well to be clear about what it involves. It is not just a fiscal solution. It will create a new locus of power. Any such body would become a central, perhaps the central, organ of the UN. The General Assembly has been notorious for its refusal hitherto to delegate authority to subordinate committees. It has been repeatedly pilloried as the only parliamentary body in the world that tries to do almost all its business in committees of the whole. But of course this tenacious conservatism is rooted in a pervasive conviction that to delegate is to enfeeble. Of course the impairment of the Assembly's sovereignty may be cloaked in epithets like "advisory" and "recommendatory", but if the Committee is to serve the purposes its proposers intend, its advice or recommendations must carry strong presumptive power. It will have to resist amendments to its proposals, make clear that their rejection entails serious consequences, establish in fact a sort of moral ascendancy over the incoherent parent body.

Can this be done? When the Uniting for Peace resolution was carried it was in accord with the spirit of the times, almost a codification of a power shift which was already under way. But any attempt now to recover authority ceded to the

General Assembly will meet majority, not just minority, resistance. It will involve not a transfer of power but the creation of a new instrument of authority. It will, in fact, constitute the greatest *de facto* amendment of the Charter, the most substantial reconstruction of the organisation since San Francisco. These are not arguments against it if, as seems likely, only some such radical reform can preserve the dynamic potentialities of the UN in a usable form. But if escape from the present impasse lies along such lines as these, then it is optimistic to think that it can be realised between now and September. And it is unlikely to be realised at all so long as the public is encouraged to believe that there is no salvation outside Article 19.

The Role of International Organization: Limits and Possibilities

Stanley Hoffmann

No field of study is more slippery than international relations. The student of government has a clear frame of reference: the state within which occur the developments which he examines. The student of international relations, unhappily oscillates between the assumption of a world community which does not exist, except as an ideal, and the various units whose decisions and connections form the pattern of world politics—mainly, the nation-states. International organizations therefore tend to be considered either as the first institutions of a world in search of its constitution or as instruments of foreign policies. The scholar who follows the first approach usually blames, correctly enough, the nation-states for the failures of the organization; but he rarely indicates the means which could be used to bring the realities of world society into line with his ideal. The scholar who takes the second approach stresses, accurately enough, how limited the autonomy of international organizations has been and how little they have contributed to the achievement of their objectives; but because he does not discuss his fundamental assumption—the permanence of the nation-state's driving role in world politics—he reaches somewhat too easily the conclusion that the only prospect in international affairs is more of the same.

It may well be that this conclusion, too, is justified, but it should not be arrived at through a shortcut. The approach which seems the most satisfactory, though

Stanley Hoffmann, "The Role of International Organization: Limits and Possibilities," *International Organization,* Vol. 10, No. 3 (August 1956), pp. 357-372. Reprinted by permission of *International Organization.*

not the simplest, should be the following one. First, the objectives defined by the Charter of the United Nations are to be considered as the best moral goals statesmen can pursue; that is, the maintenance of peace and security, the promotion of economic, social and cultural cooperation, respect for human rights, and the establishment of procedures for peaceful change. (Implicit in this assumption is, of course, another one: it is legitimate that statesmen should assign moral ends to their policies, and that states' activities should be submitted to moral judgments, the absence of a single, supranational system of values notwithstanding.)[1] Secondly, the means through which these objectives are to be sought are necessarily international agreements; no conquest of the world by one nation, or even by an alliance of nations, could bring them about; consent is indispensable, even if it means that they can only be reached gradually and partially. Thirdly, it cannot be assumed at the outset that the present structure of international society *must* be the permanent framework of action, for it may well be that the objectives cannot be reached within such a framework, as, for instance, the World Federalists have argued. Changes in the structure may thus appear necessary. But one has to avoid utopias; if it is unwise to postulate the perpetuation of the present system, it is equally unwise to advocate ways which an analysis of world politics reveals to be blocked.

The problem which we want to discuss briefly can thus be phrased in the following terms: given the present structure of world society, what *should* and what *can* international organizations do to promote the objectives which we have mentioned?

I

A short analysis of present world society reveals a number of paradoxes and contradictions.

In the first place, the scene is dominated by two opposite developments. On the one hand, there is the phenomenon usually described as bipolarity of power. On the other hand, at the same time that military and economic strength has become centered, temporarily perhaps, in only two superpowers, there has been a trend toward further political disintegration of the world. As the process of "social mobilisation" of hitherto "passive" peoples progresses,[2] the number of

[1] We have argued this elsewhere at greater length. See "Quelques Aspects du Rôle du Droit International dans la Politique Étrangère des Etats" in: Association Françiase de Science Politique, *La politique étrangère et ses fondements*, Paris, Armand Colin, 1954, pp. 264-270. See also A. H. Feller, "In Defense of International Law and Morality," *Annals of the American Academy of Political and Social Science,* July 1952 (Vol. 282), pp. 77-78.

[2] See Karl Deutsch, *Nationalism and Social Communication,* John Wiley and Technology Press, 1953.

sovereign states has increased,[3] and the continuing break-up of former empires will undoubtedly add new ones. Both developments, contradictory as they appear, make the return to a concert of the great powers impossible; the necessary solidarity and fluidity of power are both gone.[4] And yet, the technological gap between the advanced and the backward nations is greater than ever before.

In the second place, the process of interlocking interests and activities, which internationalists once hopefully described as leading inevitably to a world community, has indeed continued. The distinction between internal and international affairs is now ruled out; it has therefore become impossible to prevent one nation from influencing and intervening in the policies of another. The superb autonomy and specialization of diplomacy is over, and nearly the whole world has become a "Turkish question". At the same time, however, the psychological effect of this development has been rebellion and seeking refuge in a conception made for, and reminiscent of, a more idyllic age: the concept of national sovereignty and independence. The contradiction is nowhere more apparent than in the UN itself. The organization has contributed immeasurably to an internationalization of all problems, and to a kind of equalization of diplomatic standards and practices for all members; but at the same time its operations are based on the principle of equality and the myth of sovereignty. The smaller states use sovereignty as a fortress, and the superpowers as a safeguard of their own freedom of action against friendly or hostile restraints.[5]

In the third place, the two sets of factors previously mentioned have produced a fundamental change in the politics of the two leading powers. The great powers of the nineteenth century used limited means for limited objectives. The relations between these powers could easily be described in equations, or at least in mechanistic terms—balancing process, equilibrium, etc. The superpowers of today have trans-national objectives; each one stands both for a certain organization of the world, and for a certain distribution of social forces and political power in each nation.[6] The means they use, with one important exception (the resort to general war), are also much broader. Their emphasis, in the choice of means, is far less on *national* power, far more on gaining allies. As some theorists have

---

[3]See E. H. Carr, *Nationalism and After,* New York, Macmillan, 1945, p. 53, for predictions to the contrary.

[4]See Kenneth Dawson, "The UN in a Disunited World," *World Politics,* January 1954 (Vol. 6, No. 2), p. 209, and this writer's *Organisations internationales et Pouvoirs Politiques des Etats,* Paris, Armand Colin, 1954, part I.

[5]See Max Beloff, *Foreign Policy and the Democratic Process,* Baltimore, Johns Hopkins Press, 1955, lecture IV.

[6]Raymond Aron, "En quête d'une Philosophie de la Politique Étrangère," *Revue Française de Science Politique,* January-March 1953, pp. 87-91.

shown,[7] this "multiple equilibrium" opens new channels of influence for the two superpowers and creates, at the expense of both, new procedures of restraint quite different from the restraints imposed on the big powers by the European concert. No big power can "go it alone" and define its interests to the exclusion of other nations' interests; the only, though very real and important, choice it has is between more and less broad international definitions of ends and means, depending on the kind and amount of international power it wants to mobilize.

In the fourth place, the smaller nations are torn between two modes of behavior in which they usually try to indulge simultaneously, as well as between two attitudes toward both the nation-state and the UN. The two modes of behavior represent two levels of world politics. On the one hand, the smaller states try to protect themselves, *collectively,* against the rivalries of the two superpowers. Individually, they would be the victims of the great conflict; together, they have the best chance of restraining the big powers and of gaining a number of advantages in return. Some seek such a common escape in a broad alliance with the United States (Rio Treaty, NATO, SEATO), others in a neutral belt. But in either case, thus protected against the "nationalistic universalism" of the superpowers,[8] they practice traditional nationalism quietly. The smaller nations live in two ages at the same time. As for the two attitudes toward the nation-state and the UN, each one is taken by a different group of states. The new nations focus on the nation-state their highest ambitions of international power, economic development, and social unity. Furthermore, their attachment to the nation-state is proportional to the intensity of their will not to get involved in the big-power conflict: a feeling that neutralists in Europe have echoed and expressed sometimes in impressive theoretical arguments.[9] These nations, at the same time, look on the UN with great enthusiasm; they see in it an instrument for the advancement of the smaller nations (in number and in power), and a mechanism for restraining the superpowers. On the contrary, the older nation-states of continental western Europe are more disabused of the nation-state, even though it retains the citizens' basic loyalty; and they look at the UN with greater misgivings, both because they have been outvoted so often in the UN on colonial issues, and because they contest the wisdom of spreading all over the world the disease of nationalism which they, too, contracted once, and from which they have suffered grievously.

---

[7]Jiri Liska, "The Multiple Equilibrium and the American National Interest in International Organization," *Harvard Studies in International Affairs,* February 1954; Ernst B. Haas, "Regionalism, Functionalism and International Organization," *World Politics,* January 1956 (Vol. 8, No. 2), p. 238.

[8]Hans J. Morgenthau, *Politics Among Nations,* New York, Alfred A. Knopf, 1954, pp. 230-234.

[9]See for instance J. M. Domenach, "Les Nationalismes," and G. E. Lavau, "La Souveraineté des Etats," in *Esprit,* March, 1955.

This brief description leads to a few remarks concerning the scholar's or the politician's usual approaches to the understanding of world politics. First, it shows the fallacy of simple models or categories of analysis. The assumption of a Hobbesian state of nature among states is misleading. It exaggerates the degree of opposition between loyalty to the nation and cooperation among nations,[10] as well as the degree to which the more unmitigated forms of "power politics" are being used by nations; it leads to the presently hopeless solution of world government as the only alternative to a world of militarized, anti-liberal, indeed carnivorous nations.[11] Now, this is not at all the way in which many people think of the nation-state. It oversimplifies the reasons for the rise of anti-liberal forces which are not engendered only by the clash of sovereignties and nationalism; it leaves out all the restraints which, in the 19th century, made the state of nature a rather Lockian one, and, in recent years, shaped a system so new and complex that no theorist has anticipated it. The model of Hobbes is not more accurate than the model of the world community—which may explain why it is so easy to jump from the first to the second.[12]

In the second place, the analysis of foreign policies in terms of power, or of power and purpose,[13] is also insufficient. The concept of national power is no guide in a century where ideas are the most powerful weapons, if it does not include the strength of ideological appeals. Even if it does, it fails to explain the differences between the ends and means of foreign policy in periods of limited conflicts and relative stability, and in revolutionary periods.[14]

Thirdly, the usefulness of reasoning on the basis of internal or even international precedents appears very limited. Those who show, not without truth, the distorting effects of the nation-state on the thinking of the citizens, are sometimes the first to use examples drawn from the development of constitutionalism.[15]

---

[10] This exaggeration has been criticized by Arnold Wolfers, "The Pole of Power and the Pole of Indifference," *World Politics,* October 1951 (Vol. 4, No. 1), p. 39, and by Karl Lowenstein, "Sovereignty and International Cooperation," *American Journal of International Law,* April 1954 (Vol. 48, No. 2), p. 222.

[11] See Thomas I. Cook, "Theoretical Foundations of World Government," *Review of Politics,* January 1950 (Vol. 12, No. 1), p. 20.

[12] See Ernest S. Lent, "The Development of United World Federalist Thought and Policy," *International Organization,* IX, pp. 486-501.

[13] See, respectively, Morgenthau, cited above, and Thomas I. Cook and Malcolm Moos, *Power Through Purpose: The Realism of Idealism as a Basis for Foreign Policy,* Baltimore, Johns Hopkins Press, 1954.

[14] See Aron, cited above, and Association Française de Science Politique, cited above, pp. 370-373.

[15] This tendency is criticized by H. J. Morgenthau, cited above, Ch. XXIX, and by Gerhard Niemeyer, "A Query about Assumptions of International Organization," *World Politics,* January 1955 (Vol. 7, No. 2), p. 337.

Those who deplore the forces which have destroyed the simple and autonomous mechanisms of nineteenth century diplomacy are too easily inclined to use it as a standard and as a still attainable ideal.

Finally, the statemen's view of world politics is sometimes equally oversimplified. Western statesmen have tended to assume too readily that there are two completely separate spheres of world politics today: the conflicts with the communist bloc, all around the iron curtain, and the relations with the rest of the world, where all the objectives of the UN may be gradually reached, where anti-Soviet collective security and solid, supranational communities can be organized without any Soviet leap over the barriers of containment.[16] The Soviets have tended, and still tend, to assume too easily that, in the non-Soviet world, all is tension and conflict, as if the alignments established as buffers against the cold war did not dampen minor antagonisms.[17]

II

Before examining what international organization should and could do in such a world, let us see what its recent role in international politics *has been*.

The UN was built on two assumptions; both have proved to be unjustified. The first was, of course, the survival of a concert of great powers. The second was what one might call the Kant-Wilson hypothesis. The organization was supposed to harmonize the interests of sovereign states, conceived as nineteenth century nations. Their international policies would therefore be distinguishable from their internal problems. Their usual antagonisms would be limited in scope, or at least seldom involve their national existence. This was the assumption of a world squarely based on the nation-state–the hypothesis of inter-state cooperation for and with peace and security.[18] There was nothing revolutionary about it; historically, it was rather reactionary, in so far as it tried to revive conditions whose disappearance had brought about two world wars. Both assumptions implicitly envisaged the establishment of a widely acceptable *status quo*, on the basis of which the organization would operate. The tragedy has been the conflict between these underlying hypotheses and the two major realities of world politics: the bipolarity of power and the further disintegration of the world.

---

[16]That this view was held by Secretary of State Acheson appears in many of the documents reproduced by McGeorge Bundy, *The Pattern of Responsibility,* Boston, Houghton Mifflin, 1952. It remains true that the picture was a fairly accurate basis for policy in Stalin's time.

[17]See Khrushchev's speech at the 20th Congress of the Communist Party of the USSR, *New York Times*, February 15, 1956.

[18]See Max Beloff, "Problems of International Government," in *Yearbook of World Affairs*, 1954, London, Stevens & Sons, pp. 4-8.

The consequence of the conflict between the first postulate and bipolarity has been the failure of the collective security mechanisms of the Charter. The conflict between the second postulate and the multiplication of nation-states, due to the anti-colonial revolution has led the UN to use as channels of peaceful change the procedures created for the settlement of ordinary disputes. It was hoped that the UN might thus harness that revolution. However, change has taken place, not as the consequence of, but either outside of or before the decisions of the UN, and it has been violent and often savage. The UN has given the impression of merely smoothing some of the edges and of running after the revolution so as not to be left too far behind.[19]

In order to avoid complete paralysis on cold war issues because of the first conflict, and to transcend the procedural limitations which have made it difficult to cope with the second, the organization has escaped from its original Charter and changed into a "new United Nations".[20] However, the new, unofficial charter is based upon an assumption which conflicts not only with the old ones, but also again with the reality. Both the "Uniting-for-Peace" resolution, charter of the "cold war" role of the UN, and the more fragmentary code of practices adopted by the UN in dealing with the anti-colonial revolution[21] were obviously necessary in order to keep the UN in line with the main currents of international politics. But the policy of collective assertion, parliamentary debates and majority votes assumes the existence of a sort of world community, where decisions similar to those reached in the framework of a constitutional system would make sense[22] – a far cry from both the hierarchical big-power rule and from the inter-state league of the Wilsonians. All these contradictions have engaged the UN in a series of vicious circles.

On the cold war front, bipolarity has made the resurrection of a concert of power against the one threatening big state fairly ineffective. The fear many small nations have of becoming engulfed in the cold war has, of course, undermined the whole argument behind the Uniting-for-Peace Resolution. Furthermore, the impossibility of tracing a clear line between internal and international

---

[19] See Raymond Aron, "Limits to the Powers of the UN," *Annuals of the American Academy of Political and Social Science,* November 1954 (Vol. 301), p. 205.

[20] See H. J. Morgenthau, "The New U.N. and the Revision of the Charter," *Review of Politics,* January, 1954 (Vol. 16, No. 1), p. 3.

[21] Elimination, through a variety of devices, of the domestic jurisdiction clause; assertion of a right of the UN to define a collective and substantive policy, rather than limiting the organs to the more purely conciliatory procedures of the Charter: See Leland M. Goodrich and Anne P. Simons, *The UN and the Maintenance of International Peace and Security,* Washington, Brookings Institution, 1955, pp. 155, 160, 609; and H. J. Morgenthau, cited above, pp. 315-338.

[22] See Aleksander W. Rudzinski, "Majority Rule Versus Great Power Agreement in the UN," *International Organization,* IX, pp. 366-385, p. 368.

affairs has obscured the idea of aggression; when aggression is easily disguised as social liberation, it is not astonishing to see the very nation which advocates a clear-cut definition of aggression suggest that civil or national-liberation wars be left out of the organization's reach.[23] Finally, the fact that recommendations have to be made by a 2/3 majority increases the small nations' power to destroy the new system either by refusing to make it work or by irresponsible recommendations which not they, but the big states, will have to carry out; the balance between proclamation and performance is a difficult one.[24] Both the difficulties and the dangers of putting into effect the "Uniting-for-Peace" machinery show that the primary emphasis in the UN cannot be put on collective security.[25]

The attempts to cope with the nationalist revolutions and the problem of change are not much more satisfactory. Conditions are so revolutionary that the UN has been unable to use effectively conciliatory procedures tailored only for conflicts between stabilized sovereign states. But world politics remain so strongly based on the sovereign state that the UN cannot get its assertions of competence and declarations of policy accepted by those of its members whose sovereignty is thereby infringed. If the members of the majorities point out that sovereignty means little in an era when internal tensions become matters of international concern, the outvoted members can always argue that the majorities' policies lead not to greater integration of the world, but to an increase in the number of sovereign units eager to shield their own activities behind Article 2, paragraph 7.[26] The issues between states, in an era where conflicts do indeed involve the very existence of nations, the birth of some, the dismantling of others, cannot be settled by resort to a world court: hence the constant refusal of the Assembly to submit such questions to it. But precisely because the issue is the life and death of the basic units in world politics it is useless to expect the more threatened ones to submit to majority votes.[27]

---

[23]See Ales Bebler, "The Yardstick of Collective Interest," *Annals of the American Academy of Political and Social Science*, November 1954 (Vol. 301), p. 85.

[24]See the comments of George Kennan, *Realities of American Foreign Policy,* Princeton University Press, 1954, p. 40, and the suggestions of H. Field Haviland, Jr., in *Annals of the American Academy of Political and Social Science,* November 1954 (Vol. 302), p. 106.

[25]See the remarks of Sir Gladwyn Jebb, "The Role of the United Nations," *International Organization*, VI, pp. 509-520, and René de la Charriere, "L'Action des Nations Unies Pour la Paix et la Sécurité," *Politique Étrangère,* September-October 1953.

[26]See the debate between Clyde Eagleton and Quincy Wright in *Proceedings of the American Society of International Law*, 1954, pp. 32-34, 67, 116, 119. The long discussions in UN organs on human rights, show similar arguments.

[27]See Clyde Eagleton, "Excesses of Self-Determination," *Foreign Affairs*, July 1953 (Vol. 31, No. 4), p. 592, and "The Yardstick of International Law," *Annals of the Academy of Political and Social Science,* November 1954 (Vol. 302), p. 68.

The result, not unexpectedly, is frequently deadlock followed by retreat of the UN. The policies advocated by it are not carried out, and after a decent resistance the UN ceases to recommend them.[28] The committees established for the implementation of these policies fail to obtain the cooperation of the other party, and when the walls of Jericho refuse to collapse, it is the committee which is broken up.[29] At the same time the more modest task which the original Charter did allow the UN to perform—what we called smoothing of edges, the curbing of the worst forms of unavoidable violence—becomes more difficult for two reasons. The decision of the UN to take a substantive stand reduces the chances of conciliation by increasing the opposing party's resistance and distrust. Furthermore, the two main trends of present world politics have interacted. The cold war has first thrown a shadow over, then a monkey wrench into, UN attempts at securing peaceful change. The break-up of the original concert of powers in these matters[30] has increased the chances of change through violence; it has emancipated the anti-colonial nations from a possible big-power tutelage; in so far as the Soviets support them, while the US is allied to the colonial powers in such institutions as NATO and SEATO, it has become far more difficult for the UN to oblige the antagonists or the reluctant side in a colonial conflict to renounce violence.[31]

It may have been vain to expect, in a world where the two main trends create for existing states a good deal of trouble, that an international organization established for coping with the irrepressible, minimum degree of insecurity that persists during stabilized periods could do much to eliminate the glaring insecurities of today. Maybe the organization could, indeed, be nothing but a "gentle civilizer". But the civilizer has not always been gentle, It has rather tended to increase the degree of insecurity, while both the cold war and the peculiar voting system which gives the loudest notes to sing to the weakest voices have prevented it from harnessing the forces it helped to set in motion. The reliance on, and exploitation of, the vague, broad and yet-to-be achieved principles and purposes of the Charter have combined the maximum of ambiguity with the maximum of

---

[28] An examination of UN substantive recommendations on Palestine, Kashmir, Spain, and South Africa's apartheid policies, and of their gradual watering down or abandonment is the basis of this assertion (see Goodrich and Simons, cited above, Chapters IX to XII). The success of UN intervention in Indonesia remains an isolated instance in this respect (i.e. substantive recommendations on issues not directly connected with the cold war).

[29] See the fate of the committees created for dealing with German elections, with apartheid policies and with the problem of Indians in South Africa (see Goodrich and Simons, cited above, chapters VIII and XIII).

[30] See a study of these "ad hoc concerts" in Ernst B. Haas, "Types of Collective Security: An Examination of Operational Concepts," *American Political Science Review,* March 1955 (Vol. 49, No. 1), p. 40.

[31] See Coral Bell, "The UN and the West," *International Affairs*, October 1953 (Vol. 29, No. 4), p. 464.

resistance from the members. The result has been a somewhat disturbing division of labor between the world body and the regional organizations; the problems that could be solved were quite legitimately dealt with by the latter,[32] but the UN has become the recipient of those problems which just cannot be solved diplomatically, *a fortiori* by parliamentary votes in the Assembly.[33] This was particularly apparent in the case of all the cold war conflicts which were submitted to the UN by both parties for propaganda purposes; on these issues, and on most of the colonial problems as well, Mr. Kennan's rather cruel description of the Assembly's votes as a series of "tableaux morts"[34] is an apt one.

Self-restraint or resignation to very limited and superficial soothing tasks might have killed the organization. But taking worthy stands and cheering itself up until it gets hoarse, has not really saved it as a force in world affairs—though such attitudes might have made it useful as an instrument serving a number of widely different foreign policies. The rules of the "new UN", like the rules of the original Charter, create both too rigid and too big-meshed a net of obligations for member nations. It is too rigid, in so far as compliance with these rules has proved to be impossible. It is too big-meshed, because in order to be applicable to so many different states, these obligations inevitably had to be few and vague. Thus, the rather obvious and recognized solidarity of interests among smaller groups of states is not sanctioned by any set of norms and institutions common to them. These great gaps increase insecurity, the chances of conflicts, and uncushioned power politics.

III

The following considerations on what the role of international organization *should be* in the present world are based on the following postulates. (a) The nation-state, conceived as a legally sovereign unit in a tenuous net of breakable obligations, is not the framework in which the ideals we have defined at the outset can *all* be realized or approximated. It can hardly be maintained that it affords the greatest possibilities of economic advance, and even, in many areas, of orderly political and social change. (b) Experience to data has shown that political organization on a world scale cannot, by itself, advance beyond the stage of the nation-state: its fate is linked to the nation-state. Three consequences flow from these postulates.

---

[32] In particular in the case of the Organization of American States.

[33] I. L. Claude, *Swords into Plowshares*, New York, Random House, 1956, p. 122, comments that the Commonwealth has been the greatest exporter of insoluble disputes to the UN (Kashmir, Indians in South Africa).

[34] George Kennan, *Realities of American Foreign Policy*, cited above, p. 42.

The first consequence concerns the role of the political organs of the UN. If they cannot shape new forces, they should at least prevent the nation-states from getting even further away from the distant objectives which the UN proclaims. The two tests—rather negative ones, one may fear—which each decision or recommendation should meet are, first, a test of responsibility: will it decrease, increase, or leave unchanged the state of tension with which it is supposed to deal? If it will not contribute to decreasing tensions, it should not be made, except if inaction is clearly bound to produce even worse consequences than intervention. This test is particularly necessary in colonial affairs. . . . Secondly, a test of efficiency: is the measure advocated, sound as it may be, backed by a sufficient combination of interests and forces? Otherwise, it will be an empty gesture.

The second consequence suggests the need for building new institutions which will help the nation to go beyond the stage of the nation-state. A case can be made—and has often been made[35]—against excessive and premature attempts at establishing "rigid legal norms" and institutions; it has been said that the process of integrating nations must be left to the free interplay of political, economic and social forces within them. Undoubtedly, no organization can be effective if there are no such favorable forces; it can not create them. But where they do exist, a network of legal obligations and institutions can consolidate the common interests at the expense of the divergent ones, and act as the indispensable catalyst of an emergent community; otherwise there would be no opportunity to select, seize, save and stress the unifying forces. The reason why the nations tend to organize themselves as states and why the highest allegiance of the citizens usually belongs to the state is that this form of political organization affords them protection, security, justice, gratifications and services. Therefore, the only way to transfer loyalty to another set of institutions is to create new agencies which will provide the citizens with some of these advantages and help in gradually building communities larger than nations.

But these new agencies will be solid and effective only if they are accepted freely by the peoples they are supposed to link. This means, in the first place, that the peoples will have to reach the "national stage" first. Recognition of the insufficiency of the nation as framework of social organization can only come *after* the nation has achieved a large measure of self-government. Consequently, in areas where no nation-state has yet been established, the national stage cannot, in all probability, be skipped. However, independence might be accompanied by an agreement on "interdependence" with other countries for clearly defined and accepted functions.

In the second place, wherever the nations, new or old, have all the attributes, blessings and curses of the sovereign state, a difficult task of incitement and negotiations will have to be performed. Political federation is probably ruled out in

---

[35] See George Kennan, *Realities of American Foreign Policy*, cited above, pp. 105-106.

the early stages. Except perhaps in the limited European area where disillusionment with the nation-state is strongest (but how far does it go?) one cannot expect, even under the stress created by necessities of defense or economic development, that nation-states will agree to the kind of wholesale transfer of powers which political federation requires. Suicide, so to speak, if it takes place at all, will have to be piecemeal. Political power cannot be expected to be abandoned first. Nor is it sure that political federation is always a desirable goal. The main enemy of international stability and individual liberty, in those countries where the nation-state has ceased to be a refuge and become a prison, is not the nation, but the state; it is the concentration of political, economic, military power, etc. . . . in one set of institutions. The creation, by amalgamation of existing nation-states, of a new state similar in its essence to the previous ones and even larger in area can hardly be called an improvement. A federation strong enough to survive the strains of birth and youth might soon develop into a super-nation; the trend toward centralization, observed in all federations, could lead to such a result.[36] A decrease in the number of leviathans is no gain if it is compensated by an increase in their respective power. Thus, the only practical way to reach the aim—a decentralization of allegiance—seems to be the establishment of functional institutions based on trans-national interests. In order to be effective, these agencies would have to be geographically limited. Or, if in certain cases a regional limitation makes little sense economically,[37] they should possess some ideological, historical or technical justification. They would therefore, as a rule, not be universal institutions like the UN and its specialized agencies, but, for instance, organizations in which certain under-developed countries sharing one common economic problem would cooperate with more advanced nations which have solved or faced the same problem at home or in their colonies. The nation-state would thus be caught in a variety of nets. Gradually, unobtrusively perhaps, a large measure of economic power would be transferred to the new agencies. They would for a long time to come leave to the state a kind of negative power to destroy the net; nevertheless, they could reach and provide the individuals with tangible services.[38] They would not constitute an immediate rival for the states

---

[36]See François Perroux, *L'Europe Sans Rivages*, Paris, Presses Universitaires, 1954, especially part II; Percy Corbett, "Congress and Proposals for International Government," *International Organization*, IV, p. 383-399, p. 390, and Jean Rivero, "Introduction to a study of the development of Federal Societies," *International Social Science Bulletin*, Spring 1952 (Vol. 4, No. 1) p. 375.

[37]See the case against regionalism in economic organizations in Raymond F. Mikesell, "Barriers to the Expansion of UN Economic Functions," *Annals of the American Academy of Political and Social Science*, November 1954 (Vol. 302), pp. 39-40, and Perroux, cited above, especially pp. 399-415.

[38]See I. L. Claude, "Individuals and World Law," *Harvard Studies in International Relations*, 1952.

and would therefore expect more consent or at least less violent resistance. The most effective attack on sovereignty is not a frontal one—it is one which slowly but clearly deprives sovereignty of its substance, and consequently of its prestige. The build-up of interlocking functional communities is required both by the presently strong attachment to formal sovereignty and by the actual interlocking interests which can become a positive force in world politics only if they are institutionalized.

As a third consequence of our two postulates, the UN should concentrate on, and develop, its role as a "center for harmonizing the actions of nations in the attainment of (the) common ends", which these joint interests suggest. Indeed the UN should either take the initiative or at least assume responsibility for the establishment and coordination of the regional or functional communities we have advocated. Two reasons militate for such a policy. In the first place, it is necessary to provide the UN, checkmated on political issues, with a new area of activities in its own interest. Secondly, the west, increasingly unable in political matters to get its views accepted by others through a process of "collectivization of interests",[39] but unable also to discard the world body, must find constructive ways of seizing the initiative. In the inevitable clash of ideas between east and west, the west cannot merely offer to the nations the ideal of internal democracy; it must also present the image of a more satisfactory world order. The Soviet Union, which wants to prevent a consolidation of the non-communist world, plays upon the strong attachment which is still felt to the nation-state and to nationalism, sovereignty and independence. The west cannot fight back on this ground; it would mean giving up the objectives we have mentioned. Nor can the west propose such revolutionary changes that the Soviets might successfully exploit this continuing attachment to the shelter of sovereignty, as well as charge the west with hypocrisy, since none of the leading western states is ready to sacrifice large areas of its own sovereignty.

Again, a progressive middle road seems to be the right one. This is precisely where the UN can operate. Militarily, the role of the UN, as we indicated, can only be a very limited one; it is therefore normal that initiatives for collective defense be taken outside of it. But initiatives for economic action should be made within the UN. This would be politically advantageous. The suggested regional or functional institutions can hardly function without western economic assistance. Now, the new nations have shown a distrust of purely western initiatives, interpreted as cold war moves, and a respect for the UN, which suggest that the UN should be selected as the channel for such assistance. It is also wise technically; there is a need for coordination of the present and future technical

---

[39] Hans Morgenthau, cited above, in *Annals of the American Academy of Political and Social Science* and *Review of Politics*; Edward H. Buehrig, "The United States, the United Nations and Bipolar Politics," *International Organization*, IV, pp. 573-584, p. 583.

institutions, which can best be exercised by the UN.[40] As the French Foreign Minister, M. Christian Bineau, has recently suggested,[41] an agency for world economic development should be created within the framework of the UN. This agency would coordinate and control specialized agencies such as the International Bank for Reconstruction and Development, as well as the UN technical assistance activities and more recently created or proposed UN institutions such as the International Finance Corporation and the Special United Nations Fund for Economic Development.[42] It should give its aid, gifts, loans, technical assistance, raw materials or energy, etc., to the regional or functional organizations we have recommended, rather than to states directly. These organizations would be sponsored by the UN agency and established among the underdeveloped nations (with or without direct participation of the industrialized ones). They would be the pioneers of supra-national development. The UN agency, being international by virtue of the Charter, would play the more modest but essential role of an instigator.

IV

The last question we have to discuss is obviously the most difficult one: *can* international organizations play the role we have tried to assign to them?

First, as for limiting the political organs of the UN to the rather limited tasks we have suggested, there is little doubt about the answer. On colonial and self-determination issues, the small powers, which are indispensable in the decision-making process, cannot be led to abandon the policy they have promoted in recent years; the Soviet bloc may be expected to fan the flames, and the United States cannot easily try to stop the movement—the more so, since it needs the small powers in case of a return to acute cold war tension. The answer here is: no. However, on the issue of collective security and also in the settlement of ordinary disputes, the organization might be condemned not just to violate the two tests we have indicated, but not even to reach the stage where proposals would be submitted to the tests. Both the reluctance of a majority of members to face the cold war and the neutralization of UN procedures by the conflicting maneuvers of the big powers could lead to such a paralysis. Writers who have shown

---

[40] See Edgar S. Furniss, Jr., "A Re-examination of Regional Arrangements," *Journal of International Affairs*, May 1955 (Vol. 9, No. 2), pp. 79-89.

[41] See a summary of M. Pineau's project in *Le Monde,* May 5, 1956, p. 2.

[42] M. Pineau's plan envisages also the establishment, within the world agency, of a board which would buy and sell surplus commodities produced by underdeveloped areas, and stabilize the market prices of raw materials.

how useful an instrument of American foreign policy the UN is[43] have attached too much importance to the Korean miracle and the mechanical "50 to 5" votes and underestimated the eventuality of Russian exploitation of UN procedures. However, any American attempt at penalizing the small powers either by direct pressure or by de-emphasizing the importance of the UN[44] would leave the field wide open to the Soviet Union. The Soviets, who adopted in the worst years of the cold war an attitude of disdain for the UN, have now realized what possibilities of counterattack they have neglected; nor can the United States afford to abandon the UN in favor of pure bilateralism or regionalism. Each of the superpowers is, in a way, caught in the UN. In spite of the partial excesses and the partial paralysis, the political organs must be preserved. By promoting diplomatic intercourse among all nations, they allow the more under-developed ones to use their participation as both a compensation for and as a weapon against the gap that separates them from the more advanced states. Also, if the world should return to multipolarity and stabilization, the UN must be there to perform at last the services that had been prematurely expected in the days of euphoria.[45]

Secondly, could the UN play the new economic and social role which we have suggested? The obstacle here seems to be the reluctance of the United States and Great Britain to allow the UN to play such a role, and to transfer a major part of their foreign aid funds to the UN. It has been suggested that the west might lose its freedom of movement on the economic front of the "cold war" if it accepted a system in which the smaller powers, and the USSR itself, could control the use of western resources. This argument is debatable on two counts. It is better to risk providing the nations concerned with a sort of right of veto or a brake on the activities of a UN economic agency than to sow the seeds of grave economic rivalries, misallocation of resources, and social and international tensions by taking no initiative at all. Such would undoubtedly be the effects of the uncoordinated policies of nations which may all want to industrialize themselves without regard for the regional distribution of opportunities and the scarcity of investment funds. To resort to purely western initiatives made outside of the UN is to court failure, as the new nations fear colonialism in disguise and western "cold war" intentions. To wait for local initiatives is not very wise either. A study of existing economic agencies shows that, with the significant exception of the European Coal and Steel Community and new continental European projects, American or British

---

[43] Advocated, for instance, by George Kennan, cited above, pp. 59-60.

[44] Hans Morgenthau, cited above and "The Yardstick of National Interest," *Annals of the American Academy of Political and Social Science*, November 1954 (Vol. 302), p. 77; Jiri Liska, cited above.

[45] See the concluding remarks of E. B. Haas, cited above, *World Politics,* January 1956.

initiatives have been decisive.[46] The institution we suggest, which could be an irritating check on western policies, would also provide the west with a big and subtle channel for getting the main points of its policies across far better than through direct aid to a few selected allies; the dose of economic medicine administered to the peoples of under-developed areas through such an institution may be excessively sweetened in consequence of their objections, but it will still be administered to more.[47]

Furthermore, the opportunities that a UN agency might give to Soviet maneuvering are not greater than the opportunities the Soviets already have for exploiting nationalism and driving wedges between those nations closer to the west and the uncommitted ones. If the main western powers carry their hostility against the restraint exercised at their expense by the small nations so far that the more traditional emphasis on bilateral diplomacy and "self-interest", narrowly defined, is preferred, then indeed Soviet strategy will have won. Bilateralism breeds separation, and further opportunities for political and economic conflicts. It allows the Soviets to outbid the west, or at least to drag the west into an endless bidding game. On the contrary, if the west did take the initiative in proposing a world agency on the lines we suggest, and if the Soviets refused to join in order to "go it alone", their own unilateral offers of aid would then become as politically suspect as western offers have sometimes become. The example of SUNFED should be kept in mind. The Soviets, in the beginning, were as cool to the Fund as were the western industrial nations. Strengthening an important area of the non-communist world could hardly have been welcome to the Soviets; but in 1954 and 1955 they saw that they could exploit western reluctance at no cost to themselves, and they rallied to the underdeveloped nations' claim for a rapid establishment of a Fund. Western reticence and insistence on priority for bilateral aid may prove to be a serious mistake. American opposition, at first, to close bonds between the proposed Atoms-for-Peace organization and the UN, and the shift, between 1953 and 1954, from a revolutionary and truly supranational institution to a mere clearing house, can also be criticized on these grounds. The more rapidly the world moves out of the situation of bipolarity, the more useful it will be for the west to deal with the under-developed, uncommitted members of the "third force" through a world organization, where their moves and

---

[46]The contrast between the Colombo Plan and the failure of the Simla Conference, where the initiative was left to the local leaders, is a case in point. See William Henderson, "The Development of Regionalism in Southeast Asia," *International Organization,* IX, pp. 463-476.

[47]See Benjamin V. Cohen, "The Impact of the United Nations on United States Foreign Policy," *International Organization,* V, pp. 274-281.

maneuvers can be more easily controlled than if they too enjoyed total freedom from international restraints.

Finally, it remains necessary to discuss the chances of success of regional or functional institutions sponsored by a UN agency of the kind we have suggested. The record of existing regional and functional organizations such as NATO, the Colombo plan, the OEEC, the European Coal and Steel Community, and the OAS, does not really answer the question, because most of them have not been launched for the purposes and in the conditions we have advocated. However, the main conclusions have to be taken into consideration. In the first place, outside of the Soviet bloc in which regionalism is an instrument of Soviet hegemony, there has been no political integration. In political matters, interstate cooperation remains the most one can expect. Secondly, the greatest measure of effective supranational integration has been achieved, ironically enough, in military alliances.[48] This is an ominous sign indeed, whose meaning can best be seen in connection with a third conclusion. The most successful non-military organizations are those which are squarely based on their members' calculations that the common agencies will bring benefits to them as nations; the framework of expectations remains the nation-state, not the larger area served by the agencies. States are more willing to confess their military insufficiency than their economic and social weaknesses. When it is a question of welfare, not of survival, the urgency seems smaller. This explains why NATO has never been able to play the same role in economic and political matters as in military affairs.[49] The only relative exception to the last conclusion is western Europe, for the reasons which were indicated above. It is no accident that the only area in which individuals may appeal, in case of a violation of their rights, to a supranational body is part of the territory covered by the Council of Europe; and even there the process is a slow and limited one.[50]

Thus, the precedents show a need for caution and realism. Many serious objections must be contemplated. First, there are obstacles to the very establishment of the institutions we have advocated. The most obvious one is, again, the cold war. How will it be possible even for a UN agency to convince the new

---

[48] The record of the European Coal and Steel Community, impressive as it is, does not rival NATO's and justifies Lincoln Gordon's question whether similar results could not have been reached without the apparatus of supranationality ["Myth and Reality in European Integration," *Yale Review,* September 1955 (Vol. 45, No. 1), pp. 80-103, p. 92].

[49] See on this subject Norman J. Padelford, "Political Cooperation in the North Atlantic Community," *International Organization,* IX, pp. 353-365.

[50] In addition to trusteeship territories, of course. See P. Modinos, "La Convention Europeenne de Droits de l'Homme," *Annuaire Europeen,* Vol. I, The Hague, Martinus Nijhoff, 1955.

uncommitted nations to harmonize their development plans and, as it may appear necessary, to "de-nationalize" a part of their economic resources and policies, when they are encouraged to stick to the nation-state by Soviet strategy and may even receive Soviet help if they refuse to join western-inspired arrangements? There is no doubt about the crippling effect Soviet policy could have; but this is not a reason to give up trying, since this is precisely what the Soviet Union would like to force the west into. Furthermore the Atoms-for-Peace case shows that the west disposes here of such a powerful lever that even the Soviet Union cannot afford to remain aloof and hostile—or else, as in the Marshall Plan precedent, in spite of all her threats and baits, the nations which see the advantages of such common enterprises will join at great cost to Soviet prestige.

A second obstacle can be called the vicious circle. The new institutions cannot be created without the consent of, and, especially in case of UN sponsorship, without a controlling role for the recipient nations. Will they not therefore be able to veto, for nationalistic reasons, more ambitious plans of supranational development, and end up with nothing more than the more timid and traditional inter-governmental cooperation schemes, loaded with safeguards and rights of veto? This may well be. But even modest schemes are better than unbridled competitions, and additionally, in so far as most of the functional plans would depend on support from the industrialized nations of the west, the bargaining power of the latter should not be underrated. The needs of the under-developed nations are such that if they had to choose between the discomforts of isolation and the sacrifice of sovereignty involved in joint development projects, it should not be lightly assumed that they would prefer the first—unless the west couched its appeal too much in cold war terms, or asked at the outset for too many sacrifices of sovereignty. The possible advent of a "third industrial revolution" should give to the western nations, who have such an advance in atomic energy experience, a very powerful counter. The debates in the 1955 General Assembly on Atoms-for-Peace have shown that the under-developed nations are willing to accept and even to promote joint undertakings as an alternative to the western tactics of bilateral agreements which they resent.

A third obstacle could prevent either the establishment or the efficient functioning of the suggested institutions. Will not the basic political antagonisms between states paralyze these agencies? Will not, for instance, the fear that the members might have of each other's ambitions or power prevent any joint undertaking? Or will not the nation which has the greatest resources and skills, or whose economic development will appear to be the most necessary for the whole area's advance, seize these advantages and impose gradually its domination over the other members under the cloak of supranational arrangements? Here again, one must recognize that the risk does exist and that such fears may either play a deterrent role or saddle the institutions with crippling provisions for balancing purposes. It would indeed be naïve to expect these institutions to put an end to "power politics". They would provide new channels, new restraints and new fields of action for it. But it would be equally naïve to expect, in the absence of any joint undertaking, that the effects of uneven distribution of power would not be felt. They cannot be eliminated; but they can be softened and used for the common good if adequate common mechanisms are established. Thus, this objection is, and should be, a cause for great caution in the establishment of new institutions,[51] but definitely not for inaction.

The last objections bear upon the effects such mechanisms, if they are successfully established, might be expected to produce. On the one hand, it is suggested that the decentralization of allegiance to which we have referred will not take place because the various states will still act as a screen between the individuals and the supranational bodies. State borders might lose their political significance, but their psychological effects will be preserved, and the states will have a vested interest in not allowing too big a transfer of loyalty to the new units.[52] On the other hand, one might say that even if the states did not insist on keeping their subjects' full allegiance, the transfer of loyalty to utilitarian, technocratic bureaucracies deprived of any contact with the peoples they work for is very unlikely indeed. There really is no easy refutation of this argument; the dreams of rational internationalists have been shattered more than once; there is little doubt that the splitting of loyalties can only be the result of a very long process, and that it will require a period of peace in which the state's prestige and resistance to encroachment on its powers can be eroded. Common economic interests have not prevented nationalist explosions; nor can the institutionalization of these interests be expected to suppress them. In most parts of the world, on the most elemental and vital problems, the nation-state will keep the final say. But this is not an argument against trying both to remove the greatest possible number of questions from the sacred zone of nationalism and sovereignty to the unglamorous sphere of international cooperation and to create such patterns that even when the last word remains with the state, this word will be in no small way conditioned by the state's commitments and by the growing habit of common action.

---

[51] Safeguards that make cooperation possible, even though it will be slow, are better than schemes which disintegrate because they were too bold. The failure of EDC shows how necessary it is to provide for common mechanisms which do not create, among the weaker members, fear lest the potential superiority of one of the partners will be accentuated by the process of integration.

[52] See Hans Morgenthau, *Politics Among Nations,* cited above, p. 500; contra Quincy Wright, "International Organization and Peace," *Western Political Quarterly,* June 1955 (Vol. 8, No. 2), p. 149. See also I. L. Claude's discussion in *Swords into Plowshares,* cited above, pp. 382-387 and 400-402.

V

If we state, then, what can be done, and compare it with what should be done, the prospects appear both modest and not at all hopeless. Far less can be done than the most ardent internationalists desire or sometimes expect. But somewhat more can be done than the spokesmen for reliance on "wise statesmanship" or on the manifestation of "perennial forces" seem to believe, and certainly quite a lot more should be tried.

The defenders and promoters of international organizations would have a much stronger case if they recognized frankly the two following limitations. First, there is no sudden mutation in world politics, and the forces that may some day break the crust of the nation-state can only be helped, not created, by international organization. This is why the basis of action remains the state, why the chances of truly supranational institutions, even limited to certain functions, are far smaller, in most parts of the world, than those of organs of international co-operation, why even ambitious supranational schemes might not operate very differently from these, and finally why in the new bodies "power politics" will continue. But this is not what matters. Power politics also survive in the internal affairs of any nation. What counts is the framework and the general direction of the process.

Secondly, the mushrooming of international institutional institutions will not solve the fundamental issue of security.[53] They can be created on all sides of the big abysses that separate the nations and threaten world peace–the cold war, the colonial revolution; they cannot bridge the gaps. Here the balance of power between the super-powers, and between the crumbling empires and the rising new nations, are the decisive factors. The most international organization can do is to provide restraints on the superpowers and centers of cooperation between old and new nations after the colonial issue has been decided by force or by local agreements.

Once these limitations are accepted, the role of international organization should appear in its true light. Even if it were not much more than that of an "amiable civilizer", it would still be a far bigger one than many challengers seem to suggest. They usually leave this role to traditional diplomacy. International organization as a fragile but still badly explored diplomatic method can, within its own limits, help the nations to transcend the limits of the nation-state.

---

[53]See Arnold Wolfers, cited above, and E. H. Carr, cited above, pp. 52-53.